RENEWALS 458-4574

DATE DUE

GAYLORD   PRINTED IN U.S.A.

ELECTORAL PROCESSES AND GOVERNANCE IN SOUTH ASIA

ELECTORAL PROCESSES AND GOVERNANCE IN SOUTH ASIA

Edited by

Dushyantha Mendis

International Centre
for Ethnic Studies
Kandy, Sri Lanka

Los Angeles • London • New Delhi • Singapore
www.sagepublications.com

First published in 2008 by

SAGE Publications India Pvt Ltd
B1/I-1 Mohan Cooperative Industrial Area
Mathura Road, New Delhi 110 044, India
www.sagepub.in

SAGE Publications Inc
2455 Teller Road
Thousand Oaks, California 91320, USA

SAGE Publications Ltd
1 Oliver's Yard, 55 City Road
London EC1Y 1SP, United Kingdom

SAGE Publications Asia-Pacific Pte Ltd
33 Pekin Street
#02-01 Far East Square
Singapore 048763

Published by Vivek Mehra for SAGE Publications India Pvt Ltd, typeset in 9.5/11.5 pts. Calisto MT at InoSoft Systems, Noida, and printed at Chaman Enterprises, New Delhi.

Library of Congress Cataloging-in-Publication Data

Electoral processes and governance in South Asia / edited by
  Dushyantha Mendis.
      p. cm.
  Includes bibliographical references and index.
    1. Elections—South Asia. 2. Election law—South Asia. 3. South
Asia—Politics and government—20th century. 4. Democracy—South
Asia. I. Mendis, Dushyantha, 1954–

JQ98.A95E44   320.60954—dc22   2007   2007044258

ISBN: 978-0-7619-3577-3 (HB)   978-81-7829-738-5 (India-HB)

The SAGE Team: Sugata Ghosh, Koel Mishra and Sanjeev Sharma

CONTENTS

LIST OF TABLES AND FIGURES

Tables

Figures

ACKNOWLEDGEMENTS

The origins of this volume lie in the acute concern the International Centre for Ethnic Studies (ICES) Kandy shared with the rest of civil society in Sri Lanka and other South Asian countries about the numerous violations of democratic norms in the electoral processes of our countries.

In pursuit of that concern, ICES Kandy first undertook a study of electoral malpractice and fraud in Sri Lanka in recent years. That project was funded by the Asia Foundation, Colombo, Sri Lanka.

The importance of the subject encouraged us to broaden the scope of our research into electoral processes in other South Asian countries as well. The centrepiece of this project was an international conference held in Colombo in June 2002 on Electoral Processes and Governance in South Asia, with the participation of teams of scholars and practitioners from Bangladesh, India, Nepal, Pakistan and Sri Lanka who presented papers at this conference and many other distinguished invitees. We thank the Ford Foundation in New Delhi for financial support for this conference as well as the research on this project as a whole; this is another significant instance of the support the ICES has long received from the Ford Foundation, which we acknowledge with pleasure and great appreciation.

This volume contains the revised, updated and edited versions of the papers originally presented at the conference of June 2002. We owe a special debt of thanks to all our writers for the patience and co-operation they have extended to us in completing this work.

Ms Dilshad Shahabdeen and Ms Jenny Claydon assisted me in the early stages of editing this draft, and Ms Sumedha Abayaratna assisted with the secretarial work. In the somewhat hectic subsequent and closing stages of this project Ms Kanthi Gamage copy edited the manuscript and Ms Iranga Silva formatted all the drafts. I was indeed fortunate to have such cheerful and competent support as I received from all of them, but Kanthi and Iranga deserve special mention as they had to bear a heavy load of work and they did so with their customary aplomb and meticulous attention to detail.

I also gratefully acknowledge the generous support and advice I have always received from Prof. Kingsley M. de Silva and Prof. Stanley W.R. de A. Samarasinghe, Chairman and Executive Director respectively, of the ICES.

Finally I thank the staff of SAGE Publications for their professionalism and expertise. Dr Sugata Ghosh liaised with me in the commissioning of the work and the copy editing was handled initially by Ms Janaki Srinivasan and subsequently by Ms Koel Mishra who saw the manuscript through to press. It has been a pleasure working with them and they have each made important contributions to this work.

Part I

Introduction

1

EDITOR'S INTRODUCTION
South Asian Democracies in Transition

Dushyantha Mendis

I

Introduction[*]

It is evident from the articles published in this book that electoral processes in the South Asian countries are troubled to greater or lesser extents whatever the formal structures and legal provisions relating to those processes may be.

As visible and controversial as they are, however, electoral processes constitute only the thin edge of a much larger wedge. They are a reflection of the democratic processes in the countries in which they apply. It is these processes as they operate in the South Asian countries that we seek to understand and analyse in this chapter, in order to provide a context to the chapters which follow.

[*]The helpful suggestions and comments made by Professor Stanley W.R. de A. Samarasinghe on this Chapter are gratefully acknowledged by the author.

At this stage it is important to be clear about what we mean by democracy. For many, democracy is synonymous with a system which countenances a multiplicity of political parties and regular elections, certain fundamental freedoms such as those of expression, political organisation and freedom from arbitrary arrest, and certain fundamental institutions such as a free media, independent judiciary, the rule of law and supremacy of the Constitution. However, all these are symptoms of a more fundamental underlying structuring and organisation of society, rather than being themselves the very stuff of democracy.

As Robert A. Dahl states,

> If one … imaginatively penetrates the obvious appearances of free speech, the operation of the press, parties, elections, and defeated governments voluntarily abdicating office, at last one discovers an underlying factor on which this entire structure depends. It is the consciences, norms, and habits of the people in the society.… For it is these that define what uses of control are legitimate and what are illegitimate, what behaviour is acceptable and what is not. And if these definitions, commands, permissions, and approvals prescribed by the norms, habits, and consciences of the people are not appropriate …, then no written constitutions, no guarantees, no prescribed codes, no laws will achieve it.[1]

The type of regime with the requisite consciences, norms and habits is defined by Dahl as a 'polyarchy'. Dahl set out some basic pre-conditions necessary for the operation of this type of regime. First, 'Polyarchy requires social indoctrination and habituation in the process of polyarchy and the desirability of democracy'.[2] Second, 'Polyarchy also requires agreement on those basic issues and those methods that facilitate peaceful competition'.[3] Third, 'Polyarchy requires a considerable degree of social pluralism—that is, a diversity of social organisations with a large measure of autonomy with respect to one another'.[4] The importance of this, in Robert A. Dahl's words, is that 'The number and variety of preferences and interests represented in policy making are … greater if the political regime is a polyarchy'.[5] Fourth, polyarchy requires that 'Recruitment (into political leadership) must not be significantly limited by the unilateral control of existing political leaders … the political elites constantly renew themselves by recruiting new members from individuals and groups not hitherto included'.[6] Finally, 'A prerequisite to many of the preceding conditions is a society with a considerable degree of psychological security'.[7]

The second and fifth conditions would appear to be logical consequences of the first, for if there has been a long process of indoctrination and experience in democratic processes, then there would be general agreement on basic methods of peaceful competition. The long processes of indoctrination and habituation in the processes of polyarchy would also give rise to the fifth condition, a considerable degree of psychological security. The fourth condition—the constant renewal of political elites—would be largely a function of the third condition, that is, a considerable degree of social pluralism. Thus the crucial conditions would be the first and the third, and it is these which we seek to analyse in the discussion which follows.

II

Social Indoctrination and Habituation in the Process of Polyarchy

Here we shall deal briefly with the period prior to 1947 in the case of Bangladesh, India and Pakistan, as the Indian subcontinent received its independence from British rule in that year; the period prior to 1950 in the case of Nepal, as in that year the administration of the country by the Rana family was brought to an end after around a century; and the period prior to 1948 in the case of Sri Lanka, that being the year in which Sri Lanka received its independence from British rule.

Bangladesh, India and Pakistan

These three countries will be considered together as they have their immediate antecedents in the Moghul and British empires. It is worth noting that in their heyday, around 1700, the writ of the Moghuls ran from Chennai in the south and Bengal in the east to Kabul in the north-east. The British empire in India, its immediate successor, was a smaller affair, not including within itself the areas now belonging to Afghanistan.

Where the Moghul empire was concerned, there would by and large be no controversy regarding Barrington Moore's assessment:

Essentially, the political and social system of the Mogul era was an agrarian bureaucracy imposed on top of a heterogeneous collection of native chieftains differing widely in resources and power. As the Mogul authority weakened in the eighteenth century, it reverted to looser forms. Under Akbar and succeeding strong rulers, there was no landed aristocracy of national scope independent of the crown.... Native chieftains did enjoy substantial independence, though the Mogul rulers were at least moderately successful in incorporating them into the Mogul bureaucratic system.... The weakness of a national aristocracy was an important feature of seventeenth century India that, as in other countries, inhibited the growth of parliamentary democracy from native soil.[8]

Neither did economic change provide the catalyst for political change:

... by skimming off most of the economic surplus generated by the underlying population and turning it into display, the Mogul rulers for a time avoided the dangers of an aristocratic attack on their power. At the same time, such a use of the surplus seriously limited the possibilities of economic development or, more precisely, the kind of economic development that would have broken through the agrarian order and established a new kind of society.[9]

British rule did not make many changes in the power structure established by the Moghuls. The concept of a British empire in India conveys a monolithic unity. This in fact was not the case; apart from the areas of India under direct British rule, there were more than 500 petty rulers who governed their areas at the pleasure of the British, subject to varying degrees of central control.

Barrington Moore is worth quoting again on the effects of British rule in India:

After suppressing the Mutiny, the British were able to impose upon India nearly a century of law and order and a fair facsimile of political unity....

A policy of law and order favours those who already have privileges, including some whose privileges are not very large. Such was the consequence of British policy in India, though it set in motion, however slowly, other and deeper forces. British rule rested mainly on the Indian upper classes in the countryside, native princes and larger landowners....[10]

Such a structure of power was not one likely to give rise to democratic governance; law and order perpetuated exploitative relationships. 'The Zamindari system ... ensured a regular source of revenue for the British rulers but, in the process, condoned all kinds of corruption perpetrated by the feudal class at the village level.'[11]

However, by the end of the nineteenth century, a class of industrial capitalists arose in India, and this class, finding its interests at odds with those of British capital, financed the Indian nationalist movement. For this movement to attain any significance, however, it was necessary to mobilise the rural masses, and it was Gandhi who achieved this with his vision of rural regeneration. These eccentric visions could be countenanced with equanimity by both industrial and landed capital, given Gandhi's central tenet of non-violence. As Barrington Moore states, Gandhi's 'outlook contained nothing very terrifying to the holders of property, even to the landed aristocracy who were generally antagonistic to him.'[12]

> ... the whole program of *Swadeshi* or local autonomy was in effect a doctrine of 'buy Indian' and helped to cut down the competition of British goods. Furthermore, from the standpoint of the wealthy classes, there were useful aspects to Gandhi's doctrine of the dignity of labor.[13]

Thus, Gandhi's doctrines, by bringing in the peasant masses to the nationalist movement, 'brought water to the mills of the wealthy urban classes.'[14]

An interesting insight into India's nationalist class is set out below:

> What came to be looked upon as the nationalist class was nothing but the disparate and traditionally dominant castes and communities gathered together in their interest to preserve their traditional dominance on the one hand over the lower caste masses, and to enlarge their area of dominance in the new political society on the other.[15]

The peasantry had thus by the time of independence from British rule, been delivered to the nationalist movement, but that movement in turn basically held no quid pro quo for the peasantry. Having thumped their drums and blown their trumpets when required, what independence held out for them was nothing other than consignment once again to the rural misery which had been their accustomed home for millennia. Nothing in this tale is indicative of any movement towards polyarchy.

Nepal

Nepal was politically unified in 1768, and its dominant elite came from emigrants from India, upper caste Hindus fleeing subordination to the Muslim conquerors of India, between the twelfth and fifteenth centuries. These immigrants brought with them their Hindu social stratification into castes, though they also absorbed into their fold old local ruling families who were already there, through intermarriage and proclamation.[16] Indeed, even before the Rana autocracy, the Nepali political system had shown a remarkable capacity to absorb and co-opt the elites scattered around the country. As Leo E. Rose notes:

> After 1770, the national elite in Kathmandu expanded over time to include several other social groups whose support was critical to the central government but who were products of somewhat different political and social traditions from the dominant bahun group.[17]

This political elite was to have a very long life ahead of it. 'Despite these divisions within the political elite system, between 1770 and 1950 a reasonably coherent national political culture was evident about which there was a broad consensus within the elite.'[18]

In mid-nineteenth century, there took place the usurpation of power by the Rana family, which was to supply the hereditary prime ministers of Nepal until 1950, reducing the king to a mere titular position. The Ranas were themselves a large family group, connected with the royal and other important families by marriage. What disturbed the equilibrium for the Ranas was the Indian nationalist movement, which inspired educated young middle-class Nepalis such as B.P. Koirala and D.R. Regmi to pursue their democratic aspirations through an anti-Rana movement. It was this movement, backed by junior branches of the Rana family who presumably felt 'underprivileged' compared to their more powerful fellow family members, that overthrew the Rana family rule in 1950, a promising start, one would have thought, in the direction of polyarchy.

Sri Lanka

Sri Lanka's great hydraulic civilisation which collapsed around the thirteenth century appears to have been based on a bureaucratic monarchy. The collapse coincided with, and may have been caused by, a trend towards feudalism, which was to have a long life ahead of it. The littoral of Sri Lanka was conquered piecemeal by the Portuguese and subsequently the Dutch, over the sixteenth and seventeenth centuries. It was left for the British to complete the unification of the island by the absorption of the Kandyan kingdom, with its core in the central highlands. This important step was accomplished painlessly in 1815 when the Kandyan aristocracy, in overthrowing their own king, invited the British in.

The Kandyan kingdom was no greenhouse of democracy. It was dominated by a few aristocratic families, most of them connected to each other through marriage. As the outstanding Sri Lankan historian, Colvin R. de Silva, has written:

> Their (i.e., the aristocratic families) wide landed possessions brought them political pre-eminence and gave them economic control in a national economy based entirely on agriculture; a social system based on caste gave them considerable influence; an imperfectly supervised, though centralized, administration presented them with wide opportunities of corruption, and the extensive control of the governmental machine which had been vested in them proved a source of unrestricted power.[19]

The British tried a novel experiment commencing 1832, with the introduction of a Legislative and an Executive Council, the direct ancestors of the present Sri Lankan parliamentary system. However, members of those bodies were appointed, and Sinhalese representation in the Legislative Council was limited over the nineteenth century to members of one single aristocratic family. The franchise was extremely limited.

The Sri Lankan independence movement, was largely a very elitist phenomenon. Unlike in India, the Sri Lankan capitalist class was extremely small, and a complacent junior partner of the British capital. Their interests were not in the direction of independence, political or economic.

In 1933, however, the British placed Sri Lanka politically well ahead of the colonial pack yet again, by the grant of universal adult franchise. It is interesting and sobering to note that this step was unanimously opposed by members of the Sri Lankan political elite. However, the masses were now on the very doorstep of the elite; again, one would think, an important step in the direction of polyarchy.

III

Social Pluralism

This condition assumes importance in the establishment of polyarchy in that it provides the condition precedent for the representation of diverse groups in policy formulation. Accordingly, it is important to examine to what extent social diversity is reflected in policy making in the selected South Asian countries.

Bangladesh

East Pakistan, as East Bengal was known following the partition of India, was liberated from its large landowners and moneylenders when this class, largely Hindus, fled the area on partition. With them also went whatever industrial capital the area possessed.[20] The Ayub regime cultivated the rural elite by legislative concessions increasing the landownership ceiling. Thus, as Richard Nations points out, the leading class in East Bengali society has been '... an amorphous petty bourgeoisie of traders, functionaries, professionals, intellectuals and rural notables, who float uneasily above the swelling peasant sea below them.'[21]

The social roots of the Awami League, which took power at the time of independence in 1971 were in this class.[22] The Awami League's socialist programme suited this diverse ruling elite down to the ground, paving the way for large doses of state patronage (a phenomenon we shall note with regard to Sri Lanka as well, which has a very similar social structure). As Ayesha Jalal points out:

> In March 1972, the government's nationalization policies led to a dramatic expansion of the public sector which now accounted for an estimated 86 per cent of the total industrial assets. Instead of selecting from the available pool of skilled bureaucrats, the regime opted to appoint political favourites to top jobs in the

nationalized industries. This was consistent with the imperatives of disbursing state patronage—plum jobs, permits and licences—through the political networks of the Awami League. Good for the consolidation of the regime's support base, this was a bad recipe for public sector efficiency.[23]

What lost the regime its support was its ineptitude, as indicated by rising famine in the countryside, and its authoritarian tendencies, as evidenced by Mujib's attempt to set up a one-party socialist state,[24] and this loss of support led almost directly to the military coup of 1975. Regime change did not make a difference in the locus of power, though there may have been some widening at the upper end, particularly in a military–business nexus.

> It is discernible that the groups, eg the bureaucracy (both civil and military), the petty bourgeoisie, the trading and industrial bourgeoisie and the rich peasants have administered the policy in Bangladesh. They have sought to control the state machine in order to dispense patronage as a basis for expanding power over the polity, and also to seek material benefit from the dispensation of this patronage.[25]

Neither has economic liberalisation led to any democratising trends.

> ... economic reforms were used primarily to consolidate the power of the ruling elites. Successive regimes, both military and civilian, treated market reforms as an instrument to build and maintain coalitions in particular with traders and industrialists. In exchange for political support, they allowed business elites to use economic restructuring as the primary tool to attain their financial and economic objectives.[26]

Virtually the same point is made by another noted commentator on Bangladeshi affairs.

> Whilst the public sector stagnated both owing to acts of policy and the crisis of governance, the attempt to privatise the economy did little more than breed a class of rentiers masquerading as capitalists....
> Bangladesh has privatised over 600 public enterprises in the last 15 years—more than Chile under Pinochet—perhaps a record

in the world. A ... study in 1991, commissioned by the interim government, the first ever attempt by the government in 15 years to physically look at the outcome of its privatisation policies, found that around 60 per cent of those enterprises were closed. Privatisation has thus become a vehicle for extracting resources from the State and from the people without contributing either to growth, investment or productive efficiency.[27]

Thus in Bangladesh the precondition for a polyarchy, of a social diversity involved in policy making, is not met.

India

Some scholars tended until recently to analyse India in terms of a political oligarchy. The challenges facing India's politicians at the time of independence were:

> ... the political, economic and infrastructural integration of the territory of the new state, which now excluded those parts of British India that made up the new state of Pakistan but included over five hundred territorial units of different sizes that had been ruled by Indian princes exhibiting varying degrees of independence from British control in their management of administrative, financial and infrastructural matters.[28]

The response to these challenges as devised in what has been called the 'Nehruvian order' is said to have provided 'a unique model of integration based on a coalition of diverse interests that the Congress party had represented in the decades following independence.'[29]

The system which gave rise to this unique model, as explained by Partha Chatterjee,

> ... consisted of a differentiated structure of the party organisation from the central to the provincial to the district and local levels, each level enjoying a degree of autonomy and influence over the corresponding level of government activity and therefore accommodating different class and group interests within the ruling political formation. The effectiveness of the process depended on the mediating efforts of political leaders at different levels of the party organisation who had recognised areas of authority within

which they could build coalitions for voicing demands on the state as well as for mobilising electoral support for the party.[30]

One way in which the traditional elites enlarged their area of dominance was through the ideology of state-led development, which necessarily led to a large public sector. Thus,

There is no question that over the last three decades the state has accumulated powers of direct ownership and control in the economy to an extent unparalleled in Indian history, both in the spheres of circulation (banking, credit, transport, distribution and foreign trade) and of production—directly manufacturing much of basic and capital goods, owning more than 60 per cent of all productive capital in the industrial sector, running eight of the top ten industrial units in the country, directly employing two-thirds of all workers in the organised sector, holding through nationalised financial institutions more than 25 per cent of paid up capital of joint stock companies in the private sector, and regulating patterns of private investment down to industrial product level and choice of technology....[31]

Having centralised resources in the state, the dominant elites could then make use of them for their own benefit.

India, he [Bardhan] says, is governed by three 'proprietary' classes: industrial capitalists, rich farmers and professional bureaucrats. The industrial capitalist class has benefited from the government's import substitution policies, the industrial licensing system, the policy of taking over sick firms, and restrictions on foreign investment. Rich farmers have benefited from the government's price support programme and from subsidised inputs (water, power, fertilisers, diesel fuel) and subsidised credit. And the bureaucrats have gained in political power and income through their control over what has become an elaborate system of patronage. Although these classes have some competing interests ..., all three welcome state subsidies....[32]

Left out in this analysis is the large middle class, a major beneficiary of state intervention. Rajni Kothari has written that

... the middle class (which in absolute numbers is large in India) has succeeded in utilising the State from providing it with a production base that can sustain its parasitic lifestyle. To this must be added the numerous lumpen elements that are finding employment at the lower rungs of an ever growing bureaucracy....[33]

However, other groups have to some extent at least found their voice in various political groupings. For instance, the Jana Sangh

... appeared during the 1960s very much as the potential representative of ... the middle classes threatened 'from above' by the intervention of the state in the economy and the development of capitalism, and 'from below' by the increasing political awareness and mobilisation of the backward classes.[34]

Christophe Jaffrelot also makes the point that

... the BJP expanded its base among the middle class in two directions in the late 1980s and early 1990s. Its primary source of support had formerly been found among the high castes from the urban 'middle world'—shopkeepers, lawyers and white collar workers of intermediate rank. At the time of writing, the BJP has made inroads among the lower middle classes—especially students or unemployed youths—and the new elite. These two poles of the middle class often shared a common high caste background and an antipathy towards the Mandal Commission report[35] and its implementation.[36]

Other economic and social groups have been mobilising themselves as well. An important transformation in the Indian political scene has been

... the emergence of Other Backward Classes (OBCs) and the Scheduled Castes as ever more distinct and self conscious political constituencies through organisation and appeals by a host of political parties and movements striving to construct a distinct OBC and Dalit caste interest and political discourse. The subversion of upper caste political dominance and assertion of non-brahmin and popular identities in the political field has a long history in south India and Maharashtra, where it provided central underpinnings for the assertion of regional identities.[37]

Indeed a striking feature of Indian democracy is the increasing participation of the poor in the electoral process.

Recent studies have shown that in 1972 only 38 per cent of the poor voted, but in 1996 51 per cent of the poor voted. This growing sense of political efficacy is reflected in the fact that while 42 per cent of the lower castes in 1972 felt that their vote made a difference, this increased to 60 per cent by 1996. Similarly, while rates of party membership of the Scheduled Castes increased from 13 per cent in 1971 to 19 per cent in 1996, party membership of the upper castes declined from 36 per cent to 28 per cent during the same time period. The major factors influencing the rising political consciousness of the poor were a growing realisation that the state can play a vital role in dispensing public goods and an increasing awareness that politics can serve as a route to greater pride, dignity and confidence in protecting their interests.[38]

The assertion of regional identities and the associated restructuring of Indian politics is another important political transformation. Hansen and Jaffrelot point out

> ... the emergence of still more distinct regional polities in each state, with distinct political cultures, distinct political vernaculars and distinct configurations of caste mobilisation and alliances ... the central leadership's (i.e., the leadership of the Congress party under Indira Gandhi) concomitant populist mobilisation of lower caste strata in order to undercut the power of local elites and state-level Congress organisations ultimately stimulated the growth of vernacular political elites and thus further eroded centralised political authority in Delhi.[39]

The net result is the decline of 'national' parties and the trend to ever larger coalition governments being formed between the national and regional parties.

The erosion of support for national parties was demonstrated by the fact that the combined vote of India's two largest national parties—the Congress and the BJP—was only 52 per cent of the total number of votes cast in 1999. The biggest gains were made by various regional parties and parties representing caste and communal identities. The BJP was able to form a government in 1998 by cobbling together an eighteen party coalition representing a number of these new political forces....

In 1999, the pre-election coalition of twenty-four parties that the BJP cobbled together won a comfortable majority....[40]

This argument about the diversification of the sources of political power in India is indeed now conventional wisdom. As another author also points out,

> Ever since [the 1989 elections] ... India has been ruled by coalition governments that reflect the newly diffuse distribution of political power. A national party—typically Congress or the BJP—is at the core, with regional parties acting as crucial makeweights in a fragile, multilateral marriage of political convenience....
>
> In fact, the fragmentation of the polity dictates that any nation-wide political party must rely on smaller, regional, caste based and interest based parties to obtain a governing majority. Such a development, while making for more contentious politics, may have an unintended positive consequence: National governments will increasingly reflect the diversity of the country and willy-nilly will make India a more 'federal' republic in fact as well as in theory....[41]

This more inclusive nature of Indian politics means also more parties to share in the pork barrel.

> ... at the Centre with the shaky coalition governments of recent years the regional party leaders bring in their particularistic agenda and exercise their clout to redefine the central government policies....
>
> The public sector has been a milch cow for the upperclasses and castes for many decades, it is now the turn of these other groups, and the economist's argument about the efficiency of management is often a secondary issue.[42]

Economic liberalisation beginning with Narasimha Rao's minority government of 1991 has nevertheless continued, and gathered momentum. The economic reforms undertaken in 1991 were impelled by a balance of payments crisis, but they have been continued not only at the centre but by the states as well. As one writer puts it:

> There has also been a shift in the site of reforms from Delhi, the nation's capital, to various state capitals. Taking their cue from the center, a number of state governments have come forward

with reform policies at the state level ... elections to state legislative assemblies in 1993, 1994, and 1995 brought a variety of opposition and regional parties to power in the states ... most of these governments have shown commitment to reform....[43]

Myron Weiner also notes the economic reform process initiated by the states, but notes that the process has proceeded slowly.[44] Whatever the speed of the reforms, it represents a new development, and has to be seen in the political context in which it occurs. In India we have seen that new players have entered the political scene almost forcibly, giving rise to the regional bent of today's political activity in the country. The fact that the new regional powers are undertaking reforms of their own probably means that the old political and economic oligarchy centred on the 'Nehruvian order' is gone for good.

Symptomatic of the trend towards increasing democratisation in India is the rise of the Election Commission (EC) and the Supreme Court as extremely powerful and independent sources of authority. From the depths of its degradation during the period of Indira Gandhi's emergency (1975–77), the Supreme Court has ploughed its way into a much more independent, self-assertive role, and

... the result has been a tremendous expansion and protection of civil, political, economic and social rights against arbitrary encroachments by the state.... In the early 1990s, the Court became even more activist by becoming involved in combating corruption and promoting good governance.[45]

Ujjwal Kumar Singh's chapter in this volume also shows how the Supreme Court has played a decisive and critical role in broadening and deepening the role and functions of the EC, a body which is now held up as a model to the other nations of South Asia.[46]

Nepal

The important players on the Nepali political scene for the greater part of the period since 1950 have been:

(i) The monarchy, and this term includes within itself the king, the royal family, various 'client' families and the palace secretariat. Freed from the Rana autocracy in 1950, the monarchy has by and large been assertive in Nepali politics until the upheaval of 2005–06.

(*ii*)   The traditional elites, of whom Leo E. Rose writes:

> ... while there have been substantial changes and expansion of opportunities (for instance, in access to education) for local and ethnic elites and even non-elites since 1950, the dominant status of the national political elite, and its basic familial composition, has remained reasonably constant. There have been serious challenges to this largely Kathmandu-based elite from a variety of sources after 1950 including challengers with strong political support bases both inside and outside the capital. But until 1990, the national political elite demonstrated an impressive capacity to counter, accommodate, absorb, and eventually defeat the attempted intrusions by 'outsiders' into their playing field.[47]

However it should be noted that the elite itself does not present a monolithic block. Nowhere is this better illustrated than in case of the bureaucracy which is largely filled with members of the Kathmandu elite.[48]

> ... the central bureaucracy was subdivided into several well-defined factions that competed vigorously for the key posts in the economic and development ministries which had the most resources to distribute. These factions remained organised along the lines of the pre-1951 chakari patron–client family system, though with less cohesiveness and sense of identity with the unit than under the Ranas.[49]

Though Leo E. Rose argues that there has been some progress since 1990 in that a fairly large number of the leaders of political parties are now from the local elite families from outside Kathmandu, or are otherwise disinclined to accept the dictates of the Kathmandu-based party leadership, and there has also been some change in the social composition of the bureaucracy at the regional level, subject to some doubt about how significant the changes described by Rose are in view of the following conclusion by Hari Prasad Bhattarai in his chapter in this volume:

> The political parties are still dominated by those elite sections of society that have ruled the country for centuries and

even though they may articulate values of equality and progress, the hierarchical values and traditions, which are deeply rooted in these elitist groups are an impediment to the devel6pment of a fully-fledged democratic system.[50]

(*iii*) Finally, we have the political parties, but these are not shining avatars of democracy. Nilamber Acharya and Krishna P. Khanal's comments in this volume on the functioning of the Nepali political process would indicate that political parties exist only to further their own ends.

> Elections continue to be a formal means of acquiring power and winning elections at any cost appears to be the only motive of those engaged in politics. The mad race to capture power by securing votes by any means, and the impression given by many of those who shared power during the last decade that power is the passport to quick prosperity, has shaken the trust in elections and the democratic process itself. Opportunists, commission agents, criminal gangs and all types of miscreants have found it convenient to promote their own interests through candidates of major political parties during elections. Correspondingly, candidates elected to office need to be in a position of power to reward and protect their backers. As a result the post-election scenario of the country is marked by extreme pressure for a ministerial berth or any other position with power and privileges. Those who are denied these rewards switch their loyalty from one leader to another resulting in the chronic instability of government.[51]

A monarchy striving to protect its own position, and an elite at loggerheads within itself over division of spoils—these form a necessary and sufficient background for stagnation: political, economic and social. Clearly, social reform could not be expected from the system as it was and is constituted. For instance, the monarchy successfully moved against the Parliament in 1960—not only dismissing the elected government but also moving into a totally different constitutional structure—partly at least due to the fact that the government was going to introduce land reforms which would have antagonised the traditional elites.[52] Neither could the monarchy carry through any programme of land reform itself, being confronted with the same obstacle—the traditional elites—as had faced the Parliament.[53]

Political reform has come only in the face of public pressure and agitation. The Panchayat system introduced by the monarchy in 1962 provided for directly elected representatives only at the most local level, the regional and national panchayats being indirectly elected, thus providing a solid foundation for manipulation of the system by the palace. In 1981 public pressure forced a major change, with the introduction of a national panchayat elected on the basis of universal adult franchise. This system however still gave the monarchy virtually sovereign powers. This system was changed to one of constitutional monarchy with sovereignty vested in the people in 1990, again in the face of public agitation. The struggle between Parliament and monarchy was clearly not over, considering the developments in Nepal since 2002. The mass demonstrations of April 2006 in Kathmandu have now forced the monarchy to reinstate the Parliament.

However, the chapters dealing with Nepal in this volume also make it apparent that the political parties themselves have not responded proactively to the challenge of creating a viable democracy in Nepal in the period between 1990 and 2002. It is not perhaps surprising then that a force outside the formal system—the Maoist insurgents—should become as powerful as they are, for the simple reason that established institutions do not seem to be responsive to mass concerns.[54] As Hari Prasad Bhattarai notes:

> ... the inability to effect structural reform through the parliamentary system and the continued deterioration of the economic well-being of the majority of the people provided the impetus for the Maoist movement ... the Maoists have obtained a high degree of support and many recruits from the socially and economically marginalised sections of society.

Pakistan

The military has been either directly or indirectly calling the shots in Pakistan for much of the greater part of Pakistani history. It has been ably backed in its exercise of power by the civil bureaucracy. The process whereby the state acquired such immense power in Pakistan is a complex one involving also an external factor, India.

> Pakistan's failure to evolve a democratic political system has been blamed on the organisational weaknesses of the Muslim League.

Jinnah's death so soon after its creation has also been a much favoured explanation. But the death of an individual leader, however great, cannot be sufficient explanation for why Pakistan slipped off the democratic course. A close scrutiny of the historical evidence in any case suggests that, in the immediate aftermath of partition, neither elected nor non-elected institutions had a decisive edge. Quite as much as the Muslim League, the civil bureaucracy and the military were a shadow of their counterparts in India. Not only did they lack the necessary pool of skilled manpower, they also suffered from grave infrastructural inadequacies. It was the imperative of building a new centre together with the outbreak of war with India over Kashmir within months of Pakistan's emergence which created the conditions for the dominance of the bureaucracy and the army.[55]

There was also failure at the political level, or perhaps more accurately, the emergence of political issues which gave every appearance of being intractable of final solution. In his chapter in this volume, Maluka has set out the problems with which the Pakistani Constituent Assembly had to grapple: Islamic or secular state, the question of a national language, joint or separate electorates (for religious minorities), and the question of representation where the Bengalis were in a numerical majority. It is this last issue which was to be critical. According to Ayesha Jalal:

> What confounded the problems plaguing Pakistan during the initial years of independence were the vexing implications of its demographic arithmetic. While power was concentrated in the western wing, Bengalis in the eastern wing had an overall majority in the country. In any system of representative democracy, the Bengalis would be in a position to use their majority in parliament to dominate the central government. This was anathema to the civil and defence officials and their allies among important West Pakistani landed and business families.[56]

Confronted with problems of this magnitude it is no wonder that it took two Constituent Assemblies until 1956 to draft a Constitution, or that this Constitution could never be made operational because the military seized direct control in 1958, just before elections scheduled under the new Constitution for 1959. Until then there had been a facade of civilian control where civil bureaucrats were shuttled into and out of offices nominally regarded as elective.

The citation from Ayesha Jalal above would also offer another clue as to what gave staying power to a non-democratic order: the ability of the civil and military bureaucratic complex to find allies among important social strata at least in West Pakistan. The leadership and political base of the Muslim League which had led the call for and achieved the creation of Pakistan was in fact largely in India.[57] However, the leadership of the new state turned out to be dominated by the migratory minority, the Mohajirs.[58]

> Political power came to be concentrated in the hands of the civil bureaucracy and the military very early in the day. But while their dominance within the state structure has been undeniable, they would not have succeeded in their project of exercising control over the economy and society without the tacit support of at least some of the dominant social classes. These have been identified as the big landowning families of West Pakistan and the nascent industrial bourgeoisie. Although both have remained junior partners in the firm that has managed Pakistan's affairs since the early 1950s, they have not failed to extract economic compensation for their subordinate role in the power structure. Despite an inability to turn economic power into direct political control, the dominant social classes in Pakistan have done quite as well as their Indian counterparts in negotiating terms with the state in support of their material and other interests.[59]

One significant creation of the Mohajir-dominated ruling class was, one may note without much surprise, the Mohajir-dominated industrial class.

> When partition occurred, there was practically no industry in the provinces of Sind, Baluchistan, Punjab and the North-West Frontier. Throughout the subcontinent, the Muslim bourgeoisie, of whatever ethnic origin, had played a negligible role in the development of a manufacturing capitalism. Some minority communities of Muslims, however, had traditionally specialised in selected commercial and speculative functions (bullion broking, for example), mainly in Bombay and Calcutta.... These groups migrated to West Pakistan after Partition with what capital and skills they possessed, and there formed the initial nucleus of the entrepreneurial class in the Western provinces. Later, they were joined by a similar Punjabi trading minority, the Chiniotis, but even today some half of the millionaire elite which dominates the

urban sector of the Western economy is composed of Gujerati-speaking immigrants from communities who represent less than 0.3 per cent of the total population. In 1947, these were newcomers to Karachi, with very slender assets. They therefore became over-whelmingly dependent on the patronage of the state bureaucracy for the finance and import licenses crucial to business enterprise in the early years.[60]

The party elected to power in 1970, the Pakistan People's Party (PPP), in what was then West Pakistan, has often been described as 'populist.' However that may be, it carried out a sweeping nationalisation of the industrial and banking sectors. However, these nationalisations were to simply increase the power of those who controlled the state.

The state of Pakistan accumulated immense power of patronage in the form of control over allocation of resources through nationalisation of banking and industrial sectors in the 1970s. In the populist framework of Z.A. Bhutto's patrimonial rule, patronage expanded far beyond the locality. It led to extractive centralisation on the one hand and distributive privatisation on the other. Chains of dyads based on patron–client relations oper-ated at various levels as political polarisation set in. From 1988 onwards, the Pakistan People's Party (PPP) and Pakistan Muslim League (PML) sought to outdo each other in preventing their respective client groups from joining the rival patron-group.[61]

That successive Pakistani governments used privatisation for their own political ends has been noted by another writer:

... privatisation has formed the mainstay of reforms under both the Pakistan People's Party (PPP) and Islami Jamhoori Ittehad (IJI) governments alike. It has allowed each government to fi-nance deficit spending and to dispense public assets, especially the most profitable units, to political supporters.[62]

The period from 1970 has witnessed other important changes (apart from the break-up of Pakistan into Pakistan proper and Bangladesh), which may yet have an impact on Pakistan's traditional political accommodations; foremost here would be the emergence of new, economically powerful groups.[63] For instance, although the power of the relatively small but powerful industrial class was smashed by Zulfiqar Ali Bhutto who was elected Prime Minister in 1970, subsequently some of this class have made a comeback in the post-Bhutto period:

Small scale industry and the informal sector became the backbone of industry, replacing the 22 families of Ayub's era. In the rural areas, there was the emergence of capitalist farmers, who took advantage of green revolution technology. There also occurred the emergence of a large class of shopkeepers, small scale industrialists, transporters, etc., the people emerging from the 'remittance economy,' the remittances of Pakistani migrant labour in the middle-east.

However, though

Economic power increasingly rested with a middle class, ... with regard to political power, they had to be junior partners with the military. There were 11 governments in office—and while they were in office one can't really say that they were ever in 'power' during the 1988–99 period.... Clearly, the power to decide who was worthy of being in government throughout the 1990s, rested with groups and forces who had no tradition, experience or interest with democracy. This charade of who held real power in Pakistan, came to an unambiguous end on 12 October 1999.[64]

The question that arises is whether the newly emergent middle class would continue to be content being junior partners of the military, or whether they would seek a more assertive role for themselves and when such assertiveness would commence. While new economically influential groups may have emerged, the military has not weakened its hold over Pakistani society and polity; on the contrary the military has come to be increasingly entrenched in the political and economic life of Pakistan. The military

... appropriates civilian positions and a large chunk of the administrative budget meant for non-military personnel is funnelled through to serving and retired military officers. The newspaper 'Dawn' reported that there were as many as 104 serving and retired Lieutenant Generals, Major Generals or equivalent ranks from other services (who were) among the 1,027 military officers inducted on civilian posts in different ministries, divisions and

Pakistani missions abroad after the 12 October 1999 military takeover.[65]

The military's economic stake is also huge: '... the military has arrived at the point where its businesses today control about 23 per cent assets of the corporate sector with two (military) foundations, ... representing two of the largest conglomerates in the country.'[66]

Given the military's long role as the ruler in Pakistan, Zulfikar Khalid Maluka points out in his chapter in this volume that:

The military's overwhelming proclivity for interference in national affairs and jealously guarding its financial interests has led political analysts to question the very future of the democratic process in Pakistan. The manipulations of the civil–military bureaucracy to assert its authority over the divided political parties, deny society the benefits of civil rule, grab resources, suppress dissent, thwart elections and abrogate constitutions, have resulted in the perversion of every institution of national importance such as the Parliament. Neither the police nor the civil bureaucracy can act insulated from the influence and direction of the military.[67]

Maluka points out that even the political parties are not entirely insulated from the influence of the military (and this is quite distinct from political parties cobbled together through the agencies of the military). He says 'If the civil military bureaucracy is the chief malefactor in uprooting constitutional democracy, the political parties themselves are not far behind; some sided with the dictators and others sat on the fence and waited for opportune moments...'

Thus in Pakistan we find that it is a small number of groups who control the levers of both political and economic power. However there have been some dynamics in Pakistani society which may make military dominance more untenable over time.

Sri Lanka

Sri Lanka attained independence from British rule in 1948. The politically most active and powerful class turned out to be in Sri Lanka, as in Bangladesh, the petit bourgeoisie. Here we see the applicability of the concept of the 'intermediate regime' to the case of Sri Lanka, first shown in a paper by S.W.R. de A. Samarasinghe presented in 1980.[68]

Samarasinghe states:

> The concept of 'Intermediate Regimes' first suggested by Michael
> Kalecki ... to describe the emergence of government representing
> the interests of the lower-middle class (including in this also the
> corresponding strata of the peasantry) ... is a convenient tool to
> put the economic policies followed by successive governments
> after 1956 in their proper political context. The political back-
> bone of the Intermediate Regime is the lower middle class ... in
> the context of Sri Lanka this class may be identified operationally
> as consisting of middle and lower rank government officials,
> school teachers, small businessmen, cultivators with a fair amount
> of land and so forth.[69]

It was the genius of S.W.R.D. Bandaranaike, swept to power as
Prime Minister by an electoral landslide in 1956, to tap into the
aspirations of this vast amorphous petit bourgeoisie. These were the
people who had been left out in the cold in the colonial period, of
which the biggest beneficiaries were the westernised, Christianised,
minuscule upper and middle class. The petit bourgeoisie were now
demanding their place in the sun, and the means that evolved to that
end, inter alia, were:

(*i*)   a high degree of state control over the economy;
(*ii*) the creation of a large public sector where the petit bourgeoisie
        could obtain employment; and
(*iii*) a system of controls and regulations through which erstwhile
        members of the petit bourgeoisie could set themselves up as
        an indigenous entrepreneurial class.

Any hope that the new dispensation was to be directed to the
benefit of the poor as well was to be quickly dispelled. One of the
most threatening bogeymen to emerge from the 1956 government
was the Paddy Lands Act of 1958, which was supposed to provide
protection to tenant farmers and sharecroppers. In the event it turned
out to be an utterly damp squib, so watered down were its provisions
when it was finally enacted.

The intermediate regime provided a political consensus between
the major political parties right up to 1977, but the economic stagnation it engendered rendered it no longer politically efficacious; in
1971, the 'declasses' had risen in armed revolt against the whole

system. Thus in 1977, President J.R. Jayewardene resorted to an open economy or, to be more accurate, an economic system with significant elements of an open economy. Under this system which at least provided some economic momentum, Sri Lanka has seen the rise of a fairly significant upper and middle class. On the other hand, the elements of political patronage, through, for instance, a large public sector were only slowly dismantled, still providing for petit bourgeoisie demands as well. It remains to be seen which class will come out triumphant in the ongoing struggle, but at least it could be said that the foundations of the intermediate regime, though perhaps not demolished, are at least shaken. The shift to a more open economy could be said to provide a type of consensus between the two major 'national' parties.

IV

Control over Resources

From the foregoing analysis, it becomes clear that the state or, more accurately, those who control it at any given point of time, also control vast resources. State control of resources is very large in South Asian countries also because a particular ideology of development each of these countries has followed at one time or the other proved very convenient for the dominant groups of those countries.

Governments in South Asian countries control vast resources because of what has been termed (quite accurately in the opinion of the present writer) 'The First World's Misbegotten Economic Legacy to the Third World'.[70]

It has been observed that:

Unlike Schumpeter, who emphasised the role of innovations and the concomitant private anticipation of entrepreneurial profit as major factors explaining development, most development economists writing in the late 1940s and 1950s visualised a dominant role for the state in initiating and sustaining the development process. A corollary view was the advocacy of comprehensive national development planning under state auspices....[71]

The result came to be that:

In many developing countries, the state controls the 'commanding heights' of the economy, owning a large part of the non-agricultural economy and regulating the flow of credit, foreign exchange, and investment licenses. To a large extent it can play one class against another, local capital against foreign, one transnational company against another, all for the purpose of furthering its own goals.[72]

The state with its vast resources therefore becomes a battle ground for contesting parties to gain control over it, and the resources it offers. The problem goes well beyond mere instances of individual corruption as it often is in advanced western countries; rather, on this contest, as it takes place in South Asian countries, depends the fate of whole networks of patronage, making the political contest all that much keener, and more violent, because entire livelihoods of many thousands of people are at stake.

It is from this basic problem of the state's control over resources and the livelihoods of people, that a distinctive feature of the life of the South Asian countries under discussion arises—its excessive politicisation. And it is from this excessive politicisation that all the vicious features of the political contests in these countries arise. The only basic agreement as to issues and methods is that political power effectively justifies any and every means used to achieve it.

The intrusion of criminality into politics is perceived, in the countries discussed in this volume, as a major problem in their electoral processes. The relationship between the electoral process, money and thuggery is not hard to find.

The nexus between politics and crime is logical as well as paradoxical. It is logical because politics is about power and the pursuit of power in highly competitive electoral contests and these require huge sums of money (preferably unaccounted), which is more easily available in the world of big crime than anywhere else. The game of power is also incomplete without muscle power, which gives the contestant a visible but undefined intimidating edge. The world of crime, on the other hand, has two important ingredients sought by the world of politics, the power of money and muscle. The investment of both these ingredients in politics is highly profitable in terms of legitimacy (in a purely legal sense) and systemic protection. Irrespective of who seeks the other first, the nexus has a logic, howsoever contrived or resented by society.[73]

V

Psychological Security

This is a condition stipulated by Robert Dahl, which we have earlier in this discussion observed may be a dependent variable, the dependence being on a long process of habituation in the processes of polyarchy. Nevertheless it deserves discussion because all our South Asian countries, with perhaps the exception of Nepal, are confronted in one way or the other with questions of identity, and because it is in the nature of psychological insecurity that it leads to people placing a higher premium on the rights of their larger ethnic or religious group rather than on their individual rights and duties. Where this takes place, it makes it much easier for the more powerful within the larger group to get away with much which is directly injurious to the rights and liberties of their own as well as those of the other groups.

With the solitary exception of Nepal, all the other countries of South Asia in their present form are recent political amalgams or units, created by the British colonial rulers, Bangladesh being a break away from one of those creations. Bangladesh emerged on the basis of a distinct Bengali identity which the rulers of Pakistan were too intransigent to accept or provide for. On the other hand, Bangladesh was indisputably a Muslim majority political unit as well. This question, whether Bangladesh perceives itself to be a Muslim or a Bengali nation, is one which anxiously asserts itself and still has not received any resolution.

The rise of the concept of Hindutva in India, and the continuing Hindu–Muslim problems of India are too well known to need reiteration here. Pakistan was formed on the basis of an Islamic identity—that after all was its rationale, to provide a nation for the Muslims of India who would otherwise be discriminated against in a Hindu majority entity. There are problems in Pakistan as regards treatment of its minorities—for instance its treatment of its Christian and Shia minorities—and these are again sufficiently well known and do not need to be discussed at length here. Even more glaring may perhaps be its suppression of the ethnic and regional aspirations of large sections of its Muslim population.[74] The ethnic conflict in Sri Lanka is also sufficiently well known and needs no detailed discussion here.

What is common to all these instances is that a process of nation building basing itself on language or religion, or indeed policies perceived as attempts to do so, have led to conflict in these countries. Given that all these problems exist, however, it is questionable as to what extent they disfigure the electoral processes of these countries. In Bangladesh, intimidation and violence directed against minorities appears to occur, as Sohela Nazneen points out in her chapter in this volume, not against Hindus per se so much as Hindus who are part of the Awami League vote block, when their votes would provide a decisive swing in the relevant electorates. There is no evidence that Muslims have been discriminated against in India where electoral processes are concerned; the evidence from Amit Prakash's chapter in this volume indicates that India has become ever more inclusive in its electoral processes. Nepal does not have qualitatively the same problem, but Hari Prasad Bhattarai's chapter shows that such discrimination as takes place in Nepal's electoral process is the result of historic inequalities and inequities in Nepali society. Only Pakistan could be said to have run a discriminatory electoral system during the period when it effected a system of separate electorates for Muslims and non-Muslims. While this has overtones of apartheid, it is at least arguable that it was an attempt also to ensure representation of minorities which may not otherwise occur in a system of joint electorates. The chapter on the Statutory Framework and Institutional Arrangements in Sri Lanka clearly shows that at least electoral systems have progressively become more inclusive where minorities are concerned. Thus, ethnic and religious divides do not appear to have distorted electoral systems so much as social and economic divides in South Asian countries.

VI

Prospects for Democratic Processes in South Asia

In each of the countries analysed here, the vast resources commanded by the state makes those with any degree of access to those resources jealously guard such access from intruders. If the problem is that political and economic power in these South Asian countries is concentrated in a few groups, the solution would be to liberalise the distribution of such power. Such liberalisation could flow from two sources. First, there may be domestic pressures and dynamics working towards such liberalisation. Second, there could be external pressures and dynamics driving these countries in the same direction.

To take the domestic pressures first, political dynamics, in that hitherto marginalised or neglected groups would ever more confidently and indeed aggressively assert themselves in all these South Asian countries, would be a prediction quite safe to make. Sometimes these assertions may take the form of armed militancies. A harbinger of even more fundamental change would be the process of economic growth and development itself, in creating new stakeholders and interest groups who directly seek to influence policy. Economic development is the first priority of any government in South Asia, or elsewhere for that matter, and such development would launch entirely new dynamics in the countries in which it occurs.

The most important external pressures would arise from this very concentration on economic development. Statist or autarchic models of development have been clearly proved to have been failures if not outright disasters, and every South Asian nation today is engaged in opening itself out to increased trade and foreign investment. The degree to which each country has set about doing this may vary, but there can be no doubt about the overall direction.

In making their economies more open, all these South Asian countries must also necessarily implement elements of what has come to be known as the 'Washington Consensus'. In freeing and attempting to maintain, stable exchange rates to encourage greater flows of trade and investment, governments have to keep their budget deficits under close control. In moving towards greater efficiency in resource allocation, governments must necessarily move away from direct economic activity. It is in these two policies, that is, controlling budget deficits and withdrawal from direct economic activity, that governments gradually lose their ability to maintain patronage networks and pork barrel spending. Thereby hopefully the state would cease to be a battleground between groups competing for the largesse the state has to offer.

Attempts at reform without significant underlying structural changes however are bound to prove ineffective and frustrating. In some South Asian countries exaggerated hopes have been misplaced on newfangled and dramatic initiatives, intended to operate free of both the legislature and executive, as if these were some sort of deus ex machina which could resolve all the problems which these societies have otherwise been unable to do much about.

In Sri Lanka, for instance, in 2001 yet another (the 17th) amendment to the Constitution was passed by Parliament. This amendment sought to provide for the independence (from president and Parliament alike) of various statutory institutions, among them the EC. The method of appointment to the central Constitutional Council which made appointments to the other institutions was both tortuous and tortured, to say the least, and reflected a complete distrust of both Parliament and president. Though passed with great fanfare and with grossly exaggerated hopes of a new political milieu, the amendment has turned out, quite predictably, to be a dead duck; the lack of political will to make the spirit of the amendment functional has led to gridlock in the appointment of the Constitutional Commission and the other bodies to be appointed by that Commission. Though the 17th Amendment was brought into effect in 2001, the EC is yet to be appointed. Just recently, the gridlock in re-appointing the Constitutional Council has led to the president making appointments to some of the bodies under the purview of the 17th Amendment, bypassing the Constitutional Council altogether.

Again, we have tremendous enthusiasm being shown for election monitoring. In this connection Zulfikar Khalid Maluka, in his chapter in this book, observes that '... 50–100 citizens of foreign countries observing elections cannot be as effective as the members of Pakistani society themselves.'[75]

Another idea which has gripped the imagination of well meaning would-be reformers is that of the neutral caretaker government during elections, first introduced through a Bangladeshi upheaval. Muzaffer Ahmad's 'Overview of Recent Electoral Experience in Bangladesh' makes clear one deleterious effect of the manner in which the concept of caretaker government has been formalised; as it is a retired chief justice who heads the caretaker government, appointments to the higher judiciary have become politicised as never before, as every political party has an interest in seeing to it that a retired chief justice sympathetic to them is in place at election time. As Muzaffer Ahmad very accurately points out in his chapter in this volume,

> The caretaker government option is an admission of the failure of political parties to abide by democratic norms during the election period.... The lesson to be drawn is that political underdevelopment cannot be remedied fully by an expedient measure even when at the beginning it is received with acclamation.[76]

In a similar vein, as Nilamber Acharya, Krishna P. Khanal and Birendra Prasad Mishra observe in their chapter on Nepal in this volume,

> ... an all-party election government, that is, the government of major parties represented in Parliament, may well legitimise the competing interference of the major parties in an election rather than making any contribution to the free and fair conduct of elections.
>
> The more acute question is how can the voter put his or her trust in the caretaker or neutral government to run the country if he/she is unable to trust the popularly elected and accountable government to remain in power during elections.... The concept of caretaker or neutral government should not be applied because democracy should not concede any ground to the notion that it can be interrupted for the greater public good, albeit for a limited period or limited purpose. It is a dangerous notion. The need is not to run away from democracy but to remain in it and go on perfecting it.[77]

Acharya, Khanal and Mishra have here sounded an important warning against trying to build institutions unaccountable to any one, and therefore irresponsible in the use of their authority. They, and Muzaffer Ahmad also, show, as does the Sri Lankan experience with the 17th Amendment to its Constitution, how unrealistic it is to expect anything already tainted to give rise to something else that is expected to be pure and undefiled; political pressures would inevitably push through, subvert and overcome whatever purely formal structures may be in place.

Other ingenious expedients resorted to are difficult if not impossible, to implement. Some of these which emerge from the chapters, in this volume are:

(*i*) a ban on transfers of public servants once an election is announced—easily circumvented because the government in power can make the placements they want prior to calling elections;

(*ii*) a ban on announcing new development projects, social welfare schemes and so on after elections are called—easily circumvented and virtually impossible to enforce because allocations could be made just before calling elections, and as Muzaffer Ahmad has pointed out general promises could be made at specific places;

(*iii*) ceilings on election expenditure—again impossible to enforce because there is no apparatus to keep track, and check returns made, of such expenditure; Acharya and Khanal have mentioned an interesting Nepali expedient in overcoming the problem of expenditure ceilings; the use of 'dummy candidates,' that is, candidates who are not effectively running, but whose quota for expenditure is used by the serious candidates;

(*iv*) information on candidates—in his chapter in this volume, Ujjwal Kumar Singh discusses an interesting experiment tried out in India where election candidates are compelled to divulge various details regarding themselves, including records of past convictions by the courts. However, it is unclear whether the Election Commission of India—or any institution operating in any of the South Asian countries let alone in such a vast country as India—would have the time and resources to check all the details being supplied by the thousands of contesting candidates.

That all these expedients are being tried is indicative of the level of desperation which at least some sections of society feel about the unsatisfactory nature of the election process in their countries, and though the measures proposed may be impractical, they indicate a positive trend—a sense of dissatisfaction with the status quo, and a lot of thinking going on as to what to do about it.

However, none of these measures attacks the source of the problems associated with electoral processes in all these South Asian countries: the excessive level of politicisation seen in all of them. That would not end until political and economic reform have liberalised these societies to such an extent that governments, or political parties, can act arbitrarily or capriciously only at the peril of being exposed and pilloried by a public opinion no longer dependent on government largesse. Economic liberalisation and the political liberalisation it inevitably brings about would also increase the space available for greater activity and assertiveness on the part of civil society organisations.

All the writers in this volume have in one way or another expressed a sentiment of the utmost importance: the need to go on working at making our societies more democratic. That may appear at first glance to be a quixotic effort, given the myriad problems facing democratic systems in the South Asian countries; the efforts may not bear fruit in our own lifetimes. However, there is also much that should also encourage the South Asian proponents of democracy.

After all, all these countries do have structures of laws and institutions which, at the very least, have been formulated with the democratic ideal in mind, and even more important, the democratic ideal is still very much alive and kicking in all of them. The realisation of democratic aspirations may however depend more on economic policies rather than purely legal or institutional reforms, and thus we are left with the perhaps not very surprising conclusion that those interested in improving electoral processes in their countries should first be fighting for increasing economic liberalisation. As so often happens, in electoral processes as well, the political and economic factors are inextricably interlinked.

Notes

1. Robert A. Dahl and Charles E. Lindblom, *Politics, Economics and Welfare*, New York, Evanston and London, Harper Torchbooks, 1963, pp. 286–87.
2. Ibid., p. 287.
3. Ibid., p. 294.
4. Ibid., p. 302.
5. Robert A. Dahl (ed.), *Regimes and Oppositions*, New Haven and London, Yale University Press, 1973, p. 4.
6. Ibid., pp. 315–16.
7. Ibid., p. 318.
8. Barrington Moore Jr, *Social Origins of Dictatorship and Democracy—Lord and Peasant in the Making of the Modern World*, London, Penguin University Books, 1967, pp. 318–19.
9. Ibid., p. 321.
10. Ibid., pp. 353–54.
11. Partha S. Ghosh, 'Corruption in India: A Holistic Analysis' in K.M. de Silva, G.H. Peiris and S.W.R. de A. Samarasinghe (eds), *Corruption in South Asia*, Kandy, Sri Lanka, International Centre for Ethnic Studies, 2002, p. 28.
12. Barrington Moore Jr, *Social Origins*, p. 375.
13. Ibid., p. 377.
14. Ibid.
15. G. Aloysius, *Nationalism without a Nation in India*, New Delhi, Oxford University Press, 1997, p. 221.
16. Leo E. Rose, 'The National Political Culture and Institutions in Nepal' in Amita Shastri and A. Jeyaratnam Wilson (eds), *The Post-Colonial States of South Asia*, New York, Palgrave, 2001, p. 115.
17. Ibid., p. 115.
18. Ibid., p. 117.
19. Colvin R. de Silva, *Ceylon under the British Occupation 1795–1833*, Vol. 1, Colombo, The Colombo Apothecaries Co. Ltd., 1953, pp. 131–32.

20. Richard Nations, 'The Economic Structure of Pakistan and Bangladesh' in Robin Blackburn (ed.), *Explosion in a SubContinent,* Harmondsworth, Penguin Books Ltd, 1975, p. 256.
21. Ibid., p. 257.
22. Tariq Ali, 'Pakistan and Bangladesh: Results and Prospects' in Robin Blackburn (ed.), *Explosion in a SubContinent,* p. 295.
23. Ayesha Jalal, *Democracy and Authoritarianism in South Asia,* New Delhi, (South Asian Edition) Cambridge University Press, 1995, p. 87.
24. Sugata Bose and Ayesha Jalal, *Modern South Asia: History, Culture, Polit-ical Economy,* New Delhi, Oxford University Press, 1998, p. 236.
25. A.M. Quamrul Alam, 'The Nature of the Bangladesh State in the Post-1975 Period,' *Contemporary South Asia,* Vol. 2, No. 3, 1993, p. 322.
26. Fahimul Quadir, 'The Political Economy of Pro-Market Reforms in Bangladesh: Regime Consolidation through Economic Liberalisation?,' *Contemporary South Asia,* Vol. 9, No. 2, 2000, p. 198.
27. Rehman Sobhan, 'Country Report on Bangladesh' in V.A. Pai Panandiker and Navnita Chadha Behera (eds), *Perspectives on South Asia,* New Delhi, Konark Publishers Pvt. Ltd, 2000, p. 226.
28. Partha Chatterjee, 'Introduction' in Partha Chatterjee (ed.), *Wages of Freedom: Fifty Years of the Indian Nation-State,* New Delhi, Oxford University Press, 1998, p. 7.
29. Rajni Kothari, 'The Democratic Experiment' in Partha Chatterjee (ed.), *Wages of Freedom,* p. 27.
30. Partha Chatterjee, *Introduction,* p. 8.
31. Pranab Bardhan, *The Political Economy of Development in India,* Oxford, Basil Blackwell, 1984, p. 38.
32. Myron Weiner, *The Indian Paradox—Essays in Indian Politics,* Ashutosh Varshney (ed.), New Delhi, Sage Publications, 1989, pp. 140–41.
33. Rajni Kothari, *State Against Democracy: In Search of Humane Governance,* New Delhi, Ajanta Publications, 1988, pp. 42–43.
34. Christophe Jaffrelot, *The Hindu Nationalist Movement in India,* Delhi, Viking Penguin India, 1996, p. 177.
35. This is the report of a 1980 Commission of Inquiry which recommended an extensive array of reservations in public sector employment in favour of lower caste and underprivileged groups.
36. Ibid., p. 435.
37. Thomas Blom Hansen and Christophe Jaffrelot (eds), *The BJP and the Compulsions of Politics in India,* New Delhi, Oxford University Press, 1998, p. 8.
38. Stanley A. Kochanek, 'Political Governance in India: The Challenge of Stability and Diversity' in Amita Shastri and A. Jeyaratnam Wilson (eds), *The Post-Colonial States of South Asia,* p. 29.
39. Thomas Blom Hansen and Christophe Jaffrelot (eds), *The BJP and the Compulsions,* pp. 7–8.
40. Ibid., p. 30.
41. Sumit Ganguly, 'India's Multiple Revolutions,' *Journal of Democracy,* Vol. 13, No. 1, January 2002, p. 42.
42. Pranab Bardhan, 'The Nature of Opposition to Economic Reforms in India,' *Economic and Political Weekly,* 26 November 2005.

43. Vanita Shastri, 'Liberalising India's Economy: Context and Constraints' in Amita Shastri and A. Jeyaratnam Wilson (eds), *The Post-Colonial States of South Asia*, p. 248.

44. Myron Weiner, 'The Regionalisation of Indian Politics and its Implication for Economic Reform' in Jeffrey D. Sachs, Ashutosh Varshney and Nirupam Bajpai (eds), *India in the Era of Economic Reforms,* New Delhi, Oxford University Press, 1999, p. 261.

45. Stanley A. Kochanek, 'Political Governance in India' p. 29.

46. Ujjwal Kumar Singh, 'Statutory Framework and Institutional Arrangements: India,' in this volume.

47. Leo E. Rose, ' The National Political Culture', p. 122.

48. Ibid., pp. 127–28.

49. Ibid., p. 128.

50. Hari Prasad Bhattarai, 'Group Discrimination at Elections: Nepal' in this volume.

51. Nilamber Acharya and Krishna P. Khanal, 'Statutory Framework and Institutional Arrangements: Nepal', in this volume.

52. Craig Baxter Yogendra K. Malic, Charles H. Kennedy and Robert C. Oberst, *Government and Politics in South Asia*, Lahore, Vanguard Books, 1988, p. 359.

53. Lok Raj Baral, 'The Process of Democratisation in Nepal: Problems and Prospects' in John M. Richardson Jr and S.W.R. de A. Samarasinghe (eds), *Democratisation in South Asia: The First Fifty Years*, Kandy, Sri Lanka, International Centre for Ethnic Studies, 1998, p. 192.

54. The political picture in Nepal is confused because of the widespread and powerful challenge of the Maoist insurgency. That such an insurgency exists could be used to prove the point that the Kathmandu political elite monopolised power for far too long, with the reforms coming after 1990 being 'too little, too late.' On the other hand the insurgency could also well be used to illustrate the argument that the most dangerous moment for a ramshackle political structure is when it starts to reform itself.

55. Sugata Bose and Ayesha Jalal, *Modern South Asia: History, Culture, Polit-ical Economy,* New Delhi, Oxford University Press, 1998, p. 213.

56. Ayesha Jalal, *Democracy and Authoritarianism in South Asia,* Cambridge, Cambridge University Press, 1995, pp. 50–51.

57. Mohammad Waseem, *Politics and the State,* pp. 62–63.

58. Ibid., pp. 108–09.

59. Ayesha Jalal, *Democracy and Authoritarianism*, p. 144.

60. Richard Nations, 'The Economic Structure of Pakistan and Bangladesh' in Robin Blackburn (ed.), *Explosion in a Subcontinent*, London, Penguin Books, 1975, p. 254.

61. Mohammad Waseem, 'Corruption, Violence and Criminalisation of Politics in Pakistan' in K.M. de Silva, G.H. Peiris and S.W.R. de A. Samarasinghe (eds), *Corruption in South Asia*, pp. 142–43.

62. Christophe Candland, 'Institutional Impediments to Human Development in Pakistan' in Amita Shastri and A. Jeyaratnam Wilson (eds), *The Post-Colonial States of South Asia,* p. 275.

63. S. Akbar Zaidi, 'State, Military and Social Transition: Improbable Future of Democracy in Pakistan,' *Economic and Political Weekly*, 3–9 December 2005, p. 5173.
64. Ibid., p. 5176.
65. Ibid., p. 5177.
66. Idem quoting Ayesha Siddiqe.
67. Zulfikar Khalid Maluka, 'Statutory Framework and Institutional Arrangements: Pakistan', in this volume.
68. S.W.R. de A. Samarasinghe, 'A Review of Some Macro-Economic Aspects of Sri Lanka's Post-War Home Oriented Growth Strategy,' *Ceylon Studies Seminar, Conference on Post-War Economic Development of Sri Lanka*, Peradeniya, 16–20 December 1980, pp. 6–7.
69. Ibid.
70. Doug Bandow, 'The First World's Misbegotten Economic Legacy to the Third World,' *Journal of Economic Growth*, Vol. 1 No. 4, Fourth Quarter 1986, p. 17.
71. T.N. Srinivasan, 'Introduction to Part 1' in Hollis Chenery and T.N. Srinivasan (eds), *Handbook of Development Economics,* Vol 1, Amsterdam, Elsevier Science Publishers, 1988, p. 3.
72. P. Bardhan, 'Alternative Approaches to Development Economics' in Hollis Chenery and T.N. Srinivasan (eds), *Handbook of Development Economics,* p. 65.
73. Ajay K. Mehra, 'Criminalisation of Indian Politics' in K.M. de Silva et.al. (eds), *Corruption in South Asia,* pp. 101–02.
74. The Pakistani state managers ... considered all ethnic and regional aspirations detrimental to their project of nation-building.... The centre dismissed 10 governments in various provinces in 11 years following partition. This pattern continued into the 1990s. The ethno-nationalist movements emerged following the dismissal of governments in: NWFP in 1947 and again in 1973; East Bengal in 1954 and 1958, and refusal of the centre to allow the Awami League to form the government in 1971; Sindh in 1948 and 1955; and Baluchistan in 1973. At other times, the Punjab-dominated army ruled the country which left an impression of alien oppression in other provinces.... The Pakhtun, Bengali, Baluch and Sindhi militant cadres took up arms against the government in a separatist bid several times in the post-independence period. Mohammad Waseem 'Corruption Violence and Criminalisation of Politics in Pakistan', in K.M. de Silva, G.H. Peiris and S.W.R. de A. Samarasinghe (eds), *Corruption in South Asia* p. 172.
75. Zulfikar Khalid Maluka, in this volume.
76. Muzaffer Ahmad, 'Country Papers: Bangladesh' in this volume.
77. Birendra Prasad Mishra, Krishna P. Khanal and Nilamber Acharya, 'Country Papers: Nepal' in this volume.

Part II

COUNTRY PAPERS

2

BANGLADESH

Muzaffer Ahmad

The Constitution of Bangladesh in its preamble pledges to realise through the democratic process a society in which rule of law, fundamental human rights and freedom, equality and justice—political, economic and social—will be secured for all citizens.[1] The Constitution of the People's Republic of Bangladesh in no uncertain terms states that 'All powers in the Republic belong to the people, and the Constitution is the solemn expression of the will of the people.'[2]

'People' certainly has been conceived as an organic whole but it cannot be taken to mean everybody. The practice of the parliamentary system as it occurs in Bangladesh appears to mean a limited majority of the seats in the Parliament but not an absolute majority of the voters. All the parties that formed governments under three elections since 1991 have received less than 51 per cent of popular vote. Thus minority rule (with majority seats) has been the practice.[3]

Elections are said to be the time when people exercise their supremacy directly. In Bangladesh however street politics by the opposition is believed to have replaced the voice of the people. The act of casting a vote does not necessarily attribute sovereignty to people as voting per se is mechanical unless public opinion on basic issues is formed freely by the people; free and fair elections in the context of unfree or constrained opinion may not ensure sovereignty

of the people. The party manifesto is a package without any participatory formulation. Thus electioneering under the charisma of a
dead or living leader without seeking endorsement of the programme
at the formulation stage through participatory debate does not oblit-
erate the dichotomy between the governed and the governing even
during elections.

Even in mature democracies, not to speak of new democracies,
studies have shown that voters are largely passive audiences with a
thin information base and distorted perception of issues. A voter's
preference is influenced by allegiance and predisposition. It is said
that the average voter does not act but reacts and the process of
forming opinion in reality does not start from the people but passes
through them.

Public opinion is in reality 'a pattern of attitudes and cluster of
demands.' The result of the election is merely to establish who is to
govern for a specified period of time but the system does not allow
the will of the people to become the motive power of the political
process. The reality is people remain the governed and elections
decide which of the minority group of political product formulators
will govern. Even under universal suffrage it is the powerful ma-
chine of the political parties that place their choice for people's
endorsement. The choice of candidates is also made by the parties
for election and the people are asked to select the party and not
choose his representative.

The mere existence of a number of parties also does not ensure
existence and pursuit of democratic values. In recent years the issue
of democratic choice in elections has been extended to democratic
culture within the party organisations in addition to existence of
distinctive multiple parties. Competition among leaders may be due
to trivial personal factors or regional factionalism so that parties
become merely different labels. They are rarely forced to be sensitive to people's voices so as to offer choices instead of remaining
bureaucratic and oligarchic.

Political parties are a manifestation of the freedom of association.
However, in Bangladesh there is no regulatory framework for their
activities, especially financial activities. The manifestos of political
parties are a mere formality and there is no provision to hold
the parties accountable for their promises; they have become mere
populist promises and are not debated seriously. The candidates
standing for election are often selected in a clandestine fashion by
party supremos without consideration of the electorate, and may
include thugs and holders of black money.

The challenge in the democratic polity is for the parties to reflect people's sensitivities in their manifestos and when voted to power to translate them into state policy. The democratic transition from a governed democracy to a governing democracy where an omnipotent popular will imposes itself through a pressure from below is a long and difficult journey which few democracies have successfully undertaken.

Political freedom is basically defined by absence of coercion, external restraint as well as freedom from opposition associated with arbitrary political power. Historically, in advanced western democracies, political freedom was sought in opposition to the power of the state and was not achieved by means of the state. However in many Third World countries including South Asian ones, it is the state that is relied upon to ensure fundamental rights and freedoms.

Constitutional Provision for Political Freedom

We have already noted that in the preamble of the Constitution, democracy has been identified as fundamental to the realisation of human rights and freedom. Effective participation of the people through their elected representatives at all levels of administration has been identified as integral to the concept of democracy.

The Constitution has guaranteed certain specific rights to every citizen. The freedoms so guaranteed include, among others, freedom of assembly (Article 37), freedom of association (Article 38), freedom of thought and conscience and of speech and of the press (Article 39). Enforcement of these rights has also been ensured by Article 44 wherein the High Court and Parliament are empowered to act to protect these rights.

These freedoms are subject to two types of restrictions. One, restrictions that are imposed by law in the interest of public order. These restrictions however can be arbitrary and when imposed have not been challenged so as to receive judicial interpretation of the limits of such restrictions. Government may also impose restrictions in public interest, and non-democratic governments have habitually suspended operation of human rights and rights guaranteed by the Constitution.[4]

While non-democratic regimes in Bangladesh have denied political freedom, Bangladesh has also experienced democratic regimes which have constrained political freedom through enactment of laws (for example, Public Safety Law.) Thus the rule of law turned into the rule of legislators has not always been the expression of the community sense of justice, and the judicial processes have not always been quick enough to assert their interpretation in favour of the content of freedom as provided for in the Constitution.

History of Elections in Bangladesh

Bangladesh has had an uneven experience of electoral processes over the last six decades. Election laws were introduced in 1935 under the British colonial regime to address the demands of the nationalist movement for self-governance. The laws that were formulated provided for separate electorates and special representation of designated groups under a restricted franchise. The results of the 1937 and 1946 elections were accepted by contesting parties as free and fair, irregularities were at a minimum and administration was neutral. The western electoral system thus became integral to the national aspiration for good governance. Provincial elections held in East Pakistan in 1954 unseated and virtually uprooted the governing Muslim League as their policies were considered anti-people and non-protective of the interests of East Bengal. However, the legitimacy of the outcome was never questioned.

This was followed by the non-democratic regime of Ayub Khan who abrogated a Constitution formulated through political negotiation between the political parties and elites of the two wings of Pakistan. This laid elected representative democracy to rest for the time being. Instead Ayub Khan introduced a system of basic democracy where an electoral college consisting of local body functionaries elected by people of the locality voted for the president. In the elections that ensued, the neutrality of administration was compromised, voters' lists were not accurately prepared and electoral laws did not facilitate a free and fair election.

Popular unrest compelled Ayub Khan to resign and his successor Yahya Khan held a general election in 1970 to elect members to National and Provincial Assemblies under a Legal Framework Order. Although this was a free and fair election, the rise of the East Pakistan-based Awami League (AL) as the dominant majority party in the Provincial and National Assemblies led to non-acceptance of the election results by the ruling military and political elite in West Pakistan. This led to the Liberation War and the creation of Bangladesh in December 1971.

The elections in 1973 held under a new Constitution and a legendary leader—Sheikh Mujibur Rahman—were not free and fair as the administration had once again lost its neutrality. In December 1974 Sheikh Mujib proclaimed a state of emergency, and pushed through a constitutional amendment limiting the power of the legislative and judicial branches of government, establishing an executive presidency and instituting a one-party system.

A confused period following the assassination of President Sheikh Mujibur Rahman in August 1975 was brought to end with another interregnum of non-democratic rule under Ziaur Rahman. Having tested the waters in local elections, Ziaur Rahman, in a quest for legitimacy, organised a presidential referendum, a presidential election, a political party to contest general elections and a general election.

Zia's referendum was held in May 1977. The outcome was predictable, his 19-point programme was endorsed by 98.88 per cent of total votes cast. The reasons for such massive support is attributed to active mobilisation by the bureaucrats, extensive publicity in state-run media, alleged manipulation of turnout of voters by electoral officials, patronage schemes for local area development and, most importantly, the overenthusiastic support of election officials.

Zia was plagued however by coup attempts by the members of armed forces. In this context Zia announced a presidential election for June 1978, probably to strengthen his position before parliamentary elections. General Zia won the election by securing 76.63 per cent of votes. The election was termed as rigged and grossly unfree and unfair. The election emboldened Zia not only by the victory he won but also because of the level of actual support recorded for him.

The election to the Parliament was held on 18 February 1979. Zia formed the Bangladesh Nationalist Party (BNP) in September 1978 to contest this election. Zia's BNP received 41.17 per cent of votes but 69 per cent of 300 seats in the Parliament against AL's 24.56 per cent of votes and 13 per cent of seats. Allegations were made of vote rigging, violence, intimidation and obstruction of voters by BNP. The opposition alleged that rigging was done in a pre-planned manner in connivance with election officials. This was the first time that allegation of a plan to rig elections systematically was made. The involvement of the bureaucracy, including agencies entrusted with protecting and fostering law and order, in influencing the election result surfaced as a hallmark of electoral process that still haunts the system to date.

In this period it must also be noted that businessmen emerged not only as financiers of political parties but also staked claims to office in the party and government. However, by 1980, Zia faced a number of problems: local feuds erupted within his party, the opposition became restive and Parliament recalcitrant despite some success in foreign affairs and in stabilising the economy. The army also suffered from continuous factionalism which finally resulted in the assassination of Ziaur Rahman in May 1981.

After a short period of indifferent governance by President Abdus Sattar with a fractured Bangladesh Nationalist Party, the military took over power in March 1982 under General Hussain Muhammad Ershad with the backing of the big neighbour, the civil bureaucracy, certain civilian politicians, including those from the AL, and a group of international donors. Ershad followed a much traversed path and in turn called a referendum, local elections and parliamentary elections for which he also organised a political party (the Jatiya Party or [JP]) and presidential elections.

The referendum was held on 21 March 1985 in the face of strong political opposition. The voting process was made easily subject to manipulation; the Election Commission (EC) announced a 72 per cent turnout, much higher than normal for elections and 94.14 per cent supported Ershad's programme.

Ershad's administrative reforms established *thana (upazila)* as the basic administrative unit. *Upazila* elections were held in May 1985. This was a process to co-opt rural elites as was done under the 'basic democracy' of General Ayub. In this election, mass political violence resulting in deaths, injuries and postponement of votes were reported and the neutrality of the army, police and administration was questioned by political activists and observers.

At the general elections of May 1986, a 60.31 per cent turnout was reported, the highest since independence in a parliamentary election. Ershad's Jatiya Party won a simple majority of 153 seats with 42.34 per cent of votes cast and AL got 76 seats with 26.16 per cent of votes cast. The AL had participated in the election though the BNP had boycotted it. After the election, AL and Jamaat-i-Islami (JI) accused the government of 'vote piracy', a new coinage that entered the electoral experience. It is believed that malpractices and corruption were more rampant in this election than in any other parliamentary election. A British electoral observation team considered the election as 'a tragedy of democracy'. The observation team reported massive rigging and capturing of vote centres by force. The turnout, as reported by a BBC correspondent, was about 10 per cent. All this vindicated the BNP's stand in boycotting the election.

Presidential polls followed on 31 August 1986. No major political party put up any candidate. The voter turnout was reported by the EC to be 54.23 per cent and Ershad obtained 83.57 per cent of votes cast. According to the opposition, fewer than 5 per cent of eligible voters actually cast their votes; the ballot boxes were stuffed by electoral officials and members of armed forces as well as the members of law enforcement agencies.

The Ershad regime not only fostered the continuation of the civil–military bureaucracy which made elections unfree and unfair but also formed a new alliance with big businesses on the one hand and the petty bourgeoisie at the sub-district level on the other. Even as Ershad tried to civilianise his regime, the growing mistrust of it by the parties in opposition and their uncompromising stance on boycotting elections created a turbulent political scene. The situation was further complicated by a downward slide in the economy. Ershad's attempt to use Islam as a political ploy did not succeed in calming the situation. The uprising against the Ershad regime and withdrawal of support from military commanders led to its fall in December 1990.

The concluding chapter of that fall was the institution of a neutral caretaker government (NCG), a concept set forth in the 1990 Joint Declaration of the Three (political) Party Alliances. It took effect by the resignation of Ershad's vice-president; the appointment in his place of Chief Justice Shahabuddin Ahmed, the joint opposition's nominee for head of the neutral caretaker government; the resignation of General Ershad; and the perfectly constitutional transfer of power to the Vice-President, Shahabuddin Ahmed.

The Constitution had become the plaything of the strong men in power; Shiekh Mujibur Rahman, General Ziaur Rahman and General Ershad had all amended the Constitution to suit their own ends. The Parliament elected in 1990 however amended the Constitution to institute a prime ministerial system instead of a presidential system.

Parliamentary elections were held on 27 February 1991 under a reconstituted EC. The election has been held to be free and fair by all independent observers. The electoral institutions, political parties and the administration all played their roles properly. There was no serious allegation of misconduct, malpractice or rigging. The turnout of voters was 55.35 per cent. The BNP won 140 of 300 seats with 31 per cent of popular votes cast, AL won 88 seats with 30 per cent of votes, JP, 35 seats with 12 per cent of votes cast and JI, 18 seats with 6 per cent of votes cast.

Local elections held in 1992 were also considered to be fair. However, at the 1994 elections for four City Corporations, it was evident that popular support for BNP had dwindled in the four cities including Dhaka from 50 per cent in the 1991 parliamentary elections to 39 per cent and AL had increased its support from 34 per cent in 1991 to 42 per cent in 1994. This jolted the complacency of BNP and led to an overreaction of the ruling party in the Magura–2 by-election, a seat won by AL in the last general election. Magura–2 became a competition of prestige and strength for BNP and AL. The BNP won the seat and AL claimed widespread rigging and demanded resignation of the government and EC as well as fresh elections under a caretaker government. The JP and JI also voiced allegations of non-neutrality on the part of administration, law enforcement agencies and election officials. On rejection by the BNP of the demand for an election under a neutral caretaker government (NCG), the opposition boycotted Parliament and then resigned en masse on 28 December 1994. The opposition now launched a campaign of repeated general strikes, marches and demonstrations in order to force the government to resign. BNP proceeded to dissolve the Parliament in November 1995. Election to the Parliament as per the Constitution was scheduled for 15 February 1996. The liaison committee of AL, JP and JI decided to boycott the election and asked the people to boycott it as well. In the face of a serious threat to law and order, the army was deployed in addition to police, paramilitary forces and para-police forces. Even then there was widespread violence before polling day, on the polling day and after polling day, and vote rigging, snatching of ballot papers and boxes, and capturing of booths took place on a massive scale. Voter turnout was low, reported to be around 10 per cent. All major opposition parties rejected the results in which 276 BNP candidates won. The opposition had won a moral victory and the demand for cancellation of the election and a fresh election under an NCG became irresistible.

The Jatiyo Sangsad was called to session on 15 February after the swearing in of a BNP government. In March 1996, following increasing political turmoil, the new Parliament, responding to opposition demands, enacted a constitutional amendment to allow a neutral caretaker government to conduct elections. The PM resigned on 30 March, and an NCG was immediately formed with Justice Habibur Rahman heading a ten-member Council of Advisors.

At the election held on 12 June 1996, AL emerged as the largest party with 135 seats and 37.47 per cent of the votes; the BNP won

104 seats with 33.34 per cent votes, JP, 29 seats with 16.10 per cent votes; and JI, three seats with 8.47 per cent of votes. EC ordered re-polling in 27 constituencies. This finally gave AL 147 seats, BNP 116 seats, JP 32 seats and JI three seats. AL formed the government with the help of JP and AL majority was ensured by gaining 27 seats allocated for women and conceding three seats to JP.

The BNP alleged vote rigging by AL, and also harassment and jailing of its activists, and staged several walkouts from Parliament. From June 1999 the BNP and other opposition parties abstained from attending Parliament, and staged an increasing number of nationwide general strikes and boycotts of elections (by-elections and elections to local bodies). They demanded that AL step down in favour of a new NCG which would conduct fresh general elections. Prime Minister Sheikh Hasina's Awami League government however completed its full five-year term, the first-ever elected government in Bangladesh's 30-year-old political history to record this achievement.

The general elections held in October 2001 were once again won by the BNP under Begum Khaleda Zia. The BNP in alliance with a couple of other smaller parties obtained 198 seats with 42.7 per cent of the vote; the AL, 63 seats with 40.1 per cent of the vote, the JP, 14 seats with 7.5 per cent of the vote, and the Jamaat, 17 seats with 4.3 per cent of the vote.

The Neutral Caretaker Government (NCG)

As we have seen, the first neutral caretaker government was installed in December 1990 through a constitutional expedient of the resignation of the incumbent vice-president, appointment of the person selected to head the NCG, Justice Shahabuddin Ahmed, as Vice-President, followed by the resignation of the President, General Ershad, and the devolution of power to the vice-president. The popular demand for a specific constitutional amendment for an NCG became irresistible with the agitation following the disputed Magura by-election and the dubious general elections of February 1996. The sixth Parliament met for 11 days and adopted the necessary amendment to the Constitution and the then BNP government resigned, handing over power to a non-party caretaker government.[5]

Under the terms of the Constitution:

- A caretaker government shall be in office from the date the chief advisor enters into office within 15 days on dissolution of the Parliament till a new government is formed after election.
- The non-party caretaker government shall consist of the chief advisor as the head of the executive and no more than ten other advisors who are eligible to be Members of Parliament.
- The president shall appoint as chief advisor the last retired chief justice if he is willing to hold the office and other advisors on the advice of the chief advisor.
- The non-party caretaker government shall discharge all functions as an interim government and shall carry on the routine functions of such government, more importantly providing all possible aid and assistance that may be required for holding the general election peacefully, fairly and impartially, but shall not take any policy decision.
- During the pendency of the non-party caretaker government, the defence portfolio is held by the president.
- The pendency of the caretaker government is 90 days.

In sum, the caretaker government is given the job of holding a free and fair election within 90 days of assumption of office.

Justice Shahabuddin's government faced numerous machinations by General Ershad who tried to foster instability with the help of loyalists in the army, the police and his own political party. Justice Shahabuddin emphasised the impartial role of the security forces, reshuffled the entire administrative system in order to ensure its neutrality and made sure that the environment was secure for conducting elections. The EC was reconstituted and formulated a code of conduct for candidates, agents, workers and political parties. Military and paramilitary forces were called in to maintain law and order and election observers were allowed to monitor elections. The election was conducted in a free and fair manner although the losing party accused election officials of partisanship during vote counting.

In 1996, the first constitutionally formed NCG under Justice Habibur Rahman reconstituted the EC, reshuffled the administrative service, adopted several measures for the recovery of arms and amended the ordinance for withdrawal of election officials for obstruction/prevention of fair polling. Besides further developing the code of conduct, the EC undertook a voter education campaign and updated the electoral rolls. Despite an attempted military putsch which underscored the problems of dual responsibility with the defence portfolio being held by the president and the rest of the administration functioning under the chief of the NCG, the elections were held as scheduled with a high voter turnout and the AL became the majority party to form the government.

The next elections were due in 2001 but before leaving office the AL made a number of postings at district and sub-district levels, particularly in the administrative service and the police, presumably to influence the conduct of elections. The EC was appointed by the AL regime and they also ensured that a retired chief justice of their choice—Justice Habibur Rahman—became chief of the caretaker government. However, much to the displeasure of the AL, the chief of the NCG followed his predecessor's example and reshuffled the administration. The chief advisor also amended the Representation of People's Order to provide for the quick disposal of election disputes, limitation of election expenses, prohibition of candidature for certain offences and withdrawal of election officials for certain offences. Law and order deteriorated, requiring daily monitoring and raids to recover arms and arrest offenders. Although the AL considered these actions as partisan and there were some disturbances during the elections, observers found the elections to be free and fair.

NCGs, in the periods they have been operative, have themselves had to face some political criticism, as would be evident from the account set out above. Every head of the NCGs which have been operative in Bangladesh has found it necessary to reshuffle officials among administrative positions in order to prevent election abuses that might otherwise occur. However, this has led to criticism by political parties.

Similarly, the EC may also need amendments to existing legislation to hold free and fair elections, and the caretaker government has implicit power to promulgate ordinances in this regard unless the preceding political government had already acted on the recommendations of the EC. In 2001, as the EC was a divided house due to politically motivated appointments, its recommendations for amendments were put in cold storage by the AL. The caretaker government acted on advice of the CEC to make the required amendments, but this order was considered by the AL to be a policy decision and as such a function exclusively of a duly elected legislature.

All the caretaker governments have sought the help of the armed forces for holding free and fair elections. Placing these forces under the president instead of the chief advisor may create problems. As *mastans* (thugs) have become a factor and as the law and order situation becomes charged, the chief advisors need to have easy and quick access to the armed forces.

The chief advisor has been stipulated to be the last retiring chief justice unless he declines to accept the office. This provides an opportunity to the party in office to locate a retiring chief justice of their choice by advising dissolution of Parliament accordingly. It is believed that the framing of the constitutional provision for care-taker government in 1996 was itself made keeping Justice Habibur Rahman in mind who was said to have AL sympathies. Barring a retired chief justice on grounds of age is believed to have been done to bar a former chief justice of the Ershad regime. In 2001 it is believed that the AL preferred to hold an election under Justice Latifur Rahman as he upheld the power of the Parliament to repeal the so-called Indemnity Act which banned any trial of those alleged to be involved in the killing of Sheikh Mujibur Rahman and his family, and saw to it as chief justice that the appeal against the lower court verdict in that case was heard expeditiously at the High Court. As for the elections due in 2007 it has been reported that 'By raising the age of retirement of Supreme Court judges from 65 to 67, the BNP government appears to have manipulated events such that the head of the caretaker government will be a certain ex-chief justice who was once an officer of the BNP.'[6]

Thus, when members of the bar are appointed to the bench on the prime minister's advice, political loyalty seems to be an important deciding factor. Correspondingly, elevation to the Appellate Division seems to be subject to the scrutiny of political loyalty. However, all the heads of caretaker governments assert they have acted with dedication to assist the EC to hold a free and fair election.[7]

The caretaker government option is an admission of the failure of political parties to abide by democratic norms during the election period. Unless major parties agree to uphold responsible and democratic norms themselves, the task of the caretaker government will become increasingly difficult. The caretaker government can function well under conditions of political acceptability, bureaucratic neutrality and civil support. It is now apparent that the concept of caretaker government was a matter of political expediency and the concept was not well thought out. The appointment to the post of chief justice and elevation to the bench of the Supreme Court is now more politicised than ever before. The lesson to be drawn is that political underdevelopment cannot be remedied fully by an expedient measure even when at the beginning it is received with acclamation.

The Bureaucracy

In colonial countries the civil services were called the steel frame of governance. In post-colonial Pakistan, particularly during periods of non-democratic governance, the grip of the civil–military bureaucracy became more deep, creating a stranglehold on democratic institutions. Despite the liberation war, Bangladesh did not get rid of the grip. All governments depend on the bureaucracy largely because of lack of education, capacity, farsightedness and leadership quality. No caretaker government is able or empowered to reconstruct the bureaucracy. It is interesting to note that former bureaucrats have dominated the caretaker governments; important committees of the caretaker government were constituted with bureaucrats. The chief advisors had to make significant changes in the bureaucracy before they felt sure of the reasonable neutrality of the government machinery. At the field level also, numerous, critical and continuous changes became necessary. Politicisation of the bureaucracy has undermined the ability of caretaker governments to be able to conduct free and fair elections. Unfortunately such politicisation has taken place under democratically elected regimes, affecting the efficiency of the machinery that is needed to provide and deliver public service.[8]

Civil Society

It is difficult to exactly locate the phenomenon said to be civil society; it may indeed be more proper to refer to the phenomenon as civil elites. The role of civil society is to help the people at the lower strata not only to articulate the pressure from below but also to distinguish between political propaganda and political reality in addition to educating people to understand and judge for themselves the opportunities and choices in the form of articulation of popular will. It is important to caution that civil society leaders are not supposed to replace the political elite by becoming counter-elites. In Bangladesh, civil society organisations have largely become appendages of the political parties. Very few civil society organisations—professional, academic, business and so on—have been able to unite for free and fair elections because as individuals they were mostly divided along party lines. Failure of civil society organisations to act on principles explains why the roots of democracy are not deep in Bangladesh.

Non-Governmental Organisations (NGOs)

The big and vocal NGOs are divided along party lines. Some of them have got involved in monitoring elections which has further compromised their role in voter education and local level articulation for free and fair elections. The neutral few are small and thus have no impact.

Donors

The donors have played a significant role in promoting tolerance amongst the two major political parties, in placing observers whose consolidated report is qualitatively better than those of others, and in funding local observer groups. But on the negative side, the donor-funded groups prepare reports on a given format leaving out details or matters which are not to the donor's liking. More discouragingly some donors have tried to dictate the manifestos/actions to be taken on forming the government. This smacks of hegemony, undermining democratic traditions as well as sovereignty.

Local and Foreign Observers

For the first time observers were granted legal recognition in 2001.[9] However management and administration of the observer groups were chaotic. The EC failed to do its job and the training given to literally thousands of observers was not well planned. As a result, the value of such observation, except for legitimation of result, was minimal.

Election Monitoring

International non-governmental organisations (INGOs) and donor-funded NGOs are now fielding observers to monitor elections. Donors offer large funds to train observers and some NGOs are funded to educate voters on the electoral process. The materials used by some NGOs for training, observation and voter education are allegedly partisan. Nevertheless, the EC has encouraged election monitoring by neutral persons of high integrity in order to promote a free and fair electoral process and uphold the principles of representative democracy.

Ideally monitoring should commence as soon as the electoral preparations by political parties and the EC begins. However, this is not the case in Bangladesh. It is apparent that international and local NGOs are primarily focused on election day itself. The observers' findings are moreover limited to selected polling stations, circumstances at a particular point of time and violations of the code of conduct. Issues of exclusion from or ineligible inclusion in the voters' list and vote buying and coercion which rob voters of the 'freedom to vote according to educated information and conscience' are generally ignored by NGO monitors. They tend to focus more on visible violence than on invisible barriers. Pre-election monitoring is limited and post-election monitoring is almost non-existent. The reporting lacks professionalism and accountability.

As a result there is widespread dissatisfaction with the monitoring process. Impartial observation by local citizen bodies at every important or 'difficult' polling centre on election day and preferably throughout the electoral process beginning with nomination, campaign, selection of agents and administration through counting of votes and declaration of results is a necessity. This requires a tolerant political culture and efficient electoral administration.

Media monitoring is carried out based on the space and time allocated to political parties by selected national daily newspapers and state-run television stations. However, there is no adequate coverage of local media or private television stations.

On the basis of the findings of international and local NGOs, and foreign observer groups, the elections held in 2001 were peaceful and fair; election administration including the polling process was considered to be efficient and neutral. However, some observers, particularly the Society for Environment and Human Development, expressed their concern about the non-neutrality of officials during the pre-election period. The Election Monitoring Alliance also reported abuse of electoral procedures during the pre-election period. It is probable that despite the laudable efforts of the EC and NCG, the quality of pre-electoral governance has not improved, mainly due to the presence of black money and armed cadres at the disposal of the major political parties. While there has been development in rules and procedures, values and norms in the performance of civic obligations including electoral practices have deteriorated.

Rise of Vested Interest in Politics

Business houses have always financed political parties in the hope of gaining access to the corridors of power although not to stake a claim to political office. Business houses in India such as the Tatas and Birlas still follow this tradition. Historically Bengali Muslim traders played an insignificant role in trade and industry. In the Pakistani era a few Bengalis made an appearance in these sectors but they represented less than a fifth of the volume of trade or invested fixed capital in industry. After liberation in 1971, despite the nationalisation of key sectors the government promoted a new business elite of about 100–200 family businesses which received patronage through contracts and concessions in construction, supplies, wholesale trade, distribution outlets, franchises, etc. The promotion of local business houses through patronage was boosted through denationalisation, liberalisation of credit policy and the expansion of the transport and service sectors, including banking and insurance. Most of these business houses flourished not because of their competence but because of their connections. As a result, financing political parties and their front organisations became a lucrative venture. The Structural Adjustment Policy, growth of the non-traditional export sector and the orchestrated demise of the public sector ushered in a new era of business–bureaucracy interrelationships. The regulatory power of the executive realised that patron–client relations could provide a 'win–win' financial situation for all the stakeholders, that is, business houses, bureaucracy, politicians and political parties. Hence red tape and rent seeking prompted the business interest groups to jump onto the political bandwagon. This divided the business and trade associations but raised the importance of businessmen in politics and political decision-making. Thus, business associations and business houses have formed a constituency that politicians court with passion while retired bureaucrats and military personnel have become partners of such business groups.

The Rise of Armed Cadres and the Criminalisation of Politics

No government has been able to control the new and growing phenomenon of armed cadres due to non-implementation or partial implementation of the law. The liberation war and other related incidents saw the introduction of arms in the hands of the youth. After the war, most of the arms were surrendered but some groups kept theirs. After the resurgence of political parties and front organisations, arms became a crucial factor in gaining control of student unions, trade unions, local electoral bodies and business groups. The current state of politics in Bangladesh is such that armed cadres have become a balancing force in confrontational politics. Thus criminals who extort, oppress, persecute and deprive people of their rights have become a new constituency which receives the patronage of local and national political leaders. This in turn has encouraged a section of the police and security forces to form alliances with these groups.

Group Discrimination

There is evidence to indicate discrimination and marginalisation of religious and ethnic minorities during pre- and post-election periods in Bangladesh. Violence against these groups cannot even be termed communal. It is the outcome of the patron–client power structure particularly in rural areas, criminalisation of politics, exploitation of religion and the absence of due diligence by national leaders.

The Ain-O-Salish Kendra prepared a news scan analysis of the print media. Their findings show that pre-election intimidation of minority voters occurred in selected pockets, that the use of threats was common and that physical assault and destruction of property also took place.

Post-election violence in the south and southeast of Bangladesh saw the destruction of property, looting and physical assault. This was mainly due to the NCG becoming a lame duck following the conclusion of the election and the proclivities of criminal groups. The experience of the minorities has cast gloom on the democratic process itself. A democratic polity and an efficient administration are needed to ensure the security of vulnerable citizens. Therefore, it is unfortunate that neither local civil society nor the national leaders of political parties have intervened to prevent such carnage. Thus in future, special security arrangements for the vulnerable minority groups during the pre- and post-election periods are a necessity and it is the duty of not only the administration but also civil society to prevent the occurrence of such violence. The local administration should be held accountable for any such violent attack.

A Road Map to Free and Fair Elections

Based on the experience of the three elections held under an NCG, a number of recommendations can be made.

- The president should be elected by an electoral college consisting of members of local level institutions as well as Members of Parliament (MPs). If an eminent and non-partisan personality is elected president then an NCG would not be necessary because the president can form an interim non-partisan advisory council in consultation with the major parties in the outgoing Parliament.
- The selection of a list of nominees for appointment to the EC, including the CEC, should be carried out by a panel of the Parliamentary Committee on Law and Parliamentary Affairs and the president should make appointments from the list either without consultation with the prime minister or in consultation with both the prime minister and the leader of the opposition. The budgetary allocation for the EC should be made on recommendation of the EC and vetted by the Parliamentary Committee.
- Political parties should be required to be transparent in their finances and activities by ensuring their registration and compulsory disclosure of their membership and finances, including the sources of their income, and beneficiaries/recipients of their expenditures. Business houses, NGOs and all others contributing to political parties should be required by law to disclose the amounts of their contributions. Legal sanctions should be enforced against both political parties and donors who fail to disclose the contributions made/received.
- The voters' list should be continuously updated, computerised and made publicly available for inspection. Improper exclusions and inclusions should be remedied, voter identity cards should be issued within a reasonable time frame, and voter education should be introduced in school curricula.
- Recovery of unlicenced arms should be a continuous function of law enforcement authorities and offenders should be dealt with immediately.
- Civil society and local members of the respective parties should monitor nomination of candidates. Candidature of loan

defaulters, tax dodgers and criminal record holders should be monitored and disclosed to the public by civil society prior to the elections.

- Use of public resources for election purposes should be made an election offence.
- All vulnerable groups must be protected and any reports of intimidation/violence should be dealt with promptly.
- Citizens' groups should monitor electoral offences and report these to the EC.
- Courts using summary procedures to deal with election offences should be set up well ahead of the elections and remain functional well after the election.

Conclusion

Bangladesh has entered a democratic phase after a long period of non-democratic rule. Political parties have used any available means to fight elections on the basis that the ultimate end—reaching the seat of pivotal power—justifies those means.

The non-democratic practices within the political system have also limited the effectiveness of representative democracy. Often the dynastic nature of the party system limits the opportunity for local leadership to rise in the hierarchy to serve the community. Moreover, the emergence of a nexus between business and politics as well as patronage and protection of criminal elements by various front organisations of political parties have also effectively blocked the rise of a service-minded leadership in the political organisations of Bangladesh. Dependence on black money, guns and goons for electioneering has made the proper functioning of the electoral process and representative democracy difficult in Bangladesh.

The electoral laws, institutions and processes need to be viewed in these contexts. Any institution or law is only as effective as the environment permits it to be. Elections have, however, provided an opportunity for the electorate to mature and electoral laws to be amended so as to contain malpractices. Elections provide the only opportunity for political participation by the public at large and thus remain important even though the factors conditioning the political process do not necessarily contribute to a system of governance that is responsive and accountable to the electorate.

Notes

1. Government of the People's Republic of Bangladesh (GOB), Ministry of
   Law, Justice and Parliament Affairs (MLJP), *The Constitution of the People's
   Republic of Bangladesh.*
2. GOB, MLJP, The Constitution: Article 7 (1).
3. See Yahya Akther, *Electoral Corruption in Bangladesh,* London, Ashgate,
   2000.
4. See GOB, MLJP: *The Constitution of the People's Republic of Bangladesh.*
5. Ibid.
6. Zafar Sobhan, 'Game On—Bangladesh's Pre-Election Season in Full Swing,'
   Bombay, *Economic and Political Weekly*, Vol. XLI, No. 18, 6–12 May 2006,
   p. 1736.
7. Personal Interview.
8. Ibid.
9. Election Commission, *'Rules for Local and Foreign Observers, 2001.*

3

INDIA

Partha S. Ghosh

Introduction

It is said that holding a general election in India amounts to holding
polls in Australia, Canada, Europe and the United States all put
together. When state assembly elections, by-elections and panchayat
elections are also taken into account the figures become truly stag-
gering. India has more than 3.2 million directly elected people's
representatives spread over various tiers of government. Generally
there is mass enthusiasm for elections, which has been appropriately
characterised as a sort of carnival.[1]

The electoral process in India involves much more than the periodic acts of voting and competition among political parties to form
the government. It also involves some enduring rules and structures
to ensure procedural certainty, which is regarded as the principal
task of electoral governance, and helps ensure the democratic principle of uncertainty of electoral outcome.[2]

This chapter is divided into eight sections. The first explains the
magnitude of the exercise. The second deals with the constitutional
and statutory framework of elections in India. The third section
examines the structure and workings of the Election Commission

(EC), the principal institution entrusted with the task of conducting elections. The fourth deals with the Model Code of Conduct for Elections, election procedures and malpractices. The fifth section deals with election observers and the sixth addresses group discrimination at elections. The seventh deals with such questions as pre-poll surveys conducted by professional and commercial agencies as well as the politico-moral issues involved in exit polls, which are becoming increasingly popular. The final section draws some broad conclusions based on the overall electoral experience of the country.

I

The Magnitude of Indian Elections

In India's first general election, held in 1952, the size of the electorate was 176 million of which 85 per cent were illiterate.

- Four thousand five hundred elections were to be conducted which included both the Parliament and the state assemblies.
- Each voter had to be identified, named[3] and registered.
- Two hundred and twenty-four thousand polling stations were constructed and equipped with 2 million steel boxes, requiring 8,200 tonnes of steel.
- Sixteen thousand five hundred clerks were appointed on six-month contracts for typing and collating the electoral rolls, constituency-wise.
- Three hundred and eighty thousand reams of paper were used for printing the rolls.
- Fifty-six thousand presiding officers were chosen to supervise the voting, aided by another 280,000 supporting staff.
- Two hundred and twenty-four thousand policemen were put on duty to prevent violence and intimidation.
- There were only six cases of violence in the entire country. A *Manchester Guardian* correspondent reported that for the most part the 'behaviour was of an orderliness elsewhere found only in English queues. The canvassing, too, was quiet and dignified. Indeed the entire tone of the elections, even on the Communist or Hindu Mahasabha platforms, was reminiscent of

Hyde Park on a rainy day.' However, a veteran Chennai editor
was not so charitable. He complained that 'a very large majority [will] exercise votes for the first time: not many know what
the vote is, why they should vote, and whom they should vote
for; no wonder the whole adventure is rated as the *biggest
gamble* in history'.[4]

There were 675 million people on the electoral rolls for India's
14th General Election, held in April–May 2004. According to estimates there were around 3.5 million election personnel deployed,
2 million security personnel put on duty and 1 million electronic
voting machines (EVMs) were used. There were 10,000 candidates
running for 537 Lok Sabha (House of People) seats (with 543 seats
in total). Many of these were dummy candidates put up by the
contestants to eat into the votes of their rivals. The total cost of
conducting the election was about $245 million.

The population of India was 361.1 million in 1951, and is about
1.3 billion today (1.027 billion according to the 2001 Census).
These two figures may be juxtaposed against the number of parliamentarians elected in 1952 and 1999. In 1952 the number of seats
in Parliament was 489, which means on average each MP represented approximately 740,000 people. In the election held in 1999,
there were 543 seats in Parliament, meaning each MP represented
approximately 1.9 million people.[5] The uneven sizes of the constituencies distort the picture further. For example, in Delhi, the Outer
Delhi constituency had approximately 2,820 million electors whereas
the Chandni Chowk constituency had around 360,000 electors only.
In terms of size, the Outer Delhi constituency is bigger than all of
Delhi's remaining six constituencies put together. According to the
Delimitation Act, 1972, the Delimitation Commission was supposed
to readjust the constituencies on the basis of the 1971 Census. However, the *Constitution Amendment Act, 1976* placed an embargo on
fresh delimitation until the publication of the 2001 Census figures.
There have been no revisions of constituencies since then because of
this embargo, which has now been extended by another 20 years.
While it is a Herculean task for any person to canvass his candidature
in such huge constituencies, the task of the EC is even more daunt-
ing, and has grown multi-fold over the years.

II

Constitutional and Statutory Framework

The Constitution of India enshrined the principle of universal adult franchise. This principle was empowering as it saw citizen-voters as having the capacity of self-governance. In order to ensure that this equality could in fact translate into equal opportunities for participation, it was important that precise rules and norms were laid down so that citizens' participation could, as far as possible, be unrestrained by structural conditions. Among the first of the important questions resolved was that the country would use the first-past-the-post and not the proportional representation system. Although some Muslim members in the Constituent Assembly were in favour of the latter in order to prevent 'the tyranny of the majority,' the overall consensus was not in its favour. While the interests of some other minorities such as the Scheduled Castes and Scheduled Tribes were protected by some constituencies being reserved for them, no such thing was done for the Muslims against the background of the partition of the country. Thus reservation for religious minorities was not granted.

The proportional representation system was not used, first, because it was a cumbersome process, which the large majority of illiterate or semi-literate Indian voters would not be able to understand and respond to appropriately. Second, the system presupposed the existence of a well-developed party system, which India did not have to start with.

Constitutional Provisions

Articles 324 to 329 of Part XV of the Constitution provide the legal–constitutional framework for the conduct of elections. Article 324 provides for the setting up of a single centralised body, the EC, entrusted with the task of 'superintendence, direction and control of elections,' and we shall more fully discuss the role and functions of the EC further on in this section.

Article 325 states that no person is to be ineligible for inclusion in or claim to be included in any special electoral roll on grounds of religion, race, caste or sex. There shall be one general electoral roll for every territorial constituency for election to either the House of

Parliament or the legislature of a state. It is widely felt that this provision of the Constitution is of crucial significance in assuring equality and the democratisation of the election procedure. It is also important for maintaining the secular character of the Constitution.[6]

Article 326 lays down that elections to the House of People and to the legislative assemblies of states are to be on the basis of adult suffrage, that is, every person who is a citizen of India and not less than 18 years of age on such date as may be fixed in that behalf by or under any law made by the appropriate legislature and is not otherwise disqualified under this Constitution or any law made by the appropriate legislature on the ground of non-residence, unsoundness of mind, crime or corrupt or illegal practice, shall be entitled to be registered as a voter at any such election. Article 327 recognises the power of Parliament to make provision with respect to elections to legislatures.[7] The power of Parliament is, however, subject to 'other provisions of this Constitution' including Article 324.[8] Article 328 similarly provides the legislature of a state the power to make provision with respect to elections to such legislature.[9] Article 329 adds important bars to interference by courts in electoral matters, for example, (a) the validity of any law relating to the delimitation of constituencies or the allotment of seats to such constituencies, made or purporting to be made under Article 327 or 328, and (b) election to either the House of Parliament or a state legislature. The latter can be questioned only by an election petition presented to such an authority and in such a manner as may be provided by law by the concerned legislature. Under the *Representation of the People Act*, the power to decide election disputes vests in the High Courts with a right of appeal to the Supreme Court. Disputes relating to the election of the president or vice-president are, however, to be settled by the Supreme Court.

Parliamentary Enactments

The constitutional provisions for conducting elections were supplemented by laws made by Parliament. The major laws are the *Representation of the People Act, 1950*, which deals mainly with the preparation and revision of electoral rolls, the delimitation of constituencies, prescribing additional qualification for voters and the *Representation of the People Act, 1951*, which deals in detail with all aspects of the conduct of elections and post-election disputes. Some of the important provisions of the 1950 Act are:

(*i*)   The seats in the Lok Sabha are distributed state-wise. A constituency of the Lok Sabha cannot be spread over two or more states.

(*ii*) Every constituency of the Lok Sabha is a single member constituency.

(*iii*) The constituencies of the Legislative Council of states are determined by the president.

(*iv*) There is a chief electoral officer for each state and a district election officer, an electoral registration officer and an assistant electoral registration officer for each district. All these are deemed to be on deputation to the EC.

(*v*)   Any person who is not less than 18 years of age on the qualifying date and who is ordinarily resident in a constituency and is not otherwise disqualified, is entitled to be registered as a voter in the constituency. Electoral rolls are revised and updated from time to time by the electoral registration officers either on an application by some person or on its own. An intensive revision of the roll is carried out before every general election to the Lok Sabha or the state legislature or before a by-election, unless the EC directs otherwise.

A separate law for setting up a Delimitation Commission was enacted in 1972 and one was set up under the act in 1973. No Delimitation Commission was set up after that and there has been no revision of constituencies because of the decision of the government to freeze the constituencies so as to withhold representation in Parliament to those states where population had been growing fast. The freeze was reaffirmed recently with the passage of the Delimitation Bill permitting fresh delimitation of constituencies on the basis of the 1991 Census. The process of delimitation is expected to continue for two years and will involve only a reorganisation of constituencies within states without changing the number of total seats or rectifying the discrepancies that exist between population and representation through redistribution of seats among states.

The *Representation of the People Act, 1951* deals with all aspects of the conduct of elections and post-election disputes. It details provisions regarding qualifications and disqualifications for candidates; time schedules for elections; administrative machinery for conducting elections; and powers to requisition premises, vehicles and so on by a government for the elections. It specifies roles and functions of candidates and their agents; manner of voting, counting of votes and declaration of results; disposal of elections petitions; specification of corrupt practices and election offences; suspension of poll or countermanding of election; registration of political parties; deposits for contesting elections; prevention of impersonation, limits on election expenditure, and so on.[10] The Supreme Court has held that where the enacted laws are silent or make insufficient provisions to deal with a given situation in the conduct of elections, the EC has the residuary powers under the Constitution to act in an appropriate manner.

The Indian Penal Code, 1860 has declared certain actions in connection with elections as offences. These are promoting enmity and so on, between different groups on grounds of religion, race, place of birth, residence, language and so on (Section 153A); imputations and assertions prejudicial to national integration (Section 153B); bribery (Section 171B); use of undue influence to interfere with the free exercise of any electoral rights (Section 171C); personification at an election (Section 171D); making false statements (Section 171G); illegal payments (Section 171H); failure to keep election accounts (Section 171); and making or circulating statements conducive to public mischief, enmity or hatred between different classes.

While most of these provisions were part of the *Indian Penal Code (IPC)* before independence, Sections 153A and 153B were added in 1969 and 1972 respectively. Some of these offences such as bribery, undue influence and promoting enmity on the ground of religion, race, etc., have also been declared corrupt practices under the *Representation of the People Act, 1951* (Section 123) which also prescribes several other electoral offences such as holding a public meeting within 48 hours of polling beginning (Section 126), creating disturbances at election meetings (Section 127) and so on.[11]

III

The Elections Commission

The Role of the Elections Commission

Article 324(1) of the Constitution provides that the EC shall superintend, direct and control the preparation of the electoral rolls for and the conduct of all elections to Parliament, to the legislature of every state, and to the offices of president and vice-president.

The EC decides the election schedules for the conduct of both the general elections and by-elections. It also decides on the location of the polling stations, assignment of voters to the polling stations, location of counting centres, arrangements to be made in and around the polling stations and counting centres, and all allied matters. The EC normally announces the poll schedule in a major press conference a few weeks before the formal process is set in motion.

The Constitution has laid down that the EC shall consist of a chief election commissioner (CEC) and such other election commissioners appointed by the president subject to the provisions of any law made in that behalf by Parliament [Article 324(2)]. In case any other election commissioner is appointed, the CEC acts as the Chairman of the EC [Article 324(3)]. Originally there was only one election commissioner but now there are three. In the case of differences of opinion amongst them the majority opinion prevails.

To assist the CEC in the discharge of his responsibilities specified in Article 324(1) of the Constitution, before each general election to the Lok Sabha and elections to the legislative assembly of each state, the president may, after consultation with the EC, appoint Regional Commissions [Article 324(4)]. The president, or the governor of a state, shall make available to the election commissioner or to a regional commissioner such staff as may be necessary for the discharge of the functions conferred on the EC by Article 324(6). The conditions of service and tenure of the election commissioners and regional commissioners are determined by the rules made by the president, subject to the provisions of any law of Parliament [324(5)].

To underscore the autonomy of the EC the Constitution provides that 'the CEC shall not be removed from his office except in like manner and on the like grounds as a Judge of the Supreme Court and the conditions of service of the CEC shall not be varied to his disadvantage after his appointment.' It has been further provided that 'any other Election Commissioner or Regional Commissioner shall not be removed from office except on the recommendation of the CEC.'

The CEC and other election commissioners have a tenure of six years, or can continue up to the age of 65, whichever comes first. They enjoy the same status and receive the salary and perks as Judges of the Supreme Court of India. The EC transacts its business by holding regular meetings and also by circulation of papers.

The EC at times delegates some of its executive functions to the officers in its Secretariat. It has a separate Secretariat in New Delhi, consisting of about 300 officials in a hierarchical set-up. Two deputy election commissioners—the senior-most officers in the Secretariat—assist the EC. They are generally appointed from the Indian Administrative Service (IAS), the national civil service of the country, and are selected and appointed by the EC with fixed tenure. The directors, principal secretaries and secretaries, under secretaries and, deputy directors support the deputy election commissioners in turn.

There is functional and territorial distribution of work in the EC. The work is organised into divisions, branches and sections. Each section is headed by a section officer. The main functional divisions are planning, judicial, administration, information systems, media and secretariat coordination. The territorial work is distributed among separate units responsible for different zones into which the 35 constituent states and union territories of the country are grouped for convenience of management.

At the state level, election work is supervised by the chief electoral officer of the state, who is appointed by the EC from amongst senior civil servants proposed by the concerned state government. But his supervision is subject to overall superintendence, direction and control of the EC in Delhi. In most of the states he is a full-time officer with a team of supporting staff.

At the district and constituency levels, the district election officers, electoral registration officers and returning officers, who are assisted by a large number of junior functionaries, discharge the electoral duties. They all perform their functions relating to elections in addition to their other responsibilities. During election time, however, they are available to the EC on an almost full-time basis. A huge task force comprising nearly 5 million polling personnel and civil police forces is created to conduct the general elections. This election machinery is considered to be on deputation to the EC and is subject to its control, superintendence and discipline during the election period, extending over a period of six weeks to two months.

The Secretariat of the EC has an independent budget, which is finalised directly in consultation between the EC and the Ministry of Finance of the Government of India. The latter usually accepts the recommendations of the EC for its budgets. However, the major expenditure on actual conduct of elections is reflected in the budgets of the concerned constituent units of the Indian Union—state or union territory. For parliamentary elections, the expenditure is entirely borne by the union government. Similarly for state assembly elections, the expenditure is borne entirely by the concerned state. In case of simultaneous elections to the Parliament and state legislatures, the expenditure is shared equally between the union and the concerned state governments. Court decisions have impacted on the scope of jurisdiction of the EC. Thus a 1978 judgement by the Supreme Court interpreted the expression 'superintendence, direction and control' as empowering the EC to act in contingencies not provided for by law, and to pass necessary orders for the conduct of the election. These included whether a re-poll should be held at a particular polling station or not;[12] to decide disputes relating to the allotment of symbols to political parties;[13] to recognise such parties or to derecognise them for such purpose;[14] to determine the status of rival groups within the same party; and to determine the effect of merger or separation of parties for this purpose.[15] While the determination of citizenship is outside the jurisdiction of the EC, where revising an electoral roll according to the procedure prescribed by the *Representation of the People Act, 1950*, the electoral authorities shall have the power to decide individual cases raising questions of citizenship.[16] Also, if the EC believes the disturbed conditions of a state or a part of it mean that free or fair elections cannot be held, it may postpone the elections.[17]

Thus under Article 324(1), the EC may be construed as having residual powers relating to the electoral process in areas unoccupied by legislation,[18] which empowers the EC to issue all directions necessary for the purpose of conducting smooth, free and fair elections.[19] By and large, the EC's powers under the Article are vast, and primarily administrative. Its judicative and legislative powers are only marginal. All its powers relating to direction and control of elections are, however, limited by the fact that all its orders must be traceable to some existing law,[20] and cannot violate the provisions of any laws including state acts.[21]

IV

Election Code of Conduct, Procedures and Malpractices

Model Code of Conduct

After considerable deliberations at the political level all parties agreed to a Model Code of Conduct as early as 1968. But because of many problems associated with its implementation it could not be announced. Nevertheless, several recommendations were made, namely the Goswami Committee on Electoral Reforms (1990), the Indrajit Gupta Committee on State Funding of Elections (1998) and the Law Commission's report on Reform of the Electoral Laws (1999). Besides, there were many studies and articles by NGOs and concerned individuals. The EC published its opinion on the matter in 1991 in what came to be known as the Model Code of Conduct for the Guidance of Political Parties and Candidates.

The Model Code has seven parts headed: General Conduct, Meetings, Processions, Polling Day, Polling Booth, Observers and Party in Power. Some of its most important points follow:

- All parties and candidates shall scrupulously avoid all activities which are 'corrupt practices' and offences under the election law, such as bribing of voters, intimidation of voters, impersonation of voters, canvassing within 100 metres of polling stations, holding public meetings during the period of 48 hours ending with the hour fixed for the close of the poll, and the transport and conveyance of voters to and from polling station.
- Except the voters, no one without a valid pass from the EC shall enter the polling booths.
- The EC appoints observers to deal with specific complaints from or problems of candidates or their agents regarding the conduct of elections.
- From the time elections are announced by the EC, ministers and other authorities shall not announce any financial grants in any form or promises thereof, or (except civil servants) lay foundation stones, etc., of projects or schemes of any kind, or make any promise of construction of roads, provision of drinking water facilities, etc., or make any *ad hoc* appointments in government, public undertakings, etc.
- Ministers of central or state government shall not enter any polling station or place of counting except in their capacity as a candidate or voter or authorised agent.

The Model Code of Conduct serves as the bible for the election observers and it is this code that they are expected to see being adhered to. According to M.S. Gill, the CEC of India from 1996 to 2001:

... in the last four years the EC has worked hard to frame a comprehensive set of guidelines and directions for the Central

Observers and for the code of conduct application in order to ensure that it has served the true purpose of democracy in a fair and balanced manner.

It is the CEC's belief that after the 1996, 1998 and 1999 parliamentary elections, and numerous state elections, a steady, firm and correct use of the code of conduct has been more or less established. The EC has also framed comprehensive guidelines for the work of central observers.[22]

The Balloting Procedure

Indian elections follow a balloting system based on symbols, a necessity because of the large extent of illiteracy. Each national party has a symbol reserved exclusively for its candidates throughout India, while state parties have a symbol for the exclusive use of its candidates in the respective states. All other candidates have to choose one symbol from a list of free symbols. The first two general elections followed a system of balloting in which there were as many ballot boxes as there were candidates.[23] However, a marking system on the ballot paper was introduced in state elections in the late 1950s and in the third general election of 1962. Voters use 'x' marks against the name of the candidate of their choice. After this, one box was used into which all votes are dropped. The practice of using indelible ink on the voter's finger was introduced as a precautionary step to prevent impersonation since the first general election of 1952.

Electronic Voting Machine

Electronic Voting Machines (EVMs) were first used in the 1980s on a trial basis. But on account of resistance from some major political parties they were not brought into wider use. However, efforts continued as EVMs were expected to increase efficiency and they replaced ballot papers in a phased manner after both the polling personnel and voters were adequately trained, and used to the device. While these machines were initially used in 16 select constituencies during the November 1998 state assembly polls in four states, Goa became the first state to use EVMs to conduct the entire polling in the assembly elections in June 1999. Encouraged by the response the EC, which invested several million rupees to procure the

EVMs—each costing approximately Rs 50,000—decided to deploy them in 46 parliamentary constituencies in the 1999 general elections. In the 14th General Election, held in April–May 2004, the entire polling was done by EVMs.

Challenges to Fair Polling

The overall situation has been characterised as a combination of three 'MPs' (money power, muscle power and mafia power) and four 'Cs' (criminalisation, communalisation, corruption and casteism). There are other challenges too. The party in power tends to distort the system to perpetuate its hold on the political process through its hold on the bureaucracy and the developmental process. This development poses a serious challenge to fair polling as the personnel on whom the EC has to depend for the conduct of elections have to be found from amongst them. Besides, there is a tendency for all ruling parties to offer sops to the voters just before elections in terms of raised salaries or other direct or indirect financial benefits to influence the outcome of the polls. To meet these challenges the EC has come out with a Model Code of Conduct to check unfair campaigns and misuse of authority during election campaigns, though these still do not have legal sanction.

Rigging of Elections

This is done in the following ways:

(*i*)   By creating a law and order problem in pockets which might vote for the rival candidates. This would result in low voter turnout in those areas. In contrast, by making all possible arrangements to maintain law and order and to provide the best facilities for voters to come and vote in those polling stations where votes are expected to be cast in favour of the ruling party/parties.

(*ii*) By influencing the presiding officers and his colleagues to stamp the unused ballot papers as desired, in case the polling agents of the rival parties are not present.

(*iii*) By bribing and buying the polling agents of other parties, or by intimidating them, thereby allowing rampant bogus voting to take place. This practice is known as 'friendly rigging'.

(*iv*) By capturing polling booths through the use of muscle power and seeing to it that the presiding officers do not recommend a re-poll.

(*v*) By impersonating voters. This is possible on a massive scale if the political climate is favourable to the party that is rigging. It happened in 1977 when massive bogus voting took place in favour of the Janata Party, which was in opposition and making a bid for power at the cost of the ruling Congress Party led by Indira Gandhi.

V

Election Observers

Though India is a developing nation it has neither invited foreign observers nor has it encouraged them to come to India and pass judgements on its electoral institutions. It has instead developed its own system of internal observation. Following the long-drawn-out nationalist movement, which was both peaceful and highly intellectual in its orientation, when India became independent in 1947 the leaders had two primary concerns. One was to build India's own democratic institutions without any support from the West and the other was to make its democracy as mass-based as possible. At the core of both of these objectives was the conduct of free and fair elections. How to ensure these, given the country's large population, massive size, mass illiteracy, rampant superstition and abject poverty, was the most challenging task. In spite of all these problems, Indians were strongly opposed to any idea of receiving some sort of certification from other nations about their capability in organising elections. Moreover, since at the time of India's independence almost the entire developing world was still under colonial yoke, foreign observers really equated to observers from the West, against whom India had natural reservations. Against this background the system that seemed acceptable was to send internal observers to monitor the process and report back to the EC, which alone was entitled to take corrective measures.

To ensure free and fair polling the EC appoints election observers under powers conferred upon it by section 20B of the *Representation of the People Act, 1951*. In August 1996 this section was added to the Act. Prior to that election observers were appointed under the plenary powers available to the EC under Article 324 of the Indian Constitution, to which reference has been made above. Section 20B of the *Representation of the People Act, 1951*, reads as follows:

(*i*) The EC may nominate an Observer who shall be an officer of Government to watch the conduct of elections in a constituency or a group of constituencies and to perform such other functions as may be entrusted to him by the EC.

(*ii*) The Observer nominated under subsection (i) shall have the power to direct the Returning Officer for the constituency or for any of the constituencies for which he has been nominated, to stop the counting of votes at any time before the declaration of result or not to declare the result if, in the opinion of the Observer, booth capturing has taken place at a large number of polling stations or at places fixed for the counting of votes or any ballot papers used at a polling station or at a place fixed for the poll are unlawfully taken out of the custody of the Returning Officer or are accidentally or intentionally destroyed or lost or damaged or tampered with to such an extent that the result of the poll at that polling station or place cannot be ascertained.

(*iii*) Where an Observer has directed the Returning Officer under this section to stop the counting of votes or not to declare the result, the Observer shall forthwith report the matter to the EC and thereupon the EC shall, after taking all material circumstances into account, issue appropriate directions under Section 58A or Section 64A or Section 66.

According to the Guidelines for Observers, issued by the EC in 1998 the election observers

... will act as the eyes and ears of the EC during the period of the election and provide direct inputs to the EC from the field as an interface with the election machinery: the candidates, parties, and electors to ensure that the acts, rules, procedures, instructions and guidelines related to elections are strictly and impartially complied with by all concerned.

As such, 'the candidates, political parties and the voting public have high expectations from the Observers as the direct representatives of the EC in the Constituencies'.[24]

Types of Observers

There are two types of observers sent to monitor the elections, namely, (*a*) general observers and (*b*) expenditure observers. The general observers observe that the elections are conducted according to the law and the directions of the EC and in a free and fair manner. The expenditure observers are appointed to closely watch, analyse and report the instances of misuse of money power by candidates and political parties to influence the electors.

Ordinarily two general observers and one expenditure observer are sent to each parliamentary constituency. If a particular constituency is sensitive, two or three additional observers may also be sent. To focus on the counting process, additional counting observers are appointed to cover all counting centres in the country. Table 3.1 provides details of the deployment of observers in general elections and state elections between 1996 and 1999.

General observers are drawn from the Indian Administrative Service (IAS) cadre with 14 to 15 years of service and often of the senior joint secretary rank. They generally observe how far the Model Code of Conduct has been adhered to. The expenditure observers are drawn from the Indian Revenue Service, meaning that they are generally either Income Tax or Customs officers, and also senior level officials. The permissible limit of expenditure for each party or candidate is Rs 1.5 million for each Lok Sabha constituency and Rs 600,000 for each assembly constituency. The expenditure observer checks the party accounts and if an anomaly is noticed he reports it to the EC.

Efficacy of Observing

Can election observers ensure free and fair polling? Before an attempt is made to answer this question, a few points may be kept in mind. In the first place, it is generally the case that the politically losing parties make allegations of poll rigging and talk about unfair means employed by their rivals. It is almost invariably argued that the elections in Kashmir have been rigged in every case apart from in 1977. But even then there were allegations that they were not fair. Wajahat Habibullah, the former director of the Lal Bahadur Shastri Academy, Mussoorie, where IAS probationers are trained, and who was deputy commissioner in Srinagar in 1977, said in an interview

Table 3.1

Opinion-poll-based Election Forecasts for the 14th General Election

Sponsoring Publication/Channel	Date of Publication	Agency	Sample Size		Field Work Period	Seats Forecast		
			Seats	Persons		NDA	Congress	Others
India Today	9 Feb.	ORG–MARG	98	17,649	9–17 Jan.	330–340	105–115	95–105
Outlook	15 Mar.	MDRA	102	12,249	19–25 Feb.	280–290	159–169	89–99
Indian Express/NDTV	27 Mar.	AC Nielson	207	45,578	5–18 Mar.	287–307	143–163	90–100
Zee News	4 Apr.	Taleem	65	12,788	15–20 Mar.	265	196	83
Star News	4 Apr.	C Voter	120	12,000	March last week	277	164	102
Rashtriya Sahara	10 Apr.	DRS	500	65,089	28 Mar–5 Apr.	271	168	104
The Week	18 Apr.	TNS	143	17,513	25 Mar–1 Apr.	230–265	170–200	95–110
India Today/Bhaskar	15 Apr.	ORG–MARG	199	51,000	25 Mar–7 Apr	282	165	96
Indian Express/NDTV	15 Apr.	AC–Nielson	57/140	16,393	6–13 Apr.	260–280	165–180	96–105
Star News	17 Apr.	C Voter	120	12,000	10–16 Apr.	272–286	154–170	95–111

Source: Yogendra Yadav, 'Making Sense of the Opinion Polls', *The Hindu*, New Delhi, 19 April 2004.

in 2002 that 'today they [the 1977 elections] are described as the freest and fairest elections the state has witnessed. But at that time, I was abused by all the parties that participated'.[25] During the Tamil Nadu Assembly elections held in 2001 the opposition All India Anna Dravida Munnetra Kazhagam made a big hue and cry that the ruling Dravida Munnetra Kazhagam was rigging the polls. However, the results overwhelmingly went in favour of the former.

Second, the question of fair polling does not include the acts of omission and commission that precede the polling, which have much to do with the outcome of the poll. To take the example of the experience of Jammu and Kashmir, in the election to Kashmir's Constituent Assembly in 1950, which consisted of 75 members, all the nominations filed by the opposition were rejected. In the 1962 assembly elections the National Conference won 68 out of 76 seats. The remaining seats were bagged by Jammu's Yuvak Sabha and Praja Parishad. In the Valley 11 nominations filed by the Praja Socialist Party were rejected. In several other constituencies the situation was so manipulated that the Plebiscite Front (floated by Sheikh Abdullah's supporters) stayed away from the election. The National Conference won 35 seats uncontested. In 1987, the Muslim Unity Front had emerged as a political force to reckon with. But its nominees were threatened and beaten up and eventually the poll outcome went against them to everybody's surprise.[26]

Third, it is extremely difficult to muster hard data to prove poll rigging. It is only in rare cases that remedial measures such as nullifying a particular election result takes effect.

Thus the efficacy of monitoring as a mechanism to ensure free and fair polling is at best limited. It is confined to the rules and regulations for the conduct of the poll and if there is a glaring anomaly in its conduct the observers can report the matter and the EC may reprimand the poll in a particular booth or area. Moreover, since it is not physically possible for an observer to be present at all times in all the booths they can make only random checks, which cannot be foolproof. Since it is an important organ of the EC to ensure free and fair polling more research is required to make the process more effective.

VI

Group Discrimination

Positive Discrimination

Discrimination against Scheduled Castes (SCs), Scheduled Tribes (STs), Other Backward Classes (OBCs) and women has historical roots. To rectify the situation, at least in the case of the first three, there has been significant positive discrimination as a result of a constitutional mandate (positive discrimination for women is also being actively considered over the past decade or so).

The overall framework which emerged from the process of constitution-making over the period of the functioning of the Constituent Assembly and its Advisory Committees was that of the conscious removal of all possible disabilities which might hinder or retard the exercise of full political rights by any member of any minority community. Universal adult franchise and joint electorates were repeatedly emphasised by various bodies concerned with the framing of the Constitution. Thus, these two concepts emerged as the bulwark of the democratic set-up of India. Obviously, there is little scope of institutional discrimination against the minorities in such a framework.

However, the framework of equal citizenship and political rights for all individuals, irrespective of community, sex or creed was tempered by cultural and educational rights for the minorities. This ensured that while political equality was emphasised, such equality does not translate into majority-led homogenisation of the polity.

One significant digression from this framework of equal political rights was that of additional political rights and safeguards for SCs and STs.[27] There seems to have been near unanimity in the Advisory Committee and the CA that these two groups, on account of historical injustices suffered and/or having been excluded from normal administration under the British rule, were entitled to additional political rights in order to secure adequate representation of their interests in the legislatures. However, the way in which this provision has been operationalised may act as a source of discrimination against non-SC/non-ST communities.

It is widely agreed that positive discrimination in the Indian context has led to a wave of democratisation. For instance, the assertion of hitherto marginalised sections of the society (especially in the north Indian states) is testimony to the fact that such positive discrimination has been of immense value in fostering democratisation of the polity. It has not only challenged old structures of domination which have discriminated against the marginalised sections for centuries, but also set in motion a pattern of socio-economic and political empowerment which is irreversible and will significantly alter the popular political discourse, the political idiom and the patterns of discrimination.

As far as the case of community and religion-based identities in India vis-à-vis the electoral system are concerned, the absence of positive discrimination for these identities was a conscious choice made by the representatives of these communities in the Constituent Assembly. While historically these social groups enjoyed special provisions under the British rule, they voluntarily relinquished their claim to positive discrimination during the process of the framing of the Constitution owing to the perceived need to stress a common citizenship. However, this does not imply that these communities have equal access to the electoral system. These social groups have no legal or formal impediment to the enjoyment of equal political rights and any discrimination that might exist against them is not directly attributable to any actual desire by the state to reduce or eliminate the election of citizens who happen to belong to a minority. Owing to their smaller numbers and territorial dispersion, minorities are systematically outvoted in terms of their participation and representation in public life. This constitutes an impediment to their enjoyment of individual political rights and hence, discrimination in the political process.

It may not be an exaggeration to state that perhaps caste is the most important category wherein electoral discrimination may operate. This social category is not only rooted in the historical dynamics of Indian public life but has also been the bedrock of all kinds of social discrimination. Owing to the inherently exploitative and inegalitarian nature of the caste hierarchy, this social category is perhaps the most amenable to discriminatory practices in the electoral realm as well.

VII

Psephological Predictions: Issues Involved

In India elections can appear just like carnivals: popular enthusiasm is tremendous and there is great inquisitiveness to know the outcome of the polls. The science of psephology has therefore gained increasing popularity.

Psephological predictions about the poll outcome entered the Indian electoral scene with the 1967 General Election. The 1967 and the 1971 elections were studied by the Michigan State University in collaboration with the Delhi-based Centre for the Study of Developing Societies using large sample sizes and detailed questionnaires. *India Today* pioneered the exercise in the media in 1978. Ever since, it has virtually become a regular feature for all important newspapers and TV channels to recruit professional agencies to predict the poll outcomes, which are mainly predicted correctly. Of late, exit polls have also become common. Table 3.1 shows the popularity of these psephological exercises in respect of the 14th General Election held in April–May 2004.

Since the general elections in India are not held on one single day—for example, the 14th General Election was held over five days spreading almost to a month—some people have raised the question of political propriety in respect of the exit polls on the ground that they may influence voting patterns in subsequent days of polling. The matter was even discussed by the EC but so far no ban has been enforced.

VIII

Conclusions

Elections are the most significant indicators of the health of a democracy. Indian electorates display complex symptoms making the political health check-up of India extremely difficult. On the one hand there is an ever-increasing upsurge of democracy, noticeable from the growing percentage of participation in the election process from the underprivileged sections of the society as well as the rural masses in general.[28] Interestingly the election data during the last 50 years and more clearly show that the rural and marginalised sections of the society have been participating in larger numbers while the share of the urban participation is declining in proportionate terms. On the other hand there is a growing voice against electoral malpractices, use of money and muscle power, and the overall criminalisation of politics.[29] One major bane suffered by developing societies is their all-pervasive disregard for law—first, there may be no law, and second, if there is any, it may not be enforced. Since electoral laws in India are well in place it is imperative to develop a mechanism to see to it that they are enforced. The rationale for having the EC together with its elaborate administrative paraphernalia is thus clear. Incidentally, most of the opinion polls held in the country over the years have rated the EC as the most efficient and impartial of all the democratic institutions of India. Therein lies the future of Indian democracy.

Notes

1. Ramesh Thakur, 'General Election this Month: India Girds for World's Biggest Tamasha [Carnival]', *The Japan Times*, Tokyo, 11 April 2004.
2. For a comprehensive discussion of this theme see Shaheen Mozaffar and Andreas Schedler, 'The Comparative Study of Electoral Governance—Introduction', *International Political Science Review*, 23(1), pp. 5–27.
3. Many women in north India were identified as A's mother or B's wife, etc. Sen was outraged by this 'senseless relic of the past' and directed his efforts to insert the names alone instead 'mere descriptions of such voters'.
4. For a detailed account of the election of 1952, see Ramachandra Guha, 'The Biggest Gamble in History', *The Hindu*, New Delhi, 27 January 2002 and 3 February 2002 (in two parts).
5. The maximum number of elected members of Lok Sabha is 550. Article 81 of the Constitution provides that not more than 530 members will be elected from the States and not more than 20 members from union territories. Article 331 of the Constitution provides that not more than two members from the Anglo-Indian Community may be nominated by the president of India, if in his opinion that community is not adequately represented in that House.
6. *Poudyal vs Union of India*, (1994) Supp.(1) S.C.C. 324 (para. 206) C.B.
7. Parliament may make provisions from time to time by law with respect to all matters relating to, or in connection with, elections to either the House of Parliament or to the House or either Houses of the legislatures of a state including the preparation of electoral rolls, the delimitation of constituencies and all other matters necessary for securing the due constitution of such House or Houses.
8. *Sadiq vs Election Commission*, A. 1972 S.C.187.
9. Subject to the provisions of this Constitution and insofar as provision in that behalf is not made by Parliament, the legislature of a state may from time to time by law make provision with respect to all matters relating to, or in connection with, the elections to the House or Legislature of the state including the preparation of electoral rolls and all other matters necessary for securing the due constitution of such House of Houses.
10. S.S. Gadkari, *Electoral Reforms in India*, New Delhi, Wheeler Publishing, 1996, p. 10.

11. The main difference between an electoral offence and corrupt practice is that an electoral offence attracts penalty in a criminal code, whereas a corrupt practice disqualifies a candidate whose election can be set aside.

12. *Mohinder vs Chief Election Commissioner*, A. 1978 S.C. 851, paras 91, 114–15, 121. See for details D.D. Basu, *Shorter Constitution of India*, New Delhi, Prentice Hall of India, 1996, p. 1061.

13. *Sadiq vs Election Commissioner*, A. 1972 S.C. 187.

14. *S.S.P. vs Election Commissioner*, A. 1967 S.C. 898.

15. Ibid.

16. *Inderjit vs Election Commission*, A. 1984 S.C. 1911 (para 4).

17. *Digvijaya vs Union of India*, (1993) 4 S.C.C. 175 (paras 12, 14).

18. *Kanhiya vs Trivedi*, A. 1986 S.C. 111 (paras 13, 16).

19. See D.D. Basu, *Shorter Constitution of India*, op. cit., especially for judgements pertaining to the limits on the powers of the EC, pp. 1061–62.

20. *Kanhiya vs Trivedi*, A. 1986 S.C. 111 (para. 16).

21. *Dasappa vs Election Commission*, A. 1992, Kant. 230 (para. 10).

22. See M.S. Gill's Foreword, to EC of India, M.S. Gill's *Elections in India: Major Events and New Initiatives, 1996–2000*, New Delhi, Election Commission of India, 2000, pp. iv–v.

23. In Sri Lanka, where universal suffrage was introduced in 1931, each contestant or party had a box with a distinctive colour.

24. The Election Commission of India, *General Elections, 1998: Guidelines for Observers (Reprint 2002)*, New Delhi, 2002, pp. 2, 13. Emphasis is in the original.

25. *Times of India*, New Delhi, 20 May 2002.

26. Arun Joshi, 'A Long History of Rigged Elections', *Hindustan Times*, New Delhi, 19 May 2002.

27. And the provision for nomination of two representatives of the Anglo-Indian Community to the Lok Sabha, if the president thinks that they are not properly represented in the House (Article 331 of the Constitution of India).

28. Yogendra Yadav and Sanjay Kumar, 'Political Agenda of Electoral Reforms in India', in Devendra Raj Panday, Aditya Anand and Dev Raj Dahal (eds), *Comparative Electoral Processes in South Asia*, Kathmandu, Nepal South Asia Centre, 1999, pp. 35–42.

29. The Vohra Committee underlined the problem in detail. See Government of India, Ministry of Home Affairs, *Vohra Committee Report* (Chairman: N.N. Vohra, Home Secretary), New Delhi, 1993.

4

NEPAL

Birendra Prasad Mishra, Krishna P. Khanal
and Nilamber Acharya

Democratic Constitution

The 1990 Constitution of the kingdom of Nepal is the result of a
five-and-a-half decade long struggle of the Nepalese people for representative democracy. Since the 1940s the people had been raising
their voice against the oligarchic rule of the Ranas. The first mention
of any election, though undemocratic and indirect, was made in the
stillborn *Government of Nepal Act* proclaimed in 1948 by the Rana
regime. In February 1951 however the 104-year-old hereditary autocracy of Rana prime ministers was overthrown following the armed
revolution carried out by the Nepali Congress (NC) in 1950, and
King Tribhuvan returned to Kathmandu from temporary exile in
India. Although the king proclaimed in February 1951 that elections
for a Constituent Assembly would be held, and the *Interim Government Act* came into effect in April 1951 to create conditions for
holding elections, unfortunately they never took place and political
power was thereafter concentrated in the monarchy; no elections
were held either for a Parliament or a Constituent Assembly for
nearly eight years.

After a lapse of eight years a new Constitution was proclaimed and the House of Representatives (HOR) was elected on the basis of universal adult franchise in 1959. However, the Constitution of 1959 and the Parliament elected under it were short-lived; in December 1960 the king dissolved the Parliament and suspended the Constitution.

The Constitution of Nepal proclaimed in December 1962 by the king institutionalised the undemocratic character of governance with the concentration of all power in the hands of the king. However, in 1980 the Constitution was amended for the third time and elections for a powerless National Panchayat were permitted. Political parties were however prohibited. General elections were held in 1982 and 1987 on the basis of adult franchise during this period.

The 49-day-long historical Popular Movement for restoration of multiparty democracy in 1990 led to the formation in April of that year of an interim government of representatives of the Popular Movement and two nominees of the king, charged with the task of preparing a democratic constitution and holding general elections. This movement in which the Communist Party of Nepal–United Left Front (CPN–ULF) also participated was spearheaded by the NC. As per the agreement between the king and the political leaders an interim government was formed under the prime ministership of K.P. Bhattarai, the then NC President. For the first time a Constitution was drafted by the people's representatives and proclaimed on 9 November 1990. This Constitution makes Nepal a constitutional monarchy.

Parliament

Parliament consists of His Majesty the King and two Houses, namely the HOR, the Lower House, and the National Assembly (NA), the Upper House.

The 205 members of the HOR are elected for five-year terms in general elections held on the first-past-the-post system and on universal adult franchise. The country has 75 administrative districts and each district irrespective of the size of its population is treated as an election district. Each election district has at least one constituency, with larger districts having more than one constituency depending on the size of the population.

The HOR may be dissolved on the recommendation of the prime minister any time before completion of its term. The five-year term of the HOR can be extended for a maximum period of one year during the operation of a state of emergency.

The NA, the Upper House, consists of 60 members appointed/ elected as follows:

(*i*)   Ten members nominated by His Majesty on the advice of the Council of Ministers;

(*ii*) Thirty-five members including at least three women elected by the HOR on the basis of the system of proportional representation by means of the single transferable vote;

(*iii*) Fifteen members, three from each of the development regions, elected on the basis of the system of the single transferable vote by an electoral college consisting of officials of local bodies.

A third of NA members are renewed every two years.

Parliamentary-based Political Executive

The leader of the parliamentary party commanding an absolute majority in the HOR is appointed prime minister and forms the Council of Ministers which he heads. Ministers may be appointed from among the members of both houses of Parliament though only a member of the HOR can be the prime minister.

Under Article 35(2) of the Constitution, the powers of His Majesty are to be exercised upon the recommendation and advice, and with the consent of, the Council of Ministers, except as otherwise expressly provided for in the Constitution.

Other Institutions Set Up by the Constitution

The Supreme Court as the apex court is the watchdog of the Constitution. It is empowered to enforce fundamental rights. Any Nepali citizen may file a petition in the Supreme Court to have any law declared void on the grounds of inconsistency with the Constitution.

The Commission for the Investigation of Abuse of Authority (CIAA) is a permanent and independent constitutional body with the power to conduct inquiries and investigate improper conduct or corruption by a person holding any public office. The Election

Commission (EC) conducts, supervises, directs and controls elections to Parliament and local bodies at the village, town and district level. The Election Constituency Delimitation Commission (ECDC) demarcates the constituencies in districts having more than one seat. The Public Service Commission (PSC) is an independent constitutional body to conduct examinations for the selection of suitable candidates to be appointed to Civil Service posts.

The independence of the EC and the other constitutional bodies and authorities—Supreme Court, CIAA, ECDC, PSC and Auditor General—is underscored in the Constitution by the process of appointment and removal of members of those bodies or holders of the relevant office. They are appointed by the king on the recommendation of the Constitutional Council and may be removed only by a two-thirds majority of the total number of members of the House of Representatives through the process of impeachment.

The Constitutional Council consists of:

- the prime minister
- the chief justice
- the speaker of the HOR
- the chairman of the National Assembly
- the leader of the opposition in the HOR

However the process of making recommendations for the various appointments is not transparent due to absence of laws governing procedures of the Constitutional Council.

Government during the Election

The government continues to remain in power after the dissolution of the HOR till the post-election government is formed, and continues to carry out normal functions during elections.

Political Parties

As per the constitutional provisions, political parties contesting the elections are required to register with the EC. After the announcement of the date of elections, the EC calls for registration of political parties contesting the election and they are required to submit petitions along with the Constitution, rules, manifestos and names of members of its executive committee. Recognition and registration of a political party for election purposes is extended or rejected based on the following provisions of the Constitution:

- The Constitution and rules of the political party must adhere to the norms of democracy.
- The Constitution of the party must make provision for election of its office-bearers every five years.
- The political party must field at least 5 per cent female candidates out of the total number of candidates contesting for election to the House of Representatives.
- It must obtain a minimum of 3 per cent of the total votes cast in the parliamentary elections.
- It should not discriminate in favour of or against any Nepali citizen from becoming a member of the party on grounds of religion, caste, tribe, language or sex.
- It should not profess any religious or communal ideology by name, objective, insignia or flag that tends to fragment the country.

In the 1991 elections three parties were denied registration on such grounds. The Constitution provides that to be recognised as a national political party one has to poll a minimum 3 per cent of the popular vote at parliamentary elections. Smaller parties resent this provision. The EC modified its procedure for party registration after 1996; earlier, political parties had to register afresh before each election whereas now only new parties require registration, and previously registered parties are only required to give their latest update. Political parties retain the same election symbols unless the EC decides otherwise owing to a split within the party or disputed claims over the same symbol.

Voter

Every Nepali citizen who has attained the age of 18 years has the right to vote in one of the election constituencies in accordance with the provisions of law. There is a single unified election roll and no discrimination in the right to vote on the grounds of religion, race, sex, caste, tribe, ideological conviction, education, geographic location or property ownership. However, a voter has to go to the place of his permanent residence where he is registered in the electoral rolls to cast his vote. This denies voting rights to those who are away from their home. Into these category fall the government employees and election staff too who are away on duty. The homeless too are similarly deprived. Voters are issued with a voter's identity card.

Candidate

Every person who is entitled to vote in the elections for the HORs, subject to the provisions of Article 47 of the Constitution and other existing laws, may be a candidate from any of the election constituencies. Article 47 defines the qualifications as follows:

- a citizen of Nepal;
- must have attained 25 years of age for the HOR and 35 years of age for the National Assembly;
- should not be disqualified under any law;
- should not hold any office of profit.

Further, Section 31 adds that his/her name should be in the list of any of the constituencies.

Section 27 of the *Member of the House of Representatives Election Act* disqualifies a person from being a candidate for election to the HOR if he/she

- has not reached the age of 25 years;
- is not a Nepali citizen;
- is of unsound mind or mad;
- is bankrupt;
- is an employee of the government, of an autonomous body owned by the government, or of institutions receiving government grants;
- is working in a post of profit receiving honorarium or monetary benefit from government funds, except persons on elected or nominated political post or getting pension on retirement;
- has been convicted by a Special Election Tribunal and sentenced to imprisonment, and six years have not elapsed from the day of completion of the punishment;
- has been convicted on criminal charges of moral degradation and sentenced to at least two years imprisonment, and if six years have not passed since the completion of the sentence.

If he/she is a party nominee, the official nomination paper containing his/her name signed by an authorised official of the party should have reached the commission at least 15 days before the day of nomination of candidates.

If, after nominations for election to Parliament have been filed but before the election is completed, a question arises whether a candidate is disqualified or has ceased to possess the qualification set forth in the Constitution, a final decision thereon shall be made by the EC.

The quality of elections and democracy in general very much depends on the quality of candidates. How the members of the HOR are chosen is very important, particularly how the candidates are chosen by the major parties. Thus the process of selection of candidates by the parties should be reviewed and made transparent.

Second some additions to the qualification of candidates should be considered:

- Candidate should submit property statement along with the certificate of payment of all taxes.
- Candidate should submit his bio-statement according to a format which should include among other things information if he/she was involved in litigation of a criminal character.
- Any person convicted on corruption charges should be debarred from entering the fray for six years.

Anti-defection Provision

Article 49(1)(f) of the Constitution states that the seat of a Member of Parliament (MP) shall become vacant if the party of which he was member when elected provides notification in the manner prescribed by law that he has abandoned the party.

Disqualification of Members

According to the Article 48, if a question arises as to whether an MP is disqualified or has ceased to possess any of the qualifications set forth in Article 47, the final decision shall be made by the chief justice of Nepal or any other judge of the Supreme Court designated by him.

Constituencies

The administrative districts (75 in total) are treated as election districts. Every district elects at least one representative to the HOR while larger districts send more depending on the size of the population. In effect one seat is reserved for every district though some districts may be far smaller than any constituency in multi-constituency districts. This notion of geographic representation is criticised by some sections as being undemocratic. Each member of the lower house represents his constituency. There are presently 205 constituencies corresponding to the total seats in the HOR.

Delimitation of Electoral Constituencies

For the purpose of parliamentary elections, all 75 administrative districts of the country are divided into 205 electoral constituencies. The Election Constituency Delimitation Commission, a body appointed by the king on the recommendation of the Constitutional Council, is authorised to delimit the constituencies as per the provisions of the Constitution taking into consideration 'the boundaries of the administrative districts, geographical factors, density of population, transportation facilities and communal homogeneity or heterogeneity of the local residents'. The Constitution provides that after every census result, delimitation of constituencies is reviewed and reorganised. Article 45 of the Constitution states that

> ... for the purpose of election of members to the House of Representatives, administrative districts shall be treated as election districts, and the ratio of the number of seats allocated to any district shall be, so far as practicable, equal to the ratio of the population, as determined by the last census preceding the concerned election.

Every district is guaranteed a minimum representation of one seat regardless of the size of population. Decisions of the Delimitation Commission are not subject to contest in any court of law.[1]

Delimitation of constituencies for the 1991 elections was made on the basis of the 1981 Census. But for the elections held in 1994, delimitation of the constituencies had to be done based on the 1991 Census. Since a new census was carried out in 2001 the number of seats to be shared by the districts will change again.

As per the 1991 Census result the changes, as shown in Table 4.1, occurred in the distribution of seats to the districts.

Table 4.1
Electoral Districts and Constituencies

District/Constituency	1991 Election	1994 Election	1999 Election
Districts with single constituency	11	14	14
Districts with two constituencies	26	24	24
Districts with three constituencies	21	19	19
Districts with four constituencies	8	9	9
Districts with five constituencies	7	6	6
Districts with six constituencies	2	1	1
Districts with seven constituencies	0	2	2
Total Districts: 75			
Total Constituencies: 205			

Source: Election Commission, 1991/1994.
Note: The distribution of seats among districts in the 1999 elections was the same as in the 1994 elections.

The population of Nepal, a little over 15 million in 1981, had gone up to nearly 18.5 million in 1991. It was only natural that there would be changes in the distribution of seats among the districts. However, each census in Nepal has revealed that there is a strong tendency for migration of people from the north to the south and that some of the northern mountain districts even have a minus population growth rate. As a result there are large differences in electoral size between some of the mountain districts and other constituencies. Based on the 1981 Census, the ratio of population per constituency was around 73,282. Seven mountain districts had a population below this figure. As per the constitutional provision, since each district is entitled to have representation of a minimum of one seat to Parliament, such a ratio does not apply to these districts. In 1991, with the exception of these districts, the Constituency Delimitation Commission had fixed a figure of 89,500 per constituency to allocate seats to the remaining 68 districts.[2]

Delimitation of the constituencies at the 1994 Election was carried out on the basis of the 1991 Census. This time around the number of districts below the average population ratio had increased to eight and seats were redistributed for the remaining 67 districts. The ratio of population per constituency had increased to approximately 92,250. Thus, each census is likely to cut down the representation of hill and mountain districts in Parliament in favour of the *Tarai* districts in the south of the country. In such a situation, the existing constitutional provision for review of delimitation of constituencies after every census is likely to create an imbalance in the political demography of the country. Therefore, major political parties such as the NC and the Communist Party of Nepal (Unified Marxist-Leninist), CPN(UML), have voiced their opinion in favour of keeping the status quo for at least 25 years.[3] The Constituency Delimitation Commission appointed after the dissolution of the House of Representatives on 22 May 2002 adhered to this suggestion ignoring the constitutional provisions for allocating parliamentary seats to the districts on the basis of the population ratio and maintained the status quo with only minor changes in two constituencies.

Polling Centres

Poor transport infrastructure and scattered settlements of people in the hills and mountains of the country cause problems in applying any common criteria or ratio of voters per polling centre. Normally, there would be one centrally located polling centre for every 3,000 voters so that voters need not walk more than 4.5 km to cast their votes. Although these centres are usually set up in public buildings, there have been several occasions where polling centres were set up at private orchards and locations convenient for a particular party or candidate.[4] Moreover, the limited number of polling centres and the distances to be covered to reach them, particularly in the hill and mountain districts, may often be very inconvenient to voters allotted to those polling centres. For instance, there was one polling centre per 1,792 voters in the Kathmandu district in the 1999 elections whereas in remote districts such as Kalikot and Panchthar, the ratio was one centre per 2,109 and 2,119 voters respectively.[5] People in those remote districts had to walk the whole day to reach their polling centres.

Elections

Since the promulgation of the Constitution the country has experienced:

- Three general elections on the basis of the first-past-the-post system for the 205-member HOR—those of 1991 (on 12 May),

1994 (on 15 November) and 1999 (on 3 and 17 May) in which voter participation was 65, 62 and 66 per cent respectively. The results in each election have put the NC and the CPN(UML) in the position of the two strongest parties of the country.

- The first indirect election for the 60-member National Assembly in 1991 with elections held every two years thereafter starting from 1993 for one-third of Assembly members.
- Elections for local bodies in 1992 and 1997.
- Constitutionally required internal party elections.

Table 4.2 sets out the results of the general elections of 1991, 1994 and 1999.

Table 4.2

Political Parties, Popular Vote and Seats Obtained
in the House of Representatives

Political Party	1991 Popular vote in %	1991 Seats (%)	1994 Popular vote in %	1994 Seats (%)	1999 Popular vote in %	1999 Seats (%)
NC	37.75	110 (53.65)	33.38	83 (40.49)	36.14	111 (54.15)
CPN(UML)	27.98	69 (33.65)	30.85	88 (42.93)	30.74	68 (34.63)
RPP	–	– –	17.93	20 (9.76)	10.14	11 (5.37)
RPP(C)	6.56	3 (1.46)	–	– –	3.33	– 0
RPP(T)	5.38	1 (0.48)	–	– –	–	– –
SJMN	4.83	9 (4.39)	1.32	– 0	0.84	1 (0.49)
NSP	4.10	6 (2.92)	3.49	3 (1.46)	3.13	5 (2.44)
NWPP	1.25	2 (0.97)	0.98	4 (1.95)	0.55	1 (0.49)
RJM	–	– –	–	– –	1.37	5 (2.44)
CPN(D)	2.43	2 (0.97)	–	– –	–	– –
CPN(ML)	–	– –	–	– –	6.38	– 0
RJMP	0.47	– 0	1.05	– 0	1.07	– 0

Source: Election Commission (compiled from Election Results 1991, 1994, 1999).

Changes in the Government and Untimely Elections

In the period 1990–2002 the Lower House of Parliament never completed a full term. After the restoration of the multiparty system, the first government formed was an interim one, which lasted for one year as per the Constitution. The second government, formed after the first general elections held in 1991, lasted for only three years. The House was then dissolved by the king on the advice of the prime minister due to internal differences within the ruling party, the NC, when the annual motion for approval of government policy and programme was defeated in the Lower House. Consequently a mid-term election was thrust upon the nation in November 1994. The CPN(UML) formed the government as the single largest party having 88 MPs in the Lower House and functioned for about seven months. However, the political scenario in Parliament changed with the formation of a coalition of two major parties, the NC with 83 MPs and the Rashtriya Prajatantra Party (RPP) with 20 MPs in the Lower House. They jointly registered a motion of no-confidence against the CPN(UML) government and the Lower House was summoned to debate the no-confidence motion. Before the commencement of the debate, the prime minister of the CPN(UML) government recommended the dissolution of the Lower House to the king and the king accordingly dissolved the Lower House. However, the House was restored after the Supreme Court held that the prime minister's advice to the king for dissolution was not justified. A two-party government of the NC and RPP then took charge of the nation and functioned for about 16 to 18 months. The RPP, the junior partner of the government, however now formed another coalition with the single largest party, CPN(UML), choosing a senior party member as the leader of the party and to become prime minister, ignoring the leader of the party in Parliament. This also functioned for about six months until there was a split within the RPP. The leader of the RPP having 11 members in his fold became the prime minister with the help of the NC. This government too functioned for about 6 to 8 months and collapsed with the withdrawal of the support by the NC. A division now occurred within the CPN(UML) and a new party, CPN(ML), came into being. With the help of this splinter party, the NC formed another government but this too did not last long because once again CPN(ML) withdrew its support. Consequently, the NC had to form yet another government as the single largest party in the Lower House. The government of the NC, including the CPN(UML), the Nepal Sadbhavan Party and others, called for the third general election in 1999, six months ahead of the completion of the five-year term of the House. Hence, six governments were formed in four and a half years. After the 3rd General Election held in May 1999, the House had barely completed three years, when it was dissolved again on 22 May 2002.

Frequent changes of government relegated all major issues facing the kingdom to a secondary position. Development work could not be carried out on a sustained basis. Maoist activities could not be controlled and corruption was rampant.

The Electoral System

The electoral system in Nepal as in most South Asian countries is based on the simple majoritarian model called the first-past-the-post system. The voters have a single ballot and a candidate is declared elected when he scores the largest number of valid votes cast. This system is effective in setting up a stable government in countries where a two-party system is prevalent. But in a country where there are multiple political parties and election is usually a multi-cornered contest, the winning candidate is likely to be elected with less than a majority of total votes cast. For instance the candidates who won the elections in some of the constituencies had scored less than 25 per cent of the votes cast, which implies that Parliament is becoming less and less representative. The shortcomings of this system have been exposed by the results of the elections and the ratio of representation of political parties in Parliament. Table 4.2 illustrates some of the inconsistencies.

Table 4.2 shows that a remarkable gap exists between the support the political parties derive from the electorate and its impact in Parliament and government. None of the parties in government have obtained even 40 per cent of the popular vote since the 1991 election. Likewise, some of the parties have been denied due representation mainly because of the electoral system. It is an irony that in 1999 a political party having scored more than 6 per cent of the popular vote failed to get representation in Parliament whereas another party having only 1.37 per cent of popular votes scored five seats. Similarly, a party with 36 per cent of the vote enjoyed a comfortable majority in the House and was privileged to form a government of its own. Such anomalies, inherent in the first-past-the-post system, provide adequate grounds to question the mandate of the parliamentary majority.

The first-past-the-post (FPTP) system is under attack from smaller parties and sections not represented in Parliament. The arguments against the FPTP system are well known. The discrepancy between votes and seats under the FPTP system in Nepal have been pointed out. It is argued that if the loser loses everything and the winner takes all out of the election, vast sections of the population remain un-represented and lose their faith in the system. Thus there is a demand for Proportional Representation (PR). Nepal being a multi-ethnic country, the need to secure representation of all groups has been emphasised. It is also true that the status of party represented in Parliament and membership in the powerful Constitutional Council emphasise the government's and opposition's strong position of in-fluence in state affairs. The existing system may put unnecessary obstacles to the emergence of other alternative parties. However, none of the parties has clearly stated what model it would prefer to introduce under the PR system from the variety of models available to determine the ratio of representation under this system.

People's experience shows that we are in the stage of emphasising the need for stability and accountability of democratic governments. The period of hung Parliaments which witnessed the succession of six governments in four years starting from November 1994, and brazenly corrupt practices to boot, should caution us against jump-ing into new waters. Nepal does not have the time and resources to permit the luxuries of fragmentation of political parties, insatiable serial governments or spate of midterm elections. Instead, we should look into the task of strengthening the political parties and reforming and making them capable of meeting the challenges before the coun-try. Besides, the well-known arguments in favour of the FPTP sys-tem, including MP's links with the constituency, need no repetition.

Although a shift to the PR system may bring about some positive changes in the ratio of representation, this alone is not going to rectify the electoral malpractices which are evident in the existing system. In order to ensure that the PR system is effective in terms of governance, the political parties need to be plural, consensual and reconciliatory in their orientations and approaches.

Caretaker or Neutral Government during Elections

The concept of a caretaker government only to conduct elections is based on the presumption that, irrespective of what the Constitution says about the independence of the EC and the conduct of election by it, it is the government which conducts election. If that be so, an all-party caretaker government, that is, the government of major parties represented in the Parliament, may well legitimise the competing interference of the major parties in an election rather than making any contribution to the free and fair conduct of elections.

The more acute question is: how can the voter put his or her trust in the caretaker or neutral government to run the country if he/she is unable to trust the popularly elected and accountable government to remain in power during elections. Again, if the voters return to the party which was in power before announcement of the election, with increased strength, the imposition of an all-party or neutral government on the people would appear to be a trampling of the will of the people. On what basis could the continuity of the ruling party at election time be terminated without the expressed will of the people? The concept of caretaker or neutral election government should not be applied because democracy should not concede any ground to the notion that it can be interrupted for the greater public good, albeit for a limited period or limited purpose. It is a dangerous notion. The need is to not run away from democracy but remain in it and go on perfecting it.

A neutral government, that is, a government which is again accountable to no one, is no answer to the ills of our election process. A divided, weak or unaccountable and obviously futureless government during elections will be less capable of providing necessary assistance to the independent EC in its fight against malpractices than any strong government accountable to the people and with stakes in the future. Of course, the party that called the election will be devoid of the privileges of incumbency and of direct access to state machinery in the case of a caretaker government. But a caretaker government by itself would not be able to reduce corrupt practices. Things could only get worse when the incumbent government and apparent alternative to the government apportion the application of foul means between themselves.

The trend of the three general elections conducted so far by the EC also does not appear to support the demand for special election government or caretaker government. The first election was conducted when there was an all-party interim government comprising four members from the NC, three from the United Left Front of seven Communist parties including both parties which are now united in the CPN(UML), two representatives from civil society and two nominees of the king. The NC got a clear majority and CPN(UML) emerged as a strong opposition leaving all other opposition parties far behind, the prime minister who was also the president of the NC losing the election. The NC got 37.75 per cent of total votes and 110 seats in the 205-member HOR, and the CPN(UML), 27.98 per cent of votes with 69 seats.

The second election was conducted when there was a majority government of the NC which was so confident of its victory that it went in for a midterm election, but lost not only its clear majority, but also the position of the largest party in the House. The NC was relegated to the second position conceding the first place to the CPN(UML). The NC got 33.35 per cent votes and 83 seats, and the CPN(UML), 30.85 per cent of votes with 88 seats. The hung Parliament produced six governments in four years and one month, with a nine-month average duration of a government.

The third election was conducted when the country was run by the joint government of the two largest parties in the country, the NC and the CPN(UML). The NC emerged as the governing party with a clear majority (36.14 per cent votes and 111 seats) and the CPN(UML) as a strong opposition (30.74 per cent of votes with 71 seats).

What do these facts say? Perhaps they say:

- Irrespective of the type of government the elections confirmed the broad trend of support for the two strongest parties.
- The outcome of each election did not favour the government during the period of elections. The national government was replaced after the first election by one-party majority government. That government in turn was replaced by one-party minority government as the result of the second election. Joint government of the two strongest parties was replaced by the majority government of NC as the outcome of the third election.
- If there were malpractices, they were not the monopoly of any type of government, or of any single party, or of any specific period during which a certain type of government was at the helm.
- Though there were malpractices, the result did not substantially affect the strong parties because malpractices tended to balance and neutralise each other's efforts. Strong parties resorted to malpractices in proportion to their strength at the expense of weak ones.
- The government was not able to substantially influence the outcome of election.

Democracy: The Ultimate
Toll of Political Failure and Insurgency

The NC government elected in 1999 was faced with (*a*) internal crises within the party (it went through four prime ministers in the period 1999–2002), (*b*) national crises caused by the massacre of the royal family including King Birendra on 1 June 2001 and (*c*) an increasingly effective and widespread campaign of violence by the Maoist insurgency, all of which led to systemic political failure.

A state of emergency was declared in November 2001 in response to violence by the Maoist insurgents. However a political confrontation loomed in May 2002 on the question of the extension of the state of emergency. Parliament was thereupon dissolved, and fresh elections called for November that year.

Expelled by his own party, the NC, the then Prime Minister, Sher Bahadur Deuba, headed an interim government which renewed the state of emergency. The prime minister in consultation with all major parties represented in Parliament advised the king to extend the date of election by one year. The king then dismissed Prime Minister Deuba and indefinitely postponed elections. The king thereafter conducted a type of revolving door premiership between Deuba, Lokendra Bahadur Chand and Surya Bahadur Thapa.

On 1 February 2005, the king dismissed the prime minister and his government, and assumed direct executive power. In doing so he cited corruption among the politicians and the need to tackle the insurgency. These events led to a virtual dictatorship of the king backed by the army, the only real check to royal authority being the Maoist insurgency. However Maoist activities could not be controlled. The frequent shutdowns declared by the Maoists paralysed the economic activities of the kingdom and disrupted the normal life of the people.

Events from November 2005 onwards would however give some hope of a rejuvenation of the political system. In November 2005 the Maoist rebels and the main political parties, pressed by civil society, agreed on a programme intended to restore democracy. In April 2006, weeks of demonstrations, strikes and protests against the king led to the king reinstating Parliament, and the appointment of veteran politician G.P. Koirala as Prime Minister. As work on this chapter was being completed, the Maoists called a three month ceasefire. A three-man negotiating team of the Maoists arrived in Kathmandu and a team of three ministers was announced by the government to negotiate with the Maoists for their participation in the interim government and to formulate ways and means of conducting elections to a Constituent Assembly. The government has reciprocated the Maoists' three-month ceasefire with an indefinite ceasefire, and has also withdrawn the Interpol notice issued on the Maoist leaders. It is hoped that sustainable peace will be restored and Nepal will usher in a new era of full-fledged democracy.

Notes

1. His Majesty's Govt., Nepal, *The Constitution of the Kingdom of Nepal 1990*, Kathmandu, Ministry of Law, Justice and Parliamentary Affairs, 1992.
2. Election Commission, *General Election in Nepal 1991*, Kathmandu, Election Commission, 1992, pp. 16–19.
3. The High-level Election Reform Commission (1999) had made such a recommendation in its report submitted to the HOR. (Report of the High-level Committee formed under the Chairmanship of the prime minister, 2001 [in Nepali]).
4. Thakur P. Sharma, 'Pratinidhi Sabha Sadsya Nirbachanko Kanuni Ebam Byabaharik Pakshya', (in Nepali) in NCCS Occasional Paper No. 3, June 2001, pp. 38–39.
5. Iswor Pokharel, 'Nirbachan Byabasthanka Bibidh Pakshya, Tyasaka Samasya ra Sudhar', (in Nepali), pp. 18–19.

5

PAKISTAN

Rasul Bakhsh Rais

I

Introduction[*]

Frequent interruptions in the democratic process have hampered the development of a healthy polity and electoral process in Pakistan. Elections in Pakistan could be grouped into five distinct phases. In the first phase (1947–58), there were two federal legislatures/assemblies, one elected before independence and the other after independence. Both these assemblies, which functioned as Constituent Assemblies as well, were indirectly elected; in both cases, the provincial assemblies served as an electoral college. Before independence, elections to the provincial assemblies were held on a limited franchise and after independence on the basis of direct adult franchise. The 1956 Constitution, the first Constitution framed after

[*]This section has benefited from the revised draft of the paper presented by Dr Rafique M. Afzal on 'Election Procedures and Malpractices' at the International Conference on 'Electoral Processes and Governance in South Asia', June 2002, Colombo, organised by ICES-Kandy, Sri Lanka.

independence, was abrogated in October 1958, without any elections held under its auspices. In the second phase (1958–69), there were two elections of Basic Democracies (1960 and 1964), two elections of the unicameral Parliament/National Assembly (1962 and 1965), and the Provincial Assemblies of East and West Pakistan (1962 and 1965), one presidential referendum (1960) and one presidential election (1965). Eighty thousand directly elected Basic Democrats from East and West Pakistan constituted the electoral college for the presidential referendum as well as all the elections.

The first general elections in Pakistan were held in 1970 on the basis of direct adult franchise, with a voting age of 21, after 23 years of independence. Conducted under the martial law regime, the elections were free and without any interference by the government. The result of the elections was to give such a majority to the Awami League party in the then East Pakistan (now Bangladesh) as to form the government of Pakistan. This result was not accepted by the military and the Pakistan Peoples' Party (PPP), which was the majority party in the then West Pakistan. Although the PPP in West Pakistan accepted the Awami League (AL) as the majority party at that time, it refused to attend the first session of the newly elected National Assembly unless the central issues pertaining to the future Constitution of the country were settled between the PPP representing West Pakistan and the AL representing East Pakistan.[1] Because of the electoral concentration of the two major parties in the two wings of the country, the PPP rejected the idea of the AL representing all provinces of Pakistan. However, the PPP itself had electoral plurality in only two provinces of West Pakistan, Punjab and Sindh, and could not claim representation for Baluchistan and the North-West Frontier Province (NWFP). In the postponement of the Dhaka session of Parliament, the AL saw the historical machinations of West Pakistani politicians and military attempting to deny them power. This resulted in a major political crisis leading to civil strife; crackdown by the military; breakdown of authority of the state of Pakistan; Indian military intervention and finally war between the two countries in 1971. The first ever general elections therefore ended up dividing the country in two.

The third phase (1971–77) therefore begins after the break-up of Pakistan and the establishment of Bangladesh. Members elected from West Pakistan to the National Assembly in 1970 formed the first National Assembly, which was continued under the 1973 Constitution for a term of five years. The 1973 Constitution provided for a federal parliamentary system with a bicameral Parliament. The

Second House, that is, the Senate, was also elected, and the Provincial Assemblies served as the electoral college.

The next elections to the National Assembly and the Provincial Assemblies in this phase were held in March–April 1977. These elections conducted by a civilian government headed by Zulfikar Ali Bhutto were massively rigged, and provoked the joint opposition of nine political parties, the Pakistan National Alliance, to launch a nationwide protest[2] demanding fresh elections, and these protests eventually forced the ruling PPP to negotiate. The unnecessary prolongation of these negotiations over a period of three months climaxed in yet another military takeover of power on 5 May 1977 and imposition of Martial Law in July 1977. General Zia-ul-Haq, who later created a civilian facade through party-less elections in 1985, ruled the country for the next 11 years.

The fourth phase started during the Martial Law period in 1985 and ended in October 1999 with another military takeover. During this phase, three elections were organised for the local bodies (1979, 1983 and 1987) and five for the Parliament—the Senate and the National Assembly—and five for the Provincial Assemblies of Punjab, Sindh, NWFP and Baluchistan in 1985, 1988, 1990, 1993 and 1997, besides the elections to the office of president. The elections to the local bodies and the 1985 elections to the National Assembly and the Provincial Assemblies were non-party elections but the political parties participated in all the remaining elections.

Since 1988 five general elections have been held, each after an elected government was dismissed through the use of the controversial Article 58, 2(b) that General Zia had inserted into the Constitution in order to empower himself to dissolve an unwanted government.

The fifth dismissal of a civilian government by the military was carried out when the Chief of Army Staff, General Pervez Musharraf, took over power on 12 October 1999. Interestingly, Pervez Musharraf captured power soon after Prime Minister Nawaz Sharif dismissed him and tried to install another general as army chief. The new government led by Musharraf justified the takeover on the same grounds that other military leaders who took over power before him had used: that the politicians were corrupt; the elected government had failed to perform in the public's interest; the economy was near collapse; the law and order situation was worsening and the regime was authoritarian and oppressive towards the opposition. Musharraf asserted that the country required structural reforms in all areas of national life which the previous government had been incapable of devising and wanted to replace the 'sham democracy' with 'true democracy'. He promised fresh elections after changes in the system of governance. Amidst other changes, he empowered himself with the authority to dissolve governments under the controversial Article 58, 2(b) that he had brought back into the Constitution by amending the executive power in the form of the Legal Framework Order (LFO). Much of the LFO, which has changed the parliamentary character of the Constitution, has been given legitimacy through the 17th Amendment which was supported by a big faction of the opposition, an alliance of religious political parties—Muttahida Majlis-e-Amal (MMA).

The fifth or the current phase began in 2002. There was a presidential referendum in March 2002, and elections to the National and Provincial Assemblies in October that year.

During the first and fourth phases, elections were based on the system of separate electorates for the Muslims and non-Muslims while in the second and third phases, elections were held on the basis of joint electorates. With the fifth phase there has been change yet again, and all elections are held on the basis of joint electorates. Besides other changes, the age of voters was reduced to 18.

II

Electoral Legacy

Certain general characteristics have been prevalent in Pakistan's electoral process during the eight general elections held since 1970. The last election, in 2002, shares at least one common feature with the other seven—the rejection of results by the second largest party in Parliament and the ensuing political polarisation. Rejection of the electoral results by the losing party or parties remains the most common feature of Pakistani elections with the defeated party always claiming that elections were rigged in favour of the party that won. The two major parties on the electoral scene, the Muslim League (ML) and the PPP, have made this claim during the past six elections, whilst all the opposition political parties in the 1977 elections had accused the PPP of changing the results in its own favour. In terms of the validity of these claims, it must be emphasised that it is not only for political expediency that losing parties have rejected the electoral outcomes. In fact there is substantial evidence to support allegations that elections have rarely been free or fair in the history of Pakistan except for the 1970 elections, which on the other hand unleashed new political forces and ended in political polarisation and dismemberment. No elections since have been acclaimed as fair. However the intensity of these allegations has varied from election to election.

The question of why the outcome of elections has been contested leads to another feature of Pakistani elections, the mistrust in the electoral machinery of the country. The Election Commission (EC) of Pakistan, the organisation that conducts elections lacks sufficient autonomy and independence from the executive branch of the government. Compared with similar organisations in other democracies, it lacks the credibility necessary to earn the trust of the public. The EC in Pakistan has a poor image and has failed to evolve as a national institution of any stature. This is not entirely due to the cynical nature of the Pakistani political culture. It is because the EC has failed to cultivate impartiality and trust, the two core values that are quintessential for a successful electoral exercise. This raises a further question: have the regimes in power used the electoral machinery to produce results to suit their interests?

The answer to this leads to the third feature of Pakistani elections, the partiality of the executive branch of the government. Interestingly, seven out of eight general elections since 1970 have been conducted either by a military regime or by an interim government that the military regime had created under its supervision. Therein lies the real dilemma of Pakistan's electoral politics—the civil–military relations in Pakistan. Without understanding the nature of civil–military relations it is not possible to understand the flaws in the electoral process or why questions have been raised about its impartiality. It would suffice to say that the military in Pakistan has its own vision of good politics, good society, good economy and good democracy. It does not trust the politicians, nor does it believe that they are genuine representatives of the people of Pakistan. All the military leaders who have captured power have viewed free play of democratic forces as dangerous, anti-development, and having the potential of degenerating to lawlessness and anarchy. Considering itself a modern and vital institution of the state, military leaders have tried to impose a different kind of political order. Its labels have varied from 'basic democracy' under Ayub Khan, the first military ruler, to 'true democracy' of the present ruler, President General Pervez Musharraf. But the content of such an order, the intention of those trying to establish it and the direction of political change and economic reforms have unquestionably remained the same under all four military regimes. In essence, all have aimed for controlled, guided or graduated democracy. Although a sad reflection on the political scenario in Pakistan, it is equally interesting that each military government has succeeded in co-opting a sizeable section of politicians, usually those in the opposition. Frequent changing of political loyalties, more often for lucrative positions in the government or for evading accountability, has created a mixed political system—a partnership between the military leaders and a faction or factions of politicians from different political parties. In all instances the military has been in the driving seat, while the co-opted politicians have been dispensed with just as eagerly as they were drafted in the first place. The most recent example is the eviction of Prime Minister Zafarullah Khan Jamali from office in June 2004.[3] The military governments, aided and assisted by political groups, have a vested interest in keeping pliant groups in power, and if need be in directly assuming control of the government. In a military-dominated or military-directed political system, the electoral process loses its credibility, as it is seen by the public as an exercise to bring into power political parties most favoured by the military and root out those opposed to its interventions. Unfortunately, the latter is true of the way elections have been conducted in Pakistan.[4] It is alleged that through its intelligence agencies the military has attempted to change the loyalties of politicians, funded political campaigns of the groups it favours, and used the EC to change electoral results selectively, if not entirely.[5]

With the low level of trust in the electoral process and frequent allegations of defrauding the opposition of its true electoral representation, the voter turnout in Pakistani elections has declined. It is also a reflection of distrust of the political class in Pakistan, particularly the two mainstream political parties, the ML and the PPP. Allegations of corruption, nepotism, mismanagement of the economy and general apathy toward the problems faced by the masses at the grassroots level have failed to instil any spirit or enthusiasm among the voters on election day. Only 38 per cent of the registered voters cast their ballots in the 1997 elections. The turnout at the October 2002 elections was slightly higher but below 50 per cent. Low turnout in Pakistani elections can also be explained with reference to two other issues: depoliticisation and demise of ideology. Due to long years of military rule and distrust of politicians, interest in political participation, already low, has further declined. Elections are the most authentic mode of political participation, but by losing faith in their impartiality the people lose the opportunity of political participation.

The three-dimensional political polarisation along ideological lines of ethnic nationalism, Islam and socialism prevalent in the 1970s has changed. Ethnic nationalism and Islam are dominant issues but the ideological debate is no longer intense or in the mainstream of political discourse. Both the ethnic nationalists and Islamists have retained their appeal among their supporters and, as evident from the 2002 elections, the Islamists have increased their support base. The political parties have failed to generate new ideas or debates about the plethora of problems that Pakistan faces. Most of them lack the intellectual content, leadership and political capacity to interpret issues in any meaningful form and solidus or present solutions that would be popular, rational and workable. The result is a public that is uninterested in the political affairs of the country. Unfortunately this mindset, grown from a dismal political process, feeds back into authoritarianism and moves the country further away from democracy.

There are three key issues which are central to the understanding of electoral politics of Pakistan: the statutory and institutional arrangements for holding elections; the procedures and the extent to which procedural and other malpractices in elections take place; and group discrimination during elections.

III

Institutional Arrangements

The 1973 Constitution has provisions for holding elections under the EC of Pakistan, making the latter a constitutional body.[6] Conduct of elections is a federal subject. The president of the country appoints the Chief Election Commissioner (CEC), the highest officer responsible for a free and fair electoral process. He is usually a retired or serving judge or chief justice of the Supreme Court of Pakistan. Ironically, while the tenure for the assemblies, national as well as provincial is five years, the CEC is appointed for a three-year term. The term of an incumbent can be extended for one year by the national Parliament. The short term in office does not give the CEC sufficient time to exercise a degree of control on the electoral process. The Constitution provides for two members in the EC, which the military government of Pervez Musharraf increased to four. They are serving judges of the four respective High Courts of the four provinces. They are appointed by the president after consultations with the CEC and the chief justices of the concerned high courts to which they belong. The members maintain their regular jobs as judges as well as serve on the EC whenever it convenes.

In theory the CEC has a secure tenure, as he cannot be removed arbitrarily before term. His removal by the government requires the same procedures as for firing a sitting judge of the High Court or Supreme Court of Pakistan.[7] Few CECs in the political history of Pakistan have earned the respect and trust of political parties. This is largely due to the process of appointing the CEC, which is the sole prerogative of the president of the country. Constitutionally, the president is under no obligation to consult Parliament, the prime minister or the opposition parties when appointing the CEC. The manner in which CECs have been appointed in the past and the credibility of the individuals who were selected, though from the highest court of the country, has raised doubts about the integrity and impartiality of the CECs. For instance, the media, the opposition and even the bar councils of Pakistan were agitated when the retiring chief justice of Pakistan, Irshad Hasan Khan, was appointed to this position because of his controversial role in validating the suspension of the Constitution, dissolution of the assemblies and capture of power by Pervez Musharraf.[8]

Yet another important office in the EC is that of the secretary, who in theory is appointed by the CEC. However on several occasions governments have sent a replacement from the civilian bureaucracy when the secretary retired, which has invariably given the government the necessary leverage to control the electoral machinery. However, if a regular employee of the EC were elevated to the position of the secretary and if this practice were followed strictly, it would end the nexus between the secretary and the executive, which has damaged the independence of the EC in the past.

The EC has been vested with powers of contempt of court, which can be exercised by any High Court of the country for offences similar to those covered by the *Contempt of Court Act, 1976*.

The duties of the EC are extensive. They range from registering voters and preparing voters' lists on an annual basis to drawing the territorial boundaries of electoral constituencies for the provincial and national assemblies and making arrangements for polling. The electoral rolls prepared by the EC are also used for local government elections. The age limit for voters in the 1973 Constitution was 21 years, reduced to 18 years through an amendment in Article 51(2) by the Musharraf regime.

To prevent voter fraud, the EC requires production of national identity cards (NICs) for casting ballots. However, this has not prevented malpractice by individuals, groups and political parties. Bogus NICs have been obtained from the now defunct National Registration Authority.[9] This problem can be solved to an extent by the EC using its own resources for registration and verification.

The delimitation of constituencies is riven with the political interests of the dominant groups and political parties. There has been a major change in the number of constituencies both in the National and Provincial Assemblies since the promulgation of the Constitution. The EC Order 2002, EC Amendment Order 2002 and the Conduct of General Election Order 2002 changed the number of seats for the National Assembly from 217 to 357.[10] These presented the EC with the gigantic task of redrawing the constituencies. However, this was accomplished in a short period of time by using the 1998 Census. Tables 5.1 and 5.2 show the numbers of seats allocated to the provinces, regions, minorities and women in the national and provincial assemblies.

Table 5.1
National Assemblies

Province/Area	General Seats	Reserved for Women	Reserved for Technocrats	Total Seats
Baluchistan	14	3	1	18
Federal Capital	2	–	–	2
FATA	12	–	–	12
NWFP	35	8	3	46
Punjab	148	35	15	198
Sindh	61	14	6	81
Total Seats	272	69	25	357

Table 5.2
Provincial Assemblies

Province/Area	General Seats	Reserved for Women	Reserved for Technocrats	Total Seats
Baluchistan	51	11	5	67
NWFP	99	22	9	130
Punjab	297	66	27	390
Sindh	130	29	12	171
Total Seats	577	128	53	758

There have been recent drastic changes in the electoral system of Pakistan. First and foremost came the elimination of separate electorates for the minorities that many civil society groups and religious minorities had demanded in the past. None of the civilian governments attempted to undo that system, fearing a backlash from the religious right which had argued that the minorities should elect their own representatives separately, a legacy of Muslim electoral politics in pre-partition India. In practice, however, genuine representation of the minorities was an impossible task because they were scattered all over the country.

The second most important change was the reservation of 30 per cent of the seats for women. They are now elected on the basis of proportional representation for which each province forms a single constituency. The third important change was the increase in the total number of seats for the national and provincial assemblies.

Although these are positive changes, the representation of all sections of society cannot come about by increasing the number of seats alone. It requires sustained democracy, better party politics and social mobility. Otherwise, the traditional elite classes in the vast rural constituencies will continue to dominate the electoral arena, as evident from the outcome of the 2002 elections.[11]

Elections are conducted by each province being divided into a number of administrative districts. An increasing number of districts have been carved out since independence due to the manifold increase in population. The CEC appoints one district returning officer (DRO) for each district. In recent elections, the DROs have been obliged to perform the role of district session judges during elections. The DRO's duties include accepting or rejecting nominations of the candidates, designating schools and other public buildings as polling stations and supervising the administrative duties pertaining to election duty. Nomination papers of a candidate can be rejected on a number of grounds. Appeals against rejection of nomination papers can be filed in the Election Tribunal that the EC nominates from the relevant High Court Bench with the consent of the president. Similarly, appeals can also be filed against acceptance of a candidate's paper in the Appellate Tribunal if he has defaulted loans or has not paid taxes or other government dues. Decisions on these appeals have to be taken within a given time frame.

Each polling station has a presiding officer, deputy presiding officer and other staff to issue ballot papers, check NICs and ensure that voters are registered. In case of irregularity and disruption of order the presiding officer can stop the polling and report the matter to the DRO. Ballot papers, ballot boxes and other stationery which bear the seal of the EC have to be accounted for. During polling, each candidate can assign a maximum of two polling agents who guard against any irregularities by the staff or rival candidates. At the close of polling day, ballot boxes which are sealed in the presence of the polling agents are reopened in their presence, counted and the votes matched against the ballots issued. After the ballot count the presiding officer receives the signatures of the polling agents representing the various candidates and forwards the lists to the returning officer who in turn transmits the results to the EC.

The process appears flawless, but in practice it is not. The stronger candidates intimidate the polling agents of the weaker candidates; polling staff in some places are bought off/pressurised by higher authorities to produce favourable results; and the agents of the losing candidates refuse to certify or sign the results in order to create political controversy on claims of fraud.

IV

Election Procedures and Malpractices

Malpractice during elections begins with the voters' lists which have neither ever been free of error nor included the entire voter population. Although voter registration is a universal problem in most democracies, it is acute in countries such as Pakistan where citizens are not registered or erroneously registered for political reasons. The task of registration is assigned to local schoolteachers or other low-paid, ill-trained government servants, who are likely to be influenced by the various functionaries of the government at the local level. Voters' lists are not updated prior to elections. Although official announcements are made in the media informing people to check if their names are in the registered voters' lists, they fail to motivate people to visit the designated offices for this purpose. If an individual's name has been omitted from the list for any given reason, the process to include his name in the list is quite cumbersome and requires going before a magistrate with a form signed by two witnesses to affirm the identity of the person and place of domicile to the satisfaction of the judge.

Political parties can play a significant role in voter registration but they usually leave this task to their prospective candidates in the constituencies who ensure that their traditional vote banks are on the voters' lists and that they have acquired NICs. Individual candidates use their influence to omit the names of voters of the opposition from the lists or make bogus entries. An inadequate process of verification of voters' lists has encouraged inaccuracy and malpractices at the registration stage.

Sudden changes in election laws and a short time frame within which elections have to be held also contribute to the existing problems. For instance, in the elections held in 2002 the age limit for voting was pushed down from 21 to 18 and the time frame given for updating the electoral rolls was not more than a month, which, given the large rural population, was insufficient to enrol new voters.

The delimitation of constituencies to the advantage of more powerful groups and individuals is not uncommon. Voter behaviour in Pakistan is seldom determined by individual choice. It is mostly dictated by the interests of the extended family, clan, tribe, caste and village coalitions, which in many instances cross village boundaries. Candidates running for the Provincial and National Assemblies try to influence the boundaries of the constituencies whenever they are redrawn because they are aware of the past voting record of clan and village coalitions. The need for redrawing of constituencies arose only in 2002 because of the increase in the number of seats for the assemblies. This exercise was last carried out in 1977. However, delimitation of constituencies has never taken into account population growth, movement to urban areas or migration to other provinces. The delimitation to create new constituencies for the October 2002 elections was done in haste and ignored demographic changes.

Three sets of rules govern the electoral process. They relate to qualifications of candidates under Articles 62 and 63 of the Constitution; the code of conduct which has to be adhered to by the candidates and parties during the campaign; and proper accounting and auditing of expenses by the candidates. A candidate has to meet several criteria in order to be eligible to contest elections. He should be of good character, a follower of Islamic rules, a practising Muslim who is aware of Islamic teachings, should not have worked against the integrity and ideology of Pakistan, and should not have been convicted for moral or other crimes. It is impossible to either establish or deny a candidate's eligibility or non-eligibility on these grounds, except for that relating to convictions for crimes. It was on the insistence of religious parties that General Zia-ul-Haq inserted this list by amending the Constitution in 1980. The religious Right quite often insists that the EC and the judiciary must ensure that the candidates should be practising Muslims. These are subjective criteria and should be replaced with practical regulations. The existing criteria can be used to disqualify opposition candidates; however, the expensive and lengthy legal process that any party initiating a disqualification has to sustain prevents its misuse.

There is a ceiling on the funds that a candidate can spend on the election campaign. However, this ceiling has never been observed by the candidates or enforced by the governments in the past, which has a significant effect on the outcome of the elections. A candidate has to maintain a fleet of vehicles for the election campaign because transporting voters to the polling stations is a critical factor in determining defeat or victory for candidates. In rural constituencies, voters have to be brought to the polling stations and have to be fed before or after they cast their ballots. Therefore, only very resourceful candidates can manage successful campaigns. Candidates also have to spend substantial sums of money on posters, billboards and, now increasingly, on private electronic media to publicise themselves. Very rich candidates often use black money to buy votes. With the declining trust in political parties due to widespread corruption by political leaders, the poorer sections of society have resorted to using the vote for monetary gain. Therefore, the rule of the electoral game is that the more one spends the better the chances of victory. The lack of controlled election expenses has caused severe corruption, as it does not permit fair play for all candidates. Although there are laws to check this malpractice, its implementation is so poor that almost every candidate disregards them. The result is that worthy candidates with genuine credentials and capacity to serve in public office are rarely willing to contest elections, or if they do, they are easily defeated.

Political parties can meet the election expenses of their candidates through their own resources. However, very few of them have the ability to mobilise these resources or have the organisational skills to run campaigns for their candidates. Only two parties have demonstrated this capacity, the Muttahida Quami Movement, an ethnic party based in Karachi and the Jamat-i-Islami, a religious political party.

The electronic media has been used as a political weapon by incumbent governments to damage the standing and reputation of the opposition. However, parties that have been victimised as a result of the government's manipulations have not desisted from using the same tools against their opponents once they were in power.

The elected civilian governments have used relatively subtle means for electoral intervention. The most popular of these is the grant of funds to sitting members of the national and provincial assemblies for development, which is used for the benefit of their own voting blocs and in order to change the loyalties of those who voted against them. Posting and transfers of schoolteachers, revenue officers, police, employees of the communication department or any other agency of the provincial and federal government are done on the recommendations of powerful members of assemblies or ministers. Whilst this may increase political capital for the ruling party and increase its support base, it contributes to the institutional decline of the state and undermines the autonomy of bureaucracy. These interventions have often crossed the fine line between political patronage and corruption in Pakistan.

V

Monitoring Elections

As a result of electoral malpractice in developing democracies, monitoring by independent foreign observer groups to judge the fairness of elections has become an accepted norm. Election monitoring by foreign groups shows that the regional as well as international community is interested in transparent elections and is against using elections as a tool of legitimising power. In recent years, groups such as the Commonwealth, the European Union and South Asian Association for Regional Cooperation (SAARC) countries have sent observation teams to monitor elections in Pakistan.

Governments in Pakistan and elsewhere have welcomed and facilitated observers in order to establish the credibility of the electoral process. The presence of the pervasive international media has also increased the need to invite foreign observers. The government is aware that denying access or creating difficulties for foreign election monitors would be counterproductive, as it would raise more doubts about their impartiality.

It is a sign of acceptance of foreign monitors that their reports are now widely referred to by both the government and the opposition in support of their respective claims, although these referrals are only when the reports are favourable to them.

Certain sections of society however consider foreign observers an intrusion on the sovereignty of the nation. Some critics argue that foreign monitors descend on developing countries during elections and that they are unfamiliar with the people, their culture and institutions, and the dynamics of local politics. This is not an entirely true perception because by means of comparative observation and regular studies of elections, effective tool kits and checklists are now available which can be used to ascertain the transparency of elections. In practice, election monitoring teams do include members who are familiar with the local society, its history and politics or have dealt with that country in some professional capacity. The monitoring reports on Pakistan have generally been fair in assessing the institutional capacity of the EC and the electoral procedure, whilst being transparent about their shortcomings.

The Human Rights Commission of Pakistan, which has been observing and reporting on elections, is a credible local institution that has the respect of a wide section of Pakistani civil society. More institutions/organisations such as these can replace the work of foreign observers.

VI
Group Discrimination

Three types of groups have been marginalised in the Pakistani electoral process; religious minorities, women and lower castes. Discrimination against these groups has been both institutional and informal.

Religious Minorities

From the beginning the post-partition leaders of West Pakistan demanded separate electorates for the minorities, which meant that minority representation in the National and Provincial Legislatures would be fixed in proportion to their population and only the minorities would vote for their candidates. The 1956 Constitution that was aborted by Ayub Khan's martial law in October 1956 had left the issue unsettled but had referred the matter to the National Assembly which allowed West Pakistan (present-day Pakistan) to apply separate electorates for the minorities. However, East Pakistan (now Bangladesh) which had more minorities had rejected the idea. The 1962 and 1973 Constitutions which were influenced by secular modernists like Ayub Khan and Zulfikar Ali Bhutto adopted the joint electorate system. Under the military rule of Zia-ul-Haq, who had political interest in cultivating the religious constituency, the Constitution was amended in 1973 establishing separate electorates. Although separate electorates guaranteed the election of 10 representatives of the minorities, in reality this system excluded 3.8 per cent of the population from voting.[12]

The religious minorities, namely the Hindus in Sindh and the Christians in Punjab, are scattered all over the country without any major concentration except for the Hindus in the border district of Tharparkar in Sindh. Five elections, beginning in 1985, were held under separate electorates in which religious minorities did not vote for the mainstream candidates. Their votes in well-contested constituencies could have tipped the balance in favour of one candidate or another. The Human Rights Commission of Pakistan, civil society groups and the associations representing minorities demanded a repeal of separate electorates, but the mainstream political parties fearing political attacks from the religious parties did not respond. The credit for ending the system of electoral apartheid goes to the military regime of General Pervez Musharraf. As far as voting is concerned, the minorities are now back in mainstream politics of Pakistan, having been allowed to vote with the rest of the citizens in the October 2002 elections. However, they have little or no representation in the assemblies with the ending of special seats for them. One suggestion that has been circulated in this regard is that special seats allocated to the minorities in the assemblies be restored. In the three tiers of the new local government system the minorities have been assured of representation on a joint electorate basis.

Women

Pakistan has traditionally been a male-dominated society in which women have been widely discriminated against and form the most oppressed social class, facing lack of education and discrimination in many areas.[13] Although the status of women is better in literate and urban areas of the country, they too face a variety of problems. Underdevelopment of the society in general, the agrarian economy and feudal social relations add to discrimination against them. Laws

ending institutionalised discrimination against women and the protection of their fundamental rights are the responsibility of the state.
The empowerment of women is one of the central objectives of the
feminist movement in Pakistan and in other societies. But this objective cannot be realised without political equality and participation of women in the political process.

Pakistani voters cast their vote in blocs that are formed on the
basis of castes, sub-castes, tribes and extended families. Even the
male members of a community seldom cast their vote on the basis
of individual preferences. Voting, unlike in the mature democracies,
is a group decision, and unfortunately women in large sections of the
rural population are excluded from that process. A few women from
the elite landowning families have contested elections, and in some
cases have defeated their male opponents. The political parties devised affirmative action for female representation by fixing 20 seats
for women in the Parliament for 20 years in the 1973 Constitution.
But the respective Provincial Assemblies forming an electoral college elected them. The Legal Framework Order (LFO) issued by
General Pervez Musharraf introduced a set of amendments in the
Constitution, which have now been sanctioned by the 17th Amendment. Under these changes, the seats for women in the National
Assembly have been raised to 60 (see Tables 5.1 and 5.2) with the
same proportion in the Provincial Assemblies. This is a major change,
but the seats have to be filled on the basis of proportional representation according to the lists provided by the parties. This system does
get women into the Assemblies but leaves them out of the electoral
contest. The decision as to which woman will represent the party in
the assemblies rests with the party bosses who, with very few exceptions, invariably choose their own daughters, wives, sisters and
other close relatives. Nonetheless, this is a step towards women
gaining a voice in the legislatures.

Lower Castes

It is generally assumed that caste and social hierarchies based on it
do not exist in Muslim societies. However, this is not the case. In
Pakistan the caste system runs deep in the social psychology of
people at every level. Castes are social markers and differentiate
people on social grounds. The people who have traditionally adopted
menial professions such as weaving, carpentry, shoemaking, hairdressing as well as those working in the agricultural sector and

performing domestic duties in the households of the landowning class are generally considered as low caste. The bonded agricultural labour and domestic servants in middle-class households, a rising phenomenon due to the increasing gap between the poor and the new rich, have also created social and economic dependencies, thus lowering their status. The political independence of these communities and whether or not they have the right to exercise their vote freely is questionable. This author's work on devolution in three villages of Faisalabad district reveals that the political interests of local influential figures determine the votes of the lower classes.[14]

It seems that democratic freedom, civic liberty and the right to participate in the political process through elections or by means of civil society organisations is largely conditioned by one's place in society, level of education and degree of economic independence. This is true of societies such as that in Pakistan where democratic traditions are weak and electoral processes are disrupted. Over time, however, elections and democracy can prove to be essential tools of empowerment for the lower castes and other marginalised communities.

VII

Conclusion

We may draw four brief conclusions from the above study. First, elections in Pakistan have been mostly controversial and have sometimes resulted in dangerous political polarisations, as losing parties raise serious doubts about the fairness of the electoral process. The trust in the EC is weak and its independence and integrity is doubted by most political parties. All governments, civilian and military, have been accused of manipulating the elections. The referenda held on three occasions to legitimise three military generals has further damaged the sanctity of voting. Some accusations are exaggerated, but the perception of the lack of fairness and transparency remain quite strong in the public's mind.

Second, the legal framework and procedures for conducting elections are quite elaborate and well practised in Pakistan. They are now widely understood by the contestants, and over time they have become institutionalised. The problem lies however in sudden changes in legal requirements and the short time frame within which elections have to be conducted under the new procedures.

Third, governments may intervene covertly by influencing certain critical decisions of the electoral machinery. At an individual level polling agents of the candidates disrupt elections, fake identities, put bogus entries in the voters' lists, bribe or threaten polling staff, stuff ballot boxes with bogus votes and disrupt the poll by violent means. Preventing these malpractices would require greater autonomy for the EC.

Finally, group discrimination in elections against women, lower castes and, until very recently, against the minorities has been pervasive. Privileged classes, particularly landowners in the rural areas of Pakistan, dominate the electoral scene. The emergence of a new middle class and its social mobility has not translated into its political representation. It is largely the weak political system, disruption of the democratic process and elite networking that has shaped ruling partnerships. Womens' emancipation and empowerment is both a social and political issue. The problem of political equality for the lower classes falls in the same category. The solution lies in sustained democracy that will strengthen participation. It is only through participation that all marginalised groups can empower themselves, effectively articulate their interests, influence public policy in their favour and end discrimination.

Notes

1. Sharif al Mujahid, 'Pakistan: First General Elections', *Asian Survey*, Vol. 11, February 1971, pp. 159–71.
2. Sharif al Mujahid, 'The 1977 Pakistani Elections: An Analysis' in Manzooruddin Ahmad (ed.), *Contemporary Pakistan: Politics, Economy and Society,* Durham, North Carolina, Academic Press, 1980, pp. 63–91.
3. After nearly 20 months in office, Jamali was forced to resign on 26 June 2004 through behind the scene pressures, *Dawn,* Karachi, 27 June 2004.
4. 'Fair Polling' (editorial), *Dawn,* 7 July 2004.
5. It is reported that the Inter-Services Intelligence (ISI) used tens of millions in putting together an alliance of parties opposed to the PPP in the 1988 elections. There is a case in this regard pending in the highest court of Pakistan. Some of the former top-level functionaries of the ISI have accepted reports about the distribution of funds as true.
6. Articles 213 to 226 (Part VIII and Chapter 1 & 2) of the 1973 Constitution deal with the elections issues.
7. High Court is the highest court in each province. The Supreme Court of Pakistan is a federal and apex court in the country.
8. For a glimpse of the controversy see *The News*, Rawalpindi, 5 May 2002.

9. *Electoral Politics in Pakistan: National Assembly Elections 1993*, Report of SAARC–NGO Observers, New Delhi, Vikas Publishing House, 1993, p. 18.

10. Articles 51, 51(4), and 106 of the Constitution had provisions for 207 general seats for Muslim males, and 10 seats for the religious minor-ities. There was a provision for the 20 seats for Muslim females that was good for 20 years and it lapsed in 1993.

11. *Elections Laws, General Elections, 2002*, Vol. 1, Islamabad, Election Commission of Pakistan, 2002.

12. I.A. Rehman, 'The Worse off Non-Muslim Voters', *Dawn*, 28 January 1997.

13. Khawar Mumtaz and Farida Shaheed, *Women of Pakistan: Two Steps Forward, One Step Back?*, Lahore, Vanguard Books, 1987.

14. As a member of research team I visited three villages in Union Council 17, tehsil Jaranwala, district Faisalabad, Punjab several times in four months and conducted surveys on responsiveness and participation in 2004.

6

SRI LANKA

K.M. de Silva

I

The Construction of a Democratic Electoral System

Sri Lanka's modern electoral system based on universal suffrage is over 75 years old, the oldest in the former crown colonies of the British Empire. Sri Lanka is in many ways the pioneer in the establishment and maintenance of democracy in South Asia and indeed in the whole of Asia. Indeed the comparison with regard to the suffrage and representation is with Great Britain and the countries of Western Europe, rather than with South Asia. One of the unique features of Sri Lanka's colonial experience is that in 1931, 16 years before independence, it became the centre of an unusual experiment in preparing people for independence—the introduction of universal suffrage to a crown colony. Thus, one of the essential ingredients of democracy, universal suffrage, was introduced to Sri Lanka 75 years ago,[1] more than 20 years before universal suffrage came to India, and only three years after the 'British electoral system reached theoretical democracy ... in April 1928....'[2] The decisive change in Britain had come 10 years earlier with the *Representation of the People Act of 1918* which more than doubled the electorate.[3] Sri Lanka's first general election under universal suffrage in 1931 came only two years after the first such election in Britain. Even at that time its electoral system was ahead of Britain's in that there was no provision for plural voting. Similarly, women in Sri Lanka had the right to vote, at age 21, by 1931, long before women in some European countries, France, Belgium and Switzerland for instance. In addition, Sri Lanka was the first of the British colonial territories in which elections under universal suffrage were held prior to independence: in 1931, 1936 and in 1947 (on the eve of independence). Thus the foundations of free and fair elections were laid at a national level by the colonial administration in the 1930s.

When the Special Commission on the Constitution (better known as the Donoughmore Commission) issued its report on Sri Lanka (then known as Ceylon) in 1928, that document proved to be a path-breaking state paper not least because, in Chapter V, it argued that '... a good case could be made out for regarding the extension of the franchise as more urgent than any increase of responsible government.'[4] The Commissioners added that '... we could not recommend a further grant of responsible government unless that government were to be made fully representative of the great body of the people.'[5] They recommended that males over 21 years of age and women over 30 should be granted the right to vote.

No major figure from Sri Lanka's social elite, and no important social or economic group had asked for, much less agitated for, universal suffrage.[6] When the report of the Donoughmore Commission was published, its recommendations on the franchise and representation did not come as any great surprise to Sri Lanka's principal politicians. All of them knew of the enthusiasm of one of the members of the Commission, Dr Drummond Shiels, the Labour Party representative,[7] for universal suffrage and his regular advocacy of it during the sessions of the Commission, and beyond those on other public occasions. They acquiesced in this recommendation, one which drastically changed the rules of the game in Sri Lankan politics, and prepared themselves to work within the new system.

Only one politician and one group declared opposition to it: this was the leading but ageing Tamil politician, Sir Ponnambalam Ramanathan and his followers. Ramanathan hoped his strong opposition to it, fervently expressed on behalf of the island's principal minority, would persuade the Colonial Office to either modify the recommendations of the Donoughmore Commission, or reject them.

In the event, the Colonial Office endorsed the recommendations of the Donoughmore Commission and went beyond them in the sense that women too were to be given the right to vote at 21, and not at 30 as the report had recommended.

From the very outset, elections under universal suffrage in Sri Lanka were organised by a government department charged with the responsibility of conducting and managing elections and utilising all the manpower and other resources of its own institution and of the civil service, in general, to undertake that task. Since the Sri Lankan general election of 1931 was the first such election in any crown colony, the officials in charge of conducting the election had no precedents to go by. Previously only 4 per cent of the population—a minuscule minority of adult males—had the right to vote. British officials, erring on the side of caution, were anxious that the machinery for holding elections islandwide, which had never to cope with anything more exacting than the small electorate at Legislative Council elections, should not be overwhelmed by the unpredictable pressures of universal suffrage.[8]

Three important policy decisions were taken in this regard. First of all, it was decided in 1931, to leave registration of the right to vote to the initiative of the individual voter.[9] This policy was changed in 1935 when the state took over the responsibility of registering voters. Thus while only 63 per cent of the voters secured registration in 1930–31, after 1935 every person entitled to vote was registered by the government. This latter policy introduced in time for the general election of 1936,[10] has been continued ever since. Second, elections to the national legislature were not held on the same day, but over several days.[11] Third, since universal suffrage was being introduced to an electorate in which the vast majority of voters, at that time, were illiterate, each candidate was assigned a colour for easy identification.[12] This system, with minor modifications, prevailed from 1931 to 1947. From 1947 each political party and independent candidates too were assigned a distinct symbol, and this system has remained unchanged to the present day although the rate of literacy is so much higher now.

These administrative mechanisms worked well because the professional integrity of the civil service and their political neutrality in the management of elections were never in doubt, in a system which placed a premium on impartiality and efficiency. This tradition, inherited from the days of the Donoughmore Constitution, was sustained after independence. The Department of Elections was given the task of the full-time management and conduct of elections—both parliamentary and local government—and generally its performance ranged from good to excellent. The exceptionally high standards set by the Elections Department under the leadership of men like Felix Dias Abeyesinghe[13] who held the post of head of Elections Department for about 19 years till his retirement in the early 1980s were a proud legacy for his successors in office.

Just as Sri Lanka was the first country among the former British colonies to experience universal suffrage, it was also the first in which the voting age was reduced from 21 to 18. This happened in 1959–60 with the passage of the *Ceylon Parliamentary Elections (Amendment) Act No. 11*. The political objective was to prevent the pendulum that swung in favour of the left of centre coalition led by the Sri Lanka Freedom Party (SLFP) in 1956 from swinging back to the United National Party (UNP), or to check its speed substantially. Few countries had experimented with votes at 18 then, and it was not known at that stage that the teenage vote, as it was called, was more likely to go against the government in power than against its rivals. But at the time it was introduced, the common assumption was that it would help stabilise the shift to the left and left of centre that had occurred in 1956. That did not happen.

At the General Election of March 1960, Sri Lanka introduced the practice of holding polls to all the seats in the national legislature on the same day, the result once more of the provisions of the *Ceylon Parliamentary Elections (Amendment) Act No. 11 of 1959*. Hitherto polling had been staggered, over several days, generally in three or more stages. The consequence was that the constituencies going to the polls in the second, third and fourth stages could be influenced by the results of the first day's polling, which indeed was the case in 1952 and 1956, when the bandwagon rolled in favour of the UNP in 1952, and disastrously against it in 1956. However, the most exaggerated swings of the electoral pendulum came after this system of islandwide elections on the same day was adopted, as for example in 1970 and 1977, against the UNP in the first instance, and even more dramatically in favour of it in the latter year.

The introduction of a form of proportional representation (PR) on the list system in place of the existing 'first-past-the-post' form of representation based on the British model which had prevailed in Sri Lanka since 1931, came in 1978, designed to counteract the unusually exaggerated swings of the pendulum seen in 1970 and 1977, swings which were due, partly at least, to the system of representation devised in 1947 and the weightage it provided for the rural areas and for parts of the country in which the Tamils and Muslims lived in large numbers. Once again Sri Lanka was one of the first parliamentary democracies of the former British Empire to introduce a form of Proportional Representation (PR). The first parliamentary election under PR was held on 15 February 1989. The UNP, with just over 51 per cent of the votes, secured 125 seats in the 225 member Parliament, while the SLFP which obtained 30 per cent of the votes, won 66 seats. Had the former first-past-the-post system continued in existence the UNP would have easily won a three-fourths majority in the legislature while the SLFP would have secured just over 10 seats.

II

Electoral Experiences

The first election since independence (1948) came in 1952 when the UNP, which had won the election of 1947 and led the country to independence, secured the endorsement of the electorate for a second five year term in office. The next election, that of 1956, was also a watershed in the county's democratisation, because it marked the peaceful transfer of power from one political party to another by the defeat of the UNP government in a free and fair election by a left of centre coalition, led by S.W.R.D. Bandaranaike's SLFP. Through the defeat of the UNP Sri Lanka had demonstrated the strength of its democratic system by becoming the first state in post-colonial South and South East Asia in which a peaceful transfer of power from the original legatee of the colonial power occurred through the electoral process. It took 21 years from that date (1956) before India experienced a similar change of government.

From 1956 until 1977 each successive Sri Lankan general election saw the government in office defeated at the polls. (The UNP which won the general election of 1977 was in office until 1994.) One result was that Sri Lanka developed into a genuine multi-party democracy with two parties of government, the UNP and the SLFP, who have ruled the country in turn, on their own or in coalition with other parties, since independence. No other democratic system in Asia has two major political parties who have governed the country for substantial periods of time as in Sri Lanka.

Beginning with the first general election of 1931, the country has had 15 general elections to the national legislature, one referendum on a national basis as a substitute for a parliamentary election (1982) and five elections to choose an executive president. Since 1978, the people have periodically elected four tiers of government—executive president introduced in 1978, Parliament, provincial councils introduced in 1987, and municipal and local government bodies; prior to that date elections were conducted to seats in the national legislature and to municipal and local government bodies. In terms of a four-tier system of elections the country should be one of the most vibrant democracies in the developing world.

However, the island's representative system under universal suffrage inaugurated in 1931 has three distinctive periods. The first period lasted from 1931 to 1972, the introduction of the first republican constitution. The constructive achievements of this period are a tribute as much to the maturity and sophistication of the electorate as to the political skills and good sense of the country's politicians. The next phase, 1972 to 2001, can be described as 30 years in which there were short episodes of deliberate undermining of the island's electoral process, or some short periods of intensive subversion. The initial moves in this regard came with the new Constitution of 1972; there were, as we shall see, other episodes as well, such as the referendum of 1982, but the period 1994 to December 2001 was the worst in regard to the undermining of the democratic electoral process by the government in power, that of the People's Alliance (PA).

The parliamentary elections of August 1994, organised by President D.B. Wijetunga and Ranil Wickremesinghe as Prime Minister, which were won by the PA led by the SLFP, were clearly free and fair. Chandrika Kumaratunga became Prime Minister on this occasion. However, the record of the conduct of elections at all levels especially since November 1994 saw a distinct moving away from democratic norms to the point where public confidence in the genuineness of the results of elections was rapidly eroded, until the PA government was defeated at the General Elections of December 2001.

The decisive defeat of the PA at the parliamentary elections of 5 December 2001, one of the most violent in Sri Lanka's electoral history, gave the country some hope that the electoral system would return to its traditional pattern set in the period 1931 to 1972. The third period thus begins in December 2001 and appears to mark the end, hopefully, of the phase of active subversion of the electoral processes by the government in power.

III

Three Episodes in the Subversion of the System, 1972, 1982, 1987–90

The earliest signs of trouble in the electoral process began in 1972 when, with the introduction of the first Republican Constitution of 1972, the elections due in 1975 were unilaterally and arbitrarily postponed till 1977.[14] The regularity of Sri Lanka's elections to the national legislature, generally held every five years unless the legislature was dissolved earlier,[15] was deliberately cast aside. Worse still, the government of the day, led by Mrs Sirimavo Bandaranaike, having secured an extension of its term of office by two years through the adoption of a new Constitution, later began a well-publicised campaign for yet another postponement of the election then scheduled for 1977, influenced by Mrs Gandhi's imposition of emergency rule in India in June 1975. The failure of this attempt, because it could not secure a two-thirds majority in Parliament, was followed by the rout of the government and its erstwhile Marxist allies at the general election of 1977.

The first presidential election, held in October 1982, like all previous general elections, was both free and fair, but the credibility of the genuine mandate the government had secured in October 1982 was affected by the substitution of a referendum[16] in December 1982 for the parliamentary election that should have followed. The referendum was inherently controversial because the electorate was asked to vote for or against a proposal to extend the life of the Parliament elected in 1977 for a further period of six years. Despite the legality of the referendum in terms of the Constitution of 1978, it was patently a ruse resorted to by the UNP government of J.R. Jayewardene to preserve for another six years the five-sixths parliamentary majority it had won in the 1977 general election. While the government easily won the referendum, the credibility of the final result was vitiated by the misuse of state power and electoral malpractices and abuses all of which permitted critics of the government to question the genuineness not merely of the victory at the referendum but also of the mandate President Jayewardene had won at the presidential election in October 1982.[17]

The third episode in the undermining of Sri Lanka's democratic electoral system came in the period 1987 to 1990. The source of the violence and malpractices that marred the presidential election of 1988 and the parliamentary election of 1989 was not the government of the day but the Janatha Vimukthi Peramuna (JVP), which engaged in a campaign of intimidation and terror against the holding of these elections. For the first time a violent campaign was launched to prevent people from going to the polls, and to intimidate candidates. As a result of that campaign of violence the total poll dropped to 55 per cent for the presidential election, and 64 per cent for the parliamentary election, a sharp reduction in both instances from the turn-out of 81 per cent at the presidential election of October 1982, and 70.8 per cent at the referendum of December 1982. While most of the malpractices on these occasions could be attributed to the JVP, there were allegations that the Indian Peace Keeping Force (IPKF) stationed in the north and east of the island under the terms of the Indo-Lanka agreement of 1987, stuffed ballot boxes in the Northern and Eastern Provinces, but more particularly in the Eastern Province, in favour of the UNP candidate R. Premadasa, the eventual winner. The fact however was that despite the turmoil in the country, the traditional election machinery functioned with its characteristic efficiency and impartiality despite the violent campaign of the JVP, and the killing of a few election officials.

IV
Local Government and Provincial Council Elections

As we have seen earlier in this chapter Sri Lanka's administrative machinery for the conduct of elections did not confine itself to polls for the national legislature. From the beginning, elections to local bodies—municipalities, urban and town councils, and village committees—also came within its purview. Registration of voters for local bodies was handled by the Department of Elections which also organised all other elections. These were held on a regular basis, but generally not on the same day on an islandwide basis, even after parliamentary elections began to be held on a single day after March 1960. The dates of such elections were fixed by the government which also had the power to postpone such elections if that was seen as necessary in the public interest. Postponement of such elections was generally not very common.

The years 1972–77, with the SLFP-led United Front (UF) coalition in power, were a period of sharp decline in the vitality of the local government system. Indeed there were no elections to local bodies during this whole period and the government often used its powers to dissolve many local bodies. These institutions were then either run by public servants or other individuals chosen by the government for their political loyalties. Only the Colombo Municipal Council was permitted to function but that was because the UNP mayor of the day[18] switched sides along with a small group of members of the council originally chosen on the UNP ticket: this group became a member of the SLFP.

The revival of local government bodies and local government elections came only after the defeat of Mrs Bandaranaike's left of centre coalition government in 1977. The first such elections were held in 1979, for municipalities, urban councils and town councils.[19] For the first time these too were held on a single day as with parliamentary elections. The next set of local government elections were held on 18 May 1983 in regard to 12 municipal councils and 38 urban councils, and on 20 May in regard to four urban councils. Village committees or councils had ceased to exist, and their functions were transferred to the district development councils (DDCs) established in March 1981. The date of transfer was 1 July 1981. Town councils were either elevated to the level of urban councils, or reduced to the level of rural centres under the control of the DDCs. The elections to the DDCs, 24 in all, in 1981 were also held on a single day.[20] With the introduction of the 1978 Constitution, the two-tier election system that had prevailed from 1931 became a more complex four-tier structure.

Elections to local bodies scheduled for 1986–87 could not be held because of the disturbed political situation in the country particularly the violent opposition of the JVP. In 1987, provincial councils, set up under the terms of the Indo-Sri Lanka agreement of that year, replaced the DDC. Elections to these councils were held in 1988, not on a single day, again because the violent opposition of the JVP to the establishment of such councils made it difficult to do so.[21] Local government elections scheduled for 1986 were also postponed. By the time local government elections were held in 1991, village councils had been re-established. These elections were held on an islandwide basis and on a single day. Once the term of office of the provincial councils elected in 1988–89 came to an end, fresh elections were held in 1993–94.

All these elections held after 1978 were generally free and fair. The only exception was the controversial election to the DDC in Jaffna in 1981 where the violence initiated by Tamil separatist groups led by the Liberation Tigers of Tamil Eelam (LTTE) led to the killing of the principal UNP candidate, and subsequently of four policemen sent on election duty,[22] was met by counterviolence by the police, and where the election itself was marred by allegations of rigging and by breaches of the established rules governing the conduct of elections. As a result the Jaffna poll was postponed by a few weeks but when it was held every seat was won by the Tamil United Liberation Front (TULF), difficult enough under the first-past-the-post system, but virtually unheard of anywhere under PR.

The local government elections of 1991 held under President R. Premadasa were generally accepted as being both free and fair. Provincial council elections of 1993 and 1994 held under Presidents R. Premadasa and D.B. Wijetunga, respectively, were characterised, by most observers, as being both free and fair. The fact that the UNP lost control of two provincial councils, those of the Western Province and the Southern Province and had to resort to a coalition to retain control over the Provincial Council of the North Western Province is proof of this. Chandrika Kumaratunga, Sri Lanka's fourth executive President, made her entry into national politics when she was chosen chief minister of the Western Provincial Council in 1993.

V

The Electoral Process in Crisis, 1994–2001

Local Government and Provincial Council Elections

All the elections conducted by the PA government since it came to power in August–November 1994 have been sullied by systematic and organised electoral malpractices on an unprecedented scale. The first controversial issue relating to the electoral process concerned the frequent attempts to postpone provincial council and local government elections. Thus the local government elections scheduled for sometime in 1995, were postponed on the grounds that the security situation in the country warranted it, the argument being that a large police force was required to provide security for the thousands of polling booths dotted over the country, and the release of these policemen even for a short period would be detrimental to national security. While these elections were eventually held in March 1997, the electoral malpractices organised by the government were not merely very widespread, but, more to the point, for the first time in the history of local government elections in the country, going back to the late 1930s, systematic ballot rigging, booth capturing and intimidation of opposition candidates and voters, all of these under the aegis of senior government ministers, became a feature of the poll. Unlike in India where booth capturing was a matter of private enterprise, it was a state venture in Sri Lanka, directed by some of the most important cabinet ministers of the day.

A news report published in a Sri Lankan newspaper *The Island*, 23 March 1997 captured the essence of the problem. The report referred to the observations of a polls monitor, a foreigner from South Africa:

Unprecedented Violence in Poll—*Observer*

An election observer from South Africa, at Friday's local government poll said yesterday that he had never before witnessed the magnitude of violence that occurred in the Negombo district.

Dr Raj Nadaraja who had served as an election observer in several countries told *The Island* that mobs dressed in blue, carrying guns, sticks and knives went about the Negombo district intimidating presiding officers, UNP polling agents and certain voters.

He said that he saw several voters being prevented from going to cast their votes by armed gangs dressed in blue. Subsequently several of the voters had complained to him that the persons who intimidated them were mobs deployed by the People's Alliance.

Dr Nadaraja said that PA mobs chased the presiding officers, election officers and UNP polling agents out at the Kurana, Bolawalana and Daluwakotuwa polling booths and then stuffed the ballot boxes.

At Daluwakotuwa 'I saw a UNP polling agent who was injured and bleeding being trampled [sic] by some PA activists. About eight or nine UNPers were injured in this area. When I brought it to the notice of the police including the stuffing of the ballot boxes the police seemed to be disinterested,' he said.

Dr Nadaraja observed that even during the 1994 South African election that ended apartheid rule and installed Nelson Mandela in office he had not seen such blatant violations of election laws. 'What I saw in Negombo on Friday was shocking. It was nothing short of mob rule,' he added.

From the time of the local government elections of 1997, poll rigging and booth capturing became a way of political life during election times under the People's Alliance government. And so too the gross abuse and misuse of state power and state resources—from state-owned vehicles, government buildings, including official residences of the president to state television and state-owned newspapers, to influence the poll in favour of the government.

Elections to five provincial councils were scheduled for August 1998. Once more the government decided to postpone these elections, and once more the reasons adduced were those of national security. On this occasion, the decision to postpone the elections was challenged before the Supreme Court. However, before the decision of the Supreme Court on this case was announced, the government surprised its critics by its decision to hold elections to the North Western Provincial Council in January 1999, 25 January to be exact. From the moment the election was announced to the day of the election itself, the government indulged in every imaginable type of electoral fraud and form of violence against its opponents, and systematised poll rigging to a higher—indeed much higher—level than in 1997, to a level never seen before in Sri Lanka.

Urging that 'the Wayamba (i.e., North Western) election be declared null and void,' the Centre for Monitoring Election Violence (CMEV) reported on 25 January after the polls closed that, 'widespread election violations of every stripe are being reported mainly against the PA by CMEV monitors in the field, independent observers and opposition sources....' These blatant malpractices had, 'in the considered view of CMEV, irrevocably undermined this election as an exercise of the public's free and fair choice.' The CMEV monitors identified the inactivity of the police as one of the most serious problems at this election:

The police appears to be unwilling and unable to check the violence in a number of the more serious incidents; they too were among the bystanders, and have expressed feelings of frustration and helplessness to CMEV monitors on the spot. The government seems to have pinned its faith in the end result of all this violence and election fraud, oblivious to the toll on its own credibility, and the very democratic electoral processes that brought it to power.[23]

In a statement made on 25 January 1999, the Commissioner of Elections, Dayananda Dissanayaka, pointed out that

In 212 polling stations out of 1,150 there was large scale stuffing of ballot boxes. Ballot boxes from nine polling booths have not reached the counting centres and probably never will. Six ballot boxes have been burnt. This is the worst election I have ever seen in my personal experience.[24]

When asked why he did not declare the election null and void, he explained that under the election laws promulgated in 1959 the commissioner of elections has no authority to declare an election null and void. Only the Supreme Court could do so on the basis of an election petition. But he did decide that no fewer than 50,000 ballots, constituting 4.5 per cent of the total votes polled, had been illegally cast, and therefore should be removed from the count. Independent observers believed that this was only a fraction of the votes illegally cast.

Never has an election been more roundly condemned by a larger group of professional bodies and religious dignitaries than on this occasion. Restricting oneself to the comments of the latter, there are, first of all, the views of Maduluwawe Sobitha, a highly respected and outspoken *bhikkhu* (member of the Buddhist order) who asserted that 'with the elections in Wayamba the faith our people have in democracy and in elections fell to its lowest level ever,' and urged that '... the unfair election in Wayamba should be legally cancelled.' The Venerable Madihe Pannasiha, the elderly head of the Amarapura Chapter of the Buddhist order condemned the election to the North Western Provincial Council as a disgrace to the Bandaranaike family and recommended that it be declared null and void.

The Right Reverend Frank Marcus Fernando, the Roman Catholic Bishop of Chilaw, was equally critical: 'We are deeply disturbed by the large scale thuggery, intimidation and impersonation that took place today in Wayamba. Surviving that election was like surviving a war.' He too insisted that the election be cancelled.

President Chandrika Kumaratunga attempted to distance herself from the unprecedented levels of violence and electoral fraud perpetrated by her government on this occasion, and felt constrained to criticise the poll and the campaign. Her criticisms did not lead to any repudiation of those who committed these excesses; on the contrary, some of the more notorious of them obtained positions as ministers in the North Western Provincial Council. She went through the motions of appointing a Committee or Commission of Inquiry into this election, but there has been no activity on the part of the government for this Committee or Commission and certainly no report.

Two days after the rigged election to the North Western Provincial Council, the Supreme Court delivered a landmark judgement on an application challenging the validity of the government's decision to postpone the elections to the Provincial Councils of the Central, Uva, North Central, Western and Sabaragamuwa Provinces through a regulation under the Public Security Ordinance.[25] Findings in favour of the petitioners the Court held that there had been a violation of Article 14 (1) (a) of the Constitution which guarantees freedom of speech and expression—casting a vote, it held, was a form of expression and postponement of the elections was therefore tantamount to a violation of Article 14 (1) (a) of the Constitution. Second, it held the emergency regulation in question was in the form of an order and was therefore not valid in law. Third, and more important still, it pointed out that the immunity of the president under the Constitution was neither absolute nor perpetual and the immunity shielded the doer and not the act. Fourth, holding that the commissioner of elections 'was at least partly responsible for the failure to take the poll on 28.8.98; and was wholly responsible for the failure promptly to fix a new date, on and after 28.8.98 ...', it proceeded to remind him that

> ... the Constitution assures him independence so that he may fearlessly insist on due compliance with the law in regard to all aspects of elections, even if necessary, by instituting appropriate legal proceedings in order to obtain judicial orders. But ... he made no effort to ascertain the legal position, or to have recourse to legal remedies.

The Supreme Court ordered the commissioner of elections

> ... to take immediate action to fix, within two weeks from today (27 January 1999) in respect of all five elections (a) a new date or dates not later than the four weeks from today, for the issue of postal ballot papers, and (b) a new date or dates of poll, not later than three months from today.

While the elections held on 6 April 1999 for the five provincial councils were also flawed, the poll rigging was more sophisticated. It was less blatant and cleverly concentrated in certain key polling divisions and the rigging was just enough to secure control of the councils by the United Front coalition. The election to the Southern Province conducted in June 1999 was relatively free of malpractices but not wholly so.

Presidential (1999)[26] and Parliamentary (2000 and 2001)[27] Elections

The trend set in the early 1990s of resuscitating the tradition of free and fair elections was decisively reversed in the 1994 presidential election, conducted by the PA government and won by Chandrika Kumaratunga. There is not the slightest doubt that the outcome of the poll on that occasion would not have been different even if the poll had been totally free of malpractices such as the systematic intimidation of voters in many parts of the country, widespread impersonation through a seizure of polling cards, and the prevention of people from coming to vote where they were likely to vote against the PA candidate. Polling agents of the UNP were intimidated and often prevented from performing their legitimate duties, or expelled from polling stations. Kumaratunga would still have won but the wide margin of victory, of 62 per cent for her to 35 per cent for the UNP candidate, would have been substantially less. In the context of what had happened in the elections held in the late 1990s the parliamentary election of August 1994 proved to be the last free and fair election held in Sri Lanka till the local government elections, concluded in 2002, under the UNP-dominated United National Front (UNF) coalition.

In 1999, from the time presidential elections were called in October, the signs were that the president as a candidate would exploit every advantage available to her benefit. Breaches of existing practice began very early. Thus, when the commissioner of elections fell ill just before the election campaign got under way, she ignored the claims of the deputy commissioner, and reached out to a man who had no experience of election work.[28] While the president is empowered by the Constitution to make such an appointment, the propriety of a president seeking re-election exercising his/her power in the way it was done, was to say the least, questionable. The president was uniquely privileged in being able to pick an acting elections commissioner of her choice for a presidential election at which she was a candidate. Next, she hosted an official dinner at her official residence to a group of senior government officials, most if not all of whom would be called upon to serve in very sensitive posts, in conducting the elections, and in supervising the counting of votes in the districts in the forthcoming presidential election.

This was apart from the monopoly she had in the use of the state-controlled print media and electronic media for her election campaign. Because of its lack of credibility in the country the state-controlled print media had been overtaken by the independent press and therefore its control by the president in her campaign was less important than the monopoly established over the use of the state-controlled electronic media which had a wider territorial range than the private television stations, covering the whole country, and especially the rural areas, whereas the others were concentrated in the urban areas. In addition, there was gross misuse of state resources, ranging from fleets of government vehicles, buildings and officials, for the government's election campaign on behalf of its candidate—the incumbent president. All of this was done in arrogant disregard of laws and established practices and conventions. The opportunity, and indeed the excuse, for violence against opponents, stemmed from a failed assassination attempt against Chandrika Kumaratunga by the LTTE just two days before the election.

From the time the presidential election was called in October 1999 to the day of election on 21 December, Velupillai Prabhakaran, the leader of the LTTE, cast a sinister shadow on the electoral process and the fortunes of the two principal candidates, Chandrika Kumaratunga, seeking re-election, and Ranil Wickremesinghe, the leader of the opposition and of the UNP seeking election.

By inflicting a series of defeats on the Sri Lanka army in November in the north of the island, Prabhakaran embarrassed the government and gave an unexpected boost to the chances of the UNP candidate. The latter was clearly behind the incumbent president in public perceptions of electoral fortune, but from the middle of November when the LTTE campaign against the army in parts of the north of the country was gaining a series of successes, Wickremesinghe's own chances improved dramatically. Over the last 10 days of the electoral campaign he was seen to have caught up with the president in a very close contest. Indeed most political analysts and all the Sunday newspapers, with the obvious exceptions of the state-owned newspapers, predicted a victory for the challenger. Then, on the last day of campaigning, an LTTE bomb that nearly killed President Kumaratunga reversed this emerging trend in the election process.

From the time of the assassination attempt and over two days and evenings (on 19 and 20 December), the government's electronic media conducted an energetic campaign on behalf of the president and against her principal opponent, despite the legal ban placed on such broadcasts for 72 hours prior to the actual polling under clause 117 of the *Presidential Elections Act 15 of 1981*. The shock of the failed assassination attempt was cleverly exploited by the government through the use of the state-controlled electronic media, especially TV, and the state-controlled press, culminating in the appearance of the injured president herself on state TV on 20 December, dressed in her party's colour (blue) and with her damaged eye covered with a bandage, her face clearly swollen, making an unmistakable bid for the voters' sympathy.

The Presidential Elections Act 15 of 1981 also places a ban on any form of electioneering for two days immediately before the day of the election. Electioneering, in the form of public meetings, had to stop by midnight on 18 December (Section 70). From the time of the assassination attempt, cabinet ministers, deputy ministers and government party MPs felt emboldened to hold political meetings in the guise of religious ceremonies in Buddhist temples in many parts of the country ostensibly to give thanks for her narrow escape; at these ceremonies the assassination attempt was foisted on her UNP rival claiming that he was acting in collusion with the LTTE. Vans were sent round the electorates with loudspeakers blaring, carrying the same message of collusion between the UNP and the LTTE in this bid to assassinate the president, an allegation that was also aired on state television by cabinet ministers and others. This course of action was a clear breach of the law. The opposition candidate had neither the time nor the opportunity to refute this preposterous allegation and it went virtually unanswered.

The assassination attempt made it possible for Chandrika Kumaratunga's supporters to revitalise her sagging campaign, and convert it into a fierce rampage against supporters of the UNP, making it look like a spontaneous reaction to an outrage perpetrated by the LTTE in association with the UNP. They were able to sustain this sharply escalated level of violence and to channel it, as we shall see, into large scale rigging of the poll in many parts of the country.

Poll watchers and monitors such as the Centre for Monitoring Election Violence (CMEV), the Movement for Free and Fair Elections (MFFE) and People's Action for Free and Fair Elections (PAFFREL) reported that the polls in a substantial number of polling divisions in the country (over a third in fact) were seriously affected by electoral malpractices—'irredeemably compromised'[29] were the words of the CMEV. In the immediate aftermath of the election, estimates of the impact of the rigging in favour of Chandrika Kumaratunga varied from a conservative 1 per cent to 2 per cent of the votes at the national level to those who believed it was as high as 4 per cent. If one merely accepted the conservative estimate of 1 per cent to 2 per cent Mrs Kumaratunga's vote would have dropped to 49 per cent. If the higher one was accepted it would have been 47 per cent. In either event there would have been a second count, that is the second and third preferences of all except the first two candidates would have been counted and distributed between the two. Kumaratunga may still have won but it would have been by a very narrow margin. However when more evidence of widespread election malpractices began piling up,[30] the possibility was that even an estimate of 4 per cent of the poll affected by systematic rigging, was actually too low. Once the 5 per cent threshold was reached, the evidence points to the possibility that the election was stolen. The CMEV put it bluntly that 'the extent and magnitude [of] violations renders [sic] the overall result untenable.'[31]

For the first time in the long history of organising elections in Sri Lanka, there were serious allegations of partiality and mismanagement against the head of the Elections Department and the manner in which his department had conducted the elections. There were breaches of administrative practice in the choice of returning officers, chief presiding officers and presiding officers who conducted the polls. For the first time, too, there were credible allegations of partiality and manipulation in the process of counting of votes. The Police Department which provides security for the poll, once again failed to enforce the law even where intimidation and violence prevailed in the vicinity of polling stations and in the presence of police officers.

Where politicians realise that election malpractices yield rich dividends as they have clearly done since the presidential election of November 1994, those who gain or consolidate their power in that way, simply start their period in office with a distorted view of the political process. As a government with a very slim majority in Parliament (1994–2000), there was an exaggerated fear that any electoral setback could affect its stability. The manner in which the government conducted the local government elections of 1997 provided strong evidence of this fear of the electorate. The methods resorted to were unprecedented for local government elections where, quite apart from violation of election laws relating to posters and other forms of publicity, there was systematic abuse of state power: this included exerting undue pressure on the police and the bureaucracy, the misuse of state-controlled or state-owned print and electronic media and other state resources, culminating in booth capturing and poll rigging on election day. As the rigged 'election' to the North Western Provincial Council in January 1999 amply demonstrated, those who use tactics such as those resorted at the local government election of 1997 to get their supporters 'elected' to power, develop a strong fear of losing power and the privileges that power brings. They have no hesitation in using the same tactics to remain in power. The practice of rigged elections turns into a self-perpetuating process, a commitment to continuously indulge in election malpractices simply to remain in power.

Thus the presidential election of December 1999 marred by a succession of election abuses was followed by the even more controversial parliamentary elections of 10 October 2000, and this in turn by the parliamentary elections of 5 December 2001 which came much earlier than anyone expected. The parliamentary elections of 10 October 2000 had been a setback for the PA government and a disappointment for the opposition UNP. Despite the widespread electoral malpractices and systematic violence on the part of the incumbent government, the PA secured only 45 per cent of the total votes, while the UNP had 40 per cent. In the assessment of many political analysts, expertly calibrated rigging in selected polling divisions had increased the government's poll by 5 per cent or more nationally, while the UNP was deprived of 5 per cent or more. It was evident, from the outset, that the government would be more vulnerable to shifts of opinion within Parliament, and in the country, than its immediate predecessor. How the government lost its majority by September 2001 need not detain us here, but the fact is that by October 2001, the PA was compelled to dissolve Parliament and call another general election which it scheduled for 5 December 2001.

In retrospect, both parliamentary elections, that of October 2000 and of December 2001, were deeply flawed by electoral malpractices perpetrated by the government; both involved a brazen exploitation of state resources by the PA and poll rigging, often crude and sometimes adroit; both saw the full and virtually exclusive use of the state's print and electronic media for the election campaign on behalf of the government candidates, and all of it in defiant and open disregard of election laws; and in both of them there was systematic violence against opponents of the government often directed by senior government politicians. The parliamentary elections of 5

December 2001 were the more violent of the two. On the day of the election, 10 young men were killed in the worst episode of election violence in Sri Lanka's history. A former PA cabinet minister and his two sons were among those who faced several charges including murder and conspiracy to murder in regard to this incident. (The former cabinet minister and his two sons were found not guilty of the charges against them.)

At the presidential election of 1999 and the parliamentary elections of October 2000, the government's campaign succeeded in achieving its objective, at substantial costs to its political credibility and integrity of the country's democratic electoral system. On 5 December 2001, the electoral tide turned against the government, and the violence and poll rigging failed decisively. On this occasion, unlike in October 2000, the government sponsored violence confronted quiet resistance in most polling divisions, aggressive resistance in some and retaliatory violence in a few, including episodes of post-election violence.

The violence organised by the government was a desperate attempt to stave off defeat. In the weekend before the polls, the *Sunday Times* which generally provides the most reliable polls forecasts put the opposition well ahead of the PA. Political analysts calculated that the PA's vote base had shrunk quite considerably and that it would require a massive campaign of rigging and violence to overcome the disadvantage. Such a campaign would attract so much public attention that the process itself would be self-defeating. Nevertheless the attempt was made. The rigging had been so blatant in many polling divisions that the CMEV and PAFFREL/MFFE called for a fresh poll in such polling stations if not polling divisions. The commissioner of elections was reluctant to do this. Instead he eliminated scores of ballot boxes where there was clear, if not overwhelming, evidence of ballot stuffing. In victory, the UNP-led coalition endorsed this action. They had secured a comprehensive victory despite the rigging, winning most of the polling divisions and all but one of the polling districts outside the Northern Province. While a fresh poll in some polling booths and polling divisions many have strengthened their position and increased the number of MPs they already had, it would have delayed the official announcement of the result, and delayed the transfer of power from the executive president to the new prime minister.

The UNP had won 45.56 per cent of the vote, while the PA vote had dropped to 37.27 per cent. Political analysts felt that the margin of victory for the UNP and its allies would have been much higher in a free and fair election, which the parliamentary contest of 2001 clearly was not. The parliamentary election of April 2004 organised by the UNF coalition was a free and fair election. The government in power, the UNF coalition, lost the election securing 37 per cent of the vote to their opponents' 45 per cent.

The defeat of the PA in December 2001 had consequences for the Sri Lankan political system. Certainly the result of the election restored some faith in the integrity of Sri Lanka's stricken democracy. The local government elections of 2002 and 2006, the General Elections of 2004 and the Presidential Election of 2005 have all been generally accepted as being free and fair.

Notes

1. On the introduction of universal suffrage to Sri Lanka, see K.M. de Silva, 'The Introduction of Universal Suffrage' in K.M. de Silva (ed.), *Universal Suffrage, 1931–1981: The Sri Lankan Experience,* Colombo, 1981, pp. 48–62.
2. A.J.P. Taylor, *English History, 1914–1945,* Oxford, 1965, p. 262. Taylor explained that an act by the government '... lowered the voting age for women from 30 to 21, and put them on the same straightforward residence qualification as men. One adult, one vote was at last attained except for the business and university franchises which gave about half a million people (mainly males) a second vote until they were abolished in 1948,' ibid., p. 262.
3. Peter Clarke, *Hope and Glory: Britain 1900–1990, The Penguin History of Britain,* London, Penguin Books, 1996, pp. 103–04. The act established universal male adult suffrage with a simple six months residential qualification. Women over 30 were granted the right to vote, thus conceding the principle of women's suffrage. Plural voting was not abolished but no voter might in future vote in more than two constituencies. Also, at future general elections polling would take place on one day.
4. *Ceylon: Report of the Special Commission on the Constitution,* London, 1928, p. 83.
5. Ibid.
6. A.E. Goonesinghe, the foremost trade unionist of the time, was an advocate of manhood suffrage.
7. Dr Drummond Shiels was a leading advocate and activist in Britain for votes for women.
8. *Sessional Paper XXIV of 1930.*
9. *Sessional Paper VIII of 1937,* F.C. Gimson's official report on the general election of 1936.
10. Ibid.
11. The elections of 1931 were held over the period 13 to 20 June, with constituencies polling on 13, 15, 16, 17, 18 and 20 June. In 1936, the second set of elections under universal suffrage stretched over a longer

period—22 February to 7 March. The dates of polling were 22, 25, 27, 28, 29 February and 3, 5 and 7 March.

12. See *Report of the Committee on the Method of the Ballot* (August 1930).

13. In 1957 the office of commissioner of elections which had hitherto been under the Ministry of Home Affairs, became an independent department answerable only to Parliament. F. Dias Abeyesinghe was the first holder of this office from 1960 to 1979. Through an amendment of the constitution— *The Ceylon Constitution and Parliamentary Elections (Amendment) Act No. 8 of 1964*—the position of the commissioner of parliamentary elections was greatly strengthened. His position was now derived from the constitution itself.

14. For the background see my article 'Sri Lanka (Ceylon): The New Republican Government' in *Verfassung Und Recht in Ubersee* (3), 1972, pp. 239–49.

15. The general election scheduled for 1941 had been postponed because of the pressures of the second world war.

16. See K.M. de Silva, 'Extending the Life of Parliament by Referendum in Sri Lanka' in *The Parliamentarian*, LXI (3), July 1985 pp. 134–37; C.R. de Silva, 'Plebiscitary Democracy or Creeping Authoritarianism? The Presidential Election and Referendum of 1982' in James Manor (ed.), *Sri Lanka in Change and Crisis,* London, 1984, pp. 35–50.

17. On 18 May 1983, by-elections were held in 18 constituencies in which the UNP had fared badly—i.e., lost—at the presidential election of 1982, and the referendum. In the event the government won 14 of these seats in what was clearly a free and fair election. On the same day elections were held to local government bodies in 20 districts.

18. A.H.M. Fawzie, who crossed over to the SLFP, was a member of the People's Alliance cabinet from 1994 to 5 December 2001. He was appointed to the UFPA cabinet in April 2004. He had been in the People's Alliance cabinet earlier.

19. On 19 May 1979, 43 local bodies went to the polls; UNP won 34 of them, while the Tamil United Liberation Front (TULF) won nine in the north and east of the country.

20. After the passage of the *District Development Councils Act 35* of September 1980, these councils were established in March 1981. Nominations were called for elections to these councils on 14 April 1981. On that occasion the UNP slate was returned uncontested to seven councils: Kandy, Nuwara-Eliya, Matara, Kurunegala, Moneragala, Ratnapura and Kegalle. The elections to the other councils were held on 4 June 1981.

21. On 12 February 1988 nominations were called for elections to all provincial councils, but nominations were postponed subsequently under the *Public Security Act*. Elections to the North Western, Uva and Sabaragamuwa councils were held on 28 April 1988.

22. The principal UNP candidate for the Jaffna district was assassinated on 24 May 1981. For the background to the elections, see K.M. de Silva, *Managing Ethnic Tensions in Multi-Ethnic Societies: Sri Lanka, 1880–1985*, Lanham MD, University Press of America, 1986, pp. 332–33.

156   K.M. de Silva

23. *Final Report on Election Related Violence: The North Western Provincial Council Elections, 1999,* Colombo, Centre for Monitoring Election Violence (CMEV), 1999.
24. This interview with MTV, a popular private TV station, was published in *The Island* on 26 January 1999.
25. Supreme Court judgement by Chief Justice G.P.S. de Silva and Justices Fernando and Gunasekera in Supreme Court Application, 509/98. The judgement is published in *The Law and Society Trust Review*, 9 February 1999, pp. 1–23.
26. On the presidential election of 1999, see K.M. de Silva, 'The Problems of Governance in Sri Lanka: The Subversion of a Democratic Electoral Process,' *South Asian Survey*, 7:2 (2000), pp. 227–45; 'Sri Lanka: Flawed Presidential Election: Harbinger of More Trouble Ahead,' *Economic and Political Weekly*, 27 January 1999, pp. 178–81.
27. K.M. de Silva, 'Sri Lanka: Election and After: Opportunity to Restore Stability,' *Economic and Political Weekly*, 2 March 2002, pp. 838–43.
28. Just before the presidential election, Dayananda Dissanayaka, the Commissioner of Elections, fell ill of a heart complaint. Under the current election laws the commissioner was empowered to nominate a person to be in temporary charge and to conduct the first phase of the election. The obvious choice was his own deputy to act as commissioner, but the president pre-empted this by using her constitutional powers to appoint an election commissioner, and did it from outside the Elections Department.
29. See particularly the damning indictment in the CMEV's *Final Report on Election-Related Violence. The Presidential Election, 21st December 1999,* Colombo, January 2000.
30. See, for instance, the several issues of the *Ravaya*, January to April 2000 on this.
31. CMEV's *Final Report on Election-Related Violence...*, op. cit., p. 66.

Part III

STATUTORY FRAMEWORK AND
INSTITUTIONAL ARRANGEMENTS

7

BANGLADESH

Muzaffer Ahmad

Constitutional Provision for Election and Role of the Elected

The Legislature of Bangladesh, known as Jatiyo Sangsad, consists of 345 members 'to be elected in accordance with law from single territorial constituencies by direct election.' The required qualifications to stand for election are citizenship of Bangladesh and a minimum age of 25 years. The disqualifications include insolvency, unsound mind, allegiance to a foreign state, offences involving moral turpitude and holding an office of profit of the republic, other than those specified. Membership after taking oath ceases on resignation, absence from Parliament for 90 consecutive sitting days, or resignation from or vote against the party in the legislature.

This last provision reduces the role of the representative of the constituency to merely that of an elected member of the party. Representative democracy is thereby reduced to a form of unrealistic democracy, and the job for the constituency is shifted out of Parliament to the doorstep of party bureaucracy and ministerial secretariat. Thus the role backbenchers or young rebels play in a mature democracy is abnegated by constitutional provision.

The Constitution bars a member from representing more than one constituency but does not bar a person from being a candidate from two or more constituencies. There have been attempts to limit it to a lower figure (that is, two) but the current practice of a maximum of five prevails. The practice of standing from more than one constituency is needed by the party leaders to prove their wider acceptability and to suppress dissension within the party or to protect a seat whose outcome is doubtful. This has generally given an advantage to the party that forms the government after election and has been useful in getting a favourite party leader elected. But the issue is whether this is a fraud on representative democracy. At the by-election, the people's choice possibly becomes secondary.

This process of becoming a candidate has been made possible by the absence of enforcement of the residency requirement for election from a particular constituency. The residency requirement based on paying taxes to a local body or owning a piece of land/business in the constituency can easily be met in case of need.

Leniency with regard to eligibility requirements for candidature is a matter of serious concern. It is alleged that 'non-serious' candidates make a difference where the contest between candidates is close. The remedial measures proposed in the form of higher security deposit, raising the minimum votes required for refund of deposits, and the requirement of a significant number of proposals spread over different segments, of constituencies and so on, are bureaucratic solutions against which the argument of free entry into the competitive political market has been advanced. While it has been argued that proliferation of independent and small party candidates has only a marginal impact on the outcome of an election, it is nevertheless true that contesting of elections by candidates rejected by the party has an impact on such outcome.

As to disqualification, there has been an attempt to bar loan defaulters from contesting the elections. This has been breached by major parties by changing the definition of loan default as well as by the provision for rescheduling loans. Public opinion has been in favour of limiting rescheduling opportunity, making stringent definition of loan default and adding non-payment of public utility bills to the list of disqualifications, as the businessmen/industrialists/former Members of Parliament (MP) feature prominently as bill dodgers. It is also believed that restricting loan defaulters and bill dodgers may have a desired impact on black money finance. But the major parties depend heavily on such finance.

Neutral Caretaker Government (NCG)

The NCG is of course a central element of the institutional framework for elections in Bangladesh. This topic has however been discussed by me in the Bangladesh Country Paper and therefore will not be discussed here.

The Election Commission

The Constitution provides for the establishment of an Election Commission (EC). The functions of the EC, as per the Constitution, include 'the superintendence, direction and control of the preparation of the electoral rolls' for parliamentary elections, presidential elections and elections to local government bodies. The EC prepares an electoral roll for each constituency and holds elections on the basis of adult franchise. However, the Parliament by law makes provisions with respect to all matters relating to or in connection with elections.[1] The EC sets the norms for the election campaign, and arranges for polling, counting and declaration of results.

The Constitution does not fix the number of members in the commission, but merely notes that the EC shall consist of a chief election commissioner (CEC) and such number of other election commissioners as is determined by the president from time to time according to law. The president in this respect acts according to the advice of the prime minister. It is to be noted that no qualification or for that matter disqualification for appointment to the EC has been made in the Constitution. Thus the mode of appointment as well as the size and composition of the EC has become a subject of controversy.

Traditionally the judges of the High Court, working or retired, would be appointed to the EC. In the period of non-elected regimes, they may have acted on the dictates of the ruler and some may have been rewarded for their 'services.' Justice Shahabuddin Ahmed during his tenure as acting President, confronted in 1991 with the onerous duty of conducting a free and fair election to Parliament, turned to the judiciary for appointments to the Commission. But members of the judiciary were discredited in the course of a bitterly disputed by-election and the 1996 February General Election due to non-neutrality. Justice Habibur Rahman, during his tenure as chief of the non-party caretaker government in 1996, depended on a chosen group of retired bureaucrats and the EC performed its job creditably. It may be noted that both Justice Shahabuddin Ahmed and Justice Habibur Rahman had the option to appoint the CEC and the members of the EC afresh.

This was not the case in 2001. The CEC resigned on health grounds and the Awami League (AL) Government proceeded to appoint a new CEC. Some reports have it that the AL prime minister wanted to reward a retired but loyal civil servant who is known to have more than normal allegiance to AL. The president did not agree and offered to resign if the case is pressed. Then the prime minister sent a name of another retired bureaucrat as an alternative which was accepted by the president, while the prime minister insisted on appointing the original nominee as a member of the EC which was acceded to. In this matter even the newly appointed CEC was not consulted. The AL Government proceeded to appoint a retired member of the subordinate judiciary to the EC again without consultation. For the first time, the number of members of the EC exceeded three (though two other members were to retire soon on the expiry of their tenure). The Bangladesh National Party (BNP) denounced all appointments and threatened to boycott the election. However the CEC assured the press that by his conduct he would be able to win the confidence of the political parties.

The fact however was that for the first time, a non-party caretaker government was to conduct elections to Parliament with an EC consisting of members appointed on a political basis. To avoid backroom drama and political manipulation, there is a need for a better mode of appointment of both the CEC and the members of EC. One mode could be consultation by the president with leader of opposition after the recommendation of the prime minister has been made. Again, if a working or retired member of judiciary is recommended, consultation with the chief justice should be mandatory, and if a working or retired member of the bureaucracy is recommended, the president himself being the appointing authority should review his service record for determining the suitability of appointment to the EC.

Getting back to the imbroglio of 2001, the CEC on his appointment differed with all other members of EC with respect to appointment of a consultant for computerisation of electoral rolls and preparation of identity card for voters. This raised two basic issues, that is, should the EC be single member or multi-member, and the position of the CEC vis-à-vis other members. The present CEC is on record indicating his preference for a single-member EC. The

Constitution does not exclude the possibility of a single-member EC but in practice governments have preferred the multi-member EC. In India a single-member EC has been the norm except when the government felt the need to appoint two additional commissioners in 1989 and 1993 to curb the powers of the CEC. In India the CEC did not allow the additional members to interfere with the functioning of the commission. The CEC has done similarly in Bangladesh.

The Constitution however indicates that when the EC has more than one member, the CEC shall act as its chairman. When the current CEC faced disagreement with the other members he invoked this clause to indicate that he is more than equal and is capable of taking decisions on his own. It may be recalled that in India, to curb the powers of the CEC in 1993, the law provided for decision by majority, which was challenged by the CEC but upheld by the Supreme Court. In Bangladesh no such law exists and no individual has sought a judicial interpretation of the constitutional provision.

The Constitution specifically states that the EC shall be independent in the exercise of its functions subject only to the Constitution and any other law. The independence is supposedly protected by the clause that the CEC and the EC once appointed cannot be removed from the office 'except in like manner and on the like ground as a judge of the Supreme Court' (that is, not by the appointing authority but by the Supreme Judicial Council). Independence of the EC has been further guaranteed by including the remuneration of election commissioners in the charged account along with the administrative expenses of the EC. The independence of the EC is supposedly strengthened by the provision that the CEC and members of the EC shall not be eligible for appointment in the services of the republic. Further, the EC regulates its own procedure. But the EC is dependent on the president for secondment of staff for the discharge of its duties. The budgetary allocation for holding elections (as non-administrative expenses) and for projects for improvement of the EC's own institutional capacity also require bureaucratic and political approval.

The efficient functioning of the EC depends on several factors: financial allocations made by the government, administrative officials who are in charge of the preparation of electoral rolls, delimitation of boundaries, issuance of identity cards and election monitoring, and the police and security forces for the maintenance of law and order. Thus the EC is constrained because corruption and partisanship have taken root in the administrative service as well as the police and security forces.

Basic Law of People's Representation

The *Representation of the People's Order, 1972* provides a comprehensive set of basic regulations concerning elections in Bangladesh. There have been amendments to the order in 1972, 1976, 1982, 1991, 1996 and 2001. These amendments were required to accommodate the changing needs of the different regimes, of democratic transition, of the wisdom of caretaker governments and were also the result of civil society observation of the electoral process.

Voters Eligibility and Preparation of Electoral Polls

The Constitution has vested the responsibility for the preparation of the electoral rolls on the EC and the EC prepares one single electoral roll for each constituency on the basis of adult franchise. A Bangladeshi citizen at least 18 years of age, of sound mind and deemed by law to be resident of the constituency is entitled to become a voter, that is, elector.

An ordinance to provide for the preparation of the electoral rolls was promulgated in 1982. According to the ordinance, the EC appoints a registration officer for each electoral area or constituency for the purpose of 'preparation, correction, amendment and revision' of the electoral roll. Under the superintendence, direction and control of the EC and as per the provisions of the Constitution, the registration officer causes to be prepared with such help as may be necessary to a draft electoral roll and invites claims and objections with respect thereto. The preparation of an electoral roll requires completion of a form, prescribed by the EC, by the elector. Claims for inclusion, correction of the entry in the electoral roll and objection to inclusion requires filling up a designated form after the preliminary publication of the electoral roll. The revising authority appointed by the EC decides on these claims or objections, if it is made within a specified period and after holding a summary enquiry. The registration officer makes additions, deletions, modifications or corrections in accordance with the decision of the revising authority. The corrected electoral roll is then published and access to the roll is easy.[2] In 2002, the constituency electoral roll was put on CDs and on a website. The objections to the roll were few. The general observation is that there are adequate provisions in the law to control all sorts of irregularities that may interfere with the preparation of a correct voter list. Though omissions, wrongly written particulars, exclusions, double inclusions and so on have been alleged, the total number of allegations in the context of the total number of electors is   insignificant.

The EC maintains that as elections are held not only to the National Assembly but also to local bodies and as internal migration has quickened overtime, corrections to the electoral roll are an ongoing process. Civil society organisations, by checking the correctness of the electoral roll, can help to minimise mistakes. The errors, discrepancies and distortions are alleged to be due to inefficiency of primary information collectors, distortions at bureaucratic level and socio-political attitudes at the local level. The first two causes could be corrected through civil society alertness and training of officials concerned but the third, which involves attitudes of social groups, needs a change of mindset and affirmative action on the part of EC. In 2002 the EC had taken special care to include women in areas where many have been traditionally excluded. However, exclusion of ethnic or religious minorities in some areas may not be ruled out.

Identity Card

The EC has taken up this project with great fanfare. The initial photo sessions were neither comprehensive nor free of mistakes. The question of the cost-effectiveness of the Identity Card (ID) if it is used only for voting purposes has been raised; a multiple use of the ID would have been helpful. It has also been pointed out that people who wield power can always put faces to names or names to faces as has been the case with passports. The solution seems to lie in small polling centres where everybody knows almost everybody else and civil society vigilance at the time of preparation of the electoral rolls and on the day of voting.

Delimitation of Constituencies

The delimitation of constituencies is a function of the EC and it is done in accordance with *the Delimitation of Constituencies Ordinance, 1976*. The EC is required to divide the country into 'as many single territorial constituencies as the number of members to be elected' to the national assembly according to the Constitution. Each constituency is to be a compact area and distribution of population in the latest census is the guiding principle, while administrative convenience remains a consideration. The constituencies are gazetted specifying the area and objections are heard but the verdict of EC is final.[3] The constituencies delimited in 1984 have remained subject to minor adjustments. This has avoided drawing and redrawing of constituencies but has resulted in differentiated weights to popular votes in different constituencies. One may note that recent demands for direct election and reservation of seats for women district-wise would not only require amendment to the concept of single territorial constituency but also result in differential values of votes.

Political Party Registration

Except under the martial law regime, there have been almost no restrictions on forming and running a political party. The constitutional guarantee of freedom of association and freedom of speech allows all citizens, except those in government service, to be associated with political parties.

Registration of a political party is voluntary and only requires making of an application containing required particulars and a copy of the party Constitution. The EC however reserves the right to register or not to register a party after giving due hearing. The registered party is obligated to provide further information as required and any changes to information already supplied. Advantages of registration include entitlement to a symbol reserved exclusively for the party, a set of electoral rolls at half the cost, broadcasting and telecasting facilities according to guidelines prescribed by the EC and the right to consultation by the EC. It may be noted that neither of the two major parties—the AL and BNP—has applied for registration. Though there is no ideological requirement for registration, adherence to the Constitution of the country is implicit. The provision for registration does not extend to regulation of the internal functioning and finance of any party.[4]

Election Arrangements: Pre-poll Functions

The pre-poll functions with respect to elections begin with the appointment by the EC of a returning officer for each constituency. Assistant returning officers are also appointed to assist the returning officer. However the EC has the power to withdraw any officer if it has reasons to believe that the appointee's activity interferes with the basic purpose of holding free and fair elections. These officers are normally functionaries in the government bureaucracy. Such arrangement, in the absence of field level staff of EC, assumes neutrality of conduct on the part of election staff which is difficult to expect under a politicised bureaucracy. The returning officer prepares the list of polling stations and the EC, after necessary alteration, publishes the list of polling stations specifying which electors will be entitled to vote at which polling station. This information is normally not noticed by electors till volunteers of candidates bring it to their attention. The returning officer appoints the presiding officer, assistant presiding officer and polling officers to man the polling booths from amongst employees in government and non-government establishments in his area. The services of such selected officers are then placed at the disposal of the EC.[5] These officers conduct the poll in accordance with laid down rules. As the population has increased, so have the number of polling centres. It is becoming increasingly difficult to find efficient, committed and neutral officers to man the polling centres.

Candidates for Election

Except for independents, candidates are nominated by a political party. The nomination process is centralised. The intending candidates buy prescribed application papers and submit it duly filled after making a non-refundable deposit to the party fund. A parliamentary (nomination) committee interviews the prospective candidates and finally announces the nomination. In case of 'internal disagreement' or 'possibility of revolt,' the decision is left to the chairperson of the party. The entire process is non-transparent and non-democratic. There is no consultation at the grassroots level. Just before the impending election, a procession of retired civil and military officials, businessmen and professionals join the two major parties seeking nomination. This is encouraged, often prompted. In this line-up people of questionable background and criminal police record also join the bandwagon. There has been a demand for a ban on retired government officials from joining any political party within two years after retirement. Though this was approved by the current and former election commissioners, it could not be enacted into law as it is alleged to be violative of fundamental human rights. As a result, people in the service of the republic and seeking a career after retirement become politicised and create negative trends with respect to the neutrality of bureaucracy.

In 2001 the AL is said to have sent out 'student teams' to prepare reports on popularity of intending candidates. How effective these probes were and how satisfactorily they have been used is anybody's guess. Rumour has it that the AL chief as a former prime minister had received advice from intelligence services with respect to constituencies, but this could not be, and possibly could never be, substantiated. Bangladesh Nationalist Party on the other hand established an office characterised by restricted entry even for the senior members of the party, with a view to preparing possible candidate profiles and dossiers on candidates to identify a winning candidate, along with a strategy for the campaign.

These two contrasting approaches, whatever may be their merits, are based on the principle of non-consultation with grassroots level party organisations, if any, for understanding the choice and opinion of the electors in the constituency and are alleged to be influenced by the capacity to donate to the party fund, to spend in election campaigns, to buy up local loyalty and to marshal the *mastans* (thugs) into action.

There is significant dissatisfaction with the nomination process and the resulting decisions. The general opinion about nomination by the two major parties is that loyalty and commitment are not rewarded. As the party organisations are not run on democratic principles, nor even according to the provisions of their own constitutions, the parties fail to democratise the nominations process. It remains a hidden, non-transparent approach which in the long run fails to deepen the democratic urge of the people. It is wrong to ignore the opinions/aspirations of party regulars and not provide support to a person of modest means but with a good image in the constituency. Such an approach encourages black money, allows goons to capture nominations and keeps the party organisation weak. Absence of proper consultation of electors at the constituency level is also violative of the basic principle of representative democracy.

Election Campaign

The EC by notification in the gazette specifies a day for filing nominations, a day for scrutiny of nomination papers, a day for withdrawal and a day for polls. The election campaign starts even before that, as party volunteers rush to reserve spaces on walls and bill-boards to express support for particular candidates. Normally sub-mission of nomination papers on behalf of major candidates is done with a lot of fanfare in a procession of supporters. This is a show of strength. This process also shows the linkage with the local political, social, economic as well as 'goon' base.

Any elector of a constituency can propose or second the name of a Bangladesh citizen if he is not holding an office of profit or con-victed for specified offences or is a loan defaulter [Article 12(1) of 1972 order]. The nomination papers are submitted along with a receipt of security money (TK. 10,000). Scrutiny of nomination papers is done in the presence of candidates or their agents, to decide whether the candidate meets the provisions of the law, whether the proposer and seconder are qualified to act as such and whether the signatures are genuine.

Appeals may be made against rejection or acceptance of nomin-ation papers. After appeals are heard, decisions given and withdraw-als made, the final list of candidates is published. This most often contains names of 'rebel' candidates and also those who are later persuaded to declare withdrawal or non-participation with an appeal to vote for a particular candidate. This is said to be part of the money game. Demands to regulate such surrogate or non-serious candidates have been voiced. After publication of list of candidates, election symbols are distributed. The returning officer is required to exhibit at each polling station the name and symbol of each contesting candidate. The campaign most often revolves around the symbol and not the person. Party leaders seek votes for the symbol rather than the party programme. Thus issues and commitment of candidates to electors in the constituency play a minor role.

The campaign is supposed to be guided by the code of conduct formulated by the EC.[6] The code of conduct is basically a list of what should not be done. The objective of the code of conduct is that 'election shall not be influenced by money, arms, muscle power or local influence.' Some terms are obvious but no definition of these terms has been provided in the code of conduct. An important aspect of the code of conduct is:

Following the announcement of the election schedule till the day of polling, no candidate or any person on his behalf shall openly or in secret give any subscription or donation or make promises to giving such subscription or donation to any institution of their respective constituency or to any other institution, nor shall commit to undertake any development project in the respective constituency.

This is easily violated by the party in power before dissolution of the Parliament by making special allocation of funds or goods for distribution or development work, often bypassing the MPs in the opposition. Further, both parties can make broad promises without being specific (for example, all village roads will be made *pucca* [concrete or cemented] road if elected, all private schools will be given increased assistance) during the campaign at specific places. Again making promises of donations in secret or through third parties is difficult to detect.

The DON'TS involve the following:

- disruption of opponent's meeting, processions and campaign;
- sticking of posters, bills over the posters and bills of opponents;
- use of government media, transport, employees and rest houses for the campaign;
- use of mechanised transport within the premises of polling stations;
- printing of posters beyond a certain size or in certain colours;
- inflicting damage to private property;
- carrying fire arms, etc.;
- making bitter and provocative remarks;
- spending more than the amount fixed by EC.

In case of pre-poll violations of the code of conduct, courts of enquiry are set up by the EC. In the year 2001, complaints were lodged by candidates in 109 constituencies and all that the Election Enquiry Committee did was to ask the offender to refrain from violating the code of conduct. Thus violation was almost universal and the EC could do little about it. The EC has asked for power to cancel candidature for serious breach of the code of conduct but this has not been granted. Such power without due process of law was considered to be *ultra vires* of the Constitution.[7]

It is to be noticed that in the code of conduct, there is a provision to prevent one from making provocative statements that may hurt the sentiments of followers of any religion. Islam is the religion of the majority and in certain constituencies there is the presence of substantial minority populations. There is nothing in the code of conduct which prevents one from making an appeal in the name of religion.

In Bangladesh, communal harmony has been a matter of pride and results of elections indicate that electors vote for the centrist parties. Even then social cleavages remain and the minorities need a socio-political coalition that enhances communal harmony. This has become all the more important in the context of post-election violence in 2001, even though much of it is based on local enmity and property grabbing seems to be the prime motive. It is in this context that civil society can play a role to evolve an enforceable code of conduct endorsed by candidates and also provide protection to marginalised groups as the political parties seem to have failed in this respect.

Polling and Counting

As mentioned earlier, the returning officer notifies the polling centres. The presiding officer receives all electoral materials (that is, electoral rolls, boxes, sealing material, ballot papers, marking stamp, indelible ink and so on). On the election day these are delivered at the polling centres under proper security arrangements. The candidates nominate their polling agents who are required to have valid identification papers. At the polling centre the names of the contesting candidates are displayed together with their symbols. There are restrictions on the number of agents per centre. As some centres have multiple booths and multiple enclosures in a room, the demand is that there must be at least one agent per booth. Further it has also been pointed out that submission of names of agents to the EC for issuance of ID cards is helpful from an administrative point of view but knowing such a person in advance helps extra-legal negotiation by rival candidates (that is, for remaining absent at some hour, overlooking impersonation, etc.). The counter argument is that an ID helps to stop entry of unwanted (*mastan*) persons and extra-legal arrangements could happen even on polling day as agents are not necessarily party loyalists but the local unemployed working for a fee. The ID card is issued by the candidate who often is not familiar with party regulars, and it is alleged that there are impersonated agents. There is an allegation that the number of enclosures and booths are not always proportional to the number of enrolled electors. Polling hours are fixed. However nobody is refused the exercise of his right to vote if s/he is within the enclosure/queue.

One ballot box is used per booth. The presiding officer shows the box to be empty to the candidates or their agents. The boxes are numbered and agents may sign the prescribed form as witness. The box is sealed and placed conveniently within the view of agents and assistant presiding officers. The entry into the booth is regulated and adequate arrangements for privacy is made. An elector's identity is checked by agents and the assistant presiding officer, the elector receives a personal mark with indelible ink before the ballot paper is issued, the paper bears the official mark and counterfoil is signed by the elector. The agents are there to stop impersonation. The system does work under normal circumstances. An elector, if he finds that his vote has already been cast, can be given a tendered ballot which is marked. Postal ballot is allowed for officers on election duty. Help is provided to the blind and incapacitated for voting. Thus all provisions for participation as well as free and fair elections are there in the law. In case of interruption beyond control, the polling officer may stop the polls and inform the EC through the presiding officer and the returning officer and a date for fresh polls is fixed by the EC. Where ballot boxes are taken away from the polling station, the voting is stopped and cancelled. However temporary interruptions are not treated in that category though they also lead to the commission of irregularities as well as tampering with ballot boxes.

After the closure of the polls the ballot boxes are sealed and brought to the presiding officer. The presiding officer in the presence of contesting candidates, election agents and/or polling agents proceeds with the counting of votes. The agents are given reasonable facility to observe the counting after opening of the box. The valid votes in favour of each candidate and votes excluded are put in separate packets. All packets are then put in to a principal packet. A statement of the count is prepared in words and figures. The presiding officer obtains the signature of agents on packets and statements, and gives a copy of the result to the candidate/agent. The packets and statements are forwarded to the returning officer who on receipt of the documents proceeds to consolidate the result. There may be recount of votes on the presiding officer's own volition or upon request from a candidate or his agents, only if the result is challenged. After the counting, the results are announced and returning officer informs the EC immediately by phone and fax. The consolidated result is published in the gazette. The returning officer retains the documents and all documents are open to public scrutiny except the ballot papers which can be opened only on order from the High Court if the results are contested. Allegations of excess ballots being issued, interruption in counting, falsification of agent's signature are commonly made, but no case is commonly filed on these grounds in order to test the allegations.[8]

Election Expenses

Election expenses include any expenditure incurred or payment made, whether by way of gift, loan, advance, deposit or otherwise, for the arrangement, conduct or benefit of, or in connection with or incidental to, the election of a candidate, including the expenditure on account of issuing circulars or publications or otherwise presenting to the electors the candidate or his views, aims or objects.[9] The definition of expenses is quite wide. Rules regarding contribution, expenditure and the procedure for managing funds, submission of accounts and obligations of political parties in this regard are elaborately given in the ordinance. The provision with respect to political party finance is also unambiguous with respect to expenditure limit, receipt of donation, statements to be filed, including bank statements. The expenditure limit set for each candidate is TK. 5 Lak (roughly equivalent to US$ 8,770) which is more than 23 times the average per capita income per annum. Many candidates have openly said that they spend much more but submit a statement as per rules. Neither have these statements been scrutinised by the EC.

Two issues are in order. First, what is a reasonable amount that can be enforced by law? Second, what kind of financing arrangement would allow an honest local community candidate to contest effectively as an independent?

It is now recognised that money power has distorted good political practice in the elections. An estimate by the media indicates that the minimum that a major candidate has spent for election is TK. 10 million. Reports have it that a particular industrialist has spent as much as TK. 250 million. Candidates are required to submit their sources of finance, sources of income, statement of income and expenditure, and copy of income tax returns and so on. The EC has never made these public so far, and no candidate has made any protest in this regard. Thus it can be concluded that all such statements are mere formality and done without any consequences as per the law. Media reports with respect to expenditure are sporadic and the media has made no attempt to uncover and analyse the financial statements made. It is widely recognised that bloated election expenses are one way of using black money (that is, tax-evaded money).

The growth of a society where property is acquired through fair or foul means has led to inequity in the distribution of income and wealth, as well as access to social, economic and political resources. The growing nexus of politics and money power is a legitimate concern for a democratic society. As mentioned earlier monetary resources of a candidate is considered by political parties to have a direct bearing on the candidate's capacity to win an election. It has been seen that those with larger monetary resources have an edge over others unless they have already climbed the party leadership ladder or have a special relationship with the party decision-making machinery. Some candidates with virtually limitless resources have lost but the practice of generously paying/feeding so-called volunteers, buying votes with money and gifts, and marshalling *mastans* to ward off the opponent, do indicate that money power has become increasingly a decisive factor and a resourceless candidate virtually has no chance of getting a major party nomination.

The EC has failed to enforce its own regulations. Civil society can possibly play a role. One suggestion is to make investigative estimations of actual expenditure. These could help in a subsequent election to set upper limits and also to devise ways of realistically creating a level playing field for the candidates.

The present ceiling is low to merit its enforcement and there is no way to crosscheck actual expenditure. Interviews with some MPs indicate that TK. 50 Lak is a reasonable ceiling and it should be indexed to increases in the cost of legitimate election expenses. The MPs however remain silent on truthful expenditure and crosschecking of expenditure, auditing such expenditure and making public the statements required under law. Raising the ceiling may reduce impracticality of the limit but it is likely to increase the influence of money power which is a much broader social, political and economic issue. The free market enthusiasts support a higher limit as do the proponents of a commercial industrial society. The political culture reformists indicate that malfunctioning of consultation and participatory processes in running the party and absence of institutionalised democracy within the party lead to increase in election expenditure. They argue that the weaker the grassroots level linkages, the higher is the election expenditure. The equity and propriety advocates argue that funds should be created for the benefit of honest and locally endorsed (say, by local government) resource-less candidates. The funds so created may be administered by a Government-Operated Non-Governmental Organisation (GONGO) committee at each constituency; such committees would be formed with consent and a national committee would see that such funds are equitably spent. They argue that much of the competitive expenditure may be cut out, *mastan* expenditure reduced and a collegial atmosphere created for healthy competition. There is general agreement among the civil society proponents about the need for an 'institutionalised fund' but there are serious reservations about the modalities for creation and operation of such fund. The idea of state subvention for exclusive election expenses (for example, at the rate of TK. 10 per vote polled in the 2001 election by the candidate or the party nominee if he has received a specified minimum percentage of vote) which is to be released to candidates directly and who will account for it is one proposal which has been made, but there are doubts about its practicability and political market propon-ents argue that this may restrict entry as well as constrain campaign (marketing) strategy of the party and the candidate.

Election Offences

The 1972 order and code of conduct clearly define election offences which include bribery, impersonation and undue influence. Bribery relates to obtaining or procuring or attempting to obtain or procure the assistance of any person in the service of the state as well as to giving or agreeing to give any gratification for voting or refraining from voting or inducing a candidate to withdraw candidature. We have mentioned how money power matters. Both winning and losing candidates mention that it is important to keep some government officials happy, particularly those involved in maintaining law and order. Envelopes are just sent through envoys. It is commonly mentioned that all major candidates indulge in it, otherwise meetings cannot be held, processions organised and campaigns carried on. It is interesting to note that all caretaker governments found it necessary to make significant changes in the field administration because of the known linkages of some officials with a party/candidate. At the same time it is to be noted that despite known bribery no case has ever been filed by any candidate. Impersonation has been reported, but not of a significant magnitude. Interference with the free exercise of electoral right was known to have been more in elections held before the 1990s than in the last election held in 2001.

Conclusion

Unless the EC is manned by reasonably independent staff, the conduct of free and fair elections will be increasingly difficult as political parties, without any consultation with the opposition, place their own nominees in the EC.

The laws with respect to elections are elaborate, extensive and generally promotive of democracy. The implementation of these laws is vitiated by ineffective enforcement and field level bureaucracy. The rise of money power and muscle power not only require political will to contain them but also an effective neutral administration at the field level. Democratisation of political culture, tolerance and increasing depth of party organisation are needed for promoting democracy and democratic process. Laws are only as good as are their enforcers, institutions are only as good as the controllers are and thus the blame for the malfunctioning of the laws and institutions lies less with the system, laws or institutions but more with the political practices and personalities.

The way to true democratisation lies in cultivation of democratic values from bottom upwards in all institutional areas so that the practice of democracy becomes second nature. This needs the political will of a leadership prepared to act in consonance with the far-reaching and long-term value of democratic culture even at the expense of short-run costs.

Notes

1. For the constitutional provision see the relevant articles in the Constitution.
2. For the process and provision see the *Election Commission Handbook* and Md. Saidur Rahman, *Law on Election in Bangladesh*, Dhaka, 2001.
3. For details see 'The Society for Environment and Human Development SHED', *Handbook on Election Reporting 2001* and Md. Saidur Rahman, *Law on Election in Bangladesh*.
4. Election Commission, 'Rules for Registration of Political Parties,' 2001.
5. See Election Commission 'Rules for Conduct of Elections' and SHED, *Handbook*.

6. Election Commission, 'Code of Conduct for Election Campaign', and SHED *Handbook*.
7. Election Commission, 'Courts of Enquiry, 2001' and Justice Latifur Rahman, *The Days of Caretaker Government and My Submission* (in Bengali), Dhaka, 2002.
8. Ibid.
9. Md. Saidur Rahman, *Laws of Election in Bangladesh*.

8

INDIA

Ujjwal Kumar Singh

I

Introduction[*]

The first general elections in India (December 1951–February 1952) have been characterised as 'a massive act of faith,' unparalleled in the history of humankind.[1] This incomparable act of faith was implicit in a newly independent country's attempt to move straight into universal adult franchise, rather than traverse the trajectory followed in the West, namely, reserving the right to vote to men of property

[*]The ideas discussed in this chapter were first presented at the workshop on Electoral Processes and Governance in South Asia, organised by the International Centre for Ethnic Studies (ICES), Kandy, 21 to 23 June 2002. I am grateful to ICES, Kandy, Partha S. Ghosh and S.W.R. de A. Samarasinghe for their support and especially to Dushyantha Mendis for his comments and suggestions. This is a substantially revised version of the article published earlier in *Ethnic Studies Report* (Journal of the International Centre for Ethnic Studies) Kandy, Sri Lanka, Vol. XX, Nos 1 & 2, January and July 2002, and as Nehru Memorial Museum and Library (NMML) Monograph, No. 9, Teen Murti House, New Delhi, 2004.

with the working class and women being conceded the right after a protracted struggle. This massive task was set in motion by the setting up of an Election Commission (EC) in January 1950, with Sukumar Sen as the first Chief Election Commissioner, appointed in March 1950. The *Representation of the People Act* was passed in Parliament in the next month with the hope that elections would be held in the spring of 1951. The magnitude of the task however was so great that elections could finally be held only in 1952.

The size of the electorate at 176 million, of whom about 85 per cent could not read or write, the identification and registration of voters, designing of party symbols, ballot papers and ballot boxes for a mostly unlettered electorate, building of polling stations, recruitment of honest and committed polling officers, as well as providing ample time for political parties to compete and contest the first elections ever, was an exercise of massive proportions. The following figures will help us comprehend the magnitude of the exercise. At stake were about 4,500 seats; two lakh twenty four thousand polling booths had to be constructed and equipped with about two million steel ballot boxes made of 8,200 tonnes of steel. About 380,000 reams of paper were used for printing the electoral rolls; fifty six thousand presiding officers were recruited who were assisted by about 280,000 lesser staff. The election and the electorate was spread over an area of more than a million square miles. The terrain was vast, diverse and in some cases difficult to access. The nature of electorate required some innovations, e.g., the use of large pictorial symbols drawn from their daily lives by which the illiterate voters could identify their candidates, and the use of multiple ballot boxes. On a single ballot, it was feared the Indian voter was likely to make a mistake. Thus each party had a ballot box with its symbol marked in each polling station, the voter had to simply drop their paper in it.[2]

Fifty-four years and 14 general elections later, the electorate has increased manifold, the multiple ballot boxes have given way to electronic voting machines (EVMs), the planning and conduct of elections has become a domain where political parties engage in sophisticated manoeuvrings aided by computer professionals, and door-to-door contacts by political parties are accompanied by 'mediated' campaigns through the print and electronic media. A reconfiguration of the party system into a 'competitive multi-party system', accompanied by the 'second democratic upsurge' characterised by the hitherto unprecedented intensification in political participation by the excluded castes/classes of the Indian electorate, has opened up spaces for marginal political parties and intensified electoral contests.[3] Increase in voter turnout and political participation is indicative of rising political awareness.

The magnitude of the exercise in the present day can be gauged from the facts that in the 2004 Lok Sabha elections there were 1,351 candidates from six national parties, 898 candidates from officially recognised parties and 2,385 independent candidates. A total number of nearly 390 million people voted out of a total electoral size of about 671.5 million.[4] The task force for conducting a countrywide general election consists of nearly five million polling personnel and civil police forces, all of whom are subject to the control, superintendence and discipline of the EC during the election period which may extend over a period of one and a half to two months. When elections are held, the full-time staff is not only expanded but also supplemented by large numbers of temporary staff in charge of the polling booths, and security personnel to protect the booths and for maintaining law and order. As elections require massive mobilisation of human and material resources, polling is staggered over several days, or even over several phases in a national general election. Elections for the Lok Sabha in 2004 were completed in four phases beginning on 20 April 2004, during which different states and, in some cases, different parts of the same state went to the polls in phases.[5] The legitimacy gained by the EC from the elections it had conducted was reflected in nationwide polls conducted in 1996 by the Centre for the Study of Developing Societies (CSDS), Delhi, for the Indian Council of Social Science Research (ICSSR) and *India Today*, after the national elections in June and July 1996, and then again in another survey conducted in Delhi in September–October 2003. These show a remarkably high degree of trust among the people in the EC. The 1996 poll showed that the EC was ranked the highest among political institutions in terms of public support. Of the 15,030 respondents, 62 per cent rated the EC as trustworthy, the highest score, followed by 59 per cent for the Supreme Court. The lowest ranked were the police and the bureaucracy.[6] The polls conducted in September–October 2003 showed that trust in the EC has been sustained. While only 8 per cent of the respondents thought the bureaucracy was trustworthy and 29 per cent found it completely untrustworthy, 38 per cent placed complete faith in the EC.[7]

The increased voter turnout in every election is also reflective of the steering skills of the EC in that despite the electoral malpractices which have been repeatedly pointed out by the EC itself, people's faith in the electoral system remains.

II

The Constitutional and Statutory Framework of Electoral Governance

Constitutional Framework

The EC has its roots and origins in the deliberations and recommendations made by the Constituent Assembly appointed immediately following independence in 1947. The various subcommittees of the Constituent Assembly engaged in discussing different aspects of the draft Constitution were concerned that the statutes and institutions, which enabled electoral governance, should manifest the fundamental premises of democracy. The Fundamental Rights Subcommittee of the Constituent Assembly unanimously accepted the principle of universal adult franchise. The Advisory Committee recommended to the Constituent Assembly, the grant of voting rights to all citizens at the age of 21, the conduct of voting by secret ballot, and the superintendence and control of elections to be left under an EC.[8] To guarantee this a separate chapter dealing with elections was included in the Constitution of India (Part XV, Articles 324–29).

The Fundamental Rights Subcommittee and the Minorities Subcommittee were the first to suggest the insertion of an article providing for an independent EC to direct all elections. Prompted by the need for incorporating and protecting the immense diversity of the country, and the concern for institutional safeguards against discrimination, especially in states where there existed the fear of exclusion of ethnic and linguistic minorities from the political process, the Constituent Assembly endorsed a 'centralised,' 'integrated' and 'autonomous' election machinery. In order for elections to be free and fair, and to assure that no group was excluded from the electoral process, it was important that the election machinery was integrated, and would implement unified and universally applicable rules. In order to achieve the latter, the body conducting elections had to be 'impartial', 'above party politics' and structurally independent from the political power structure. The fact that the EC derives its authority directly from the Constitution and not from any elected government, gives it considerable autonomy of action. This autonomy of the EC has also been upheld over the years by judicial pronouncements.

The decision to centralise the election machinery under a single Central election commission was taken after protracted discussions in the Constituent Assembly in the Committees and Sub-committees. When the Draft Articles came up for discussion in the Assembly on 15 June 1949, however, there was opposition to the appointment of election commissioners by the president. Apprehensive that it would, for all practical purposes, mean appointment by the prime minister, Professor Shibban Lal Saksena suggested that the chief election commissioner's appointment should be subject to confirmation by a two thirds majority in a joint session of both Houses of Parliament. Admitting that the suggestion held 'force', Ambedkar proposed an amendment, whereby the appointment of the chief election commissioner and the EC was to be made by the president 'subject to any law made in that behalf by Parliament.' Article 324(2) contains this decision of the Constituent Assembly.

To assist the chief election commissioner in the discharge of his responsibilities specified in clause (1), before each general election to the Lok Sabha (House of People) and elections to the Legislative Assembly of each state, the president may, after consultation with the EC, appoint Regional Commissions [Article 324(4)]. The president, or the governor of a state, when requested by the election commissioner, makes available to the election commissioner or to a regional commissioner the staff necessary for the discharge of the functions conferred on the EC by clause (1) [Article 324(6)]. The conditions of service and tenure of the election commissioners and regional commissioners are determined by the rules made by the president, subject to the provisions of any law of Parliament [Article 324(5)]. The Constitution also provides that the chief election commissioner shall not be removed from his office except in the manner laid down for Supreme Court judges. The conditions of service of the chief election commissioner may not be varied to his disadvantage after his appointment. An election commissioner or a regional commissioner cannot be removed from office except on the recommendation of the chief election commissioner [Article 324(5)].

Article 325 of the Constitution gives effect to the constitutional principle of equality of the citizen-voter, providing for a single general electoral roll for every territorial constituency for election to either the House of Parliament or to the House of the Legislature of a state, stating that no person can be excluded from the electoral roll on grounds of religion, race, caste or sex.[9] Article 326 lays down the principles of voter eligibility, stating that elections to the House of the People and to the legislative assemblies of states are to be on the basis of adult suffrage. Thus every citizen of India who is not less than 18 years[10] of age on such date as may be fixed in that behalf by or under any law made by the appropriate legislature, and is not otherwise disqualified under this Constitution or any law made by the appropriate legislature on the ground of non-residence, unsoundness of mind, crime or corrupt or illegal practice, shall be entitled to be registered as a voter at any such election. Article 327 gives Parliament the power to make provision with respect to elections to legislatures. The power of the Parliament has, however, been made subject to 'other provisions of this Constitution' including Article 324, which makes the 'superintendence, direction and control' of elections, the primary, and primarily, the responsibility of the EC.[11] Article 328 similarly provides the legislature of a state, the power to make provision with respect to elections to the state legislature.

Article 329 puts important bars to interference by courts in electoral matters relating to (a) the validity of any law relating to the delimitation of constituencies or the allotment of seats to such constituencies, made or purporting to be made under Article 327 or 328, and (b) election to either House of Parliament or a state legislature. Only an election petition presented to such authority and in such manner as may be provided by law by the concerned legislature can question the latter. Under the *Representation of the People Act, 1951*, the power to decide election disputes vests in the High Courts with a right of appeal to the Supreme Court. Disputes relating to the election of the president or vice-president are, however, to be settled by the Supreme Court.

Statutory Framework: Representation of the People (Amendment) Bill, 2002

Constitutional provisions for conducting elections have been supplemented by laws made by Parliament filling in the details of the statutory framework of electoral governance in accordance with the meta-rules laid down in the Constitution.[12] The two major laws in this respect are the *Representation of the People (Amendment) Bill, 2002* which deals primarily with the preparation and revision of electoral rolls, the delimitation of constituencies, prescribing additional qualification for voters and so on, and the *Representation of the People (Amendment) Bill, 2002* that deals in detail with all aspects of conduct of elections and post-election disputes.[13] The 1950 Act provides for a state-wise distribution of seats, which means that a constituency of the Lok Sabha cannot traverse two or more states.[14] Moreover, under the Act, every constituency of the Lok Sabha is a single member constituency. The constituencies of the legislative council of states are determined by the president. The 1950 Act also lays down, that a person who is not less than 18 years of age on the qualifying date and who is ordinarily resident in a constituency and is not otherwise disqualified, is entitled to be registered as a voter in the constituency. Electoral rolls are revised and updated from time to time by the electoral registration officers either on an application by some person or on its own initiative. Before every general election to the Lok Sabha or the state legislature, or before a by-election, an intensive revision of the roll is to be carried out.

The *Representation of the People (Amendment) Bill, 2002* deals with all aspects of the conduct of elections and post-election disputes. It contains detailed provisions regarding qualifications and disqualifications for candidates; time schedule for elections; administrative machinery for conducting elections; power to requisition premises, vehicles and so on, by a government for the elections; role and functions of candidates and their agents; manner of voting, counting of votes and declaration of results; disposal of elections petitions; specification of corrupt practices and election offences;[15] suspension of poll or countermanding of election; registration of political parties; deposits for contesting elections; prevention of impersonation and limits on election expenditure and so on.[16] As we shall see, the Supreme Court has held that where the enacted laws are silent or make insufficient provisions to deal with a given situation in the conduct of elections, the EC has the residuary powers under the Constitution to act in an appropriate manner.

To a large extent, attempts at reforming electoral laws have been desultory. Even when Reform Committees have been set up and their recommendations made, Bills to make them effective have lagged or fallen through. Bills drawn up for reform often attempt to consolidate the position of the party in power, or, as in the case of the *Electoral Reform Bill* presented in Parliament in July–August 2002, attempt to reclaim the ground lost to the EC. The first endeavour towards reforms was made in 1971, when a Joint Parliamentary

Committee of the two Houses of Parliament was appointed under the chairmanship of Jagannath Rao. The Committee submitted two reports in January and March 1972, the first containing recommendations for the amendment of the *Representation of the People (Amendment) Bill, 2002* and the second dealing with questions of voting age, the electoral system and so on. Some of these amendments were incorporated in a Bill introduced in the Lok Sabha in 1973.[17] This Bill was not passed before the dissolution of the Lok Sabha in 1975 and, therefore, lapsed. Certain amendments were effected in 1974–77 on matters relating to election expenses.[18] These amendments, however, were generally seen as giving advantage to the ruling party. The Tarkunde Committee appointed by Jayaprakash Narayan during the Janata regime (1977–79), whose recommendations concerning the system of representation and party finances continue to be relevant, failed to become a law because of the short tenure of the government.[19]

In the 1980s, significant changes were introduced in the electoral law, including the reduction of the minimum age of voting to 18 years, insertion of the Tenth Schedule of the Constitution to put some check on defections,[20] use of voting machines,[21] provision of registration of political parties, more stringent punishment for booth-capturing which was declared a 'corrupt practice' if practised by a candidate or agent, and permitting companies to make contributions to political parties subject however to certain restrictions since the contribution had to be declared in the company's annual accounts, and the *Representation of the People (Amendment) Bill, 2002* imposed restrictions on election expenditure. (Company donations to political parties were banned in 1969, though they were again allowed in 1985 through an amendment to the *Company s Act*, subject to certain restrictions.) The Goswami Committee under the Law Minister, Dinesh Goswami, set up under the prime-ministership of V. P. Singh, made some significant recommendations in May 1990.[22] A Bill to implement some of these recommendations, while excluding two important suggestions pertaining to identity cards and ban on donations by companies was introduced in the Rajya Sabha. In September 1998, the 170th Report of the Law Commission on Electoral Reforms recommended limited state funding towards elections, and a steep increase in the deposits made by candidates to discourage non-serious candidates representing non-recognised pol-itical parties. In order to make the Lok Sabha more representative, the Law Commission recommended addition of 138 seats in the Lok Sabha, and the substitution of the 'first-past-the-post' method of election with a list system. In order to do justice to a large number of votes that were 'wasted' or went 'unrepresented', it suggested that at the end of polling, the proportion of votes polled by different political parties be tabulated and 25 per cent of seats be distributed proportionally to these parties.

To prevent 'criminalisation of politics', the Law Commission recommended the disqualification of those candidates against whom charges had even been framed under any section of the *Indian Penal Code*, *Customs Act* and Sections 10 to 12 of the *Unlawful Activities (Prevention) Act*, Section 7 of the 1988 *Religious Institutions (Prevention of Misuse) Act* and the *Protection of Civil Rights Act*. Again, as far as the Tenth Schedule was concerned, the Law Commission recommended the scrapping of the *Anti-Defection Act* to ensure that neither 'split' nor 'merger' be allowed, and once elected a candidate would remain a member of that political party for the entire duration of the term. It also emphasised that political parties should be obliged to maintain accounts showing the details of amounts received and spent by them. The *Representation of the People (Amendment) Bill, 2002* was enacted on the basis of these recommendations.[23] Another Bill, the *Election and Other Related Laws (Amendment) Bill 2001*, based on the proposals of a committee under the chairmanship of late Indrajit Gupta, was initiated in December 2001. The Bill proposed amendments in the *Representation of the People Act, 1951*, in order to regulate fund-raising by political parties in elections. In order to do this the Bill sought (*a*) to allow companies, other than public sector undertakings, and other like bodies which are funded by the government wholly or partially, including local bodies, to make donations to political parties and (*b*) to allow individuals and other juridical persons to make donations, barring, however, donations from foreign sources as defined in the *Foreign Contributions Regulations Act*. The donation amount could be deducted from the total income of the companies as well as individuals, for the purpose of income tax computation.[24] A process pertaining to the reports by political parties on donations received and their audit by an auditor, approved by the comptroller and auditor general of India, was also incorporated. The Bill was finally passed in August 2003 after incorporating the recommendations of the Parliamentary Standing Committee on Home Affairs. It is significant that the Act was seen as legalising corporate funding and corruption in some quarters while others saw it as introducing the element of accountability in the entire process, cleansing thereby the arena of political funding.[25]

III

The Institutional Template of Electoral Governance: The Election Commission

As we have noted earlier, Articles 324 to 329 of Part XV of the Constitution provide the legal–constitutional framework for the conduct of elections. A single centralised body—the EC—has been entrusted with the task of 'superintendence, direction and control of elections'. Article 324(1) of the Constitution provides that the EC shall superintendent, direct and control the preparation of the electoral rolls for, and the conduct of all elections to, Parliament, the legislature of every state, and to the offices of president and vice-president.

In accordance with the provisions of the Constitution, the Election Commission of India was set up on 25 January 1950. The Commission now has a Secretariat of about 300 officials at New Delhi. Two deputy election commissioners, generally selected from the Indian Civil Service and appointed by the Commission with tenure, are the seniormost officers in the Secretariat, supported by directors, principal secretaries and deputy directors. There is both functional and territorial distribution of work in the Commission. The work is distributed into divisions, branches and sections, with each section in the charge of a section officer. The functional divisions are organised around planning, judicial, administrative, information systems, media and Secretariat co-ordination. The territorial work is distributed among separate units that take up the responsibility for the different zones, into which the constituent states and union territories are grouped for convenience of management.[26] At the state level election work is supervised, subject to overall superintendence, direction and control of the Commission, by the chief electoral officer of the state, who is appointed by the Commission from among the senior civil servants proposed by the concerned state government. He is, in most states, a full-time officer and has a team of supporting staff. At the district and constituency levels, there are district election officers, electoral registration officers and returning officers, who are assisted by a large number of junior functionaries. They all perform their functions relating to elections in addition to their other responsibilities. During election time, however, they are available to the Commission on a full-time basis.

The maintenance of a permanent election machinery, and the massive requirement of human and material resources during an election make elections expensive. While the Secretariat of the Commission has an independent budget finalised in consultation with the Finance Ministry of the union government, which generally accepts the recommendations of the Commission, the major expenditure on actual conduct of elections is the responsibility of the concerned constituent unit of the union-state and union territory. Thus for Parliament and state legislature elections, the expenditure is borne entirely by the union government and the concerned state respectively. In case of simultaneous elections to the Parliament and state legislature, however, the expenditure is shared equally between the union and state governments. For capital equipment, expenditure related to preparation of electoral rolls and for elector's identity cards, the expenditure is also shared equally.[27]

As far as the officers of the Commission are concerned, the Constitution lays down that the Commission shall consist of the chief election commissioner and such number of other election commissioners as the president may from time to time fix. The appointment of the chief election commissioner and other election commissioners is made by the president, subject to the provisions of any law made in that behalf by Parliament [324(2)]. In case any other election commissioner is appointed, the chief election commissioner acts as the chairman of the EC [324(3)].

The chief election commissioner is a whole time official appointed by the president and acts as the chairman of the EC. To enable him to function impartially and fearlessly he enjoys security of tenure, cannot be removed from office except in the manner specified in the Constitution, and the conditions of his service cannot be changed to his disadvantage during his tenure.

While Article 324(a) provides for election commissioners besides the chief election commissioner, 'till October 1993 the EC functioned as a 'one-man commission,' except for a short period between 16 October 1989 and 1 January 1990, when, for the first time, two additional commissioners were appointed. It was in this period that the question of the number of election commissioners to be appointed and the associated question of their relative powers became a matter of debate and judicial decision. In October 1989, the president notified that besides the chief election commissioner, the Commission shall have two other election commissioners with co-ordinate powers. On 1 January 1990, however, the president revoked his notification with the result that the two election commissioners lost their office.[28] One of them challenged the revocation of the notification, which was subsequently rejected by the Supreme Court.[29] In the process it affirmed several principles that would henceforth determine the composition and functioning of the EC:

(*i*)   It was desirable that the highly vital functions of the EC should be exercised by more than one individual.

(*ii*) The creation and abolition of posts was a prerogative of the Executive and Article 324(2) left it to the president to fix and appoint such number of election commissioners as he may, from time to time, determine.

(*iii*) While it was obligatory to appoint the chief election commissioner, the appointment of other election commissioners [Article 324(2)] or regional commissioners [Article 324(4)] was left by the Constitution to the discretion of the president.

With the affirmation of the principle that it was desirable for the EC to have more than one person to exercise its highly vital functions, the question of the relative powers of these members vis-à-vis the chief election commissioner remained a festering issue. In the *S.S. Dhanoa vs Union of India* case a Division Bench of the Supreme Court had observed that the relative inferiority of the other election commissioners was implicit in the constitutional provisions pertaining to their removal from office. While the chief election commissioner could be removed from office only by a process of impeachment [Article 325(5), Prov. 1], the other commissioners could be removed by the president on the recommendation of the chief election commissioner [Article 325(5), Prov. 2]. Article 325(3), however, simultaneously lays down that the chief election commissioner would act as the chairman of the EC when any other election commissioner is so appointed, leading to the assumption that the chief election commissioner had to act in consultation with the other commissioners. The question of whether the election commissioners would hold co-ordinate powers with the chief election commissioner, or relatively subordinate ones, thus remained unresolved, with the Constitution itself ambivalent on the issue.

The Division Bench suggested that the issue could be resolved through legislation or by amending the Constitution itself. An ordinance was subsequently promulgated, and affirmed later with retrospective effect from 1 October 1993. The *Chief Election Commissioner and other Election Commissioners (Conditions of Service) Amendment Act, 1993* which gave co-ordinate powers to the election commissioners, was challenged by the then Chief Election Commissioner, T.N. Seshan, in the Supreme Court.[30] A Constitution Bench of the Supreme Court rejected T.N. Seshan's petition, and overriding the Court's decision in the Dhanoa case, affirmed the multi-member nature of the EC and the relative powers of the election commissioners as provided in the ordinance. The Constitution Bench laid down that:

(*i*) The notification of the president appointing Mr M.S. Gill and Mr T.S. Krishnamurthy as Election Commissioners was valid and (had) made the Election Commission under Article 324, a multi-member Commission.

(*ii*) As far as possible, all business of the Commission shall be transacted unanimously, and in case of difference of opinion, according to the opinion of the majority.[31]

The practice of appointing two additional election commissioners that was resumed on 1 October 1993, with the appointment of M.S. Gill and T.S. Krishnamurthy, has since been followed. While the chief election commissioner remains pre-eminent as the head of the machinery, the powers of the election commissioners are coordinate and coequal since all decisions, in principle and in practice, are to be taken by consensus or majority vote.

The powers of the EC relating to direction and control of elections are limited by the fact that all its orders must be traceable to some existing law,[32] and cannot violate the provisions of any law including State Acts.[33] Article 324(1) has, however, been interpreted liberally, and the EC is seen as having residual powers, in areas unoccupied by legislation,[34] empowering the Commission to issue all directions necessary for the purpose of conducting smooth, free and fair elections for this purpose.[35]

Numerous court decisions have determined the scope of the powers of the EC. A 1978 judgement by the Supreme Court interpreted the expression 'superintendence, direction and control' as empowering the EC to act in contingencies not provided for by law, and to pass necessary orders for the conduct of the election, for example, deciding on re-polls at particular polling stations,[36] on disputes relating to the allotment of symbols to political parties,[37] on recognition and de-recognition of parties,[38] on the status of rival groups within the same party, and the effect of merger or separation on parties for purposes of elections.[39] While the determination of citizenship is outside the jurisdiction of the EC, the electoral authorities have the power to decide individual cases raising questions of citizenship, when revising an electoral roll.[40] The EC may postpone elections, if in its opinion the disturbed conditions of a state or part of it, prevent the holding of free or fair elections.[41]

In the latter half of 2002, the last mentioned function of the EC generated a conflict between the EC and the National Democratic Alliance (NDA) government, in particular, the Bharatiya Janata Party (BJP). The contest followed the dissolution of the Gujarat Vidhan Sabha on 19 July 2002, and the appointment of the erstwhile Chief Minister Narendra Modi as the caretaker chief minister till the time fresh elections could be held. The BJP hoped that under Article 174 of the Indian Constitution which required that six months should not lapse between the last sitting of the legislative assembly in one session and the date appointed for the first sitting in the next session, given that the last sitting of the last session of the Gujarat Assembly was 3 April 2002, election for the new assembly could be held before 3 October 2002. At the time of dissolution, Gujarat was still recovering from the communal violence which left thousands of minority Muslims dead and homeless. While Modi survived the demand for his resignation, the attempt to dissolve the Vidhan Sabha was being seen as an attempt to draw political benefit from the sensitive political context. The BJP asked for early elections, but the opposition parties, as well as some other parties that were part of the ruling combine feared that elections in Gujarat could provoke more violence, and demanded president's rule in the state. Between 31 July and 4 August 2002, the EC sent a team of officials to Gujarat followed by a visit of the entire three-member commission to decide on a possible time frame for elections in Gujarat. Contrary to Gujarat government's argument that only 12 out of its 25 districts were affected, the EC observed that almost 80 per cent of the state's administration remained unstable, and 154 of the 182 constituencies of the state were affected by riots, which included 151 towns and 993 villages.[42] Of the 121 relief camps, only eight camps were still functioning. The inmates of the camps that had shut down had not returned to their homes, and the Revenue Department or the Collectorate had no means of tracking their whereabouts.[43] The large numbers of riot-affected persons who were displaced or missing, made the task of preparing the electoral rolls that was underway impossible to accomplish at an early date. In a detailed order of 16 August 2002, the EC accepted that under Article 174, elections should normally be held before the expiry of six months. This, however, was not possible in Gujarat because the state was still in turmoil, the electoral rolls were not ready and the electoral machinery needed reinforcements.[44] The EC concluded that in the context of incomplete rolls and missing electors, elections could not be held in Gujarat before the end of November 2002, and that even if a state assembly is dissolved, or comes to the end of its term, the opportune time of the polls can be decided by the EC only.[45]

The central government construed that matter as falling under Article 143, which empowered the president to refer a question of law and facts to the Supreme Court. The presidential reference to the Supreme Court questioned the 'constitutional validity' of the ECs order, describing it as 'non-compliance with the mandatory requirement envisaged under Article 174(1) of the Constitution'.[46] In its response, the Supreme Court rejected the indictment of the ECs decision by the central government and the government of Gujarat. It argued that Article 174(1) did not apply to a dissolved assembly, nor did it provide any outer limit for holding elections for the legislative assembly.[47] Significantly, it denied that Article 174 put any kind of limits on the EC's powers under Article 324, and emphasised that the holding of elections 'is the exclusive domain of the EC under Article 324 of the Constitution'.[48]

IV

The Unfolding of Democratic Uncertainties in Electoral Governance: Trends, Contests and Ambiguities

The discussion in the previous section has shown that the EC is the constitutional body primarily concerned with superintending, directing and controlling elections in India. While making the EC pre-eminent in the domain of superintendence, direction and control of elections, the Constitution has simultaneously invested Parliament with the power to make laws relating to elections. At the same time, however, where the Parliament is not forthcoming, the EC has been devolved with residuary powers. This implies that unless the Parliament explicitly stakes its claims in electoral governance, the EC possesses the powers/responsibilities that remain unclaimed, and it leads to some tension between Parliament and EC over unclaimed power/responsibility.

In the absence of concrete legislative measures, initiatives for making the electoral procedure more credible, and the outcome more democratic have emerged from the EC, often under the orders of the Supreme and High Courts issued in response to public interest litigation.

In the municipal corporation elections in Chandigarh and Delhi in February–March 2002, for example, the state election commission made it mandatory for all candidates to file an affidavit stating that they had not been convicted by any trial court during the past three years. The instructions were issued under Article 243V of the Constitution, which specifies that a member would be disqualified from seeking election to the municipality 'if he is so disqualified by or under any law for the time being in force for purposes of elections to the Legislature of the State concerned', and Section 8 of the *Representation of the People Act, 1951* which spells out the disqualifications. On 22 February 2002 the returning officers were issued directions by the joint election commissioner under the specific subject heading, 'Criminalisation of politics—participation of criminals in electoral process as candidates—disqualification on conviction for offences—effect of appeal and bail'. The directions noted that 'criminal elements have taken to politics in a big way and the country [was] facing the serious problem of criminalisation of politics...' and reminded the officers of the High Court rulings which had taken the view that release on bail did not 'wipe off' the disqualification under Section 8(1) of the *Representation of the People (Amendment) Bill, 2002*. A proforma issued to the candidates, to be submitted along with the affidavit, explained that the information was being sought under specific legal provisions and listed the various heads including conviction in cases and cases pending before courts.[49] It is to be noted that even the EC was then attempting to filter out candidates with a 'proven criminal record' which was a dilution of the recommendation of the Law Commission which considered the framing of charges by the court as sufficient ground for disqualification. The manner in which the filing of affidavits was treated by the candidates made a mockery of the provision.[50] Officials of the state election commission were of the view that it was extremely difficult to confirm the information provided in the affidavits.[51]

The difficulties which the EC encountered in effecting changes on a relatively smaller scale in the municipal elections in Delhi and Chandigarh, were projected most recently onto a larger horizon of state politics in the Assembly elections in Bihar in October–November 2005. In an attempt to pre-empt the possibility of criminals contesting elections, the EC sought to delete the names of 'absconders' or persons against whom non-bailable-warrants (NBW) had been pending for over six months.[52] Earlier, in June 2005, the Commission directed the Bihar government to execute over 23,000 NBWs that had been pending for several months.[53] Later, on 11 August 2005, it widened the scope of its directive, issuing general instructions to all electoral registration officers in the country to delete from the voters' list the names of those against whom NBWs were pending for over six months. Significantly, deletion from the voters' list was intended to be a step towards disqualification from the electoral arena.[54]

It may be pertinent to examine here the Supreme Court judgement in the central government's appeal against a Delhi High Court judgement of 2 November 2001, for the manner in which it widened the ECs powers to seek information on a candidate's background. The High Court judgement had come in response to a petition filed by the Association for Democratic Reforms for Court to make directions (*a*) to implement the recommendations made by the Law Commission in its 170th Report and (*b*) to make relevant changes in the Conduct of Election Rules. In its order of 2 November 2000, the High Court upheld the petition, directing the EC to 'secure to voters', the following information pertaining to each candidate:

(*i*)   Whether the candidate was accused of any offence punishable with imprisonment? If so, the details thereof.

(*ii*) Assets possessed by the candidate, his/her spouse or dependent relations.

(*iii*) Facts giving insight into the candidate's competence, capacity and suitability for acting as a parliamentarian or a legislator including his/her educational qualifications.

(*iv*) Information which the EC of India considers necessary for judging the capacity and capability of the political parties which put forward candidates for elections to Parliament or state legislature.

The EC could under the High Court's order, 'issue directions to Government, State Government, Intelligence Bureau, etc., to render assistance to gather requisite and relevant information as the EC deemed fit and proper and the said authority [was] duty bound to provide the same.' Moreover, non-compliance with the directions issued by the EC was to 'entail consequences according to law'.[55]

An appeal against the judgement was made to the Supreme Court by the union government joined by an intervention on behalf of the Indian National Congress. The appeal contended that the High Court should have addressed Parliament to make the necessary amendments instead of making the EC implement changes. The union government argued that the necessary disqualifications for certain offences and corrupt practices were listed in the *Representation of the People (Amendment) Bill, 2002* and elaborate procedures for presenting valid nomination papers were already in place.

On the point of law, whether or not the EC is empowered to issue directions as ordered by the Supreme Court, the Supreme Court repeated the position established in *Vineet Narain and Others vs Union of India*[56] that the Court had the power to issue directions to the EC to step in, as it were, to fill the vacuum, till a suitable law is enacted. Taking recourse to Article 324(1), the 'reservoir of power', the Court averred that it gave scope for exercise of 'residuary power' by the EC in an infinite variety of situations that may emerge from time to time. While the disqualifications pertaining to corruption and criminal offences were already listed in law, the Court orders made 'disclosure' of facts binding on candidates. Both the High Court and Supreme Court judgements seemed ultimately to be addressing the right of the people to know. Democracy, the judges asserted, could not survive 'without free and fair elections, without free and fairly informed voters'. Votes cast by 'uninformed voters' would be 'meaningless'. The significance of the judgement, therefore, lies in the manner in which the Supreme Court enhanced the scope of the fundamental rights of citizens to freedom of speech and expression [Article 19(1)]. The '... casting of votes ... that is to say, the voter speaks out ... by casting the vote,' as a form of 'speech and expression' required as much as any fundamental right, the conditions conducive for its exercise. Conducive conditions would cover not only conditions which allowed the voter merely to cast the vote, but also conditions in which the act of voting would be meaningful and fulfilling for both the voter and for the political community of which the citizen–voter is a part. Information about the candidate to be selected, would, the judges felt, compel the 'little man' to think over before making his choice of electing lawbreakers as lawmakers.

The Court considered the fundamental freedom of speech and expression, as commensurate with the right of citizens to know. In the process of emphasising this, the Supreme Court also widened the scope of the ECs constitutional powers to superintend and conduct elections. By binding the EC to the duty of ensuring that the voters are informed of the antecedents of their candidates and the possibilities of their disqualification after they have been elected, the Supreme Court made it necessary for the EC to publicise the details of the candidates among the people. The widening of the scope of the EC's power under Article 324 of the Constitution also meant that the EC now had the power to make rules in this area 'where law [was] silent', rather than wait for the Parliament to legislate.

Table 8.1

Disclosure Requirements Regarding Candidates for Election: A Comparison between Requirements under the Supreme Court Judgement of 2 May 2002 and the Legislative Provisions of August/December 2002

Subject	Supreme Court Judgement (2 May 2002)	Provisions under the Ordinance/Act August/December 2002
Past Criminal Record	*Para 48(1) of the judgement*: All past convictions/acquittals/discharges, whether punished with imprisonment or fine.	*Section 33A(1)(ii)*: Conviction for any offence (except Section 8) and sentenced to imprisonment of one year or more.
Pending Criminal Cases	*Para 48(2)*: Prior to six months of filing of nomination whether the candidate has been accused of any criminal offence punishable with imprisonment of two years or more, and charge framed or cognizance taken.	*Section 33A(1)(i)*: Any case in which the candidate has been accused of any criminal offence punishable with imprisonment of two years or more, and charge framed.
Assets and Liabilities	*Para 48(3)*: Assets of candidate (contesting the elections) spouse and dependents.	Section 75A: No such declaration by a candidate who is contesting elections. After election, elected candidate is required to furnish information relating to him as well as his spouse and dependent children's assets to the Speaker of the House of People.
	Para 48(4): Liabilities, particularly to Government	No provision is made for the candidate contesting

(Table 8.1 Contd.)

(Table 8.1 Contd.)

Subject	Supreme Court Judgement (2 May 2002)	Provisions under the Ordinance/Act August/December 2002
	and public financial institutions.	elections. However, Section 75A(1)(ii)(iii) provides for elected candidates.
Educational Qualifications	*Para 48(5)*: To be declared.	No provision.
Breach of Provisions	No direction regarding consequences of non-compliance.	*Section 125A*: Creates an offence punishable by imprisonment for six months or fine for failure to furnish affidavit in accordance with Section 33A, as well as for falsity or concealment in affidavit or nomination paper.
		Section 75(A): Wilful contravention of Rules regarding asset disclosure may be treated as breach of the rules of the House.

In a rare show of consensus, the political parties rejected the ECs directive making it mandatory for candidates contesting parliamentary and assembly elections to furnish an affidavit giving details of their assets, conviction for criminal offence and liability to a public financial institution. Claiming the privilege of representing the 'political domain',[57] they accused the judiciary of encroachment, and proceeded to make changes in the electoral law. The *Representation of the People (Amendment) Ordinance* promulgated on 24 August 2002, replaced in December 2002 by the *Representation of the People (Third) Amendment Act*, amended the *Representation of the People Act 1951*, by inserting new Sections 33A, 33B, 75A, 125A and 169A, pertaining to 'right to information', 'declaration of assets and liabilities', 'penalties for filing false affidavit', etc. A comparative chart (Table 8.1)[58] shows how the provisions under the new Act diluted the Supreme Court order of 2 May 2002.

Under the Act a candidate contesting election is not required to disclose (*a*) the cases in which he is acquitted or discharged of criminal offence(s); (*b*) his assets and liabilities; and (*c*) his educational qualification. As far as assets were concerned a candidate was required to disclose them to the speaker only after being elected. Moreover, if a person was acquitted or discharged of any criminal offence, there was no necessity of disclosing it to the voters. While the Supreme Court judgement had emphasised the citizen–voter's 'right to know', to equip the voter with maximum information at the time of voting, the Act preferred to inform the voter only selectively. Information pertaining to (*a*) convictions and sentence under one year, (*b*) acquittals and discharge, (*c*) accusation of a criminal offence punishable with two years imprisonment, and (*d*) educational qualifications were to be screened off completely from the public domain, while those pertaining to (*i*) assets of candidate, spouse and dependents and (*ii*) liabilities were to brought onto the public domain only after the election process had ended, and only with respect to the elected candidate. Further, Section 33B inserted in the amended Act with effect from 2 May 2002, made the Supreme Court judgement and directives of the EC subservient to the Act and rules made under it.

The *Representation of the People (Third) Amendment Act* (December 2002) was challenged in the Supreme Court by the Peoples Union for Civil Liberties, Lok Satta and Association for Democratic Reforms. In its judgement delivered on 13 March 2003, the Supreme Court declared the amendment null and void and asked the EC to issue revised instructions to ensure implementation of Section 33A in accordance with the Court's judgement. In the process of delivering the judgement the Supreme Court revisited the relative powers of the EC and the Parliament, examined the scope of the legislative powers that the Parliament claimed with the insertion of Article 33B in the amended Act and reaffirmed the right to information as an integral part of the Fundamental Right to Vote.

The 2 May 2002 judgement of the Supreme Court had, as we have seen, envisaged Article 324 as a 'reservoir of powers' giving the EC 'residuary powers' 'where law [was] silent'. In its subsequent judgement of 13 March 2003, the court elaborated on its earlier judgement by emphasising that the directives given by the Court to the EC in the earlier judgement were intended to operate only until there was a legislative vacuum in the matter. Once a law was made, the directives would cease to have effect. But the law, when made (in this case the *Representation of the People (Third) Amendment Act*), was subject to the Court's 'independent assessment' and evaluation for appropriateness. The standard of evaluation sustained from the earlier judgement was, 'whether the items of information statutorily ordained are reasonably adequate to secure the right to information available to the voter/citizen'. In other words, it was for the Supreme Court to decide whether the amendments brought in through the new statute secured to the citizen–voter the information that made possible a substantive exercise of the right to vote. As Table 8.1 shows, the judges found the information falling short of what could be termed adequate. Moreover, the judgement struck down Article 33B as invalid, holding that the 'Legislature could remove the basis of a decision rendered by a competent court by rendering it ineffective, but it could not direct the instrumentalities of the State to disobey or disregard the decisions given by the court.' The judgement thus reaffirmed the earlier one holding that the voter's right to know the antecedents of a candidate was a fundamental right 'independent of statutory rights under the election law'.[59]

Following the Supreme Court judgement, the EC issued revised instructions to ensure the implementation of Section 33A. With Section 33B of the *Representation of the People Act* struck down by the Supreme Court, the direction of the Supreme Court in its 13 March 2003 order had become the law of the land in terms of Article 141 of the Constitution. To facilitate the implementation of the Supreme Court order, the EC recommended that there should be a single form of affidavit containing all vital information as required under Section 33A and Form 26 may be amended so as to include in it all the items mentioned in the Format of Affidavit prescribed by the Commission's order dated 27 March 2003.[60]

V
Providing a Level Playing Field: A Model Code of Conduct

Along with judicial review, republicanism and secularism, 'free and fair elections' have been held as part of the basic structure of the Constitution. The Model Code of Conduct drawn up by the Election Commission of India in 1968 in consultation with political parties has become an integral part of the conduct of 'free and fair elections'. In the words of M.S. Gill, the Chief Election Commissioner who oversaw two general elections (1996 and 1998), a Model Code of Conduct basically addresses the question 'how the parties should conduct themselves in a democratic exercise such as elections'. The basic purpose of having such a Code was to eventually 'ensure fairness between all contesting parties, taking particular care of the opposition since those in power in a given place naturally have the opportunity to help themselves'.[61]

The Model Code of Conduct which came into force on 29 February 2004, before the general elections, lays down *guidelines of dignified behaviour* for political parties, including norms barring political parties from (*a*) indulging in activities that may aggravate existing differences or create mutual hatred or cause tension between different castes and communities, religious or linguistic, (*b*) criticising other political parties in matters related to the private lives of their candidates, that is, matters not connected with their public activities, their policies and programme, past record and work, (*c*) appealing to caste or communal feelings for securing votes, and using places of worship for election propaganda, (*d*) engaging in activities that are 'corrupt practices' and offences under election law, such as bribing, intimidation and impersonation of voters, canvassing within 100 metres of a polling station and so on, (*e*) disturbing the right of every individual for a peaceful and undisturbed home life, that is, demonstrating or picketing before the houses of individuals because of their political opinions and activities, (*f*) creating disturbances or obstructions to break up election meetings of rival political parties.[62]

On the other hand, another set of norms seeks to ensure *a level playing field* among political parties, with the intention that the party in power may not wield unfair advantage. Section VII (i) (b) of the Model Code of Conduct prohibits the use of official resources, including aircraft, vehicles, machinery and personnel, in the 'furtherance of the interest of the party in power'. In this context the date on which the Model Code of Conduct comes into effect becomes important, since the party forming the government can be bridled, and other political parties protected, only when the Code comes into effect and the ECs regulatory role comes into play. While the Code becomes effective from the 'date of the commencement' of elections, the interpretation of what constitutes commencement has been debated, and contested in courts. A writ petition to the High Court of Punjab and Haryana, on behalf of the Punjab Government, against the Model Code and other instructions issued by the EC on 30 December 1996, argued that the EC had no power to interfere with the implementation of schemes announced by the state government prior to the announcement of the election procedure. The election procedure, the state government argued, commenced only with the issue of a notification by the governor. The High Court, reaffirmed the existing position and the observations made the Supreme Court in 1952 (*N.P. Punnuswamy vs Returning Officer*) and 1968 (*Ghasi Ram vs Dal Singh*) that the EC is entitled to take the necessary steps for the conduct of free and fair elections even anterior to the issuance of notification, that is, from the date of announcement of the election.[63] There are views, however, that hold that even this curb on the ruling party is not enough. The decision to go for elections, especially before the completion of a full term, they feel, vests in the government of the day. The genesis of that decision occurs at least a couple of months before the dissolution of Parliament followed by the fixing of the actual dates by the EC. This interregnum between the decision and the fixing/announcing of dates is of crucial importance because it allows the government of the day to announce a spate of schemes that may give it an unfair advantage in the ensuing elections.[64]

The EC has important disciplinary powers to assure that parties adhere to the Model Code. Among them is Clause 16(A) in the *Election Symbols (Reservation and Allotment) Order* that gives the Commission the power to 'suspend or withdraw recognition of a recognised political party for its failure to observe the Model Code of Conduct or follow the lawful directions or instructions of the Commission'. The disciplinary powers of the EC in the context of non-compliance is significant since the Code has no statutory or legal basis. Unlike the *Representation of the People Act*, the Model Code was not enacted by the Parliament. Formulated in 1968 by the EC in consultation with political parties, the Model Code was the consummation of a progressively widening consensus over certain norms that were first drawn up by the Kerala Government before the General Elections of 1960. The acceptance of the principles of the Model Code by all political parties appears, therefore, to be a manifestation of a 'remarkable voluntary act of political morality and collective ethics'.[65] While the elements of morality and ethics associated with the Model Code cannot be disregarded, the aspect of voluntariness should not be overemphasised; political parties have often been found wanting in their compliance to the standards prescribed by the Model Codes.

Apart from trying to ensure compliance with norms that ensure a level playing field, the EC has also been trying to assure that actors in the field, that is, the political parties, adhere to principles of intra-party democracy and organisational norms. In December 1998, for example, the EC 'punished' the Nagaland People's Council for boycotting the assembly elections in Nagaland. The punishment meted out to the party for depriving the voters of their right to exercise political choice, derecognition of the party by the EC, is the harshest punishment the latter can hand out to any political party. The implications of the punishment are that the party is denied the exclusive use of an election symbol till it contests another election and gets the required percentage of votes to regain the EC's recognition.[66] The EC also reprimanded Tamil Nadu chief minister's announcements seeking a ban on the MDMK party under the provisions of the *Prevention of Terrorism Act* (POTA) for supporting LTTE, a banned organisation, by stating that de-recognition of parties was the sole preserve of the EC.[67]

VI

The Limits of Good Electoral Governance

The statutory and institutional framework of electoral governance, we have seen, envisage a process whereby the participation of people can be assured. The statutory and institutional frameworks of elections are, however, deeply embedded, and unfold in a specific political, economic and social context. The manner in which citizens participate in elections or, conversely, are disabled is determined by these contexts. A large number of rural poor, migrants, people in conflict areas and people displaced from their homes owing to ethnic conflict or economic reasons, may not be able to participate in the political process. A question that one must address, therefore, pertains to the extent to which the machinery for electoral governance is able to take into account the long term and systemic exclusion of large numbers of people.

Migration and the Rural Poor

A primary requirement of enumeration as citizen–voter is residence, which implies that he/she must be identifiable with a stable address. While people have always been mobile in search of livelihood or economic opportunities, the 1990s experienced an exponential increase in distress migrations, owing to a complete breakdown of rural economies. The migrants are, moreover, as P. Sainath terms it, 'locked into endless step-by-step migrations'.[68] The fact that almost all migrant workers tend to be concentrated in clusters of villages within certain districts, implies certain seats are more likely to be affected than others by the migration pattern.

While large numbers of the rural poor get excluded from the electoral process in their quest for survival, Sainath points out that there are some specific periods in this survival cycle when they are most likely to be out of their villages. The months of April and May 2004, when the general election was held, were ironically the months when absences from villages were at their peak.[69] At a deeper level, economic processes and policies that have devastated the rural economy are responsible for the political exclusion of the rural poor, posing the question whether institutionalised certainties by themselves are sufficient for a democratic electoral process.

A comparable illustration of disparate political cycles of democracies and the livelihood cycles of people may also be seen in the example of the Bakerwal community of Jammu and Kashmir. The Bakerwals are shepherds who have for centuries travelled large distances over the span of the state in an annual migration pattern.[70] While a large number of the Bakerwals are registered voters, and conscious that the demonstration of political alertness through the exercise of franchise is important, their livelihood patterns precluded the possibility of their staying on in the plains to vote in the summer of 2004.

A Question of Identification

As seen in the course of this chapter, the connotation of the words 'superintend, direct and control', used in Article 324, has been a matter of controversy. The contest over this power was witnessed in the context of an order issued by the chief election commissioner regarding the identification of voters; the Supreme Court upheld the ECs instructions regarding voter identification, even when in certain contexts, it had the potential of violating the citizen's right to vote. In order to prevent rigging and false voting, the EC had issued orders on 23 January and 7 February 2002 specifying 18 alternative documents to allow persons without photo identity cards to cast their votes. The Allahabad High Court ruled that a person whose name figured in the voters' list could cast his/her vote if his/her identity was

not challenged and found to be false. Challenging this verdict in the
Apex Court, the EC argued that the court could not interfere with
the election process after a notification announcing elections had
been issued. The Supreme Court upheld the ECs instructions, turning down in the process the High Court ruling allowing persons
whose names figured in the voters' list to cast their votes without a
photo identity card or any other alternative document in the state
assembly elections.

Voters in Conflict Areas

The question of whether in conflict situations, the 'freedom' and
'fairness' of elections can at all be assured is pertinent, given that
significant political actors choose to abstain from the political process, and those that remain are often the ones who wield coercive
power in the region. In situations of long-drawn-out conflict, the
credibility of the EC may be put to test. In such a context, instead
of an autonomous body 'enabling' the people to exercise an informed choice and sovereign will, the EC may come to be seen as
representing and furthering the hegemonic interests of the state, as
opposed to the democratic aspirations of the people.

The assembly elections in Jammu and Kashmir (September 2002),
for example, opened up a debate on the credibility of an election
process in conditions that were not conducive to a free, fair and, as
or more importantly, fearless exercise of franchise. The All India
Hurriyat Conference's announcement of a 'poll panel' as an alternative EC may be seen as a manifestation of distrust of the election
process in the existing circumstances.[71] Successive elections in Jammu
and Kashmir have elicited allegations of 'rigging', 'concoction' and
'irregularities'. In February 2001, the Bharatiya Janata Party (BJP)
had alleged 'gross irregularities' in a by-election to the Lok Sabha.
The same was said about the 1996 assembly elections which made
Farooq Abdullah the chief minister. In the 1999 Lok Sabha elections, Abdullah's assembly constituency Ganderbal registered only
10 per cent voting, with 11 per cent in the parliamentary constituency of Srinagar, compelling the then Chief Election Commissioner,
M.S. Gill to call it a 'democratic comment', and ask the Parliament
to take note of it.[72] Moreover, the Rashtriya Rifles of the army and
other armed groups with links to the security forces, the Ikhwan, the
Central Reserve Police Force (CRPF) and the Border Security Force
(BSF) were witnessed, and reported by Indian correspondents, to be

'sending people out like cattle from the narrow lanes of Srinagar', forcing them to vote.[73]

Since 1995, the EC has held five elections in the region, including Lok Sabha and assembly elections, under the full sway of the armed 'counter-insurgency' groups. This is in marked contrast to the ECs stance elsewhere where the presence of police in large numbers had prompted it to declare the elections null and void.[74] It is significant that the absence of a political process and alienation of the people from the state, conditions which make elections meaningless, were not considered relevant. The EC emphasised instead the fairness and efficiency of the election machinery.[75] In a comparable situation in Mizoram, it was only when a political process was set in motion with the Mizoram Accord of 30 June 1986, conferring statehood and a special status to Mizoram, that 'conditions were seen as conducive for holding free and fair elections', and the process of elections to the assembly initiated.[76] Clearly, in Jammu and Kashmir, the 'staging' of elections in which a miniscule percentage of the population participated, became surrogate for a democratic political process.

Debate over Delimitation—Demography, Development and Representation

The 91st Constitution Amendment Bill is yet another instance of the manner in which political imperatives may deprive people of their right to choose and be represented. The Bill passed by Parliament on 23 August 2002 froze the total number of seats in the Lok Sabha and the state assemblies up to the year 2025 so that those states that 'have done well in population stabilisation' do not feel penalised by a reduction of their strength in the Lok Sabha. A Delimitation Panel has also been set up for fresh delimitation to alter the size of constituencies and refix the number of seats reserved for the Scheduled Castes and Scheduled Tribes, on the basis of the 1991 Census, to remove the disparities which may exist within each state.[77] As a result of the freeze, states like Bihar, Haryana, Madhya Pradesh, Rajasthan and Uttar Pradesh will remain underrepresented by 3, 1, 2, 2 and 4 seats respectively. On the other hand states like Andhra Pradesh, Kerala, Orissa and Tamil Nadu will be overrepresented by 3, 3, 2 and 7 seats respectively.[78] While the freeze on the total number of seats has been justified on the basis of maintaining the equilibrium in a federal system, Yogendra Yadav, criticising the amendment, points out that a loss of 2 per cent of the share of all southern states, as a result of delimitation, may not make any difference to their collective bargaining power, whereas underrepresentation of the northern states definitely deprives people of their share in democratic participation.[79]

Conclusion

The constitutional, statutory and institutional framework for the electoral process in India have been designed to establish procedural certainty, providing the basis for the free play of democratic competition and outcome. Indeed, political transitions and changes have been brought about peacefully through elections, as manifested in the prevalence of the 'anti-incumbency factor', and there has been a positive assertion of their democratic rights by hitherto marginalised or excluded sections of society. Procedural certainties are however insufficient to ensure democratic outcomes in two sets of circumstances. First, those outcomes may be eroded by political expediency, presence of entrenched structures of domination within society, and the association between money and political power. It would take a long period of political, economic and social development for reform of those particular circumstances. Second, the institutions and rules set up to ensure procedural certainty may themselves, as we have noted in this chapter, hinder the realisation of democratic outcomes. Reforms addressing this second set of circumstances would pose their own complex challenges. Ensuring procedural certainties would appear to be an ongoing task, adapting and responding proactively to other political, social and economic changes, rather than one which could be met with a fixed institutional framework and fixed, unchanging rules.

Notes

1. See Ramchandra Guha, 'The Biggest Gamble in History', *The Hindu Magazine*, 27 January 2002.
2. Ibid.
3. For an elaboration of this phase, see Yogendra Yadav, 'Electoral Politics in the Time of Change: India's Third Electoral System, 1989–99', *Economic and Political Weekly*, 21–28 August, 1999, pp. 2393–99 and Yogendra Yadav, 'Reconfiguration in Indian Politics: State Assembly Elections 1993–

95' in Partha Chatterjee (ed.), *State and Politics in India*, New Delhi, Oxford University Press, 1997, pp. 177–207.

4. See for details 'Lok Sabha Polls', Election Commission site, http:// www.eci.gov.in/Electoral System/elecsys_fs.htm

5. *The Hindu*, 1 March 2004, p. 1.

6. For a discussion of this survey result, see Peter Ronald de Souza, 'The Election Commission and Electoral Reforms in India' in D.D. Khanna (ed.), *Democracy, Diversity, Stability*, New Delhi, Macmillan, 1998, pp. 51–52 and 'Election, Parties and Democracy in India' in Peter Ronald de Souza (ed.), *Contemporary India: Transitions*, New Delhi, Sage Publications, 2000, pp. 200–10.

7. The survey conducted by *Hindustan Times* (*HT*) and CSDS, in Delhi, on a sample size of 14,000, spread across 70 constituencies, also concluded that the poll panel was trusted most among people who are rich, educated and have a high level of media exposure. Forty-one, 44 and 46 per cent of people in these groups trusted it fully. The poor (34 per cent) and uneducated (24 per cent) trusted it to a lesser extent. Only 20 per cent of people with no media exposure shared this sentiment, suggesting that media coverage, at least to an extent, could be responsible for the popularity of the Election Commission. See *HT*–CSDS Survey, 'Battle for Delhi, 2003,' *Hindustan Times*, 9 November 2003.

8. Shibanikinkar Chaube, *Constituent Assembly of India: Springboard of Revolution*, New Delhi, People's Publishing House, 1973, pp. 102–06.

9. *Poudyal vs Union of India*, (1994) Supp.(1) S.C.C. 324 (para 206) C.B.

10. Substituted by *the Constitution (Sixty-first Amendment) Act, 1988*, Section 2, for 'twenty-one years'.

11. *Sadiq vs Election Commission*, A 1972 S.C.187.

12. Apart from the provisions of the Constitution of India (with subsequent amendments, especially Articles 84, 101–104, 172–174, 193, Part XV, Articles 324–334, 341, 342), *Tenth Schedule* (Articles 102(2) and 191(2) [Provision as to disqualification on ground of defection]), *Representation of the People Act (1950, 1951), The Presidential and Vice-Presidential Elections Act (1952), Representation of the People (Conduct of Elections and Elections Petitions) Rules (1956), Representation of the People (Miscellaneous Provisions) Act (1956), The Registration of Electoral Rules (1960), The Conduct of Elections Rules (1961), Election Symbols (Reservation and Allotment) Order (1968), Criminal and Election Laws Amendment Act (1969), The Delimitation Act (1972), Election Laws (Extension to Sikkim) Act (1976), Disputed Elections (Prime Minister and Speaker) Act (1977), Representation of the People (Amendment) Act 1989, Cancellation of General Elections in Punjab Act (1991), Conduct of Elections (Amendment) Rules (1998), The Representation of the People (Amendment) Act (1998)* and so on, and various sections of the *Indian Penal Code*, form the statutory framework of elections in India.

13. See the official website of the Election Commission at http://www.eci.gov.in/ infoeci.

14. A separate law for setting up a Delimitation Commission was enacted in 1972. A Delimitation Commission was set up under the Act in 1973. No Delimitation Commission was set up after that and there has been no

revision of constituencies because of the decision of the government to freeze the constituencies so as to withhold representation in Parliament to those states where population had been growing fast. The freeze was reaffirmed recently with the passage of the *Delimitation Bill* permitting fresh delimitation of constituencies on the basis of 1991 Census. The process of delimitation is expected to continue for two years and will involve only a reorganisation of constituencies within states without changing the number of total seats or rectifying, through redistribution of seats among states, the discrepancies which exist between population and representation.

15. The main difference between an electoral offence and corrupt practice is that an electoral offence attracts penalty set out in the criminal code, whereas a corrupt practice disqualifies a candidate whose election can be set aside. *The Indian Penal Code (IPC), 1860* has declared certain actions in connection with elections as offences. These are promoting enmity, and so on, between different groups on grounds of religion, race, place of birth, residence, language and so on (Section 153A); imputations and assertions prejudicial to national integration (Section 153B); bribery (Section 171B); use of undue influence to interfere with the free exercise of any electoral rights (Section 171C); personification at an election (Section 171D); making false statements (Section 171G); illegal payments (Section 171H); failure to keep election accounts (Section 171); and making or circulating statements conducive to public mischief, enmity, hatred, and so on, between different classes. While most of these provisions were part of the *IPC* before independence, Sections 153A and 153B were added in 1969 and 1972 respectively. Some of these offences like bribery, undue influence and promoting enmity, and so on, on the ground of religion, race and so on, have also been declared corrupt practices under the *Representation of the People Act, 1951* (Section 123) which also prescribes several other electoral offences such as holding a public meeting in the 48 hours before polling begins (Section 126), creating disturbances at election meetings (Section 127) and so on.

16. S.S. Gadkari, *Electoral Reforms in India*, New Delhi, Wheeler Publishing, 1996, p. 10.

17. Some of the important provisions contained in the Bill were: (*a*) specifying four qualifying dates in a year instead of one for the qualification of voters; (*b*) prohibiting capricious transfers of election staff on the eve of elections; (*c*) disqualification of persons with contracts with the government or any public sector undertaking from contesting elections; (*d*) counting of election expenses from the date of the notification calling for election instead of the date of nomination; and (*e*) enhanced punishments for certain offences and so on.

18. (*a*) Election expenses are to be counted from the date of nomination and not from the date of notification (Act No. 40 of 1975), (*b*) election expenses by political parties or individuals other than the candidate or his agent are not to be taken into account (Act No. 58 of 1974), (*c*) expenditure by a government servant during the course of his duty is to be excluded (Act No. 40 of 1975).

19. The short tenure of the government and internal dissension prevented the adoption of the report as a legal measure. Some of the more significant

recommendations of the Committee aiming towards loosening the influence which ruling parties may have over election outcomes were: (*a*) introduction of a partially Proportional Representation system of election; (*b*) appointment of the chief election commissioner (CEC) by the president in consultation with a committee consisting of the chief justice, the prime minister and the leader of the opposition in the Lok Sabha (instead of consultation only with the prime minister); (*c*) the government in office to work only as a caretaker government during the election period; (*d*) prohibition of contributions by companies to political parties; (*e*) audit of account of candidates and parties; and (*f*) some limited financial assistance to all parties by the state.

20. The Tenth Schedule of the Constitution added by the *Constitution (Amendment) Act, 1985*, was a subject of criticism both on political and legal grounds since its enactment. In *Kihota Hollohan vs Zachilhu* (AIR 1993 SC 412), the Supreme Court gave its final verdict on the validity of the Tenth Schedule. For more details on the majority decision upholding the amendment and other legal aspects of the Amendment, see K.C. Sunny, 'Election Laws' in S.K. Verma and Kusum (eds), *Fifty Years of the Supreme Court of India*, New Delhi, Oxford University Press, 2000, pp. 226–29.

21. It may be pointed out that in 1984, in *A.C. Jose vs. Shivan Pillai*, it was held that the action of the Election Commission in introducing electronic voting machines was without jurisdiction, since at that time there was no provision in the *Representation of the (Amendment Bill), 2002* empowering the Commission to conduct polls using a device other than ballot. *AIR* 1984 SC 921, ibid., p. 225.

22. Some of these recommendations were: (*a*) post offices to be the focal points for preparing electoral rolls; (*b*) a time-bound programme for issuing identity cards to voters; (*c*) prohibiting a person from contesting election from more than one constituency; (*d*) making certain provisions of the Code of Conduct statutory; (*e*) ban on donations by companies; (*f*) limited financial assistance from the state to candidates of recognised parties; (*g*) amendment of the Tenth Schedule to the constitution to provide that disqualification for defection should be decided by the governor or the president and not by the speaker of the Lower House or the chairman of the Upper House.

23. See the 170th Report of the Law Commission on Electoral Reforms and the newspaper reports, 'Panel Proposes State Funding of Polls', *Statesman*, 19 September 1998; 'Law Panel Suggestions on Electoral Reforms', *Statesman*, 20 September 1998; 'Ban Splits, Bar those Charge-Sheeted,' *The Indian Express*, 17 September 1998.

24. See 'Bill to Curb Influence of Black Money in Election', *The Hindu*, 21 December 2001.

25. 'Bill to Legalise Poll Funding Cleared', *Hindustan Times*, 5 August 2003, p. 9. For divergent views on the Bill see 'Parliament Act Legitimises Corporate Funding of Polls: View and Counterview', *Times of India*, 1 August 2003, p. 14.

26. See for details 'Lok Sabha Polls', Election Commission website, http://www.eci.gov.in/Electoral System/elecsys_fs.htm.

27. See Election Commission website, http://www.eci.gov.in.

28. Durga Das Basu, *Shorter Constitution of India* (12th edition), Nagpur, Wadhwa and Wadhwa Co., June 1999, p. 1063.
29. *Dhanoa vs Union of India*, A. 1991 S.C. 1745.
30. *T.N. Seshan vs Union of India, Judgement Today*, 1995 (5) S.C. 337.
31. Durga Das Basu, *Shorter Constitution of India*, p. 1064.
32. *Kanhiya vs Trivedi*, A. 1986 S.C.111 (para 16).
33. *Dasappa vs Election Commission*, A. 1992 Kant. 230 (para 10).
34. *Kanhiya vs Trivedi*, A. 1986 S.C. 111 (paras 13, 16).
35. See D.D. Basu, *Shorter Constitution of India*, especially for judgements pertaining to the limits on the powers of the Election Commission, pp. 1061–62.
36. *Mohinder vs Chief Election Commissioner*, A. 1978 S.C. 851 (paras 91, 114–115, 121). See for details D.D. Basu, *Shorter Constitution of India*, p. 1061.
37. *Sadiq vs Election Commissioner*, A. 1972 S.C. 187.
38. *S.S.P. vs Election Commissioner*, A. 1967 S.C. 898.
39. Ibid.
40. *Inderjit vs Election Commission*, A. 1984 S.C. 1911 (para 4).
41. *Digvijaya vs Union of India*, (1993) 4 S.C.C. 175 (paras 12, 14).
42. See for details Rajeev Dhavan, 'The Supreme Court Reference', *The Hindu*, 23 August 2002.
43. Ibid.
44. Rajeev Dhavan, 'The Gujarat Reference', *The Hindu*, 1 November 2002.
45. 'Polls in Gujarat are for the EC to Announce', *Hindustan Times*, 19 April 2002.
46. 'Text of Presidential Reference', *The Hindu*, 22 August 2002.
47. 'Six-month Rule won't Apply to Dissolve Assemblies: EC', *The Hindu*, 29 October 2002, p. 1.
48. Ibid.
49. Directions, dated 22 February 2002, no. SEC/MCD/15/2002, issued by the State Election Commission to returning officers of Delhi Municipal Wards.
50. Officials of the State Election Commission pointed out that the initial scrutiny of the nomination papers showed that most affidavits had the signature of the same public notary, the oath commissioner or a first class magistrate. In a number of cases, the affidavits had not even been signed by the candidates. See 'Candidates Make a Mockery of Poll Panel's Revision', *The Hindu*, 6 March 2002.
51. Interview with Mr Khaneta, Joint State Election Commissioner on 16 May 2002.
52. 'EC deletes 20 Lakh Names from Rolls', *Indian Express*, 22 September 2005.
53. The Commission noted that many proclaimed offenders/absconders have been contesting elections. To evade arrest they get their nominations filed by their proposers. 'Remove Absconders from EC rolls: EC', *Indian Express*, 12 August 2005.
54. Before the 2004 Lok Sabha election, the Patna High Court had asked the Election Commission not to allow people to contest elections from jail.

Justifying the directive the High Court had argued that if a person in jail cannot be allowed to vote, he should also be debarred from contesting elections. The matter is still pending in the Supreme Court. 'EC Whip May Not Stop Criminals from Contesting', *Indian Express*, 6 August 2005.

55. Affidavit on behalf of Respondent No. 2 (Election Commission of India) in the Supreme Court of India in the Special Leave Petition (Civil) No. 737 of 2001, *Union of India vs Association for Democratic Reforms and Another*.

56. *Vineet Narain and Others vs Union of India and Another,* 1998 SCC 226.

57. 'Govt. to Consult Parties on Court Fiat to EC', *The Hindu*, 19 June 2002.

58. The Source of the Table is the Supreme Court Judgement in *Peoples Union for Civil Liberties (PUCL) & Another vs Union of India and Another, Judgements Today*, Vol. 2, No. 10, 20 March 2003, SC. 541–542.

59. *Peoples Union for Civil Liberties (PUCL) & Another vs Union of India and Another, Judgements Today*, Vol. 2, No. 10, 20 March 2003, SC 529–533.

60. The Election Commission also pointed out that in the past few elections, the candidates have had the tendency of leaving a few columns blank or giving grossly undervalued information about their assets. While Section 125A provides for punishment of imprisonment for a term up to six months and/or fine for furnishing wrong information or concealing any information in Form 26, the Commission felt that the punishment was inadequate considering the salience given by the Supreme Court to the right of the citizen to information. As a precaution against 'motivated cases by the ruling party', the Commission proposed that only those cases which were filed prior to six months before an election alone would lead to disqualification as proposed. It also proposed that persons found guilty by a Commission of Enquiry should also stand disqualified from contesting elections. *Proposals for Electoral Reforms*, Election Commission of India, 30 July 2004, pp. 1–4, 24.

61. 'What More can be Done? Election Commission Cannot Create Law', *The Indian Express*, 22 November 1998.

62. Apart from this there are guidelines on election meetings that have to be followed. See for details, J. Venkatesan, 'Model Code: What it Means for Parties, Candidates', *The Hindu*, 1 March 2004, p. 11.

63. See for details Naresh Gupta, 'Election Commission's Powers are not Mythical', *The Hindu*, Open Page, 24 August 2004.

64. See Abhishek Singhvi, 'Killing the Spirit', *Hindustan Times*, 28 January 2004, p. 12.

65. Ibid.

66. 'Well Deserved Rap', *The Indian Express*, 22 September 1998.

67. 'De-recognition of Parties EC's Sole Preserve', *The Hindu*, 13 July 2002.

68. The National Sample Survey's definition of the 'last usual place of residence' of a migrant is 'the village where a person has stayed continuously for at least six months immediately prior to moving to the present village/town'. P. Sainath, 'The Millions Who Cannot Vote', *The Hindu*, 15 March 2004, p. 10.

69. In April–May 2003, for example, close to 2 million Oriyas were out of their state looking for work. Lakhs of people from just the three districts Nuapada,

Kalahandi and Bolangir were out of their villages, either pulling rickshaws in Raipur, or working in the brick kilns in Vizianagar, or even the construction sites of Mumbai. The exodus starts in February itself, as Sainath witnessed the migration of two-thirds of villages from the Telangana region to Mumbai, ibid.

70. The Bakerwals descend with their flock of sheep to the plains in the winter and then go back to the Zanskar in Ladakh via Doda in summer. Luv Puri, 'Bakerwals won't Vote because they're on the Move', *The Hindu*, 1 May 2004, p. 12.

71. In February, 2002 the Hurriyat Conference announced its poll panel with Tapan Kumar Bose of the Kathmandu-based South Asian Human Rights Centre and Sajjad Ali Shah as its two co-chairpersons. The Hurriyat hoped that this alternate commission will help choose 'the true representatives of the people of Jammu and Kashmir', in both Jammu and Kashmir and PoK, who would discuss the future of the people in tripartite talks. 'Hurriyat forms Poll Panel', *The Hindu*, 13 February 2002.

72. A.G. Noorani, 'One-Horse Race', *Hindustan Times*, 28 May 2002.

73. Ibid.

74. In June 1981, the chief election commissioner declared the by-election in two Garhwal constituencies to be null and void because of the reports it received from its team and officers of the large presence of Haryana police in the area. (A.G. Noorani, 'One-Horse Race', *Hindustan Times*, 28 May 2002.)

75. A.G. Noorani, 'Polls Apart', *Hindustan Times*, 9 July 2002; 'EC Passes for Foreign Diplomats to Witness Polls', *The Hindu*, 14 September 2002.

76. A.G. Noorani, 'One-Horse Race',

77. 'Cabinet Nod for Delimitation Panel', *The Hindu*, 20 April 2002; 'Parliament Approves Delimitation Bill', *The Hindu*, 24 August 2002.

78. See Yogendra Yadav, 'Democracy in Deep Freeze', *The Indian Express*, 21 August 2001.

79. Ibid.

9

NEPAL

Nilamber Acharya and Krishna P. Khanal

This chapter intends to set out the legal and institutional framework of the electoral process in Nepal and also to examine how these frameworks were undermined in the period of Nepal's experience with a functioning parliamentary democratic structure, from 1990 to 2002.

Preparation of Electoral Rolls

The Election Commission (EC) prepares and updates the electoral rolls every year. The Constitution provides that every Nepali citizen having reached the age of 18 years and above is entitled to vote. To exercise the vote, his name should be registered in the voters' list. It is the duty of the EC to collect the names of the voters from every household. In order to be registered as a voter, the *Electoral Rolls Act, 1996* requires, in addition to being a Nepali citizen of 18 years of age or above, permanent residence in any constituency as well. Mentally retarded persons and those sentenced to imprisonment under the *Election Act, 1991* and not having completed one year after release are prohibited from being registered as voters. Those registering their names and giving false information on any of the above counts are liable to be punished. Double entry of names in the electoral rolls is also illegal and liable to punishment.

Registration of voters is done every year by the chief district Officers (CDOs). To enumerate voters' names, the secretary of each of the wards of the municipalities as Assistant Voters' Registration Officer, the Village Development Council (VDC) and the Municipal Ward being the grassroots units of the government in Nepal. Enumeration of voters' names and updating of the electoral rolls is conducted every year commencing the first month of the Nepali Calendar, which starts in mid-April.

As indicated in Table 9.1, one month is allocated for enumeration and updating. Thereafter the names of the voters are published in the office of each VDC and Municipal Ward. Thirty days are allocated for this publication and within 15 days of publication the concerned individuals can verify their names and if the details are incorrect or missing they can request correction and inclusion. The EC publishes the amended list of names within a period of another 15 days. Voters can again lodge claims and protest against any error of omission or commission in the electoral rolls and can also request the transfer of their names from one place to another as per their convenience. The revised and final list of voters is then subject to no more inclusion or exclusion until the following year. However, the EC can review the electoral rolls if it is convinced of the presence of severe irregularities.[1] The entire process is completed by mid-August.

One month is allocated for enumeration and updating. Thereafter the names of the voters are published in the office of each VDC and Municipal Ward. Thirty days are allocated for this publication and within 15 days of publication the concerned individuals can verify their names and, if the details are incorrect or missing, they can request correction and inclusion.

Table 9.1
Annual Schedule for Preparing Electoral Rolls

Step	Activity Process	Days Allocated
1	Collection and updating	30 days
2	Publication	30 days
3	Addition and correction	15 days
4	Publication of added and corrected names	15 days
5	Hearing of claims and protests	15 days
6	Publication of final rolls	15 days
	Total	120 days

Source: Election Commission, 2000.

Some Critical Points Related to Electoral Rolls

Despite the clear provisions regarding the eligibility of the voter, there are frequent complaints about the exclusion of eligible voters and inclusion of ineligible, mostly underage, voters in the electoral rolls. Initially, the electoral rolls prepared at the time of elections contained a multitude of errors of omission and commission. After the promulgation of new legislation relating to the electoral rolls in 1996, the provision for temporary voters was dropped and permanent residence was made a prerequisite to be enrolled as a voter; the provision for temporary voters had provided loopholes for the entry of bogus voters and many constituencies, particularly in the urban areas, including an inflated number of voters. The new requirements seem to have avoided such loopholes to some extent.[2] After the promulgation of the new legislation in 1996, the EC claims that registration of voters has significantly improved, the problems of exclusion and inclusion minimised, and that the rolls are accurate in more than 90 per cent of the cases.[3] As a result of these reform initiatives, the number of voters in certain districts has been reduced despite the increase in the total number at the national level. For instance, whereas there were 486,726 voters in the Kathmandu district in the 1991 election, the number dropped to 468,646 in the 1999 election.

However, several flaws still remain which are a cause for concern. First, while registering the name one is not required to submit proof that one has reached the voting age. This has been instrumental in underage enrolment. Second, exclusion of eligible voters occurs because of the partisan approach of local government bodies and representatives. Third, exclusion is bound to occur because enrolment is done on the basis of permanent residence and those who have no permanent residence are left out. Particularly in urban areas, the number of people without permanent residence is growing. Disenfranchising homeless people, though they may be small in number, cannot be considered as contributing to a free and fair election. Likewise, there is also the possibility of multiple registration as voters can have residence in more than one place. Fourth, there is no way to detect those who have not completed the required period after imprisonment unless a complaint is registered and the practice of registering complaints against irregularities in voter registration is almost non-existent.

The electoral rolls contain the name, age and sex of the voter along with the serial number of the household and the name of the senior member of the family, describing his/her relationship with the voter. It is only natural that the rolls may contain spelling errors in these descriptions and most of these errors are accidental, minor and generally ignored while voting. However, they sometimes become excuses for preventing genuine voters from exercising their vote and result in the build-up of tensions and confrontations between rival parties which in turn disturb the polling.

The role of officials and other agencies involved in the registration process is also equally important in ensuring that nobody is unfairly excluded from, or included in, the electoral rolls. The shortcomings that exist in the enumeration process are less due to legal flaws than the lack of alertness of voters and political parties, and negligence on the part of officials in the field.

Despite the efforts to prepare accurate voters' lists, certain impediments prevent sections of the electorate from exercising their vote. A large number of administrative and security personnel deployed for election duty are deprived of voting. Prior to 1999 they could cast their ballot in the same booth and constituency where they were deployed. But this was not allowed in the 1999 election and, therefore, more than 75,000 personnel involved in the administration of elections were unable to exercise their vote. Similarly, those living away from their residence, within and outside the country, cannot exercise their vote. There were reports that in some of the villages in the Tarai districts in the south, female voters were prevented from casting their ballots by their male counterparts.[4] Illiteracy, superstition and poverty are some of the factors which prevent voters, particularly women, in rural areas from exercising their ballot. Likewise the old and the sick in the mountain and hill districts cannot go to vote. Political apathy among urban voters also appears to be growing. The ban on both private and public transport during elections creates yet another impediment to voting.

Voter's Identity Card

Once the electoral rolls are finalised, the EC issues the voter's identity card (ID). As per the provision of the *Electoral Rolls Act, 1996*, the EC introduced voter's ID card in the 1997 by-elections on an experimental basis and it was found to be effective in minimising many of the electoral malpractices such as proxy voting, multiple voting and so on. The EC had planned to implement it in all the constituencies within five years on a phased basis to be completed by 2004. By 2001/2002, voters of 105 constituencies were expected to receive voter ID cards. In the constituencies where the ID card is introduced, voters must be in possession of their ID cards in order to cast their vote.

The process of distributing voter's ID card to all the electorates has been adversely affected by a number of factors. Lack of required funds, Maoist violence and unavailability of citizenship certificates to all citizens, particularly in the southern districts of Tarai, are some of the major problems encountered in achieving this target. Moreover, the teams involved in photographing voters were threatened and disturbed by the Maoists in several constituencies. Other problems such as low turnout of voters to have their photographs taken and errors in identification of the person in the photograph have also complicated the process.

Election Commission

The Election Commission (EC) conducts, supervises, directs and controls elections to Parliament and local bodies at the village, town and district levels. The EC has its Central Secretariat and is in the process of establishing offices in every district of the country for supervision and monitoring purposes.

The EC is an independent body with the chief election commissioner as chairman. The chief election commissioner and other election commissioners are appointed for six-year terms by His Majesty the King as recommended by the Constitutional Council. They are eligible for reappointment. However, there is an age limit of 65 years. The Constitution is open about the size of the EC; it may be a single member or multi-member body. In practice there have been three to six members.

The chief election commissioner or an election commissioner can be removed from office only by two-thirds of the total number of members of the House of Representatives through an impeachment motion. No person is eligible to be appointed as chief election commissioner or an election commissioner unless he/she:

- holds a Bachelor's degree;
- is not a member of any political party;
- has attained the age of 45.

Former commissioners are not eligible for appointment in any other government service except in that of a research or advisory nature.

The Constitution directs the government to provide personnel and other necessities to the EC; it is dependent on government bureaucracy and support to administer most of its functions. Despite the fact that the EC can request the support of any government agency, much of the administration of elections is coordinated through the Ministry of Home Affairs and its district officials such as the CDO. These personnel are placed under the jurisdiction of the EC during the period of the election and are accountable to it. The EC has the authority to direct, monitor and evaluate their activities and take action if they fail in their duty.

The EC has authority to issue orders (by publication in the gazette) in pursuit of its duty to conduct, supervise, direct and control elections in accordance with the Constitution and existing laws. It would be the duty of the government, government institutions, corporations, semi-government or non-government institutions, political parties and their officials, candidates and representatives, and persons involved in the election campaign to obey these orders. The EC may acquire land, building, vehicles, furniture or other material means owned by the government, corporations, public institutions and educational establishments for election purposes. The EC may give orders to the police who are on election security duty on the matters directly or indirectly related to the election. Any returning officer, polling officer or other official deputed by the EC to election duty may take the assistance of government security bodies in that locality, including the police.

The EC may prepare a code of conduct for government and semi-government officers and employees, political parties, candidates and related persons. Violation of the code of conduct is an offence. A code of conduct prepared by the EC is presently in operation. The EC monitors the implementation of its orders and code of conduct, and checks violations.

The EC may impose restrictions during the period of elections on the government against proclaiming new policies and programmes, mobilising human and material resources, and using government-owned media for election campaigns.

After the announcement of the date of elections, the EC appoints a returning officer for each constituency. At elections to local bodies, the CDOs are appointed as returning officers for their respective districts. For the election of the House of Representatives, it is a legal requirement that judges of the law courts or officers of the judicial service be appointed as returning officers. At elections to the Upper House, the chief judges/registrars of Appellate courts are appointed as returning officers and in the case of election to the Upper House from the members of the Lower House, the secretary-general of Parliament is appointed as returning officer.

The returning officer has the authority to appoint his assistants and subordinate staff. Normally the central and district agencies of the government bureaucracy extend their support for security arrangements. The Ministry of Home Affairs, therefore, plays a prime role in the smooth administration of elections in accordance with the norms set by the EC.

The dates of election, for both the Parliament and local bodies, are usually decided by the EC in consultation with the government except in the case of dissolution of the House of Representatives. The dissolution of the House requires an accompanying announcement of the date of new elections.[5] If elections are to take place before the EC completes enumeration of voters' names for the current year, voting is conducted on the basis of the previous year's list.

Nationwide voting may be held on the same day or on different days depending on the adequacy of election personnel and the security situation of the country. In the 1991 and 1994 parliamentary elections, polling was held on the same day in all constituencies whereas in 1999, elections were held in two phases, with a two-week gap in between. The local elections, both in 1992 and 1997, were also held in two phases.

The EC may appoint observers for inspection, investigation or supervision of polling, counting or any other process of election. The EC may cancel an election in the whole constituency or polling in any of polling stations on the grounds of its findings on complaints or information of malpractices. The EC may, on the basis of reports initiated by polling officers and returning officers regarding disturbances on polling day, illegal booth-capturing, tampering with ballot boxes and malpractices during counting, decide on repolling and recounting.

The appointment process of the election commissioners, including the chief election commissioner, has been criticised because the Constitutional Council which recommends their names is not free from party politics. The independence and impartiality of the commissioners became questionable when their number was increased to six in order to accommodate the political interests of the incumbent government. Moreover, the independence of the EC is subject to suspicion when the commissioners are given important diplomatic assignments on retirement.[6] Therefore, it has been suggested that the number of commissioners, including the chief, should not exceed three; that their appointment should be made on the basis of public and parliamentary hearings; and that they should not be rewarded with special postings on retirement.

The EC is, as an institution, independent enough to resist political pressures from any quarter, governing political party, opposition political party or others. There have been no incidents of the EC itself moving court against undue pressures on it. However, the EC is also a body of people with different personalities, some being weak and others strong. The experience of the past three elections shows that there were no serious accusations against the EC that it yielded to political pressures from any party. It has on many occasions intervened to check the misuse of state machinery, media and government employees, and issued directives to the government.

However, there have been lapses in enforcement of legal provisions and code of conduct. The Commission is not strong enough to enforce legal provisions, code of conduct and other measures for free and fair elections as would be required to change election behaviour of political parties, candidates and their supporters, and to check entry of criminal elements in the election process. The issue is not the pressure of the government on the EC, but the necessary cooperation of government and others in the political process with the EC.

The human resources employed by the EC come from the members of the judicial service and bureaucracy. Much depends on the neutrality of the bureaucracy and the integrity of its individual members on election duty. While it may be the case that politicisation of the bureaucracy or a politically committed bureaucracy is an inescapable feature of a newly emerged democracy, when government servants are divided on party lines, or too weak to stand up to party pressure or threats from criminal well-wishers of politicians, the quality of elections gets badly affected.

Nepali society is highly politicised along party lines. A problem which has a direct bearing on all aspects of election is the political affiliations of administrative personnel. All the major political parties have their frontline organisations among students, teachers, professions and interests. Even in government service and state-owned enterprises, employees' unions are formed along party lines. The non-officer ranks in particular are more politicised. More than 60,000 civilian personnel are required to conduct a national-level election and the EC draws them from the civil service. Party-oriented election officials often tend to take the side of the party of their preference and attempt a one-sided implementation of the election process, particularly on polling day. Depriving voters of their right to cast their vote for reasons of error in names, not entertaining complaints, not taking decisions on complaints and not maintaining an orderly polling booth are some of the ways in which election personnel can influence the election. Politicised election personnel have also been accused of hiding ballot papers, invalidating valid votes or vice versa. Such malpractices are possible only when there is a political nexus between election officials and party agents. Politicised administrative personnel thus constitute one of the major impediments in administering the election process.

Electoral Norms and Code of Conduct

The norms to be followed at elections are set out in the *Election Act, 1991* and *Election Code of Conduct, 1996*. The *Election Act* comprehensively lists electoral crimes subject to punishment by court of law. In addition to these legal provisions, the EC in consultation with political parties and the government framed and enforced a code of conduct in 1996, which sets out the norms to be followed by the candidates, the parties, the government and other related agencies,[7] from the date of announcement of the elections to its end. If the code is violated by any candidate, party or worker, the election could be declared void, pursuant to the relevant provision in the *Election Act, 1991*. Moreover, the concerned candidate may be disqualified from contesting again for up to six years.

The EC has also fixed a ceiling, along with detailed breakdowns, on candidates' expenditure of funds and resources during electioneering. For the purpose of election expenditure, all 205 constituencies are divided into four categories, namely, A, B, C and D and limits fixed in accordance with geographic distance, level of urbanisation and so on. Category A has three districts comprising 12 constituencies in the Kathmandu valley, where a candidate can spend up to Rs 275,000; Category B, 21 districts comprising 91 constituencies where the candidates are allowed to spend up to Rs 235,000; Category C consists of 45 districts comprising 95 constituencies and the expenditure ceiling is fixed at Rs 165,000; and Category D has seven remote mountain districts of the north where the ceiling is fixed at Rs 115,000. Candidates are required to submit statements of expenditure within a month of elections and failure to comply may lead to punishment with fine and/or prohibition from contesting elections for another six years. If the candidate has won the election his victory may be forfeited.

However, the use of 'dummy' candidates enables the candidate who was instrumental in putting the dummy candidate forward to spend more than the ceiling fixed by the EC. The ceiling on election expenses as stipulated by the EC appears to be only on paper because no candidate is likely to give an accurate statement and as there is no mechanism to monitor the election expenses of candidates, the EC has to rely on the statements submitted by the candidates themselves.

The code stipulates that no candidate or political party should conduct electioneering in a manner that would 'damage the character' of another or violate another's 'democratic rights'. The code also specifies that nobody, including ministers or government employees, can use state facilities and/or other state resources such as transport, meeting halls and so on, in favour of or against any candidate. However, as we shall note further on, these provisions too are subject to numerous violations.

Invalidation of Election

The *Election (Offences and Punishment) Act* has defined the grounds on which an election may be annulled.

Section 19(1) says that on a petition of a concerned candidate an election is annulled if it is proved that:

- the election was not fair due to offences relating to impersonation, undue influence, character assassination, offensive propaganda, graft, partiality of employees, use of weapons or explosives, damage of ballot paper, misuse of ballot paper, damage to ballot boxes, violation of code of conduct, illegal use of ballot papers and disturbances in counting;
- if any nomination paper of a candidate in the election was wrongly rejected or wrongly accepted;
- if the elected candidate had incurred election expenses beyond the legally allowed limit or he/she had amassed wealth unnaturally or illegally, or if he/she had used money to damage fairness of election or for illegal purposes.

However, the result of the election will not be annulled if it is proved that activities mentioned above had not substantially affected the result of election, and if the candidate had no knowledge of the malpractice or if he/she had done everything possible not to allow occurrence of such malpractice.

An Election Court may order recounting of votes if it is alleged that the petitioner or any other candidate is the winner, or rejection or acceptance of ballot papers had been faulty, and decide the case on the basis of recounting.

The Election Court is constituted by the government on the recommendation of the EC. It decides the cases falling under the *Election (Offences and Punishment) Act*. Investigation is done by an official deputed by the EC. The investigation officer thus deputed can issue arrest warrants and file a case in the Election Court. If any individual wants to file a case under this Act, he/she should move through the EC since Election Courts are not permanent. There have been instances when their term was not extended by the government and petitions challenging election results remained without being decided. Appeal on the decision of the Election Court lies with the Election Appellate Court.

Electoral Malpractices

A survey conducted in 2000/2001 revealed that 25 per cent out of a total of 500 respondents believed that various forms of rigging had taken place in Nepal's elections. The forms of rigging were placed in the following order: proxy voting (72.5 per cent), underage voting (52.3 per cent), use of force and violence (35.8 per cent), vote buying (34.9 per cent), partiality by police and administration (26.6 per cent), and booth capturing (9.2 per cent).[8] Electoral malpractices have reached such alarming levels that various committees have been formed in order to develop strategies which will ensure that future elections are 'free and fair' as well as 'more peaceful, impartial, credible and transparent,'[9] because if the current situation is not rectified, people may lose faith in elections and the democratic character of the polity is likely to be weakened.

Electoral malpractices can be taken as 'any actions, irregularities, and practices by any individual, group, organisation, party or agency including the government and its agencies that undermine the conduct of a free and fair election.' It includes any act of omission or commission in deviation from the rules, procedures, norms and practices set for the purpose of elections, which undermines the free exercise of the vote and has an effect on the outcome of the election. Malpractices may take place at any time before, during and after the voting. The major electoral malpractices during the pre-election period, election day and post-election period in Nepal may now be identified.

Pre-election Period

Preventing Nomination

Prospective candidates are often prevented from filing their nominations. In the 1991 election, the Rastriya Prajatantra Party (RPP) candidates were intimidated and harassed in order to prevent them from filing their candidacy. Attacks on RPP workers and preventing them from organising meetings was widespread in the 1991 elections.[10] In 1994, even a candidate of the ruling party was harassed so as to prevent him from contesting the election. In 1999 a Nepali Congress (NC) candidate from the Manang district was declared elected unopposed; he was alleged to have used undue influence over the candidates of rival parties to get himself elected without contest.[11]

Privileges of Incumbency

It is widely known that before every election the incumbent government reshuffles and transfers administrative and security personnel from one district to another. After the announcement of the new code in 1996, the government technically followed the code of conduct which prohibits the incumbent government from making any 'new appointment, transfer or deputation' after the announcement of elections. However, there are several loopholes in the code which could be exploited contrary to its spirit. Since it is the government that schedules the elections, it is able to reshuffle and transfer administrative and security personnel before the announcement of elections so as to avoid the charge of violation of the code. In the 1997 local elections, the government prematurely removed the inspector general of police and 60 out of 75 CDOs were reshuffled four days prior to the formal announcement of the date of elections. About 80 high-ranking police officers in almost all the districts were either promoted or transferred on the same day that the election was announced.[12]

The incumbent government has various privileges during elections in Nepal. Apart from the reshuffling of personnel mentioned above, there is also the possibility of electoral manipulation through misuse of government facilities and resources; better security arrangements for the ruling party; allocation of, or promises to allocate, public facilities for the needy; misuse of government-controlled media in favour of the ruling party and misuse of state resources during the campaign. Although legal provisions and the election code prohibit the misuse of state facilities and resources by any party or candidate, including ministers, the government manages to evade these checks. Moreover, the party in power is in a convenient position to raise election funds through its business nexus. Apparently the business community funds all the major parties in proportion to the latter's political strength.[13]

The election code of conduct stipulates that after the announcement of the election, the government should not make any policy commitment until elections are concluded. But there is a strong tendency for the incumbent government to influence voters through new programmes and commitments. In 1994, after the announcement of parliamentary elections, the Minister of Agriculture announced a three-year agricultural development scheme which would create new employment and income.[14] In 1995, when the mid-term poll for the Pratinidhi Sabha was already announced (later on aborted by the Supreme Court), the Communist Party of Nepal (Unified Marxist-Leninist), CPN(UML), minority government presented the annual budget containing several new policies and programmes including an ambitious 10-year programme for poverty alleviation and increased allocations for village committees.[15]

The incumbent government is considered to be the biggest perpetrator of electoral malpractices, which is why a caretaker government for the period of election, as set up in Bangladesh, has also been demanded in Nepal. Major political parties such as the CPN(UML) and RPP have sought constitutional amendments to this effect. During the 1999 election, owing to a hung, dissolved House, an understanding was reached to form an all-party government. However, due to reasons within the parties themselves, only three major parties were included in the government. Opinion of political parties with regard to the caretaker government varies from one party to another. The CPN(UML) has insisted on an all-party government while some other parties have preferred an independent and neutral government.

Violation of Campaign Norms

Political parties tend to obstruct rival candidates' campaigns in their own stronghold areas. As a result, campaign disturbances, clashes and violence including physical assault occur among the contestants. Therefore, the campaign period is extremely tense and volatile. However, the prevention of violence has proved difficult due to political interference in security arrangements.

The use of money and muscle by candidates of major political parties during elections appears to be widespread. Major candidates need to spend ever increasing amounts of money in order to mobilise volunteers, polling agents and supporters during the campaign as well as on polling day. Particularly in the southern districts bordering India, candidates hire professional muscle power thereby linking elections with criminal activities. The exercise of money and muscle, vote buying, buying of polling agents, entertainment with feasts and drinks have degenerated the electoral process. Even political leaders like G.P. Koirala have admitted that smugglers had entered Parliament by spending stupendous amounts of money.[16] Many unseen deals and pacts are made in order to ensure victory through middlemen or vote brokers.

Although there are legal provisions and rules, including the code of conduct, regulating the election campaign, much depends on the extent to which healthy norms and practices of campaign have been developed. After the enforcement of the new election code of conduct in 1996 a degree of positive impact such as the prohibition of display of campaign paintings, banners, large-size posters and so on, was apparent in the campaign. Nevertheless, acrimonious speeches by rival groups, engaging in campaign violence, intimidation of opponents and voters, the use of money and muscle, and the misuse of state power and resources could not be prevented.

The situation tends to worsen when complaints against such activities are ignored by the authorities entrusted with enforcing law and order. Legal provisions for such election offences have, therefore, remained ineffective.

Election Day

Polling centres with a congenial environment, proper security arrangements and the representation of contesting parties during polling will enable voters to cast their ballot freely. In reality, however, polling is not free of malpractice and includes:

(*i*) Proxy and Underage Voting

In most constituencies voters ID cards are yet to be introduced. Proxy voting, therefore, remains the most common electoral malpractice. If the polling agents are honest and alert, it is easy to identify proxy voters in rural areas. Sometimes, partisan polling agents tacitly agree to allow proxy voters to cast the ballot. Political parties also tend to use force in their stronghold areas to allow proxy voters to exercise the ballot in their favour. Underage voting is difficult to prevent once the underage persons are enrolled as voters. People between 15 and 18 years are frequently found to have been enrolled in the voters' list. However, this irregularity can be rectified at the time of enumeration.

(*ii*) Mismanagement of Polling Booth

Various acts of omission and commission on the part of election officials have also been discovered. Mismanaged and disorderly polling centres, as opposed to the rules and norms of the election procedure, are a common occurrence. A study of the 1997 local election of the Dang district revealed that polling had actually begun hours after the stipulated time and had continued even the next day without coming to the attention of the authorities. Moreover, the voters had been asked to place their ballot papers in cloth bags, buckets and earthenpots instead of the ballot box supplied by the EC.[17]

(*iii*) Polling Day Violence

Violence on polling day has continued to increase with each election. Those who cast their votes for rival candidates have been intimidated and harassed. Rival party cadres, particularly in rural areas, were found to have been engaged in activities such as creating false rumours, blocking voters' access to polling centres, threatening revenge if they voted for rival parties, snatching of ID cards and so on. Many of these incidents are ignored if the party involved is in power or is influential and the opponent is weak. In 1991, 51 polling centres had to be repolled because of disturbances, and this increased to 86 in 1994, and 102 in the 1999 elections. In 1991, six people lost their lives during elections with the number going up to 10 in 1994 and over 10 in the 1999 elections.

A certain amount of intimidation takes place in most constituencies and political parties tend to display their power against rival parties wherever possible. Total or partial control of polling centres by candidates of major political parties appears to have taken place in past elections and this trend is on the increase. If repolling is an indicator of booth capturing, it has become a serious problem and has come to be a part of election culture particularly in the southern districts bordering India. There was repolling in 86 and 102 centres during the 1994 and 1999 elections respectively, out of which 64 and 80 were from the Tarai districts. The Rautahat district has also become notorious for booth capturing. Although movement across the Nepal–India border is barred on polling day, gangs engaged in electoral violence enter the country well before this day.

Post-election Phase

(*i*) Post-election Violence/Revenge

Post-election violence generally takes the form of revenge and is reported particularly in rural areas.

(*ii*) Delays in Resolution of Election Disputes

The law stipulates that exclusive Election Special Courts (ESC) be formed in each of the five development regions of the country in order to hear and resolve election-related disputes. The courts are constituted accordingly and are expected to complete their duties within one year. However, many disputes have apparently remained unheard. Moreover, the verdict of the ESC, particularly in reversing an election result, may tend to be controversial. A case in point is the ESC's decision to review counting of ballots of the Nuwakot constituency, following the 1999 election. The vote margin in this constituency between the elected candidate and his nearest rival was only 15. The ESC declared some of the ballot papers invalid which reversed the result in favour of the nearest rival, who was the complainant. However, the process through which the court gave judgement on some of the ballot papers was not considered transparent and based on objective criteria; the Supreme Court reviewed the decision of the ESC and declared it void. Following this decision of the Supreme Court, the government did not extend the period of the ESCs although they had yet to decide on complaints from other constituencies.

Conclusions

The Constitution has embodied a strong commitment of the nation to multi-party democracy, adult franchise, parliamentary system, fundamental rights and the rule of law. The constitutional commitment to independence of various institutions of the state—Judiciary, EC, Public Service Commission and Commission to Investigate Abuse of Authority—is aimed at protecting the citizen against abuse of power by the state and any of its organs. The Constitutional Council is added confirmation of the constitutional commitment to independence of constitutional bodies including the EC. The powers granted to the EC reflect the state's commitment to free and fair elections. Violations of election laws and norms flow from three main sources:

- government and administrative machinery;
- candidates and their coteries;
- political parties and their mass organisations.

It is readily apparent that the political party is the most important player in all three sources. Elections continue to be a formal means of acquiring power and winning elections at any cost appears to be the only motive of those engaged in politics. The mad race to capture power by securing votes by any means, and the impression given by many of those who shared power during the last decade that power is the passport to quick prosperity, has shaken the trust in elections and the democratic process itself. Opportunists, commission agents, criminal gangs and all types of miscreants have found it convenient to promote their own interests through candidates of major political parties during elections. Correspondingly, candidates elected to office need to be in a position of power to reward and protect their backers. As a result the post-election scenario of the country is marked by extreme pressure for a ministerial berth or any other position with power and privileges. Those who are denied these rewards switch their loyalty from one leader to another resulting in the chronic instability of government.

Thus corruption, money power, muscle power, criminalisation of politics and related ills are adversely affecting the electoral process. Existing laws are violated with impunity, public outcry and media shouting are continuously ignored, political space for democratic forces is steadily shrinking, in the span of the six years ending 2002 Maoist violence gripped the country, and a sizeable number of elected representatives of the people were unable to work in their constituencies.

Elections are tarnished not because legal or institutional structures are bad. The structure is in place, and it is a good one. It has become necessary to look for extra measures because of the avalanche of violations confirming a tendency to ignore, bypass, jump or undermine the structures as they stand today. Legal reform should be considered principally in three areas:

- reforming functioning of political parties;
- providing more teeth to the EC;
- strengthening civil society and independent media.

The key question is whether any statutory provision and institutional arrangement can instil in the leadership of the major political parties the political will and moral strength to change their ways and that of their followers. Eradicating electoral malpractice may not be possible only through legal reforms because the moral stance in politics itself has deteriorated. Free and fair elections in countries such as ours are as we have seen, not only related to the formal aspect of the electoral process. The attitude of political parties and their leaders towards politics and power plays a significant role in the electoral process because much of electoral malpractice is related to political culture. Reform and improvement is, however, a continuous and time-consuming process and any reform aimed at elections should also accompany a wider reform agenda which encompasses the socio-economic transformation of the country.

Experience so far has also shown that it is futile to expect from political parties that they would mend their ways without being compelled to both by law and by civil society. A vibrant civil society is the main source of strength for free and fair elections; the quality of democracy in general and elections in particular depends on how strongly, confidently and effectively the citizenry exercise and defend their rights and freedoms.

Ultimately, it is in making voters more informed about policies and candidates, and more confident and strong in making a choice, increasing civil society pressure to make political parties more responsible and accountable, while at the same time implementing stringent measures against criminalisation of politics, and influence of money and muscle power, that elections could be a part of the struggle for a new political culture and ethical environment which would lead to a true democracy.

Notes

1. Election Commission, *Electoral Process in Nepal*, Kathmandu, Election Commission, 1998, p. 11.
2. In a by-election held in Kathmandu constituency No. 1 in 1994, the number of voters had suddenly increased from 99,662 in 1991 to 136,655 in 1994. It was alleged that supporters of the major candidates had swarmed into the constituency to enrol as voters and the EC could not resist them due to the lack of adequate statutory and legal provisions. But after the changes in 1996, the EC was able to drop such bogus voters from the rolls.
3. Election Commission, *Electoral Reforms*, p. 11.
4. A women's activist group found that in some villages of Mahottari district, male voters had exercised the ballot on behalf of their female counterparts for a considerable period of time.
5. Former Chief Election Commissioner Bishnu Pratap Shah stated that non-consultation with the EC while deciding the date of elections along with the dissolution of the House had undermined the EC. He suggested that the EC should be consulted and taken into confidence whilst doing so. This was stated at a seminar organised by Nepal Centre for Contemporary Studies on 10 June 2002 in Kathmandu.
6. The government, which came to power after the 1991 parliamentary elections, appointed the chief election commissioner as Ambassador to the United Kingdom soon after his retirement from the EC.
7. Election Commission, *The Election Code of Conduct, 1996*, Kathmandu, Elections Commission, 1999.
8. Nepal Centre for Contemporary Studies, 'Statistical Data on Electoral System and Reform Based on Field Survey of Five Districts, namely Dhankuta, Rautahat, Kaski, Dang and Baitadi,' January 2001. The percentage mentioned above is based on respondents' multiple choice from a maximum of three options from a given list.
9. After the local elections held in 1997 an all-party joint parliamentary committee headed by the chairman of the National Assembly, the upper house of the Parliament, was constituted to investigate the 1997 local elections and recommend measures in order to make future elections free and fair. Likewise, after the third parliamentary elections in 1999, another high level committee headed by the prime minister and consisting of leaders of various political parties having representation in the Parliament

was formed. *Nepal Press Digest*, Vol. 41, No. 36, September 1997; *The Rising Nepal*, Kathmandu, 2 September 1999.

10. *Nepal Press Digest*, Vol. 35, January to April 1999.

11. This is a small constituency in the northern mountain district with little over 6,000 voters. Despite the small size of the constituency, contesting the election is considered expensive. It was suspected that prospective candidates from rival parties, who had little prospect of winning the election, tacitly agreed to allow the NC candidate to win without contest. The candidate was an incumbent and had previously won the elections twice from the same constituency.

12. *Nepal Press Digest*, Vol. 35, January to April 1999.

13. In the 1991 elections it was reported that ministers belonging to the CPN(UML) had received a substantial amount of money from cement and iron rod dealers for allowing price rise and imports from India. Likewise ministers belonging to the NC had received money from contractors involved in road construction. Ibid., Vol. 35, No. 10, 11 March 1991, p. 97.

14. *Nepal Press Digest*, Vol. 38, No. 36, 5 September 1994, p. 343.

15. Ibid., Vol. 39, No. 30, 24 July 1995, pp. 281–84.

16. *The Kathmandu Post*, 12 August 2000.

17. Nand Kumar Dhital, 'Sthaniya Nirbachan Samvat 2054: Dang Zillako Adhyayan' (Local Election 1997: A Study of Dang District). A Disser-tation Submitted to the Central Department of Political Science, Tribhuvan University, 2002.

10

PAKISTAN

Zulfikar Khalid Maluka

I

Introduction

In 1947, the 450-member Constituent Assembly, elected on a limited franchise in 1946 on an all British-India basis, was divided into two bodies for the newly independent nations, Pakistan and India. A very few of the Constituent Assembly members opted for Pakistan and, therefore, additions had to be made through arbitrary selections/co-options, and in this way the final strength of the Constituent Assembly rose to 79. The Assembly was however racked by prolonged and serious political disputes, the most important among them being the issues of Islamic state or secular state, national language—the (abortive) efforts to impose Urdu as the official language of Pakistan at the expense of Bengali in the eastern wing, the parity formula, that is, amalgamation of the federating units in the western wing to balance the monolithic Bengali block, and joint or separate electorate system—whether religious minorities should have a separate electorate system or be integrated into a joint electorate process.

During the first 11 years of its history, Pakistani cabinets and assemblies were installed and dismissed surreptitiously and the country had seven prime ministers in that interregnum, and that too without facing a single general election. Some of the prime ministers/chief ministers who were imposed on the centre/units by the civil–military bureaucracy (via palace intrigues) were not even members of the assemblies. During the same period, not a single government (both at the centre and provinces) was changed through the constitutional and legal process. It was only in 1956 that a Constitution was adopted by the Second Constituent Assembly. The First general elections under the 1956 Constitution were to be held in October 1958 when General Muhammad Ayub Khan in connivance with the then President, Major General (Retd.) Sikandar Mirza, abrogated the 1956 Constitution and imposed martial law in the country.

It was only in 1970 that general elections were first held in Pakistan. By that time the parochially motivated and mala fide exclusion of the popular Bengali leaders from the country's political permutations, national decision-making and power-sharing processes, and reduction of their electoral strength in the name of 'parity' led to Sheikh Mujibur Rahman's Awami League demanding complete autonomy for the eastern wing of the country. While the Pakistan People's Party (PPP) led by Zulfikar Ali Bhutto won elections in the western wing, the Awami League had a stunning electoral victory in the eastern wing. The Awami League's right to form the government was deliberately disrupted by the military government, leading to the Bengalis' massive uprising and ultimately to the break-up of Pakistan.

In 1977, the government of Zulfikar Ali Bhutto decided to hold general elections a year ahead of the actual lapse of the tenure of national and provincial assemblies. A motley collection of nine opposition parties formed the Pakistan National Alliance (PNA) to contest the national assembly elections. The PNA launched a massive campaign against the electoral victory of the PPP on the grounds of the elections having been rigged, and it used these grounds as a means to dislodge the Bhutto regime. This confrontational course led to the military coup of General Muhammad Zia-ul-Haq in July 1977. In February 1985, General Zia held elections on a non-party basis, excluding the political parties. The election process was skillfully manipulated in selecting who would participate from amongst the independent candidates and was dubbed as a dubious exercise by the major political parties, media and observers.

General Zia's accidental death on 17 August 1988 should have allowed Pakistan to chart itself on the redemocratisation course. However, President Ghulam Ishaq Khan and the then army chief Mirza Aslam Baig organised an alliance of right wing parties opposed to the PPP through the Inter Services Intelligence (ISI), an integral component of the Army. At the General Elections of November 1988, though the PPP led by Benazir Bhutto emerged as the single largest party winning 93 seats and was in a position to form a coalition government, Bhutto was allowed to become the prime minister only after she had committed herself to the election of Ghulam Ishaq Khan as the President and left certain key cabinet portfolios to him on the pretext of special concern to the army. Benazir Bhutto's government was dismissed on 6 August 1990 on charges of corruption and incompetence and new elections were held on 24 and 27 October 1990. The partisan role of the army and President Ghulam Ishaq Khan was excessively displayed in the whole 1990 electoral process.

When inter se confrontation of the Ishaq–Nawaz diarchy led to systematic crisis of the state, the much publicised legitimacy accorded to the 1990 rigged elections went by the board. Moeen Qureshi, an unknown entity in the politics of Pakistan, was 'imported' to hold the 1993 elections. The 1993 election was hailed as overwhelmingly conforming to the letter and spirit of election laws.

Strikes, ethnic and sectarian violence in major urban centres, a wave of allegations of pillaging of money, a plethora of corruption charges, and strained relations between the president and the prime minister ultimately led to the dissolution of the national assembly and provincial assemblies on 5 November 1996. Malik Meraj Khalid was appointed as the caretaker prime minister to hold the 1997 elections. President Farooq Ahmed Khan Leghari's partisan attitude (fully backed by the military) against the PPP notwithstanding, the 1997 elections were officially hailed as conforming to the electoral laws.

A government led by Nawaz Sharif came to power in the 1997 elections. However that regime was overthrown in the military coup of 1999, led by General Pervez Musharraf. Validating the military coup of October 1999 on the touchstone of 'necessity', the Supreme Court in the *Zafar Ali Shah* case gave Musharraf three years to hold elections. While easing out Muhammad Rafique Tarar from the presidency on 20 June 2001, General Musharraf elevated himself as the President and took the oath of office. Subsequently he also got passed a piece of legislation by which he could hold the office of the chief of army staff (COAS) along with the office of president of Pakistan.

Having no political courage to face the usual process of election through the Parliament and the four provincial assemblies, Musharraf, while treading in the footprints of Ayub Khan and Zia, opted for self-selection through the contrived and dubious process of referendum. Since his military coup in October 1999, General Musharraf had euphemistically projected himself as 'popular' among the masses. However, he had to spend billions of rupees from the national exchequer on his image-building campaign. The way the general and his commanders in uniform were hopping from one major city to another and addressing rent-a-crowd rallies, the exercise definitely made a mockery of the office of the COAS.

Whilst the highest judiciary hurriedly legalised the referendum, the Election Commission (EC) manufactured the results which purported to show that up to 98 per cent of voters supported it, and that too in the face of independent observers such as the Human Rights Commission of Pakistan (HRCP) estimating voluntary participation at not more than 3 to 5 per cent.[1] The transparency of the controversial referendum could be visualised from the order of the EC to destroy its complete record hurriedly by 31 December 2002, possibly to save the Commission and beneficiary from further ridicule. The mockery of the referendum which was conducted through the lopsided alliance of the EC and the military had brought into further ridicule those two institutions and also the judiciary. It was in this context that the French Foreign Ministry spokesman on 2 May 2002, said that 'France has chosen officially to disregard the results of Tuesday's presidential referendum....'[2] On the same day, the US withheld praise for General Pervez Musharraf's much trumpeted 'victory' in the referendum, saying Washington looked forward to 'free and fair' elections in October 2002.[3] However, terming his referendum as 'free, fair and transparent' the general promised his captive nation to hold the October 2002 General Elections in 'the same manner.'[4] In fact, he and his colleagues in uniform with active connivance of the EC fulfilled that 'promise' too.

The electoral process in October 2002 has generally been held as a dubious, fraudulent and engineered one, in favour of the regime-backed candidates. The final results of that election, in most constituencies, did not tally with the results collected by the polling agents of the candidates, and such results included results of 'ghost polling stations' as well. The dark shadows of night witnessed changing of results, whereby winners were declared losers, and the then

CEC rejecting outright demands for recounting of ballots. On 9 October 2002, the military regime had amended the law which gave legitimacy to its rule, the Legal Framework Order (LFO) introduced on 21 August 2002, providing for independent candidates to join any political party within three days after the official publication of results by the EC. This *mala fide* move had its background in the manipulative elections process itself. Many independent candidates had contested the election on a common symbol of 'crescent', and they were lampooned as playing second fiddle to the king's party. Many of them were elected and they readily joined the military-backed Pakistan Muslim League (Qayyum) Group PML(Q).

Of late, Musharraf and his cronies have floated the idea of getting him elected for a second term through the present parliamentary structure instead of the new one supposed to be in place after the 2007 General Elections, if held at all. Such a design has its precedent in the election of Ayub Khan as President of Pakistan in 1964. Ayub Khan had got approved a *Presidential Election Bill* by the then national assembly which stipulated a novel way of reelecting him. The Bill laid down inter alia that the sitting president would remain in office until his successor was elected. The election of a new president would precede the election of a new assembly. The selection and election of the presidential candidate would be carried out by the existing national assembly and not by the new one. In case of Musharraf, while some legal eagles are out to legalise the obsession of the COAS president for obtaining a mandate for his office from the outgoing Parliament, yet it also exposes the overwhelming fears of the supreme commander that the new parliamentarians might not repose confidence in him as their next president. Such an exercise, which seems to be in the offing, if carried out, would be patently *mala fide* even if it can be held legally tenable by any convoluted interpretation of the already disfigured Constitution. It is hard to believe that an assembly elected through a fair and transparent electoral process would elect the general as their president for the next five years.

Constitutional and Statutory Framework

Articles 213 to 226 (Part VIII and Chapter 1 and 2) of the 1973 Constitution deal with the EC, electoral laws and conduct of elections. Item No. 41 of the Fourth Schedule of the 1973 Constitution makes elections a federal subject.

The procedural details pertaining to holding of elections are provided in the *Representation of the People Act, 1976*, which has the sanction of Article 222 of the Constitution. This Act also provides for institution of election tribunals, stipulates qualifications and disqualifications of the candidates, and a plethora of other procedural matters pertaining to holding of elections.

The *Political Parties Act, 1962 (Act No. III of 1962)* deals with formation and registration of political parties and the conditions thereof. The EC has a pivotal role in the said statute as far as the formation, registration and functioning of political parties are concerned.

The process of allocation of symbols to political parties and independent candidates for contesting of elections is governed by the *Representation of the People (Conduct of Election) Rules, 1977*. Ninety-six symbols are prescribed under Rule 9, and the political parties are allotted symbols presented therein under Rule 21 of these Rules. The returning officer of the constituency concerned allots symbols, other than those assigned to political parties, to independent candidates. The EC enjoying plenary powers under Section 21 of the *Representation of the People Act, 1976* has enunciated a mechanism for classification of symbols and principles for allotment of the same on application by the political parties in the *Allocation of Symbols Order, 1993*.

Penal offences, for example, bribery in elections, undue influence and personation at elections, false statements in connection with an election, failure to keep election accounts and so on are contained in Sections 171–A to 171–J of Chapter IX–A of the *Pakistan Penal Code (XLV of 1860)*.

Under Section 103A of the *Representation of the People Act, 1976*, the EC has the same power as the High Court to punish any person for contempt under the *Contempt of Court Act, 1976 (XLIV of 1976)*.

In July 2002, the military government announced a constitutional package for the sake of 'political stability' and 'checks and balances in the power structure' of the country. The salient features of the package were:

- Voter's age reduced from 21 to 18 years.
- Adoption of joint electorate system as originally contained in the 1973 Constitution. However, no reserved seats for the minorities proposed.
- President empowered to remove the prime minister and his cabinet, without dissolving the national assembly.

- President to appoint governors (to provinces) at his discretion.
- President to nominate any member of the national assembly as prime minister.
- Governor to nominate any member of the provincial assembly as chief minister.
- Setting up of national security council, with president as chairman of the Council.
- Members of senate to be elected directly.
- No independent candidate to take part in senate elections.
- The minimum educational qualification of Bachelor's degree prescribed for candidature to membership of legislatures.
- An overall increase of 51 per cent in the membership of the assemblies, with the number of seats in the national assembly increased from 207 to 357.
- Number of senate seats increased from 87 to 100.
- Number of seats of Punjab Assembly increased from 240 to 390, Sindh Assembly from 100 to 171, NWFP Assembly from 80 to 130 and Baluchistan Assembly from 40 to 67.
- Reserved seats for women, technocrats and *ulema* in senate and assemblies increased.
- Qualification for reserved seats in senate, national and provincial assemblies for technocrats will be 16 years of education, recognised by the University Grants Commission or a recognised statutory body, as well as at least 20 years of experience including record of achievements at the national or international level.
- Concept of caretaker government envisaged in case of general elections on the completion of the normal term of assemblies.
- EC to be converted into permanent and autonomous institution with four members, and the tenure of the chief election commissioner increased from three to five years.
- Loan defaulters not allowed to contest elections.
- Political party securing less than 10 per cent of the total votes cast in the general election not to be entitled to any seats.
- Party getting less than 5 per cent votes not to get any seat in Senate.
- Disqualification of a convict from holding political office regardless of lapse of time since his release. Similarly, another provision debars a person who has been proclaimed an absconder or convicted and sentenced to imprisonment for having absconded.

- Local governments to have constitutional cover for operation and existence.

The fixing of the voter's age limit to 18 years, enhancing the tenure of the CEC from three to five years, making the EC a permanent constitutional body, increase of seats in the national assembly/ provincial assemblies, reserving of seats for women and the policy of joint electorates are all very welcome steps. The EC and the increase in the number of seats in the national and provincial assemblies would be discussed in separate sections further on, and at this point we will discuss the other positive measures we have noted.

The decrease in the voter's age is the latest development, a series of contradictory decisions, in this regard. The 1973 Constitution stipulated an age limit of 18 years for a voter. The Zia regime enhanced it to 21 years. The Musharraf Government has reduced it to 18 years again. As could be expected, such whimsical changes in the statutes add to the difficulties of the EC in enlisting and deleting voters to and from the electoral rolls.

The prejudiced practice of keeping women voters away from the polling stations through agreements/*jirgas* and the deliberate neglect on the part of the EC to take legal action against those responsible for such a sorry state of affairs pertaining to women's franchise cannot be justified. It was in the knowledge of the EC and all those bodies associated with it that in most parts of the North-West Frontier Province (NWFP), Baluchistan and some other areas of the country, women voters are not allowed to come to the polling stations to exercise their right to vote. The issue assumes added significance in the context of the increase in the number of seats reserved for women in Parliament and the provincial assemblies.

The decision as regards a joint electorate was also a welcome development because this was a long-standing demand of the major political parties and that of the minorities as well; the use of separate electorates virtually ousted the minorities from the mainstream politics. The question at issue is whether religious minorities should be part of the general electorate or constitute a separate electorate. The issue dyed in religious hues delayed constitution-making in the 1950s, and it was also used by the Zia military regime to create cleavages between the Muslim and non-Muslim minorities in the country. Until 1977, the system of joint electorate was in vogue. The Zia regime in its enthusiastic drive for Islamisation, opted for a separate electorate system. The pertinent question was that if the non-Muslim voters could jointly elect the president and the prime minister, how could they be debarred from jointly electing the Member of Parliament? The minorities have never demanded a system of separate electorate, yet it was forced upon them by General Zia to appease the militant Muslim religious elite.[5] The question of the alienation of minorities apart, the separate electorate system poses gigantic practical problems.

(*i*)   while the Muslim voters exercised their right for electing the members of national and provincial assemblies from their particular constituency, the non-Muslims could not do that because they were required to vote for candidates whose constituencies were spread almost all over the country. If a Christian voter from Rawalpindi wished to contact his elected representative, he might have to go to Lahore or Multan, and similarly a Parsi voter in Swat could have his representative somewhere in a distant part of the NWFP or elsewhere.[6]

(*ii*)   The candidates in this system also faced immense physical, financial and social problems in campaigning for their voters, in some cases throughout the country.

(*iii*)   The EC also faced multifarious problems in preparation of electoral rolls for four categories of non-Muslims:

- Christians;
- Hindus and persons belonging to the Scheduled Castes;
- Sikhs, Buddhists and Parsis;
- Ahmadis—persons belonging to the Qadianis group or the Lahori group.

Politically, the scheme was singularly oriented to creating wedges of religious hatred and social disintegration and was a perfect mechanism for reducing national cohesiveness into pieces.

Notwithstanding the welcome measures discussed earlier, the constitutional amendments made the president the most powerful player in power permutations through his discretionary powers and through the prime minister losing his constitutional and executive authority in favour of the president. All these legal devices were aimed at ensuring that the military and its leader Pervez Musharraf retain their hold on state power. Through his controversial LFO, General Musharraf has introduced strong features of a presidential form of government into the Constitution, which almost fully absolves the person holding the exalted office from responsibility to the people or even being answerable to the Parliament. The structural dynamics via the LFO axed parliamentary supremacy and made the prime minister a senior government functionary who worked for, and was answerable to, the president and not to the national assembly.

Election Commission

The Election Commission of Pakistan is a constitutional body and the CEC is appointed by the president, at his discretion, under Article 213 of the Constitution. As per Articles 52 and 107 of the Constitution, the CEC was, up to the time of the changes announced in the constitutional package of 2002, appointed for a term of three years, that term being liable for extension by a resolution of the national assembly for a period not exceeding one year (Article 215). The package of July 2002 however has made the term of office of the CEC a five-year one. The EC consists of four members, each a serving judge of the High Courts of the four federating units of the Republic and a secretary, usually a bureaucrat. Under Article 218 (2) of the Constitution, the members of the EC are appointed by the president in consultation with the chief justice of the relevant High Court and the CEC. Barring his resignation, the CEC cannot be removed from office except in the manner prescribed under Article 209 of the Constitution for removal of judges of the High Courts or the Supreme Court.

Broadly, the work of the EC constitutes the following:

- preparation/updating of electoral rolls of eligible voters annually throughout the country;
- delimitation of constituencies for the election of members of the national assembly/provincial assemblies;
- organisation of polling for elections of the national assembly/ provincial assemblies and also holding of elections to vacant seats as and when necessary.

The appointment of the CEC and his conduct in holding general elections has often been portrayed as partial and controversial by the media and political parties alike. Such assertions could be substantiated from the induction of the present CEC by the Musharraf Government. Preceding his occupation of the CEC office, Justice

(Retd.) Irshad Hasan Khan was the chief justice of the Supreme Court of Pakistan. His elevation to that august position was criticised and even maligned by the Bar, media and the political parties to the extent that the Pakistan Bar Council and the Supreme Court Bar Association were constrained to deny him the traditional farewell dinner in protest. There were also consistent and vociferous demands in the media advising the military government to desist from appointing the said retired chief justice as the CEC.[7]

The appointment and tenure of the CEC has been, up to the time of the changes promulgated by the present military government, loaded with implications impairing his independence and the holding of free and fair elections. As we have noted, until the changes introduced by the constitutional package of July 2002, the normal tenure of CEC was three years. The term of the national assembly and provincial assemblies was five years, unless sooner dissolved. Thus, when the CEC could not last for even one stipulated tenure of the national assembly/provincial assemblies, how could he be called independent, impartial and efficient? The incumbent CEC did not have sufficient time to effectively plan for even one scheduled general election. However, as we have seen, the military government has now increased the tenure of the office of the CEC from three to five years.

The installation (vide Article 218) of the EC for the purposes of holding 'each general election' to the national assembly and the provincial assemblies was a questionable provision in the Constitution. The Constitution and the relevant statutes on the electoral process were also silent as to when the ordinary members of the EC were to be appointed and when they would go back to assuming their judicial duties in the high courts. The package of July 2002 however now provides for a permanent EC.

Governments in power usually effect transfers of civil servants connected with the election process. Pliable, greedy, biased and ill-reputed officers indulge in excessive intervention and manipulations of the worst kind, making the election process eventually a farce. It is usually suggested that transfers which have a direct bearing on the election process should be frozen at least four months prior to the actual election date. The EC should not only be in a position to freeze transfers/postings of key officials who could influence the election process but also be in a position to determine the strength and quantum of staff required from the judiciary and civil service for a particular election.

The EC is unable to insulate the election machinery from the extraneous influence of the executive, as it is completely dependent on the executive for financing its existence, taking measures for running the electoral process and other disbursements. For holding of 'free and fair' elections, the financial dependence of the EC on the civil–military bureaucracy is another impediment which should be completely removed.

Under the *Election Commission (Officers and Servants) Rules, 1989*, the CEC is empowered to appoint officers of a particular category and above. The appointment of the secretary to the EC comes within the ambit of the CEC's powers. However, the ongoing practice of appointment of the secretary by the executive is a serious cause of concern. The appointment of the secretary provides the executive an open window for interference in selection, appointment and posting of election staff.

The election commissioner is an organiser and referee of the whole election process. For invoking public faith in his impartiality, the party in power as well as the opposition should be involved in making his appointment. After the CEC's selection in a transparent and consensus mode, the power of the EC should be increased so that the institution is in a position to withstand extraneous pressures in the manner of an independent and objective judiciary.

Qualifications of Candidates

Any government—or even a candidate in any constituency—in connivance with the returning officers can play havoc with the candidates of the opposite parties via Articles 62 and 63 of the Constitution. The original provisions of the two articles, as enunciated when the 1973 Constitution was adopted, were more or less free of subjectively assessed qualifications or disqualifications. Problems arose with some of the qualifications introduced by the Zia regime in Article 62 of the Constitution reproduced below. These conditions are also reproduced in Sections 99 and 100 of the *Representation of the People Act, 1976.*

Article 62(d):   He is of a good character and is not commonly known as one who violates Islamic Injunctions.

Article 62(e):   He has adequate knowledge of Islamic teachings and practices obligatory duties prescribed by Islam as well as abstains from major sins.

Article 62(f):   He is sagacious, righteous and non-profligate and honest and amen.

These qualifications as well as some disqualifications mentioned in Article 63 of the Constitution are vague and based on theological texts. For instance, who is going to judge that a candidate is of good character and is one who does not violate Islamic injunctions? It is very easy to disparage a person's character and then exclude him from the electoral process. There is no objective criterion to judge a person as of good or bad character. What is the criterion for an adequate knowledge of Islamic teachings, practising of obligatory duties and abstentions from 'major sins'? Such subjective notions can be easily employed to discriminate among candidates for the membership of Parliament. The words 'sagacious, righteous and non-profligate' are vague, subjective, loose and elastic concepts and can be used in a prejudiced manner against opponents. The proviso to Article 62 is also vague as it mentions good moral reputation in case of non-Muslim candidates which again is not judged on an objective criterion.

The mala fide intention behind such a formulation was to employ these constitutional provisions to exclude political parties and candidates who were opposing Zia's self-styled 'Islamic rule, from the electoral process. It was initially expected that the present military government of General Musharraf would effect amendments in the Constitution to take care of such ambiguous and subjective qualifications/disqualifications for candidates contesting elections. Far from making any such amendments, the military government has not only maintained the objectionable provisions but has also added more to achieve its own ends. The constitutional package proposed disqualification of a convict from holding political office regardless of lapse of time since his release. Similarly, another provision has been added debarring a person who has been proclaimed as an absconder or convicted and sentenced to imprisonment for having absconded.

The additional disqualifications introduced by the Musharraf regime have been criticised by two former prime ministers and leaders of two major political parties—Benazir Bhutto and Muhammad Nawaz Sharif, as being specific to them and aimed at excluding them from the corridors of power. Muhammad Nawaz Sharif had been convicted by the Anti-Terrorist Court in Karachi, and Benazir Bhutto was convicted for absconding from the Accountability Court in Rawalpindi. As if these provisions were not enough to keep the two leaders of major parties away from the hustings, a new law (via President's Order) was promulgated which stipulates that a person cannot become prime minister who has held that office twice in the past. Benazir Bhutto and Muhammad Nawaz Sharif have each held the office of prime minister twice, though without completing their entire tenures of office. Thus there seems to be truth in the allegations that such provisions are Benazir–Nawaz-specific, ill-conceived, against norms of democracy and *mala fide* in intent and purpose.

Electoral Rolls and the Right to Vote

Article 51(2) of the Constitution empowers citizens of Pakistan above the age limit of 18 years to be voters.[8] The laws for preparation, revision and amendment of electoral rolls are embodied in the *Electoral Rolls Act, 1974* and the *Electoral Rolls Rules, 1974* framed thereunder, and as per provisions of Article 222 of the Constitution. The electoral rolls are used for elections for national assembly/ provincial assemblies and for local government elections as well. Non-cooperation with and excessive interference of the executive in the EC matters has resulted in the EC's failure to keep the electoral rolls updated. Such a practice is also violative of Article 219(a) of the Constitution which is mandatory and requires that electoral rolls shall be revised annually. The implications affect the transparency and fairness of the whole electoral process. The present electoral rolls were prepared in 1986–87 with 1 January 1986 being the cut-off date for enrolment of voters. The 1988, 1990 and 1993 elections were conducted on the basis of that roll, with minor additions of insignificant numbers of voters. In 1995, an exercise undertaken by the EC to prepare fresh electoral rolls proved abortive. When general elections were held in 1997, the electoral rolls prepared 10 years ago in 1987 were adopted with minor additions.

Various groups from abroad monitoring the 1997 elections had pointed out serious deficiencies in identification of voters, exclusion of names of significant proportions of voters, presence of the names of deceased voters and ineligibility of listed voters in many cases. The European Union Election Observer Group Report on the 1997 Elections listed the following shortcomings in the electoral rolls:

There was widespread confusion about the state of the electoral register. Many voters believed that their names had been inscribed in the course of the preparation of a new register during 1996. In fact, this register was not complete when the government was dismissed in November and elections announced. In its place the register used was based on the 1986 electoral records updated for the 1993 elections. A significant proportion of the names should have been deleted or transferred to other registers. Although the EC advertised this fact, and encouraged new voters to inscribe their names on the 1993 register, many voters were not aware of the situation, and were disappointed on election day to find they could not vote. Lists were prepared of eligible voters who were not included in the current registers, but in some cases the additional lists were not available at the polling stations, or were incomplete. There was a report also of additional lists being ignored for election purposes. An electoral register was not available for the Tribal Areas, where the franchise had been substantially expanded. A new register is needed for the whole of Pakistan before elections are held again.[9]

The presence of the names of deceased voters, non-existent voters and of persons wrongly inserted in the voter's list, create wide avenues of rigging. In the 1990 elections, 600 votes of those registered on the address of a vacant plot of land in a Lahore constituency were cancelled by the Lahore High Court.[10] In the same elections, 8,000 bogus votes registered in a Gujrat constituency of the province of Punjab were cancelled by the EC.[11] Above all, the non-registration of eligible voters is a transgression of the constitutional rights of such citizens, amounting to disenfranchising them.

Besides these modes of excluding citizens from participation in the electoral and democratic process, the other deadly weapon is the denial of identity cards to otherwise eligible voters or abuse of the same for parochial motives. Possession of identity cards for securing ballot papers from the presiding officer has been made compulsory. The Registration Office sends teams to villages and remote areas for collection of application forms for issuance of identity cards to the eligible voters.[12] Based on the practice of general or mid-term elections in the past, and in the view of SAARC-NGO observers, it can be said that there is a widespread practice of blocking applications of electors and distribution of identity cards to party representatives.[13] This makes possible the use of bogus identity cards, the sale–purchase of votes through identity cards or even denial of identity cards to the potential voters of the opposite parties/candidates. The foregoing modes of disenfranchising the citizens along with associated fraudulent practices uproot the basis of a free and fair elections system.

Delimitation of Constituencies

The creation, alteration and modification of constituencies pertaining to national assembly or provincial assembly elections are governed by the *Delimitation of Constituencies Act, 1974 (Act No. XXXIV of 1974)* wherein the EC has the power of reviewing/modifying the geographic boundaries of constituencies. In view of the substantial increase by the Musharraf regime in the number of seats in the national assembly and those pertaining to general voters, women and technocrats in the four provincial assemblies, the process of formulation and delimitation of constituencies was undertaken by the EC vide the *Election Commission Order, 2002; Election Commission (Amendment Order), 2002* and the *Conduct of General Election Order, 2002.* The 1998 Census in the country was made on the basis of such delimitations.

Preceding the increase in seats, the national assembly as per Article 51 of the Constitution consisted of 207 seats for Muslim members and 10 seats for non-Muslim members. The 20 seats for women members had expired as per Article 51(4) of the Constitution. The provincial assemblies of Baluchistan, NWFP, Sindh and Punjab consisted of 40, 80, 100 and 240 Muslim member seats with 3, 3, 9 and 8 non-Muslim seats respectively (Article 106 of the Constitution). According to Section 5 of the *General Elections Order, 2002*, the national assembly consists of 357 members. The seats for eaoh provincial assembly of Baluchistan, NWFP, Sindh and Punjab

Table 10.1
National Assembly Seats

Province/ Area	Number of General Seats	Seats Reserved for Women	Seats Reserved for Technocrats	Total Seats
NWFP	35	8	3	46
FATA	12	–	–	12
Federal Capital	2	–	–	2
Punjab	148	35	15	198
Sindh	61	14	6	81
Baluchistan	14	3	1	18
Total	272	69	25	357

Table 10.2
Provincial Assembly Seats

Province/ Assembly	Number of General Seats	Seats Reserved for Women	Seats Reserved for Technocrats	Total Seats
Punjab	297	66	27	390
Sindh	130	29	12	171
NWFP	99	22	9	130
Baluchistan	51	11	5	67
Total	577	128	53	67

have been fixed at 67, 130, 171 and 390 respectively. Twelve seats have been allocated to the Federally Administered Tribal Areas (FATA). The increase in national and provincial Assembly seats vide the *Conduct of General Election Order, 2002* is shown in Tables 10.1 and 10.2:

Section 5(4) of the *Conduct of General Election Order, 2002* provides for a system of direct elections simultaneous with proportional representation for election, for seats reserved for women and technocrats. The process of constituency formulation in future elections will be as per sub-section reproduced below:

(4) *For the purpose of election to the National Assembly:*

(a) the constituencies for the election on general seats shall be single member territorial constituencies;

(b) members to fill the general seats in the National Assembly shall be elected by direct and free vote;

(c) the constituencies for the seats reserved for women and technocrats shall be such that each Province forms one constituency with as many such seats as are allocated to the Provinces under clause (1); and

(d) the members to fill seats reserved for women and technocrats which are allocated to a Province under clause (1) shall be elected simultaneously through a proportional representative system of open political parties' lists of candidates on the basis of total votes secured by the candidates of each political party contesting elections to the general seats:

Provided that a political party securing less than ten per centum of the total votes cast in the election on general seats shall not be entitled to any seat;

Provided further that where only one political party secures ten per centum or more of the total votes cast and all other political parties secure less than ten per centum of the total votes cast, then the first proviso shall have effect as if for the word 'ten therein the word 'five were substituted;

Provided also that where all the political parties individually secure less than ten per centum of the votes cast, then the first proviso shall have effect as if for the word 'ten therein the word 'five were substituted.

The pattern for election on general seats and seats reserved for women and technocrats in the provincial assemblies is identical to that of the national assembly.

In the past there were instances when potential candidates in connivance with the civil–military bureaucracy succeeded in carving out constituencies to their own liking based on arbitrarily drawn boundaries. For averting such prejudiced delimitation of constituencies, there seems to be a need for an independent Delimitation Commission headed by a judge of the High Court so that the boundaries could be demarcated on fair, natural, social and geographic criteria, leaving no room for any complaint of discrimination or bias. Such a proposed Delimitation Commission must not be under the executive.

Polling Arrangements

As per Article 218(3) of the Constitution, the EC is under obligation 'to organise and conduct the election and to make such arrangements as are necessary to ensure that the election is conducted honestly, justly, fairly and in accordance with the law, and that corrupt practices are guarded against.' Article 220 of the Constitution stipulates that in connection with organising and conducting of an election, all executive authorities functioning in the federation and in the federating units are under obligation to assist the election commissioner and Commission in that exercise.

For conduct of the election, the EC appoints a district returning officer (DRO) for each district and returning officer (RO) for each constituency. There is no legal bar for appointment of civil servants as DRO/RO, yet usually officers from the judiciary are appointed to these posts. Under Section 8 of the *Representation of the People Act, 1976 (RPA)*, the functions and duties of the RO to each electoral constituency are:

(*i*) selection and preparation of lists of polling stations for approval by the district returning officer;

(*ii*) inviting and scrutinising nomination papers from candidates;

(*iii*) allocation, subject to the direction of the EC, of a prescribed symbol to each candidate, submission of lists of presiding officers, assistant presiding officers, and polling officers to the district returning officer, at least 15 days before the actual date of polls, for approval;

(*iv*) selection of government buildings for use as polling stations;

(*v*) supply of equipment, training of polling personnel, collection and consolidation of results and their submission to the EC; and

(*vi*) filing of statements of election expenses of the candidates with the EC.

The returning officer has been accorded powers to suspend any presiding officer or any other officer working under him after recording reasons for such action. The presiding officer of each polling station is under obligation to set up a polling station, to supervise the polls, to maintain discipline at the polling station, to ensure secrecy of ballot, to exercise powers of summary trial under Section 86-A of the RPA if required, to count votes after the close of polls in the presence of the representatives of the candidates, and to issue certified copies of statement of counts and accounting of ballot papers to the polling agent. The district returning officer has a key role in the whole election scheme. He is empowered under Section 27 of the RPA to order a fresh poll in a polling station or in the whole constituency if he finds that the polls were interrupted, obstructed or rigged.

Based on past experience, abrupt and last minute changes in polling stations create problems for the voters and affect the outcome of election results. It is suggested that the announcement of polling stations should be finalised and made public at least two months prior to the holding of any election. For the convenience of voters, the distance and minimum number of voters for each polling station must be kept in mind.

Election Tribunals

Article 225 of the Constitution bars the jurisdiction of any court to hear any complaint regarding the election or calling the whole election into question except by a petition presented to an Election

Tribunal. Under Section 57 of the RPA, the CEC is empowered to appoint an Election Tribunal headed by a judicial officer who is qualified to be a judge of a High Court. Each Election Tribunal has the power of a Civil Court trying a law suit under the Code of Civil Procedure, 1908. In the 1997 elections, 27 sitting judges of the four High Courts were nominated to preside over Election Tribunals. For speedy disposal of petitions a day-to-day hearing is prescribed. The Election Tribunal is competent to declare the whole polling void in a constituency or polling station and order fresh polls. The decision of the Election Tribunal is appealable before the Supreme Court of Pakistan, subject to a 30-day limitation period.

The EC in its reports on the 1985, 1990 and 1997 elections has mentioned the commonly used grounds for challenging an election cited in the election petitions: illegal practices committed by the candidates, illegalities committed by the polling staff and civil servants associated with the election process, and unjust disqualification of candidates on the basis of Articles 62 and 63 of the Constitution. The usual complaints relate to indulgence of civil servants towards one party or candidate, biased drawing of boundaries of a constituency, non-registration of voters by the authorities, misuse of official position, intimidation of voters, denial of issuance of identity cards and long distance to polling stations. The most vital grievances pertain to acceptance or rejection of nomination papers of the candidates.

The media, political parties, and foreign and local observers point out that the elections of 1977, 1985, 1988, 1990 and 2002 were rigged, yet the EC in all its reports insisted that the elections were fair and transparent. Another interesting aspect of election complaints/grievances is that not all of them are disposed of in the wake of each general election and their pendency for adjudication before the Election Tribunal was applied as a blackmailing tactic against a Member of Parliament so that he would continue to toe the leadership's line of action in government.

Election Monitoring

The society, media, intellectuals, political parties and the legal profession do monitor the elections. Recently the salutary trend of foreign observers watching elections has been introduced. However, 50–100 citizens of foreign countries observing elections cannot be as effective as the members of Pakistani society themselves.

When the civil–military bureaucracy backed by politicians has monopolised all the levers of state power, then it is the people of Pakistan who must uproot and do away with this unholy conglomerate.

Abrupt Changes in Statutes

The statutory, procedural and penal provisions pertaining to the election processes are often subject to abrupt change at the personal whims and particular 'requirements' of those who take it upon themselves to indulge in such abject exercises for stealing the people's mandate in their favour. In a country which has experimented with almost eight constitutions and where abrogating, holding in abeyance and making amendments therein on the basis of personal inclinations have become a sordid saga of the nation, the moulding, bending and amending of ordinary legislative acts for parochial motives seem a routine exercise. The main victim and subject of excessive amendments is the *Representation of the People Act, 1976,* and this fact was also noted by the EC in its report on the 1997 elections:

> It has been observed during many general elections in the country that a number of amendments in various provisions of the *Representation of the People Act, 1976* are made on the eve of each general election through amending Ordinances and then few of these amendments are re-promulgated after four months. It is also observed that some amendments, which do not suit a particular group of politicians, are allowed to lapse. This leaves a vacuum in the legal framework provided for the elections....[14]

The SAARC Observer Group echoed its opinion on the same phenomenon as follows:

> The observers were concerned about the number and scope of changes in the electoral laws and procedures put into effect by the caretaker government. While some of the changes were 'clear moves in the right direction,' e.g., the extension of adult franchise to the FATAs, the large number of major decisions and Ordinances—some issued only hours before election—ensured that compliance with some was often difficult, if not impossible ... representatives of political parties, candidates and concerned

members of the public had difficulties in even securing copies of these Ordinances. The group found that even senior government officials did not have time to study the changes.[15]

The introduction of personally motivated and biased legislation pertaining to elections notwithstanding, the implementation of even those provisions which are devoid of mala fide intent has often been prejudiced. This invariably occurs because of the involvement of the bureaucracy, police and military force in the election process and the achieving of predetermined results through these institutions.

Caretaker Set-Up

On dissolution of assemblies, a caretaker cabinet is visualised in the Constitution. The rationale of a caretaker government is to make the electoral process transparent, free and fair. In Pakistan the caretaker set-ups

> ... in the past have been grossly abused by the head of the state when prestigious ministerial slots were bestowed upon favourite political parties and allies enabling them to make full use of the state's financial and administrative power and obtain favourable elections results.[16]

Soon after their installation, the credibility of the past caretaker cabinets in Pakistan became questionable, and their conduct was visibly partial and vindictive. The installation of a caretaker set-up to the liking of an 'invisible power' or the mighty president has been the most convenient mechanism for exploiting the statutory framework of the electoral process. For instance, the 1990 elections were manipulated by the Inter Services Intelligence (ISI) for according 'popular legitimacy' to Muhammad Nawaz Sharif. The president and the caretaker government abused their powers to cause the defeat of the Pakistan People's Party (PPP).[17] In the same elections, open executive hostility and bias could be ascertained from the speech on Pakistan Television, of the then President, Ghulam Ishaq Khan, on the night preceding election day declaring that he had given '*ghusl*' (bath) to the dead body (PPP) and now the nation only had to bury it.[18] The abuse of the caretaker cabinets for partisan electoral gains has been highlighted by an analyst:

... except in 1988, caretaker prime ministers formally took control of the government's machinery: Mustafa Jatoi in 1990; Balkh Sher Mazari (April–May) and Moeen Qureshi (July–October) in 1993 and Meraj Khalid in 1996–97. Each of these governments began with an accountability drive which typically lost steam within weeks. The caretaker government was accused of conspiring with the main opposition party to keep the outgoing government out of office....[19]

Money Makes the Mare Go

Pumping of money into election campaigns has assumed notorious dimensions in Pakistani politics. The huge expenditure incurred by candidates and political parties often outmanoeuvres the prescribed official ceilings. Due to

... excess expenditure by the candidates ... the system tilts in favour of those who have the financial means and to actually incur huge expenditure on their election campaign. An election contest, thus, is perceived to be a competition in spending, with the person spending more having better prospects of getting into the elective bodies.[20]

This subject can be divided into the role of money spent by individuals and party candidates themselves, and the role of money spent from the national exchequer for election campaigns of the party in power or any favourite party in an election. On a private level, individuals and party candidates use money in buying voters, excessive wall-chalking, display of banners and posters, and other steps which involve huge sums in electioneering. Consequently false statements of accounts are submitted as a formality to the EC. The use of money hampers the prospects of well meaning, educated and deserving candidates who lack funds to get into Parliament. In this respect civil society has its obligations to fulfil, and its members should monitor campaign expenses, the amounts of money spent by not only the candidates but also their supporters and parties.

On the government level, excessive and illegal monetary patronage has often been extended to particular candidates and their parties. During the Zia era, the nominally empowered government of Muhammad Khan Junejo doled out development funds to legislators to spend in their respective constituencies to keep them well entrenched for future elections. This was indeed a massive step in the introduction of corruption and corrupt election practices by the state itself. The practice was followed by the PPP Government of Benazir Bhutto by providing funds to her party's legislators in the name of 'People Works Programme'. President Ghulam Ishaq Khan and ISI surpassed all others in the abominable practice by pumping state money for propping up the ISI-engineered Islami Jamhuri Ittehad (IJI). When the Nawaz Government came into power, he introduced 'Tamir-e-Watan Programme' on the same pattern.

Civil–Military Bureaucracy, Clergy and Judiciary

In Pakistan, power vests in and is exercised by 'officers'. Even apart from their direct usurpations of political power, military interferences in the political process are often decisive in enthroning or toppling governments through the electoral process. For instance, the military has never allowed constitutional, democratic, electoral and political values/processes to take shape in an uninterrupted fashion. The self-nourishing and self-perpetuating institutions of civil– military bureaucracy have monopolised all levers of government, consequently making a mockery of the democratic, political and election processes in the country. It has justified the dismissal of governments, dissolution of assemblies and abrogation of constitutions on the basis of purging the holy precincts of politics from degraded, corrupt and incompetent politicians and their misrules. The 'heroes' of such missions are eulogised as 'soldier–statesmen' and 'saviours' and have plunged the country into wars, economic disaster, abject poverty, ignorance and socio-political collapse.[21] The military's overwhelming proclivity for interference in national affairs and jealously guarding its financial interests has led political analysts to question the very future of the democratic process in Pakistan.[22] The manipulations of the civil–military bureaucracy to assert its authority over the divided political parties, deny society the benefits of civil rule, grab resources, suppress dissent, thwart elections and abrogate constitutions, have resulted in the perversion of every institution of national importance such as the Parliament. Neither the police nor the civil bureaucracy can act insulated from the influence and direction of the military.

Notwithstanding the systematic induction of army officers into all important civil positions of the government, the military also has its own politico-theological agenda to fulfil. All dictatorships in the country have been wrapped in theological justifications. Those who oppose the continuation of constitutional democracy have invariably used religion as a device to gain power, to condemn others, sustain dogma and perpetuate socio-economic stagnation in the society. Except Jinnah, all rulers exploited religion and appeased the agitating religious elite so as 'to legitimise their authority and to avoid electoral politics and accountability'.[23] Zia surpassed all and got full backing of the clergy which dismissed electoral politics, the Constitution and the Parliament as foreign ideas unsuitable for assimilation in an Islamic state. With this bent of mind, the dictatorial regimes have introduced Hudood Laws, the Council of Islamic Ideology, Majlis-i-Shura, Federal Shariat Court and provisions such as Articles 62 and 63 in the Constitution relating to qualification and disqualification of candidates to be vetted on the theological parameters.

The Zia regime infused the doctrine of jehad into the army and this was 'further developed and remained a driving force for well over two decades'.[24] In the present circumstances, that doctrine is being wrapped up under pressure from the USA—the one-time supporter of the same doctrine in the Soviet–Afghan context. The winding up of the jehadi doctrine has rendered a sizeable number of military officers redundant, and they are ultimately landing in civil positions.[25] Countless army officers have already been inducted into almost every branch of civil administration.[26] When this 'officer class' loaded with its rigid theological orientations interacts with religious parties having the same bent of mind and both engage in trying to persuade the people to return to orthodoxy, the net result would be tremendous pressure on liberal social values in the society.

Besides the politico-theological context, the army's hydra-headed financial stakes in civil affairs could be visualised from the following opinion of a constitutional analyst:

> The army has such a large monetary stake in the country that it will never allow a populist civilian government to interfere with the status quo. A civilian government may be permitted to continue only so far as it does not interfere with the financial interests of the army. Only a revolution may bring about a change in this state of affairs. Any civilian government brought into office by normal sedate democratic channels will neither have the strength nor will it be permitted to pursue a political or economic policy which the military does not regard as conducive to its interests.[27]

Conclusions

Regarding the elections held from 1970 onwards, as per general perceptions and media and foreign observers' comments, the 1970, 1993 and 1997 elections were relatively free and fair. The 1977, 1985, 1988, 1990 and 2002 elections were farcical because of crude rigging through the intelligence agencies, massive misuse of television and radio by the government in power, grotesque spending from the national exchequer for partisan purposes, overwhelmingly biased tone and tenor of administrative actions, and open violation of election laws for personal and base ends. Pakistan has held elections, yet not a single election led to the stability and continuation of the democratic process. Seemingly the elections have been held not to fulfil the democratic aspirations of the people of Pakistan but to lend credence and legitimacy to a certain set of the ruling elite.

Undeniably, there have always been legal and institutional arrangements in place for holding the elections. Elections have been held under these arrangements; some of them can be characterised as fair and transparent and others as massively rigged. Apparently there seems nothing wrong with the statutory framework and institutional arrangements, yet prejudiced practice results in a negative outcome. The penchant of military dictators to govern the country absolutely and without any semblance of accountability via the ballot makes a case for the futility of electoral law.

If the civil–military bureaucracy is the chief malefactor in uprooting constitutional democracy, the political parties themselves are not far behind; some side with the dictators and others sit on the fence and wait for opportune moments. The political parties must put an end to such an organised hypocrisy and keep the political and electoral process in their hands instead of inviting the military to meddle in civil matters for partisan ends.

Pakistan has experimented with various constitutional formulae in the hope that every successive Constitution would be an everlasting sacred national document. However, no Constitution or high treason clause appended therein could discourage the strong men from abrogating it or holding it in abeyance. How can such abhorrent and uncivilised practices be averted? The simple answer is the unswerving resolve of the people to stand against the military dictator's will. Even if the statutory framework for elections is perfected, that would not discourage corrupt and power-hungry individuals and parties from manipulating elections unless right thinking members of civil society, being conscious of their civil rights, resist their evil and illegitimate practices.

Notes

1. Quoted from the 1997 *General Elections Report* (Vol. I), Islamabad, Election Commission of Pakistan, p. 297.
2. Ibid., p. 237.
3. I.A. Rehman, 'The Worse off Non-Muslim Voters,' *Dawn*, Karachi, 28 January 1997.
4. Ibid.
5. See *The News*, Islamabad, 5 May 2002.
6. The age limit in the 1973 Constitution is 21 years but the military government of General Musharraf has reduced it to 18 years.
7. Quoted from the 1997 *General Elections Report,* ibid., p. 30.
8. The condition of identity cards for seeking ballot papers was challenged in the Lahore High Court in a case styled as *Aitzaz and Others vs Chief Election Commissioner and Others* (*PLD 1989 Lahore*) and the Court held that production of identity card was not likely to lead to free and fair elections. On appeal by the Election Commission, the judgement was reversed by the Supreme Court of Pakistan (*PLD 1989 SC 61*).
9. *Electoral Politics in Pakistan, National Assembly Elections 1993*—Report of SAARC–NGO Observers, New Delhi, Vikas Publishing House (Pvt.) Ltd, 1995, p. 36.
10. Jalees I. Haider, 'Were the 1990 Elections Rigged,' *The Frontier Post*, Peshawar, 15 October 1993.
11. Ibid.
12. Under Articles 48 and 58, the national assembly can be dissolved on completion of its tenure, or the prime minister can advise dissolution, or prior to the 13th Amendment in the Constitution, the president could dissolve the national assembly.
13. Faqir Hussain (ed.), *Electoral Reforms in Pakistan*, Islamabad, Friedrich Ebert Stiftung, 1996, p. 49.
14. *Electoral Politics in Pakistan...*, p. 18.
15. Haider, 'Were ... Elections Rigged'.
16. Muhammad Waseem, 'Pakistan Elections 1997: One Step Forward' in Craig, Baxter and Charles Kennedy (eds), *Pakistan—1997*, The American Institute of Pakistan Studies, pp. 1–2.
17. Hussain, *Electoral Reforms*, p. 12.
18. Zulfikar Khalid Maluka, *The Myth of Constitutionalism in Pakistan*, Karachi, Oxford University Press, 1995, p. 137.
19. Ibid., p. 8.
20. Shahwar Junaid, 'Public, Politics and Economic Management,' *The Nation*, Islamabad, 2 May 2002.
21. Ibid.

22. Farrukh Saleem, 'The Rocca Mission,' *The News*, Rawalpindi, 19 May 2002.

23. Makhdoom Ali Khan, '1973 Constitution—The Founding of the Federation,' an unpublished paper read at the seminar, 'The Heritage of Prime Minister Bhutto,' Karachi, 3–5 April 1989, p. 10.

24. Masood Hassan, 'All's Well, Dearie,' *The News*, Islamabad, 5 May 2002 and Kunwar Idris, 'An Unnecessary Referendum,' *Dawn* (Islamabad), 5 May 2002.

25. Farrukh Saleem, 'Is the US Media Changing Direction?', *The News*, Islamabad, 5 May 2002.

26. Ibid.

27. See *The News*, Islamabad, 4 May 2002.

11

SRI LANKA

Dushyantha Mendis

What do we mean when we say that first of all we seek liberty?
I often wonder whether we do not rest our hopes too much upon
Constitutions, upon laws and upon courts. These are false hopes:
believe me, these are false hopes. Liberty lies in the hearts of men
and women: when it dies there, no Constitutions, no law, no court
can save it: no Constitution, no law, no court can even do much
to help it.

—Judge Learned Hand, US Court of Appeals

Universal Suffrage in Sri Lanka*

The present Constitution of Sri Lanka has (through Article 88)
accorded every person the right to be an elector at the election of the
president and of Members of Parliament (MPs), and to vote at any
referendum (unless disqualified under various criteria set out in the

---

*The author gratefully acknowledges the comments and suggestions made by
Professor K.M. de Silva regarding this Chapter.

Constitution itself and provided that such person's name is entered in the register of electors). It is also provided (by Article 93) that the voting for the election of the president and of MPs and at any referendum shall be free, equal and by secret ballot. In a leading fundamental rights case, the Supreme Court has also recognised the right to vote as an integral part of the fundamental rights guaranteed under the Constitution . Rejecting a view urged before the court that there is a clear distinction between the franchise and fundamental rights, the court held that when the freedom of speech and expression is entrenched, it guarantees all forms of speech and expression, including the franchise.[1] As Justice Mark Fernando observed, writing the unanimous judgement of the three-member bench,

> ... the most effective manner in which a voter may give expression to his views, with minimum risk to himself and his family, is by silently marking his ballot paper in the secrecy of the polling booth. The silent and secret expression of a citizen's preference as between one candidate and another by casting his vote is no less an exercise of the freedom of speech and expression, than the most eloquent speech from a political platform. To hold otherwise is to undermine the very foundations of the Constitution.[2]

Sri Lanka is a frontrunner among Third World nations in establishing and maintaining a functioning democracy. Universal suffrage was introduced in Sri Lanka in 1931, only three years after it was finally granted in the United Kingdom itself, and 20 years before it was introduced in India. Women in Sri Lanka had the right to vote long before their counterparts for instance in France, Belgium and Switzerland. In 1935, registration of voters was made compulsory. By the state thus taking over the responsibility for registration of voters, Sri Lanka again placed itself ahead even of some advanced countries where registration is as yet voluntary.

The grant of universal franchise in Sri Lanka took place when the country was still a British colony, and through the implementation of the recommendations of a Constitutional Reform Commission sent out by the British Government, the Donoughmore Commission, named after its head, Lord Donoughmore. It is worth noting that the introduction of universal suffrage took place in spite, rather than because, of any pressure from Sri Lanka's own political elite. The Donoughmore Commission saw universal suffrage as an essential pre-requisite of social advancement: 'In view of the backward character of social and industrial legislation in Ceylon, ... a good case could be made out for regarding the extension of the franchise as more urgent than any increase of responsible government'.[3]

The commissioners also drew a direct link between responsible and representative government: '... we could not recommend a further grant of responsible government unless that government were to be made fully representative of the great body of the people'.[4]

Elective representation to the national legislature had been introduced only in 1910 and then the franchise was severely restricted in terms of income and property qualifications, as it indeed was until the time of the introduction of universal adult franchise. Nevertheless, Sri Lanka's experience of the franchise antedates Sri Lanka's experience of representative government by a wide margin, for there was some experience of it, albeit subject to stringent income and property qualification, in the area of local government. In the municipal councils set up under *Ordinance No. 17 of 1865*, the elected element of the membership exceeded the (government) nominated element. The District Road Committees established under the *Thoroughfares Ordinance No. 10 of 1861* also included an elected membership, as did the Local Boards of Health and Improvement constituted under *Ordinance No. 13 of 1898*, where the number of elected members equalled the number of nominated members.

It has been commented about these local government bodies that 'It would, therefore be more correct to call them extensions of the bureaucracy rather than genuine local government bodies'.[5] The case of the *Gamsabhas*, the village councils established under the *Irrigation Ordinance of 1856*, however, was different.

This was an attempt to revitalise an age-old institution which regulated the affairs of the village, and in 1856 the *Gamsabhas* were given the power to make rules for irrigation and cultivation, subject to the approval of the governor and the Executive Council. The proceedings of the *Gamsabhas* were summary and informal, and fines could be levied for breach of its rules. So successful was this experiment that in 1871 the *Gamsabhas* were vested with some limited powers to settle many disputes within its local area, for instance, those involving agriculture, fisheries, footpaths, village schools, petty crime and so on.[6] It has been said that the franchise for the election of the members of the committee '... was one of the simplest in the history of electoral law';[7] every male inhabitant who had not been convicted of a serious crime within the preceding five years was entitled to vote. Whereas in the early period of the setting up of the *Gamsabhas*, it was the government agent of the province who presided over its meetings, from 1871 it was the chief headman of the area, and from 1924 onwards the chairman of the committee was himself elected.[8]

Thus universal franchise when it came in 1931 would not have had the effect of imposing an alien system on a befuddled populace. There has been only one change in the franchise, in 1959–60, when the voting age was lowered from 21 to 18. Since the first general election of 1931, there have been 15 general elections, and five presidential elections. Nationwide elections for other tiers of government—local and provincial—have also been held with some regularity.

Constitutional Developments 1948–2002: A Brief Outline

The constitutional structure in Sri Lanka at the time of attaining independence was very much on the Westminster Model. The head of state was the British Queen, represented in Sri Lanka by the governor general. The governor general exercised mainly ceremonial functions, but there were some discretionary powers vested in him. These arose because under the Soulbury Constitution, certain powers and functions of the governor general were to be exercised in accordance with the constitutional conventions governing their exercise in the United Kingdom.

The political executive was the Cabinet and the legislature a bicameral one consisting of the House of Representatives and an Upper House, the Senate. The legislature was elected on the first-past-the-post system. A few electorates were multi-member constituencies, and six members were also appointed to represent interests which would otherwise not be represented in Parliament. The Senate was set up in the belief (held by the commission which formulated Sri Lanka's independence Constitution, the Soulbury Commission, so named after its head, Lord Soulbury) that it could make

> ... a valuable contribution to the political education of the general public ... there are in Ceylon, as in other countries, a number of eminent individuals of high intellectual attainment and wide experience of affairs, who are averse to entering political life through the hurly-burly of a parliamentary election. But it would

be an advantage to the country to enjoy the services of men upon whom party or communal ties may be expected to rest more lightly, and who can express their views freely and frankly without feeling themselves constrained to consider the possible repercussions upon their electoral prospects.[9]

There was also another important reason for the setting up of the Senate put forward by the Soulbury Constitution: '... those who, rightly or wrongly, feel themselves menaced by majority action, may regard a Second Chamber not merely as an instrument for impeding precipitate legislation, but as a means of handling inflammatory issues in a cooler atmosphere'.[10]

However the Senate could only delay legislation; it could not prevent it. Finance bills could be delayed for a month, and other bills for one parliamentary session.

The doctrine of the separation of powers was read into the Soulbury Constitution by the Privy Council. In *Liyanage vs The Queen*, the Privy Council observed that 'the importance of securing the independence of judges and maintaining the dividing line between the judiciary and the executive was appreciated by those who framed the Constitution'. The Privy Council went on to point out that significantly, the Constitution was divided into parts (indicating the doctrine of separation of powers), with separate parts dealing with the governor general, the legislature, the executive and the judicature.[11]

Judicial review of legislation was not expressly provided for by the Constitution, but was a power assumed by the courts.[12] That this power was implied by the constitutional history of Sri Lanka was recognised by the Privy Council in its observation about the power of judicial review 'having remained, where it lain for more than a century, in the hands of the judicature'.[13]

Protection for minorities was sought to be provided by Section 29(2) under which no law passed by Parliament

... shall (a) prohibit or restrict the free exercise of any religion; or (b) make any persons of any community or religion liable to disabilities or restrictions to which persons of other communities or religions are not made liable; or (c) confer on persons of any community or religion any privilege or advantage which is not conferred on persons of other communities or religions; or (d) alter the Constitution of any religious body except with the consent of the governing authority of that body....

This provision was held by the Privy Council, then Sri Lanka's highest appellate court, to set out 'entrenched religious and racial matters, which shall not be the subject of legislation. They represent the solemn balance of rights between the citizens of Ceylon, the fundamental conditions on which *inter se* they accepted the Constitution: and these are therefore unalterable under the Constitution'.[14]

The Privy Council had stated this proposition only by way of *obiter dicta*, and it was debatable; for instance in another case, the Privy Council had observed that the Parliament of Ceylon had 'the full legislative powers of a sovereign independent State'.[15] Nevertheless the observations of the Privy Council on Section 29(2) in *Bribery Commissioner vs Ranasinghe* was, as we shall see, to cast a very long shadow over the Constitution itself.

Members of the higher judiciary were appointed by the governor general. The powers of appointment, transfer, dismissal and disciplinary control of other judicial officers were vested in the Judicial Services Commission. This Commission consisted of the chief justice, a judge of the Supreme Court and another person who was, or had been, a judge of the Supreme Court. That the provisions relating to the Judicial Services Commission manifested an intention to secure to the judiciary a freedom from political, legislative and executive control was recognised by the Privy Council.[16]

While the highest appointments in the administrative hierarchy were made by the governor general, the powers of appointment, transfer, dismissal and disciplinary control of public officers were vested in an independent Public Services Commission. The Soulbury Constitution, in its functioning, however, did not perhaps realise its full potential.

The constitutional conventions of the United Kingdom on which the governor general was supposed to act have not been authoritatively codified, and debate is possible about what should be done in particular circumstances. Thus controversies arose in Sri Lanka about the appointment by the governor general of the prime minister both in 1952 and in 1960, and regarding the dissolution of Parliament in the latter year.

As regards the Senate, Joseph A.L. Cooray points out that

From the inception ... many of its members were selected not so much on the basis of merit as on service rendered to the party in power. Criticism had been made on the ground that there had been far too little of the careful and efficient scrutiny or the mature discussion of legislative measures that one was inclined to expect of a revising Chamber. The occasions on which its debates had reached a high standard, free from party politics, had been relatively few and far between.[17]

Of the Soulbury constitutional structure, the first to go was the Senate, abolished in 1972, with its passing regretted by none (other than perhaps its own members).

The Public Service Commission was subject to unforeseen pressures.

The difficulty that had arisen was mainly the result of having hitched an Independent Public Service Commission on to a Constitution that had to be worked on the principle of ministerial responsibility. In fact, the tragedy of the Public Service Commission was that under the Constitution it was expected, like Janus, to face both ways at the same time—in the direction of public service independence from ministerial control over appointments, transfers, dismissals and disciplinary control, as well as in the opposite direction, giving effect to the principle of ministerial responsibility to Parliament for the acts of the public service.[18]

Section 29(2) would also appear to have been a disappointment. For instance, the *Ceylon Citizenship Act, 1948* and the *Parliamentary Elections Act, 1949* were effective in disenfranchising the vast bulk of Indian Tamil plantation workers, relatively recent immigrants, by a relatively restrictive definition of citizenship. The Privy Council held that the relevant legislation was on citizenship and could not be said to be making persons of the Indian Tamil community liable to a disability to which persons of other communities were not made liable.[19]

K.M. de Silva has pointed out two other instances where minority groups were discomfited under the Soulbury Constitution.

When S.W.R.D. Bandaranaike's Official Language Act[20] was introduced in the House of Representatives in 1956, the Speaker ruled that it was not a Constitutional amendment and therefore required only a simple majority. In 1960 the Roman Catholics found to their dismay that the Constitution provided no protection for them in their campaign to preserve the *status quo* in education.[21]

It appears that the government could have driven a coach and six through Section 29(2) almost at will.

An effort to amend the Constitution was commenced in 1959 with the appointment of a Joint Parliamentary Select Committee in 1957, and although that effort came to nought, both major parties represented in Parliament, the United National Party (UNP) and the Sri Lanka Freedom Party (SLFP) held the view, throughout the 1960s, that the Constitution should be amended. However, ultimately in 1972 what took place was not the amendment of an existing Constitution but the adoption and enactment of a new Constitution, and this was done by a United Front (UF) Government consisting of the SLFP and small left wing parties.

Where the Soulbury Constitution came a cropper was in an intersection of Section 29(2) with the power of judicial review. Section 29(2) was in any case anathema to the SLFP, the party which was instrumental in bringing the assertion of the rights of the majority Sinhalese and Buddhists to the fore in the agenda of the 'national' political parties in Sri Lanka. What made it of immediate and acute concern was a 1969 case, *Kodeeswaran vs The Attorney General*, an action brought by a public officer against the government (represented by the attorney general) for an increment of salary not granted to him on the basis that he had not passed a mandatory proficiency test in the use of the Sinhala language. Among the contentions of the plaintiff was that the *Official Language Act, 1956* was unconstitutional and void, and accordingly the government had no basis on which to insist that he pass a proficiency test in Sinhala. The District Court[22] held with him. The Supreme Court[23] held that it was not necessary to rule on the matters raised by the plaintiff because in any event a public servant could not sue for an increment in salary. The Privy Council[24] overruled the Supreme Court on the latter point and sent the case back for decision on the original issues.

Kodeeswaran's case was to give point and impetus to the efforts to draft a new Constitution. As the then Minister of Constitutional Affairs, Colvin R. de Silva observed in the Constituent Assembly:[25]

... 15 years after the event the position is that the Official Language Act is under challenge in the courts, the only judgment by any competent Court on this matter being the judgment of the District Court that the Official Language Act is invalid, and in the meantime, quite rightly, the government of Ceylon continues to apply the Official Language Act, for the matter is in appeal and therefore the decision is not binding on the Crown.... If we have

this power (of judicial review of the constitutionality of legislation), if the courts do declare this law invalid ... the chief work
from 1956 onwards will be undone. You will have to restore the
egg from the omelette into which it was beaten and cooked.

The irresistible force of Sinhala language policy would appear
then to have swept away the seemingly immovable object, Section
29(2), and in fact the entire Soulbury Constitution.

The device of the Constituent Assembly—an extra-constitutional
proceeding—was perhaps resorted to get over the problem of the
pronunciamento of the Privy Council in *Bribery Commissioner vs
Ranasinghe*, that Section 29 was unalterable under the existing constitution. The Constituent Assembly also carried a certain cachet in
marking a break with the constitutional structure inherited from the
British colonial rulers. The UF Government could select this option
because it was blessed with a parliamentary two-thirds majority in
a first-past-the-post electoral system. The fact that the share of total
votes it received was considerably smaller than the number of seats
it won, did not communicate itself to the UF government as indicating the absence of a national political consensus for a new Constitution.

The constitutional structure devised in 1972 has been described
as a 'centralised democracy in which the dominant element is the
political executive, which has few institutional checks on its use of
political power'.[26] The 1972 Constitution, like the Soulbury Constitution, used the system of parliamentary executive, that is, the Cabinet form of government. However, any significant similarities
between the two Constitutions ended there.

The head of state was now the president, but the president was the
nominee of the prime minister. The president's office was diminished in other ways as well, by reducing his discretionary power. For
instance the rules for dissolution of Parliament were now spelt out
in the Constitution.

The new Constitution did away absolutely with the doctrine of
the separation of powers. The unicameral national state assembly
was declared the supreme instrument of state power of the republic.
The Assembly exercised (*a*) the legislative power of the people;
(*b*) the executive power of the people, including the defence of Sri
Lanka, through the president and the cabinet of ministers; and (*c*) the
judicial power of the people through the courts and other institutions
created by law except in the case of matters relating to the powers
and privileges of the national state assembly. Provision for members

appointed to represent special interests otherwise unrepresented in Parliament was done away within the new Constitution. Elections were still however on the first-past-the-post system and the multi-member constituencies were continued.

Appointments to the higher judiciary continued to be made by the head of state, but now the president was required to act on the advice of the prime minister or a minister authorised by the prime minister to advice the president on those matters. The Judicial Services Commission was abolished, and two new bodies set up, the Judicial Services Advisory Board and the Judicial Services Disciplinary Board. The former body made recommendations to the Cabinet on judicial appointments, but the Cabinet was not bound by such advice, though it had to take responsibility for its decision before the National State Assembly. The Judicial Services Disciplinary Board acted subject to rules made in consultation with the Cabinet, but its decisions could not be debated by the national state assembly.

The Public Service Commission was abolished, and the Cabinet vested with the authority for the appointment, transfer, dismissal and disciplinary control of all public servants. It has been pointed out that in fact 'this change cannot be looked upon as drastic; it merely gave constitutional force to what was by then normal practice'.[27]

Judicial review of the constitutionality of legislation was expressly prohibited by the Constitution, but an innovation, not entirely original, was introduced; a Constitutional Court was set up to rule on the constitutionality of legislation enacted by the national state assembly. The Constitutional Court could be moved by a wide variety of parties, but within a week of the bill being impugned having been placed on the agenda of the Assembly. The Court was also required to give its determination within two weeks of the question having been referred to it.

Section 29 of the Soulbury Constitution disappeared, but a chapter on fundamental rights and freedoms was incorporated in the Constitution. The fundamental rights sought to be protected included the equality of all persons before the law, non-discrimination in public employment on the grounds of religion, race, caste or sex, freedom of thought, conscience and religion, protection of life and personal liberty, freedom of speech, of peaceful assembly, and association and freedom of movement and residence. However, this statement of fundamental rights turned out to have very little effect in practice; a select committee of the national state assembly appointed to consider proposals for the revision of the Constitution in 1977 pointed out the three major criticisms of the chapter in the 1972 Constitution on fundamental rights: '... that the rights recognised were limited in scope, that they were subject to restrictions which were so wide as almost to nullify the grant of fundamental rights and their enforcement was not guaranteed in the Constitution'.[28]

One of the most notable things that were done with the introduction of the 1972 Constitution was that the UF Government took the opportunity to extend the life of the sitting Parliament by a further two years, an action 'probably unprecedented in the annals of Constitution making in democratic States'.[29] An area of increasing concern was the use of the *Public Security Ordinance of 1947*. Sections 3 and 8 of the ordinance have the effect that the decision to declare a state of emergency, and all regulations, orders, rules and directions made under the ordinance, cannot be questioned in a court of law. Section 7 of the ordinance provides that regulations made under the ordinance prevail over all other laws except the Constitution. It was the head of state who under the Soulbury Constitution could declare a state of emergency. Under the 1972 Constitution, almost all the powers which were vested in the head of state under the ordinance were firmly vested in the head of the political executive. What was troubling was that the government did not scruple to make tendentious use of the emergency powers.

In 1977, the UNP was elected in its turn with a two-thirds majority, but this time with a clear majority of total votes cast at the elections—50.9 per cent. The constitutional changes they made through the second republican Constitution introduced by them in 1978 were much more significant—and positive—than those made through the 1972 Constitution.

Under the 1978 Constitution, (*a*) the legislative power of the people is exercised by their elected representatives and by the people directly at a referendum; (*b*) the judicial power of the people is exercised by Parliament through the courts and other institutions set up by law; and (*c*) the executive power of the people is exercised by an elected president.

While sovereignty is vested in the people as in the 1972 Constitution, this sovereignty is protected by requiring that some basic provisions of the Constitution such as those relating to the term of office of the president, the duration of Parliament and certain fundamental rights can only be changed with the consent of the people at a referendum. One major innovation of the 1978 Constitution is

a strong executive presidency. The powers entrusted to the president
are indeed wide.

The president is head of state, head of the executive and of the
government, and commander-in-chief of the armed forces. The president appoints the prime minister (though here his discretion is fet-
tered to the extent that he is constitutionally required to appoint the
person most likely to secure a majority in Parliament) and other
ministers, and assigns their subjects and functions which he may
again change. Until the 17th Amendment to the Constitution in
2002, the president appointed the chief justice and other judges of
the superior courts and the head of the police. He also appoints other
senior officials including the heads of the army, navy and air force
and ambassadors. The president is vested with the absolute power of
recognising foreign states and governments and the executive power
to enter into treaties is not conditional on the passing of legislation.
The president is also immune from suit for any act or omission done
in his official or private capacity. Removal of the president from
office requires an impeachment process and a two-thirds majority in
Parliament, a condition at first glance unlikely to be fulfilled if the
president's own party is in power in Parliament.

Concern focused almost immediately the new Constitution was
announced on the vast powers of the president, and these powers
have remained a source of concern ever since. Often overlooked in
much discourse which attempts to cast the executive presidency as
an unfettered Leviathan is that in fact some important checks and
balances do operate on the presidency, subtle, no doubt, but no less
real for that.

For instance, two of the five executive presidents of Sri Lanka
have been stymied at one point or another by the workings of the
political process in Sri Lanka. (One of them merely completed the
term of his predecessor who had been assassinated, and the fifth is,
at the time of writing, only eight months into his term.) President R.
Premadasa was faced with the threat of an impeachment process in
1991 from an apparently substantial block of his own parliamentary
group. In July 2001 President Chandrika Kumaratunga, faced with
a vote of no-confidence on her government which had every chance
of success in Parliament, prorogued Parliament and scheduled a
referendum asking the people whether they want a new Constitution.
The resulting popular outcry made it impossible for her to proceed
with that desperate ploy. In December 2001, with the United National Front (UNF)—previously the main party in opposition to the
president's parliamentary power base, the People's Alliance

(PA)—obtaining a majority in Parliament, the president apparently found it politically impossible to exercise her discretionary powers of appointment of ministers and assignment of their subjects and functions.

Subsequently however, the president arrogated some key ministries for herself in 2003, and in 2004 dissolved the Parliament. This dissolution was probably unprecedented in the annals of parliamentary history, for though the president was constitutionally empowered to dissolve the Parliament, the governing party in Parliament had a working majority and had not been defeated on either the budget or on a confidence motion. More recently, as we shall note further on in this chapter, an application for a writ of mandamus to compel the president to make appointments to the Election Commission (EC) (under the 17th Amendment to the Constitution, again discussed further on) foundered on the doctrine of presidential immunity from suit. Thus there would appear to be a case for re-examining the ambit, scope and extent of presidential power in Sri Lanka.

However, the fact is that it is very difficult to protect against each and every such abuse, the only effective protection being public opinion and the high standards of conduct which holders of high office should set themselves. Limitations on the president's immunity from suit, and its ramifications in the field of executive action, have been clearly delineated by the Supreme Court.

> Article 35 (the article of the Constitution dealing with the immunity from suit of the President) only prohibits the institution (or continuation) of legal proceedings *against* the President *while* in office; it imposes no bar whatsoever on proceedings (*a*) against him when he is no longer in office, and (*b*) other persons at any time ... it does not exclude judicial review of the lawfulness or propriety of an impugned act or omission, in appropriate proceedings against some other person who does not enjoy immunity from suit; as, for instance, a defendant or respondent who relies on an act done by the President, in order to justify his own conduct.[30]

The 1978 Constitution has reined in what has been described as 'almost an executive dictatorship which could silence Parliament and the opposition during a state of emergency.'[31] The imposition of a state of emergency is now debated in and voted on by Parliament on the first available occasion after such imposition, and if a state of emergency is in operation for a period of 90 days in a period of six calendar months, it cannot be prolonged for more than 10 days in the following six months without the approval of a two-thirds majority in Parliament. A major departure of the 1978 Constitution was in the introduction of proportional representation (PR) in legislative elections in place of the first-past-the-post system which had prevailed up to that time. This will be further discussed at an appropriate stage further on.

The independence of the judiciary was originally (that is, prior to the 17th Amendment) safeguarded in two ways. The judges of the superior courts were appointed by the president, but could only be removed for proved misbehaviour or incapacity, and the president could make an order only on address of the majority of MPs. No resolution for the presentation of such an address could be proceeded with unless it was signed by at least one third of the total number of MPs. (These requirements for the removal of members of the higher judiciary still remain.) The judges of the lower courts are subject to the control of a body titled, once again, the Judicial Services Commission, consisting of the chief justice and two other judges of the Supreme Court.

The president's discretionary power to appoint judges of the superior courts was also restricted to some extent by a 1996 ruling of the Supreme Court.[32] There the Supreme Court held that the president's discretion to appoint judges to the Supreme Court was not unfettered, and the president was required to consult the chief justice before an appointment was made. Exclusive jurisdiction to hear and determine any question relating to the interpretation of the Constitution is vested in the Supreme Court, which must determine any such question within a period of two months.

The appointment of the most senior officials is, as we have seen, in the hands of the president. The 1978 Constitution continued the practice adopted by the 1972 Constitution of vesting appointment of heads of departments in the Cabinet. Appointment and control of other officials could be delegated by the ministers to the Public Service Commission.

The 17th Amendment to the Constitution passed by Parliament in 2001 makes some important changes in the method of making appointments to the higher judiciary and also the appointment and control of specified public servants. These changes will be discussed at a more appropriate stage further on.

The executive presidency has implicitly strengthened the hands of the minorities in Sri Lanka. Each of the two major political parties in Sri Lanka generally receives around 30–35 per cent of the total vote at parliamentary elections. However, the presidency is won on the basis of an absolute majority, and in order to secure this the president must have appeal to both the minorities and those whose allegiance is generally to other political parties. Indeed it has been noted that

> ... previous elections were won or lost in the Sinhalese areas, and the major parties could ignore the north of the island. This situation has changed since the 1980s, and the experience of the presidential elections held so far shows that no party or individual aiming at the presidency could afford to alienate the minorities, or fail to campaign in the Tamil areas of the north and east, as well as among the Indian plantation workers.[33]

However, in the 2005 presidential elections a large number of voters from predominantly minority areas were prevented from voting by the armed militant group operating in those areas, the Liberation Tigers of Tamil Eelam (LTTE). Of the two districts of the Northern Province, the voter turnout was only 1.21 per cent in the Jaffna district and 34.3 per cent in the Vanni district, whereas the average turnout in the other provinces was 78.6 per cent.

Even otherwise the 1978 Constitution has gone very far in asserting the rights of minorities. It has been said to have gone 'furthest in the effort to meet Tamil demands. Various provisions for the official use of the Tamil language and fundamental rights for the protection, among other things, of minority religious and ethnic groups were incorporated in the various chapters of the Constitution'.[34] A measure of devolution of powers and functions from the central government to the provinces through the setting up of Provincial Councils was attempted by the 13th Amendment to the Constitution passed by Parliament in 1987.

Perhaps the greatest contribution of the 1978 Constitution in terms of contributing to individual rights and freedoms is in the area of fundamental rights; every person is entitled to apply to the Supreme Court in respect of the infringement or imminent infringement, by executive or administrative action, of a fundamental right to which he is entitled under the Constitution. As we shall see, this provision has been of incalculable importance in preventing infringement of fundamental rights of voters in Sri Lanka by the executive.

The Constitutions of Sri Lanka would appear to have, over time, increasingly recognised the rights and freedoms of individuals.

Nevertheless, the right to vote and the right to a free, equal and secret ballot have sometimes been seriously impinged upon in Sri Lanka, and the next section will discuss how this has been done. Elections will be discussed under the categories (*a*) presidential; (*b*) parliamentary; (*c*) provincial; (*d*) local elections and (*e*) the referendum.

The Right to Vote Abridged? Elections in Sri Lanka

1. Presidential Elections

Presidential elections are conducted under the *Presidential Elections Act* (*No. 15 of 1981*), as amended from time to time.

1.1 Method of Election

These elections are decided on the basis of an absolute majority. Several candidates may compete, but at the end of the first count, if no candidate obtains 50 per cent of the vote, all candidates other than the first and second in terms of the votes secured are eliminated from the count, and the votes cast for the first and second candidates as second and third preferences in the ballots cast for the candidates eliminated from the count are counted in a second count and added to the total of votes cast for the first two candidates. In no presidential election in Sri Lanka has it been necessary to go in for a second count.

1.2 A Standing Invitation to Mayhem? Challenging a Presidential Election

The ground on which the election of a candidate as president is avoided is set out in the *Presidential Elections Act*, Section 90, '... by his conviction for any corrupt or illegal practice'. These practices are spelt out in great detail in the Act, but it is difficult to think how such a conviction could be obtained given the immunity from suit of the president.

The method by which the election of a candidate to the office of president shall be declared to be void is on an election petition heard by a five-member bench of the Supreme Court. The grounds on proof of which the election shall be declared void are set out in Section 91(a) to (e) of the *Presidential Elections Act*.

The only petition ever heard by the Supreme Court against the election of a president was *Sirimavo Bandaranaike vs Ranasinghe Premadasa and Chandananda de Silva*.[35] In this case Sirimavo Bandaranaike, the candidate who finished in second place in the presidential election of 1988, challenged the election of Ranasinghe Premadasa as president, basing herself on Section 91(a) and (b), which read as follows:

(*a*) that by reason of general bribery, general treating, or general intimidation, or other misconduct, or other circumstances, whether similar to those before enumerated or not, the majority of electors were or may have been prevented from electing the candidate they preferred;

(*b*) non-compliance with the provisions of this Act relating to elections, if it appears that the election was not conducted in accordance with the principles laid down in such provisions and that such non-compliance affected the result of the election.

Sirimavo Bandaranaike preferred three charges, based on Section 91(a) and (b); the first was that of general intimidation [Section 91(a)], the second that of non-compliance with the provisions of the Act relating to elections [Section 91(b)], and the third, 'other circumstances' [Section 91(a)], that is, the failure of the commissioner of elections (the 2nd respondent) and/or certain members of his staff to conduct a free and fair election, in accordance with the provisions of the Act. It was alleged that due to each of these reasons, the majority of electors were or may have been prevented from electing the candidate of their choice. The second charge was abandoned by the counsel for the petitioner in his closing address. This left only the first and second charges, based on Section 91(a).

Now, it is straightaway apparent that Section 91(a) is, in the terms of the layman, tautologous, for it follows that if there has, in fact, been general bribery, general treating or general intimidation, then the majority of electors would have been prevented from electing the candidate they preferred. However, in legal terms it is necessary to give a definition of what 'general intimidation' means, and that is what the latter part of Section 91(a) does. The alternative course is to allow the judiciary to determine for itself exactly what a situation of 'general intimidation' may mean. However, this implies that the judiciary would have to legislate on matters of acute political concern, and that option is therefore hardly practical, ignoring the question as to how desirable it may be (which, in the opinion of the present writer, is, not at all). For the benefit of the uninitiated, it must also be pointed out that it is not open to court to hold that a piece of legislation appears to be tautologous and that, therefore, they will concentrate merely on that part of the particular piece of legislation which they think is relevant; court cannot do this because it is here bound by the rule of statutory interpretation which requires that meaning and purpose be assigned to every word in a piece of legislation. Taking the section as it stands therefore, whether the majority of electors were prevented from electing the candidate of their choice must be proved in order for the election to be declared void on the grounds of 'general intimidation' and so on.

This was in fact exactly what the Supreme Court held in *Sirimavo Bandaranaike vs Ranasinghe Premadasa and Chandananda de Silva*; in its judgement, the Supreme Court held as a 'clear, categorical and unequivocal ruling on the key words in Section 91(a) of the Act,' the following paragraph from a preliminary order which court had issued:

> ... it seems to us that on the basis of instances or acts of general intimidation established by evidence, the court may draw a reasonable inference there from that the majority of electors may have been prevented from electing the candidate of their choice. In a case of general intimidation, the question that arises is—from the proved acts of intimidation of electors, is it reasonable to suppose that the result of the election may have been affected? This, it seems to us, to be the true meaning of the words 'the majority of the electors may have been prevented from electing the candidate they preferred. But it will be open to the returned candidate to show that the gross intimidation could not possibly have affected the result of the election....[36]

The court's reasoning as regards the charge of 'other circumstances' was similar; 'We have already held, in accordance with the ruling of this court in the preliminary order, that the burden is on the petitioner to prove that by reason of the "other circumstances", the result of the election may have been affected'.[37] In making these rulings, the Supreme Court was only doing exactly as it had to do under the law. In the event, of the evidence presented in the Supreme Court falling short of the required proof, the petition was dismissed.

However, it may be questioned as to when, if ever, it can be proved in a court of law, that, for instance, general intimidation had the effect of preventing the majority of electors from electing the candidate they preferred. It could be asked whether the wording of the Act has not in fact placed an impossible burden on the petitioner. The origin of Sections 91(a) and (b) is extremely interesting; it is, as the Supreme Court noted in *Bandaranaike vs Premadasa*,[38] exactly the same wording as was used in Sections 77(a) and (b) of the *Ceylon (Parliamentary Elections) Order in Council, 1946*. In fact the Supreme Court, in *Bandaranaike vs Premadasa*, studiously applied precedents from parliamentary election petition cases to the reasoning in the particular case at hand. It may be pointed out that again, they had no choice in the matter, the wording in the two pieces of legislation being the same.

However, it is important to note that the criteria for declaring the election to a parliamentary seat void is now applied to the election of the president which is held islandwide and it may be questioned as to how realistic it is to expect laws which were designed to deal with problems arising in the geographically limited area of a parliamentary seat to succeed in dealing with the totally different challenges that are posed by an islandwide presidential election. The complete uselessness of Section 91 was well recognised when the UNP, having filed a petition against the election of the president in 1999, withdrew it shortly afterwards.

Thus the more ruthless type of candidate could move into the presidency serenely unperturbed by the general intimidation, non-compliance with election laws and so on, that may have got him or her there, secure in the knowledge that no effective legal challenge can be posed against his or her election. This legal position is in fact a standing invitation to mayhem at the time of a presidential election. It is not an invitation which has been accepted by all political parties and candidates, however.

It is interesting to speculate as to why the legal provisions determining election petitions in presidential elections are so weak; stupidity and inertia would not do as explanations in a country widely regarded as being of some political sophistication. Neither would the prospect of making cynical misuse of the absence of effective legal provisions in future presidential elections alone account for the continued existence of these provisions.

These provisions become all the more curious—and apparently inexplicable—considering the fact that an apparently more appropriate wording is available in Section 92(a) of the *Parliamentary Elections Act (No. 1 of 1981):*

> ... that by reason of general bribery, general treating or general intimidation or other misconduct or other circumstances whether similar to those enumerated before or not a section of electors was prevented from voting for the recognised political party or independent group which it preferred and thereby materially affected the result of the election.

This section would appear to be an advance on the corresponding section in the *Presidential Elections Act*, and it could be asked why that wording could not be applied in the latter Act. The only logical reason that comes to mind is that such a wording in the *Presidential Elections Act* would make any election petition necessarily successful in a situation where a large part of the north of the country is controlled by a terrorist group. That is of course only speculation, but it is an interesting question as to whether one could ever bring in provisions with 'teeth' if not 'bite' to the *Presidential Elections Act* in that type of situation. If the answer is in the negative, that would provide yet another instance of the not only corrosive, but outright destructive effects on Sri Lanka of its long war against the northern terrorist group.

2. Parliamentary Elections

These are conducted under the *Parliamentary Elections Act, No. 1 of 1981* (as amended from time to time). The Parliaments of Sri Lanka under the Soulbury Constitution (that is, up to 1972) comprised two types of representatives, elected and appointed. The elected representatives themselves comprised two categories, those elected from single-member constituencies—these comprised the vast bulk of the representatives—and those elected from multi-member constituencies. The latter were devised to provide for significant concentrations of minorities—religious, ethnic, and from 1947 to 1959, caste as well—in areas which would otherwise be dominated by the majority community. In a multi-member constituency, each elector would be entitled to as many votes as there were seats for that particular electorate; for instance, in a three-seat constituency each voter would be entitled to cast three votes each, and these could be cast in whatever manner the voter thought fit, all in favour of one candidate or each in favour of three different candidates. Under the Soulbury Constitution, six members were also appointed in each Parliament to represent interests which would otherwise be under-represented or not represented.

Under the 1972 Constitution, there were no appointed members. All members were elected, still on the first-past-the-post system, and multi-member constituencies yet continued.

2.1 Delimitation of Electorates under the First-Past-the-Post System

Under both the Soulbury Constitution and the 1972 Constitution, the demarcation of the nine administrative provinces of Sri Lanka into electoral constituencies on the basis of two principles was entrusted to delimitation commissions which were periodically appointed following the usual decennial census. The two principles involved in the delimitation of constituencies (apart from the fact that the administrative provinces were to form the basis of delimitation) were:

(i) There was to be one electoral constituency for every 75,000 persons.

(ii) Additionally there was to be a constituency for every 1,000 miles of square area.

As K.M. de Silva has pointed out, this formula was a compromise—a 'squaring of the circle'—between territorial representation as demanded by the majority Sinhalese and a more ethnically balanced representation as demanded by the Tamil minority.[39] These dichotomous demands were met by the formula already noted in several ways.

On the one hand,[40] determination of seats on the basis of population attempted to satisfy Sinhalese demands; the disenfranchisement of a large part of the Indian Tamil estate labour force, coupled with the carving out of electorates on the basis of population gave an advantage to the rural Sri Lankan voter in the central hill country. On the other hand, demarcating an additional constituency for each 1,000 sq miles resulted in, for instance, the densely populated Western Province getting only one additional constituency whereas the Northern Province, with a large Tamil population, the Eastern Province, with a mixed population of Tamils, Sinhalese and Muslims, and the largely Sinhalese but relatively less-populated North–Central Province getting four additional constituencies each.

This basis of delimitation was used in all parliamentary elections up to 1977. By 1978, Parliament consisted of 168 members elected from 160 constituencies. The 1978 Constitution, however, introduced an entirely new system for electing MPs, the PR system, and under this system an entirely new basis was adopted of demarcating not electorates, but electoral districts.

2.2 Demarcation of Electoral Districts under the Proportional Representation (PR) System

Under the PR system the administrative province yet remains the basis for the demarcation of electorates. Under the terms of the Constitution, there shall be not less than 20 and not more than 24 electoral districts. Each province of Sri Lanka may itself constitute an electoral district or it may be divided into two or more electoral districts. Where a province is divided into a number of electoral districts, regard shall be had to the existing administrative districts so as to ensure as far as is practicable that each electoral district shall be an administrative district or a combination of two or more administrative districts or that two or more electoral districts shall together constitute an administrative district. Accordingly, the nine provinces of Sri Lanka have been divided into 22 electoral districts.

The number of representatives now sent to Parliament is determined as follows:

(i) There are a total of 160 representatives from the different electoral districts. In order to ascertain how many representatives should be sent from each electoral district, the first step is to obtain what is known as the 'qualifying number'; the total number of registered voters is divided by 160. The total number of voters in each electoral district is then divided by the 'qualifying number' and the result indicates the number of representatives that particular electoral district is to return. If all 160 seats have not been allocated among the different electoral districts following this exercise being carried out for all electoral districts, the remaining seats are allocated on the basis of the greatest remainder. Thus 160 seats are allocated annually among the different electoral districts on the basis of the number of registered voters in each district.

(ii) Thirty-six seats are allocated in the proportion of four per province, and these seats are allocated equitably among the electoral districts of the province. In this provision we see a vestige of the old system of giving weightage on the area basis. However, whereas under the old area basis the Northern and Eastern Provinces got eight out of a total of 25 area seats, under the PR system they still get eight, but it is now eight out of 36.[41]

(iii) Twenty-nine members are elected in proportion to the total number of votes polled at the national level—the so called 'national list' MPs.

Thus Parliament now comprises 225 representatives.

2.3 Proportional Representation

This system was introduced to do away with the wild distortions created by the first-past-the-post system in translating the popular will into the number of seats each political party receives at elections. As the 1978 Parliamentary Select Committee on the revision of the Constitution[42] pointed out, at the general election of 1970 the SLFP with 36.9 per cent of the vote secured 91 or 60.3 per cent of parliamentary seats, whereas the UNP with 37.9 per cent of the total vote secured only 17 or 11.3 per cent of parliamentary seats. In 1977, the boot was on the other foot; the UNP, with 50.9 per cent of the total vote secured 140 or 83.3 per cent of parliamentary seats, whereas the SLFP, with 29.7 per cent of the total vote secured eight or 4.8 per cent of parliamentary seats.

As we have seen, Sri Lanka is now demarcated into 22 electoral districts. The nomination list for an electoral district of any political party or group of independents contesting an election should contain a number of candidates equal to the number of seats in that particular district plus one-third of that number. These candidates are each identified by a number, allocated by listing the candidates in (the English) alphabetical order.

At the election, the ballot paper requires voters to vote for the party or group they support, and then they may mark not more than three preferences separately for three different candidates identified by number. Every political party and group contesting the electoral district is required to obtain at least 5 per cent of the total votes cast in order to have any of their representatives elected.

At the count, the votes polled by the political parties and groups who have polled less than the statutory minimum are deducted from the total votes cast in that particular electoral district. This deduction yields the 'relevant number of votes'. This latter number is then divided by the number of seats in that electoral district minus one. The result is the 'resulting number' or 'quota'. (If the result is or includes a fraction, then the figure is rounded off to the integer immediately higher than the relevant fraction.) The number of votes received in that electoral district by each political party and group (which has obtained the statutory minimum percentage of votes) is then divided by the 'quota', and this yields the number of seats each party and group is entitled to. Seats yet to be allocated to a political party or group after the completion of the preceding exercise are allocated on the basis of the greatest remainder. The party or group which polls the highest number of votes in that electorate is awarded a 'bonus' seat (which is why the 'resulting number' is obtained by dividing the 'relevant number of votes' by the number of seats in the electorate minus one). Who in each party or group will occupy the seats allocated to such party or group is decided on the basis of the preferences each candidate has received.

When PR was first introduced to Sri Lanka, there was no provision for voters to mark their preferences for individual candidates, and the seats were filled on the basis of the list put forward by the party. Apart from being criticised for taking away from the voter the right to choose his individual representative, filling of seats by the party hierarchy alone also led to frictions within the parties themselves. The system of marking preferences was therefore introduced in 1983.

The cut-off point for elimination of the votes of parties polling less than the statutory minimum was originally fixed at 12.5 per cent. Criticism that this discriminates against small political parties led to a change in 1988 when the cut-off point was reduced to 5 per cent.

The advantages and disadvantages of PR may now be briefly examined. The greatest advantage of PR has been in that it has brought to an end the wild electoral swings experienced under the first-past-the-post system. While doing this, the Sri Lankan system has not produced the type of hung or paralysed Parliament which is the usual bane of PR systems manifested in nearly all other countries which have adopted that system. Here the system of awarding 'bonus seats', something the critics of PR love to hate, would appear to have played an important role in providing some of the benefits of stable government offered by the first-past-the-post system.

Proportional representation has also been of tremendous benefit to religious and ethnic minorities. A change of central importance is in the method of determining the voting strength of electoral districts—from 'population' to 'registered electors'.[43] Thus the advantage given to the rural Sinhalese voter which we have noted in our discussion of the delimitation of constituencies has now been removed, and the minorities in the north and east are somewhat better off in the number of representatives they can elect. Of even greater significance is that concentrations of minorities in majority dominated areas are now much better placed to have elected representatives of their choice.

Another important advantage of PR is that the danger of victimisation of electorates for electing a representative from the party in opposition, very real under the first-past-the-post system, is now appreciably reduced, because it is hardly likely that under PR, an entire electoral district could be carried by one political party only.

One of the greatest advantages of the PR system may be what is commonly held up as its greatest weakness; the breaking up of the link between a particular electorate and the member specifically representing it. Though much bemoaned, it may yet be one of the healthiest contributions of the PR system to Sri Lanka, in liberating an MP from purely local concerns and demands.

Much criticism has been levelled at the absence of scope for the exercise of conscience by those elected under the PR system;[44] Sri Lankan courts have consistently upheld the sacking from the party, and therefore from Parliament, of representatives who have not toed the party line, except in instances where the principles of natural justice have not been observed. This criticism ignores some important points. First, the representative is clearly elected as a representative of a party; it is by virtue of his party nominating him or her that he or she has been elected. Thus it should come as no surprise that such a representative should be subject to party discipline. Second, there are many situations where collective interests take precedence over individual interests; the notion that a member must adhere to the discipline of his party is no more exceptionable than for instance that of the collective responsibility of Cabinet. Third, those afflicted with a bad attack of conscience in fact have a safe, simple and sure remedy ready at hand—resignation from party and Parliament. Where it is commonly alleged in Sri Lanka that many bouts of bad conscience in MPs are activated by monetary blandishments, resignation would prove the purity of the holder of the conscience. Those who criticise the absence of a provision for conscience in the PR system are in fact effectively saying that an MP should not only have his conscience, but also his parliamentary salary, perks and privileges intact as well. In a situation where the conscience has been activated by monetary blandishments, what is required to be intact then is not only the conscience of the MP, but also his parliamentary salary, perks and privileges *plus* the monetary or other benefit! Thus, if the critics have their way, conscience, even if it doth not make cowards of us all, would at least make a few of us rich, and that beyond the dreams of avarice.

The PR system has indeed had a couple of notable ill effects, but in the nature of things, little can be done about them. Campaigning has now to be done on the level not of the electorate, but of the electoral district which would comprise several electorates. Thus those candidates hailing from larger electorates (that is, in terms of the number of registered electors) are at an advantage over those from smaller electorates, assuming in both cases that they are able to carry their electorates. Second, the highly competitive quest for the voter's preferences leads to intra-party rivalries which sometimes take violent turns. Third, those who have larger campaign resources are at a distinct advantage over their less well-endowed brethren. The need for large resources also leads to many political IOUs being given for campaign funding, and this leads directly to corruption.

While it is known that these disadvantages are present, what is not known is to what extent they have—exclusively—blighted the political landscape. Intra-party squabbling for nominations could in any case take violent turns even under a first-past-the-post system, in an era where violence is readily resorted to, to resolve many problems. Campaigns will consume vast resources, and political IOUs will be given whatever system of representation is adopted; the net effect of PR may have been merely to 'democratise' violence and corruption among several candidates rather than concentrate them in one person as in the first-past-the-post-system.

2.4 By, of and for the People? Government Interventions in the Scheduling of General Elections beyond the Due Date

There have been two instances of this in Sri Lanka (after the attainment of independence). We have already noted the first, the extension of the life of Parliament from five to seven years under the UF

Government of 1970–77. General elections which should have been held in 1975 under the normal scheme of things were held only in 1977. We have also noted that this extension of the life of Parliament was probably unprecedented in the annals of Constitution-making, for it was brought in under cover of the new Constitution of 1972.

The second instance was the referendum of 1982. The question put to the people here was whether the existing Parliament should continue for another term, a question squarely within Article 83(b) of the Constitution which provides for the extension of the duration of Parliament by resort to a bill passed by a two-thirds majority in Parliament and approval of the people at a referendum. It was surely not entirely fortuitous that the ruling party, the UNP, possessed in the Parliament, which would in the normal course of things have been dissolved in 1983, a five-sixth majority. In the event, 54 per cent of those voting at the referendum approved the extension of life of Parliament, but questions have also been raised as to the manner in which the referendum was conducted.

The first intervention took place when the political executive was solidly based in Parliament and the second when the political executive was headed by a directly elected president. Thus it would appear that where such interventions are concerned, it is very much a case of six of one as against half a dozen of the other as to whether a parliamentary system or presidential system was involved, though it may also be noted that the referendum, however imperfectly carried out, did involve a consultation with the people and was squarely within the constitutional provisions for the holding of a referendum, whereas the extension of the life of Parliament in 1972 took place without any consultation at all.

2.5 Highway or Blind Alley? Election Petitions

The *Parliamentary Elections Act* carefully distinguishes between making a whole election void, and voiding and avoiding the election of a particular member.

Taking first the election of a particular member, Section 91 provides that 'The election of a candidate as a member is avoided by his conviction for any corrupt or illegal practice'. The corrupt and illegal practices are spelt out in detail in the Act. Section 92(2) provides that 'The election of a candidate as a member shall be declared to be void on an election petition on any of the following grounds which may be proved to the satisfaction of the election judge...', and specifies from (a) to (d) the relevant grounds which however need not detain us here. Under Section 95, election petitions have to be brought by individuals, either a person claiming to have had a right to be returned or elected at the disputed election, or a person who was a candidate at the election.

Now clearly these sections are brought over from, and relevant to, a time when individual candidates contested elections under the first-past-the-post system, under the banner of various parties. However, under the PR system it is the party which contests an election, and as an incident of so doing, nominates its members for election. Thus the concentration on the individual candidate in Section 92(2) would appear to be misplaced. It also leads to absurd consequences. The individual candidate whose election is declared void, for instance, on the basis of corrupt or illegal practices [Section 92(2a)] at the election would have brought votes in for his party through those very corrupt or illegal practices, but nevertheless the party is not penalised for the candidates misdoings, but instead benefits from them, for even if the particular candidate's election is declared void, the party merely appoints another of its representatives to take the place of the departing candidate.

Under Section 91(1),

> ... the election in respect of any electoral district shall be declared to be void on an election petition on any of the following grounds which may be proved to the satisfaction of the election judge, namely:
>
> (a) that by reason of general bribery, general treating or general intimidation or other misconduct or other circumstances whether similar to those enumerated before or not a section of electors was prevented from voting for the recognised political party or independent group which it preferred and thereby materially affected the result of the election.
>
> (b) non-compliance with the provisions of this Act relating to elections, if it appears that the election was not conducted in accordance with the principles laid down in such provisions and that such non-compliance materially affected the result of the election.

On the surface, this would appear to be an eminently satisfactory proceeding, but closer reflection indicates that this section too harks back to a time when a single candidate won an electorate. Voiding an entire election was well and good then, but under the PR system an electoral district is inevitably shared by representatives of several competing political parties, and voiding the entire election means that the electoral gains of those petitioning are also lost together with the electoral gains of those petitioned against. The victims are thereby victimised a second time over, and the perplexed student of electoral law may be forgiven for wondering whether this state of affairs is one ordained by the Queen of Hearts in *Alice in Wonderland*.

What the Act provides both for voiding an entire election and the election of a candidate is therefore not a highway to justice, but a blind alley. It is not surprising that no one ventures in that direction; election petitions, a favourite and often successful pastime of defeated candidates under the first-past-the-post system, are now unheard of.

3. Provincial Council Elections

These are conducted under the *Provincial Council Elections Act (No. 2 of 1988)*. Provincial councils are set up under the 13th Amendment to the Constitution, which came into effect on 19 November 1987. Some measure of devolution has taken place from the centre to the provinces through these councils, though not enough by far for the devotees of devolution; the supreme power and authority of the central government is as yet intact. As the majority of a full bench of the Supreme Court observed in the 13th Amendment to the Constitution:[45]

> No division of sovereignty or of legislative, executive or judicial power has been effected. The national government continues to be legally supreme over all other levels or bodies. The Provincial Councils are merely subordinate bodies. Parliament has not parted with its supremacy or its power to the provincial councils.

The provincial councils are elected for a term of five years, and on the PR system. The membership of each council is determined on the criteria formerly used for carving out electorates, population and area, though in the case of these councils the population basis is one member for every 40,000 persons and the area basis is one member for every 100 sq km of territory. Executive power in a provincial council is vested in the governor (appointed by the president for a five-year term) and a Board of Ministers consisting of a chief minister and four others.

3.1 Of Mere Provincial Concern? The Provincial Council Elections of 1998 that never were

The period of office of five provincial councils, that is those of the Central, Uva, North-Central, Western and Sabaragamuva councils came to an end in June 1998, and in terms of the law, they then stood dissolved. Accordingly, the commissioner of elections took the first steps towards holding elections, by fixing a period in which nominations for the prospective election were to be handed in. Thereafter a date for the election had been fixed (for 28 August 1998), to be preceded, as is usual in Sri Lanka, by a date for the casting of postal ballots (fixed for 4 August 1998). However, one day before the postal ballots could be cast, on 3 August, postal voting was suspended by the commissioner of elections without any reason being adduced for that move. On 4 August, however, the mystery was solved when the president issued a proclamation bringing the entire country under a state of emergency and issued an emergency regulation which effectively cancelled the date of the poll. The commissioner of elections subsequently took no steps towards holding elections in the provinces now bereft of duly elected councils.

Two intrepid journalists, also civil society activists, filed an application in the Supreme Court alleging that their fundamental rights had been violated by the failure of the first respondent, the commissioner of elections, to hold elections to the five provincial councils. That case is the now celebrated *Karunathilaka and Another vs Dayananda Dissanayake, Commissioner of Elections et al.,* which we have caught up with in the course of this chapter.

The facts raised in the Supreme Court at the hearing of the fundamental rights application clearly showed that in fact nothing had happened immediately before the proclamation of the state of emergency to justify such a proclamation. As the Supreme Court observed:

> The petitioners have established, *prima facie*, that from 25.6.98 up to the end of July 1998, there was no known threat to national security, public order, etc., which warranted the postponement of the elections. The respondents have failed to adduce any material whatever which suggests that, in August, 1998, there was any such threat. Accordingly, the suspension of the notices by means of the impugned Regulation was arbitrary and unreasonable.[46]

The real purpose behind the proclamation of a state of emergency was not however hard to seek. In November 1998, the provincial council elections (Special Provisions) Bill was tabled in Parliament. It sought, as the Supreme Court noted,[47] to achieve two objectives. First, it purported to vest in the commissioner the duty, within a specified period, to appoint a new date for the postponed elections. This the Supreme Court found, in a separate case, to be quite redundant, because the *Provincial Councils Election Act* already made provision for fixing another date of poll, as well as, for reasons which need not detain us here, inconsistent with some provisions of the Constitution. Second, a clause of the bill purported to empower the secretary of a recognised political party or the group leader of an independent group to substitute, in place of the name of any candidate, the name of another person with his consent, but without the consent of, or notice to, the original candidate. The Supreme Court succinctly inferred the real purpose of the emergency regulation and the bill:

> If the issue of postal ballot papers had taken place on 4 August 1998, voters would have received ballot papers and could have proceeded to cast their vote. If the postal voting process had commenced in that way, substitution of candidates in the nomination papers would have required the drastic step of cancelling ballot papers already issued, and postal votes already cast. That would have been a serious interference with a pending election. The suspension of the issue of postal ballots would have facilitated the subsequent substitution of candidates without the need to cancel any part of the voting process, and it seems probable that was the purpose of that suspension.[48]

The net result of the Supreme Court's reasoning in the matter of Karunathilaka's application was that the commissioner of elections was ordered to schedule a fresh date for the elections to the provincial councils within a specified period. The judgement in that case is however notable for a number of points—its stress on the duty of the commissioner of elections to discharge his duties and functions independently, to be discussed in Section 4 of this article (on the commissioner of elections), its inclusion of the franchise in the fundamental right to freedoms of speech and expression, and its ruling that the immunity from suit of the president is not extended to those seeking cover under the president's actions, thus bringing to bear an important qualification on the scope for arbitrary executive action. The latter two aspects have already been discussed earlier in this chapter.

At this stage what is relevant to note is that the president's actions as regards the provincial council elections in 1998 clearly demonstrate the very real danger of the misuse of the power to declare a state of emergency, vested in the political executive, with a view to interfering with the normal process of elections. Again, it would not make an iota of difference whether that executive is the Cabinet based in Parliament or the president.

It is equally important to note that the application by *Karunathilaka and Another* could only be made in the first instance because of the fundamental rights provisions of the 1978 Constitution. Whether, however, those provisions will always prove as efficacious as they proved to be in Karunathilaka's application, in applications made under similar but not identical circumstances, is an interesting if speculative question. The Supreme Court cannot be considered a monolithic entity, and different benches may approach similar questions differently. If that is so, it may be wondered as to what constitutes adequate protection against abuse of executive powers.

It would also appear practically impossible to hedge the power of the political executive to declare a state of emergency with restrictions such that it would have been impossible for the president to declare such a state under the circumstances of August 1998. The untrammelled power to declare a state of emergency is one that the political executive must necessarily have, and one can only hope that it would be used with good sense, in good faith and within a firm commitment to democratic ideals.

3.2 Blind Alley Revisited: Election Petitions in Provincial Council Elections

The provisions for election petitions in the *Provincial Councils Elections Act* are identical to those in the *Parliamentary Elections Act* and as such are subject to all the debilitating infirmities and irrelevance of the provisions in the latter Act.

4. Local Government Elections

These are held under the *Local Authorities Elections Ordinance, No. 53 of 1946* (as amended from time to time). There are presently 18 municipal councils, 36 urban councils and 257 pradeshiya sabhas (the local authority for less urbanised and rural areas) islandwide. As we have already noted, Sri Lanka has a long experience of local government, the formal structures that are familiar to us today having their origins in the nineteenth century. At the time of independence, there were four types of local government institutions in Sri Lanka; municipal councils covering the larger urban areas, urban and Town Councils covering the progressively smaller urban areas, and the village councils covering the rural areas. Commenting on the system of local government in Sri Lanka in 1957, Lady Ursula Hicks was to observe that 'it was very clear to the outside observer that local government in Sri Lanka is in the doldrums'.[49] However, that may be, local elections continued to be held regularly, and the system chugged on peacefully enough, until the early 1970s. The problem was the misuse and abuse of the extraordinary powers vested in the Minister of Local Government over all types of local government institution; under the various ordinances setting up the different types of local government institutions, the minister is vested with the power (a) to remove the Mayor/Chairman from office, (b) to remove all or any members from office or (c) dissolve the relevant council on any of the grounds specified in the respective ordinances.

4.1 Controlling the Country Bumpkins? Experiments in Local Government

The UF Government elected in 1970 was not shy about making use of the minister's extraordinary powers over local government institutions. On the contrary,

> ... there has been an ever-increasing control over them by the central government, in the name, generally, of efficiency and coordination of services and economic development, but in fact in the pursuit of political objectives designed to benefit the party in power. That tendency reached its peak in the period 1970–77 when a large number of local government bodies ranging from municipalities (including the Colombo Municipality) to village councils were suspended. The result was that an important range of institutions which could have contributed to a genuine devolution of power through participatory democracy and local initiatives lost a great deal of their vitality.[50]

In 1980 however, there was a major departure in the area of local government with the setting up of district development councils (DDC) under the *Development Councils Act (No. 35 of 1980)*. The electorate for the purpose of these councils was the administrative district, and the council itself consisted of the MPs elected from the corresponding electoral districts, and a number of elected members specified by the president, that number being specified in order to ensure that the number of elected members should exceed the number of MPs in the council, (except in those districts where the number of MPs was less than three). The Executive Committee was headed by the district minister, the other members being the chairman and two other members of the district council.

With the setting up of these councils, all village and town councils within the areas of the district council's operation stood dissolved. This had the unfortunate—and startling—effect of reducing the number of councillors elected at the local level from 7,781 to just 156.[51] Possibly it was dissatisfaction with that outcome which resulted in the *Development Councils (Amendment) Act (No. 45 of 1981)*, but the measures introduced by this Amendment did not in any way increase the number of locally elected councillors. Two new bodies were set up: the gramodaya mandalaya (GM) at the lowest level of the administrative system, the grama sevaka niladhari (GSN) division, the pradeshiya mandalaya (PM) at the subcommittees-provincial level of administration, and the Assistant Government Agent (AGA) division. However, none of the members of these bodies was elected; the GMs consisted of public officials and officers of public corporations serving in the relevant GSN division nominated by the minister by name or office, and the chairman, president or head of every such organisation, association or body which is not of a political nature, as may be specified by the minister, which in the minister's opinion should be represented in any GM having regard to the interests that such organisation, association and so on, represents or serves. The PMs consisted of the chairmen of the GMs within the relevant AGA's division.

The expectation behind setting up these mandalayas could plausibly have been to ensure representation for genuine grassroots level bodies. As Tressie Leitan observes,

> The realities of the situation were however different. Studies carried out in the districts of Kalutara and Gampaha revealed that in many village areas, voluntary organisations which were

'anti-government' generally did not present themselves for inclusion of their chairmen in the GM, through a conviction that 'it would serve no purpose'. On the other hand, mushroom voluntary organisations (which presumably felt that they had government 'support') sprang up overnight, for the exclusive purpose of membership in the GM—which carried with it prestige and political recognition, not to mention the possibility of personal enrichment through government contract—work.[52]

Not only were these bodies unrepresentative, they were not even useful in channelling proposals which may emanate at village level, to the DDC; although the chairman of the GM sat on the PM, there was no structural mechanism through which the proposals from the PM could be channelled to the DDC. As Tressie Leitan observes, 'They could do so only through devious routes, that is, either through the administrative elite, or, as happened most often, through the political elite: the MPs and the district minister'.[53]

Leitan also points out another central weakness of the whole scheme of DDCs, PMs and GMs:

> Funds for local development projects had to be obtained from the decentralized budget, which unfortunately did not come to the DC, to be utilised by it. Instead, these funds were allocated to each Member of Parliament, who considered its disbursement as his right for patronage purposes. It was thus not uncommon for members of PM (or even elected members of the DC) to supplicate the MP for a share of his 'spoils'.[54]

The reason for the setting up of this seemingly futile structure of local government has to be sought not in the theory and practice of local government itself, but in the theory and practice of presidential hopefuls. R. Premadasa, the then Minister of Local Government, Housing and Construction, was a man with presidential ambitions, ambitions which were ultimately realised. The setting up of GMs and PMs, so useless from the point of view of local representation, would have been extremely useful for R. Premadasa from the point of view of building up a cadre of loyalists spread throughout the country, owing allegiance not to any electorate but to himself alone.

With the setting up of provincial councils in 1987, the structure of local government changed again; from that time there have been municipal and urban councils for the urban areas, and pradeshiya sabhas for all the rest. All are elected on the basis of PR, as indeed the DDCs had been.

Proportional representation, as we have noted earlier, is fine from the point of view of divorcing MPs from immediate and local concerns and demands. To divorce representatives in local government institutions from local concerns and demands would, however, appear to be a negation of the very fundamentals of local government, but that is what PR nevertheless does when applied in that field. We may again refer to Tressie Leitan:

> Local elections in Sri Lanka took place before 1979 on the basis of 'wards'—i.e., each local authority area was demarcated into a number of areas which were termed 'wards' within each of which the voters elected the 'ward member' on the 'first-past-the-post' principle.... The rural voter, especially, maintained a close relationship with his 'ward member', to whom he went regarding the need for repairing a village road, or a culvert, or construction of a drinking water well....
>
> Under the system of PR, however, relationships within a party become more important considerations in obtaining placement on a party list. It is also possible for voters in a particular locality to find that they are unfamiliar with any of the candidates on the party list. Personal contact and close interaction between voter and councillor is thus very often lost under PR....
>
> Voters could also find that under the list system of PR, no representatives have been elected to the local council from their specific locality....[55]

4.2 New Wine and Old Bottles? Election Offences in Local Government

Until the coming of the *Local Authorities Elections (Amendment) Act, No. 1 of 2002* (certified on 13 March 2002), the *Local Authorities Elections Ordinance* did not contain any provisions for the filing of election petitions. However, Section 83 effectively voided the election of a member of a local authority convicted of any offence relating to elections to a local authority.

In the absence of any provisions for the purposes of an election petition in the *Local Authorities Election Ordinance*, the writ of *quo warranto* was used in Sri Lanka to test the validity of the qualification for holding office as a member of a local authority, and the writ of *mandamus* to compel the holding of a fresh election where the election already held has been merely colourable and therefore void. The writs were against individual members.

While the writs worked satisfactorily under the first-past-the-post system, even if they could still operate under the PR system, this would have been of little help, because as we have already seen in our discussion of election petitions under the *Parliamentary Elections Act*, the benefits of the misdeeds of an individual candidate would still work to the benefit of his or her political party, which has simply to nominate another representative to take the place of its departing member.

Clearly, it would have been preferable to devise some new provisions for the filing of election petitions under the new system of PR rather than leave the new wine of the PR system to be contained within the old bottles of the writ system. This was done only with the Amendment of 2002, and this amendment brought in provisions for petitions in elections to local authorities identical in substance to those relating to parliamentary elections. These provisions therefore are subject to all the limitations to which petitions in parliamentary elections are themselves subject.

5. Referendum

Referenda have unfortunate associations with fascist dictatorships, but they have been used in more respectable circumstances as well. As Joseph A.L. Cooray points out,

> In 1975 a referendum was held on Britain's continued membership of the European community, while another was held in 1979 in Scotland and Wales on the question of devolution under the Scotland and Wales Acts of 1978. Other countries such as Switzerland, Denmark, Australia and Ireland have explicitly provided in their Constitutions for referenda in respect of certain important matters.[56]

Article 4 of the Constitution provides *inter alia* that the legislative power of the people shall be exercised by Parliament, consisting of elected representatives of the people and by the people at a referendum.

Chapter XIII of the Constitution which deals with the referendum carefully distinguishes between submission of bills (Article 85) and submission of any matter which in the opinion of the president is of national importance (Article 86), to the people at a referendum. In either case the submission must necessarily be by the president. Three types of bills are contemplated by Article 85: (*a*) those certi- fied by the Cabinet as being intended for submission at a referendum; (*b*) those which the Supreme Court has determined as requiring the approval of the people at a referendum; and (*c*) any bill (not being a bill for the repeal or amendment of any provision of the Consti- tution, or for the addition of any provision to the Constitution, or for the repeal and replacement of the Constitution, or which is inconsistent with any provision of the Constitution) which has been rejected by Parliament.

We have already mentioned the referendum of 1982 as an instance of government intervention in the scheduling of elections beyond the due date, but have also noted that provision existed, in Article 83(b) of the Constitution, for the holding of a referendum for that purpose.

The abortive referendum of 2001 also has its points of interest. On 8 July 2001 a no-confidence motion against the government of President Chandrika Bandaranaike Kumaratunga was presented in Parliament. Debate on the motion was expected to be taken up on 18 July, and it was also expected to be successful, the government having lost its majority in Parliament on 20 June 2001 with the defection of one of its constituent parties. On 10 July, however, the president prorogued Parliament and at the same time announced a referendum under Article 86. The question to be posed at the refer- endum was, 'Is a new Constitution, a matter of national importance and necessity, needed for the country?'

Three central issues arise from this entire proceeding. First, there was the flagrant flouting by the president of parliamentary convention in proroguing Parliament while a motion of no-confidence was pend- ing. Second, the attempt to change the Constitution was a barely con- cealed ploy to get over the problem of the imminent defeat of the government—in other words, an attempt to change the fundamental law of the land in order to get over an immediate political problem. Third, the method chosen to change the Constitution was clearly extra- constitutional in the sense that it was not a method contemplated by the Constitution itself. It was quite the contrary, because Article 85 ex- pressly disallows the use of the referendum for any type of constitu- tional change. Clearly, a political and constitutional crisis of the first magnitude was at hand, and there is no saying how the crisis would have resolved itself had it been allowed to run its own course without external, that is, public pressure. Fortunately, for Sri Lanka, the resulting political outcry made it impossible for the particular course chosen to be pursued any further and the referendum was cancelled.

This episode provides an abject example of how constitutional provisions can be perverted when applied without any considerations of political and constitutional morality in a ruthless quest for power. It is also clear that it would be impossible to provide constitutional safeguards against such perversion, for the political executive must necessarily be granted the power to call for referendums on matters of national importance. It would be completely farcical for the provisions which grant the political executive such powers to be hedged about with various detailed provisos; it is after all a fundamental assumption made of those who seek high political office that their allegiance is not only to the letter but also to the spirit of the Constitution they swear to uphold. Such constitutional hedges would perhaps be completely ineffective as well, for if the political will and ability to abuse the Constitution is present, whatever constitutional limitations are in force could be ignored or reinterpreted to provide for the chosen course of action. The episode of the abortive referendum provides the only solution to that type of national crisis: popular outcry and resistance.

The Commissioner of Elections

Prior to the 17th Amendment to the Constitution made in 2001, Article 103 of the Constitution dealt with the commissioner of elections and Article 104 dealt with his powers, duties and functions. Under Article 103, (a) the commissioner was appointed by the president; (b) his salary was chargeable on the consolidated fund and could not be diminished during his term of office; and (c) he could be removed or remove himself from office, through the usual instrumentalities of death, resignation, attainment of the specified retirement age—60 years, or on the grounds of ill health or mental or physical infirmity by the president, or by the president upon an address of Parliament. The president could appoint an acting commissioner whenever the commissioner was unable to discharge the functions of his office, and in exceptional circumstances permit a one-year extension of his period of office after reaching the age of 60 years. Under Article 104, the commissioner was required to exercise, perform or discharge all such powers, duties and functions as may be conferred, imposed on or vested in him by law.

The immense responsibilities of the commissioner were appreciated by the Supreme Court in Karunathilaka's case:

> The Commissioner has been entrusted by Article 104 with powers, duties and functions pertaining to elections, and has been given guarantees of independence by Article 103, in order that he may ensure that elections are conducted according to law; not to allow elections to be wrongfully or improperly cancelled or suspended, or disrupted, by violence or otherwise.[57]

The elevated status of the commissioner of elections in the constitutional scheme of things in Sri Lanka even prior to the 17th Amendment to the Constitution is clearly indicated by the fact that substantial similarities then existed between the position of the judges of the superior courts and that of the commissioner. The salaries of the commissioner and the judges of the superior courts were chargeable on the consolidated fund and could not be reduced after their appointment, though in the case of judges of the superior courts, the Constitution stated also that their pension entitlement could not be reduced after appointment, a provision (significantly?) lacking where the commissioner was concerned. Both the commissioner and the judges could be removed by the president upon an address of Parliament, but in case of the judges the grounds for such removal were proved misbehaviour or incapacity whereas, as we have seen in the case of the commissioner, the president could act without an address of Parliament in case of the incapacity of the commissioner. Further, in the case of the judges of the superior courts, the address of Parliament should have been supported by the majority of the total number of MPs, including those not present, and no resolution for the presentation of such an address could be entertained by the Speaker or placed on the order paper of Parliament unless notice of such resolution was signed by not less than one-third of the total number of MPs and set out in full the particulars of the alleged misbehaviour or incapacity.

The commissioner of elections has also been vested with some wide-ranging powers by the *Elections (Special Provisions) Act, No. 35 of 1988*, which introduced amendments to the presidential, parliamentary and provincial councils election Acts. Under the terms of the *Special Provisions Act*, the commissioner is vested with the following powers with regard to all three types of election:

(i) He may declare the polling at any polling station void for any of the following reasons:

- it was not possible to commence the poll at the appointed hour;
- having commenced at the appointed hour, it was not possible to continue polling until the hour fixed for closure of the poll; and
- any of the ballot boxes assigned to the polling station cannot be delivered to the counting officer.

(ii) Where the commissioner is of the opinion that the result for the particular electoral district will not be affected by the failure to count the votes actually polled, or those which would have been polled, at the polling station in respect of which the polling has been declared void, the commissioner may direct the relevant returning officer to declare the election results for that electoral district. Where the commissioner is of the opinion that the election result will be affected by the failure to count the votes pertaining to the polling station in respect of which the polling has been declared void, the commissioner is vested with the power to appoint a date for taking a fresh poll at the relevant polling station.

(iii) The commissioner is required to consult the secretary or authorised representative of every political party and the group leader of every independent group contesting the election prior to taking any decision as to whether to or not to order a fresh poll.

A 2001 judgement of the Supreme Court (in *Jayantha Adikari Egodawela et al. vs The Commissioner of Elections et al.*—SCM, 3/4/ 2001) considerably expanded the scope of the commissioner's powers, duties and discretion to be exercised under the terms of the *Special Provisions Act*. Rejecting a view urged before court by the representative of the attorney-general that the commissioner could exercise the discretion and powers given to him by the Act only on questions as to whether the poll started on time and ended on time, and what happened in between were matters to be taken up in an election petition, the Supreme Court held that the commissioner had also to determine whether the continuation of the poll was without interruption from beginning to end.[58]

The last provision of the *Special Provisions Act*, requiring the commissioner to consult with the secretaries/authorised representatives of every political party and independent group contesting the disputed election, detracts considerably from the independence the commissioner should be able to exercise in reaching decisions as to whether or not a fresh poll should be held. In the first place, it is incongruous that the commissioner is required to consult, given his elevated position in the constitutional scheme of things. Second, the pressures that could be brought to bear on the commissioner in the process of consultation with the secretaries of the contesting political parties are obvious.

The only argument for the proceeding whereby the commissioner is required to consult is expediency. This was the case at the General Election of 5 December 2001, where the commissioner had voided the polling at a number of polling stations. However, even the secretary of the United National Front (UNF), the political party which had most to gain from a free and fair polling at the polling stations where the polling had been voided, agreed that no fresh poll was required, given the urgent need to have the overall election result—a win by a narrow margin—declared as early as possible for the UNF to consolidate the status of its party leader as the person who should be called upon by the president to form a new government. Thus, though unsatisfactory, arguments for expediency would also appear to have their validity in certain restricted contexts. The commissioner of elections is also vested with the discretion to extend recognition to political parties for the purpose of contesting at elections under its own name and with its distinct symbol. Until 1964 there was no system of registering the political parties contesting the elections; all that a candidate had to do to contest an election under the banner of a political party was to produce to the commissioner of elections a letter of candidature from the political party of the candidate's choice. In 1964, however, an amendment to the Ceylon (Parliamentary Elections) Order in Council provided objective criteria by which the commissioner of elections may take a decision as to whether or not a political party should be extended recognition.

The criteria were: (*a*) a continuous period of five years of political activity or (*b*) two of its candidates should have been elected to the previous Parliament. A political party would lose recognition if (*a*) not even one candidate was nominated for election or (*b*) all candidates nominated forfeit their deposits, that is, fail to obtain separately one-eighth of the total votes polled in each electoral district. In 1981 the system of registration of political parties was completely revamped with the *Parliamentary Elections Act* of that year. Under the procedures spelt out by that Act, the commissioner would publish a notice inviting applications to be submitted for recognition, along with specified documents and information, and the commissioner would be vested with the absolute discretion as to whether or not to extend recognition to the party. It is indeed of immense satisfaction that as at 1997

> ... the confidence reposed in the Commissioner of Elections appears to have worked satisfactorily as evident from the fact only one (1) out of 101 cases that the Commissioner refused to recognise, was successfully challenged in the Supreme Court under fundamental right of unequal treatment.[59]

Finally it may be noted that the commissioner of elections is assisted by the staff of his own department, and, at election time, by a vast mass of public servants of every category drawn in for election duty. These public servants fill the positions of returning officer for each electoral district, presiding officer of each polling station and the counting officers of each counting centre, who would themselves be assisted by every category of staff in the public service. It is a fact that the public service has become politicised, and some election malpractices and abuses are known to take place because of this, but in the absence of any serious study of the subject, it is futile to speculate just what, and how much, interference in a free and fair election takes place because of such politicisation.

To concentrate on such politicisation and possible abuse is however to ignore the tremendous contribution, involving hard work in often very difficult circumstances, which the election staff of Sri Lanka consistently make in every election in this country. Episodes of utmost dedication to duty, self-sacrifice and even heroism are not unknown, as the following account, regarding an incident which took place in the course of the General Election 1989, held in a period of terror unleashed by the Janatha Vimukthi Peramuna (JVP), would illustrate. Election staff sent to operate a polling station had been attacked on the way to the station, and two persons had been shot dead. The remaining staff had, however, got a message through to the relevant authorities and a relief party had been sent out.

[These] were despatched at 12.00 noon in three vehicles. They reached Ballekatuwa junction at 1.00 pm. After they had walked one mile from the Ballekatuwa junction they met the staff return-ing from Illukpellessa polling station after the tragic event, car-rying the corpses of the two dead persons. However, they proceeded to the polling station finally reaching there at 2.45 pm. On their way they heard burst of gun fire at close range, yet they continued and reached the polling station. They sent messages to the villagers that the booth was opened and that they could come and vote. Apparently no one arrived through fear. The polling station was closed at 4.00 pm.[60]

Less than Elevated? The Commissioner of Elections (Prior to the 17th Amendment)

Constitutionally, the commissioner of elections is placed on a high pedestal. In terms of practical politics, ways have been found on occasion of cutting the pedestal from under the commissioner's feet. An illustration of the pressures that could be brought to bear on the commissioner is given by the episode of the polling card stickers, just prior to the General Election 2000. In this instance the commis-sioner of elections decided to place small stickers on the polling cards issued to each voter for production at the polling station. The objective behind placing these stickers on polling cards was widely believed to be the prevention of the large scale rigging of elections by the use of forged polling cards. The proposed use of the stickers was however kept a secret by the commissioner, until of course there was a leakage to the government. The response of the government was hysterical beyond measure. It is reported that at a hastily sum-moned meeting of some leading cabinet ministers at Temple Trees, then the official residence of the president, a proposal was even floated of arresting the commissioner of elections, a proposal aban-doned, it is reported, only when the attorney-general shot it down.[61] Nevertheless calumny and opprobrium were heaped in liberal mea-sure on the commissioner, and the government-controlled media— three national TV channels, several national radio channels and a large newspaper group—screamed treble to their political master's bass. A national list nominee to Parliament, a lawyer, filed a com-plaint with the Human Rights Commission (HRC) that his fundamental rights as a candidate and voter were violated by the commissioner secretly attempting to paste stickers on polling cards.

> In record quick time, despite hundreds of petitions for human rights violations alleged to have been committed in the country's war torn North and East collecting dust at the HRC, its Chairman, eminent lawyer ... who is also a President's Counsel, sent a letter to the Elections Commissioner requesting him to attend a discussion at the HRC....[62]

Many a person would have broken under the strain. The commissioner of elections did not, but one wonders as to whether any one who occupied that position would under such circumstances ever feel impelled again to be innovative in combating electoral abuse.

Apart from incidents which directly undermined the independent and elevated position of the commissioner of elections, his ability to execute the functions of his office in a manner which would ensure a free and fair election was even otherwise circumscribed. For instance, one of the most serious problems in conducting a free and fair election has been, in recent times, the rampant misuse and abuse of state resources, including the resources of state corporations, the resources chiefly being men, money and vehicles. While action can be taken against this under other laws, such misuse and abuse does not constitute an election offence, and consequently the commissioner had no handle with which to try to control the situation.

Again, some circulars and directives issued by the commissioner of elections and the inspector general of police in the run up to the General Election 2000 have come to light following petitions made to the HRC by activists and election monitors on the basis of the right to know of voters. It is reported that:

> They are interesting for the manner in which they reveal the helplessness of the department (i.e., of elections), the total inadequacy of circulars and directions and the uselessness in setting up special elections units within a hopelessly politicised Police force and extreme political intimidation.[63]

Indeed the police readily become the lap dogs—and sometimes the attack dogs—of whatever political party is in power. The political impartiality of the police is only apparent in that they readily assume these roles irrespective of the ideological orientation of the party in power, political power being the only criterion they use.

The 17th Amendment to the Constitution

A hoary old story relates how a hapless student of constitutional law, searching for the Sri Lankan Constitution in a library, was directed to the periodicals section. The latest instalment to the growing number of constitutional amendments is the 17th Amendment, widely hailed, if not as a panacea for all ills in the body politic, as at least a good prophylactic against abuse of government power.

This Amendment, enacted in 2001 has set up a constitutional council which has exclusive power to make appointments to centrally important institutions such as the higher judiciary, and the police and Elections Commissions, taking this power away from the executive president. The Council consists of the following persons:

(1) The prime minister
(2) The speaker
(3) The leader of the opposition
(4) A person appointed by the president
(5) Five persons appointed by the president on the nomination of both the prime minister and the leader of the opposition
(6) One person nominated upon agreement by the majority of the members of Parliament, belonging to political parties or independent groups other than the respective political parties or independent groups to which the prime minister and the leader of the opposition belong, and appointed by the president.

The council is chaired by the Speaker. The term of office of those appointed under categories (4), (5) and (6) is three years.

The constitutional council recommends to the president persons for appointment as chairmen and members of the following commissions and no appointment may be made to them except on a recommendation of the council. Removal of members from the commissions may take place only as provided in the Constitution or the relevant law and where no such provision is made, only with the prior approval of the council. The commissions are: (*a*) The Election Commission; (*b*) the Public Services Commission; (*c*) The National Police Commission; (*d*) The Human Rights Commission; (*e*) The Permanent Commission to Investigate Allegations of Bribery or Corruption; (*f*) The Finance Commission; and (*g*) The Delimit-ation Commission.

No person may be appointed by the president to any of the following offices unless such appointment has been approved by the council upon a recommendation made to the council by the president, and no person shall be removed from such office except as provided for in the Constitution or in any law. The offices are: (Part I) (*a*) chief justice and the judges of the Supreme Court; (*b*) The president and the judges of the Court of Appeal; (*c*) members of the Judicial Service Commission other than the chairman; (Part II) (*a*) attorney-general; (*b*) auditor general, (*c*) inspector general of police; (*d*) parliamentary commission for administration (ombudsman) and (*e*) secretary general of Parliament.

The amendment also vastly expands the powers of the ECs. For the first time ever in Sri Lanka's constitutional history, the 17th Amendment states [at Article 103(2)] categorically, clearly and unequivocally that 'The object of the (Election) Commission shall be to conduct free and fair elections and Referenda'. The commission, once an election or referendum has been scheduled, has the power to (*a*) prohibit the use of state property or the property of any public corporation for election purposes of any political party, group, or candidate, and the written orders of the commission in this regard are binding on those to whom they are issued; (*b*) provide guidelines to any media unit as may be considered necessary for conducting a free and fair election and on failure of the state-owned radio and TV stations to follow such guidelines, to appoint a competent authority to take over the management of any broadcast which may impinge on the election; (*c*) to instruct the inspector general of police of the number and deployment of police officers and other police facilities for the election; and (*d*) make recommendations to the president as to the deployment of the armed forces for the purpose of conducting a free and fair election.

Interestingly as regards the misuse and abuse of state resources for election purposes, it has been pointed out that,

... one of the last drafts of the 17th Amendment specifically included a clause which related not only to the Commissioner's (i.e., Elections Commissioner) authority with regard to state resources but made any person who contravened or failed or neglected to comply with any direction or order issued by the Commissioner or indeed, any provision of the law relating to elections, guilty of an offence. The Commissioner was thus entitled to institute criminal proceedings in the appropriate court under his own hand. Where any particular offence was not punishable by any particular law, the Commission or the attorney-general could, in fact, move the High Court in the matter. Rigorous penalties could be imposed on a person found guilty of such offence....

For reasons which are fairly obvious, this clause had been removed from the final draft of the 17th Amendment ... placed on the Order Paper of Parliament.[64]

Overall, however, the 17th Amendment may indicate some progress towards a de-politicisation of, if not society, at least the bureaucracy, the judiciary and the police.

At the time this Chapter is being written the EC has not had members appointed to it because of disagreements between the recommending body—the constitutional council—and the appointing authority, the president.

The constitutional council had, in October 2002, forwarded its list of nominees to this commission to the president. The president however took objection to one of the nominees and therefore the commission was never appointed. While there is nothing in the 17th Amendment which appears to give the president discretion in the appointments to the commissions coming under the purview of the Constitutional Commission, there does not appear to be anything in the Amendment which compels the president to appoint the nominees of the constitutional council either.

In 2003 a public interest group filed an application in the Court of Appeal for a writ of *mandamus* to be issued on the president compelling her to appoint the EC.[65] This application foundered on the principle of the immunity from suit of the president.

Meanwhile the commissioner of elections has reached retirement age, and furthermore claims that he is in poor health. However he cannot retire because the 17th Amendment (Section 27[2]) states that the '... person holding the office of Commissioner of Elections on the day immediately preceding the date of commencement of the Act, shall continue to exercise and perform ... (his power and functions) until an Election Commission is constituted....' A petition to the Supreme Court[66] by the commissioner, Dayananda Dissanayake, of a violation of his fundamental rights in not being allowed to retire foundered on the express constitutional provision regarding the continuance in office of the present commissioner until a new Commission is appointed.

By the end of 2005, the period of appointment of those appointed to the constitutional council under categories (4) (5) and (6) mentioned earlier had come to an end. Gridlock in Parliament in finalising the new appointments has led to a situation where there is, at the time of writing, no constitutional council functioning. That has not deterred the president from making appointments to the National Police Commission and the Public Service Commission.

The fact that the 17th Amendment had to be brought is itself an admissions—a glaring one—that something is fundamentally amiss in the Sri Lankan polity, that a directly elected president cannot be trusted to make appropriate appointments to important institutions. However, if partisan politics can pervert, undermine, digest and regurgitate, in a hideously distorted and misshapen form, every institution of national importance, would it not make short work of a constitutional amendment?

Conclusion

A perusal of this chapter would have revealed four basic facts. If one aims to mould the statutory framework and institutional arrangements in Sri Lanka with a view to having free and fair elections, there are:

(i)   steps which have already been taken with this end in view, such as the 17th Amendment to the Constitution;
(ii) steps which could be taken, such as introducing amendments to the legislation relating to election petitions to make them more appropriate to the presidential and PR systems;
(iii) matters about which steps may be taken, but where the outcome is still uncertain—for instance the filing of a fundamental rights application where the executive has misused or abused its powers with regard to elections; and
(iv) instances where no steps, legislative nor institutional could be taken, such as in the case of abuse of power by the political executive, for instance, in interfering with the due scheduling of elections and refusing to perform his/her constitutional duty in appointing the EC.

However, it is necessary to raise questions about the political culture which makes legislation such as the 17th Amendment necessary. The independence of the judiciary, and of such important institutions such as the Election, Public Services and Police Commissions would be something which should be taken for granted in any advanced democracy, and that independence would have evolved in the form of traditions and conventions governing appointments to them and the exercise of their powers and functions. The very fact that the political executive has to be hedged in by a commission appointed through a complex procedure in making appointments to these institutions, in order to ensure some degree of independence for them, directly implies that ultimately Sri Lankan society cannot trust its own leaders to act in the best democratic traditions.

The mere creation of institutional structures without a deep political commitment to make them work in the manner which could be best expected of them would be futile and possibly even mischievous; in such a background it is very likely that the new institutional forms would simply become subjects of political horse-trading and arm-twisting.

The introduction of amendments to legislation dealing with election petitions, in order to make them more relevant to present day challenges and electoral systems would also depend on the political will to ensure free and fair elections. Of vastly greater importance is particularly how the political executive is going to conduct itself in future where elections are concerned. Thus with regard to every important measure which may be taken to ensure more free and fair elections, we find that what is crucial is the political will to attain that outcome. This brings us to the wisdom of Judge Learned Hand's dictum quoted at the beginning of this chapter: it is only when liberty lives in the hearts and minds of people will Constitutions, laws and courts be able to effectively work as elements of a functioning democracy.

Notes

1 . *Karunathilaka and Another vs Dayananda Dissanayake, Commissioner of Elections et al.,* (1999) 1 Sri Lanka Law Reports (SLR) 157, p. 173.
2 . Ibid., p. 174.
3 . *Report of the Special Commission on the Constitution,* Cmd. 3131, HMSO, 1928, p. 83.
4 . Ibid.
5 . G.R. Tressie Leitan, *Local Government and Decentralized Administration in Sri Lanka,* Colombo, Lake House Investments Ltd., 1979, p. 49.
6 . V. Kanesalingam, *A Hundred Years of Local Government in Ceylon 1865–1965,* Colombo, 1971, p. 8.
7 . Ibid., p. 11.
8 . Edgar Fernando, *Local Government Elections in Ceylon,* Colombo, 1967, pp. 8–16.

9. *Report of the Special Commission on the Constitution*, Cmd. 6677, HMSO, 1945, pp. 78–79.
10. Ibid., p. 79.
11. *Liyanage vs The Queen* (1965) 68 NLR 265 at p. 282.
12. Joseph A.L. Cooray, *Constitutional and Administrative Law of Sri Lanka*, Colombo, Sumathi Publishers, 1995, p. 116.
13. *Liyanage vs The Queen* (1965).
14. The *Bribery Commissioner vs Ranasinghe*, (1964), 66 New Law Reports (NLR) 73 at p. 78.
15. *Ibralebbe vs The Queen* (1963), 65 NLR 433 at p. 443.
16. *Liyanage vs The Queen* (1965).
17. Joseph A.L. Cooray, *Constitutional and Administration*, p. 53.
18. Ibid.
19. *Kodakan Pillai vs Mudannayake* (1953), 54 NLR 433.
20. This served to make Sinhala, the language of the majority community in Sri Lanka, the only official language of Sri Lanka.
21. K.M. de Silva, 'The Constitution and Constitutional Reform since 1948', in K.M. de Silva (ed.), *Sri Lanka: A Survey*, London, C. Hurst, 1977, p. 316.
22. DC, Colombo 1026/Z.
23. 70 NLR 121.
24. 72 NLR 337.
25. *Constituent Assembly Debates*, Vol. 1, 2833–34.
26. K.M. de Silva, 'The Constitution and Constitutional...', p. 319.
27. Vijaya Samaraweera, 'The Administration and the Judicial System', in K.M. de Silva (ed.), *Sri Lanka: A Survey*, p. 366.
28. Quoted in Cooray, *Constitutional and Administration*, p. 79.
29. K.M. de Silva, 'The Constitution and Constitutional...', p. 323.
30. *Karunathilaka and Another vs Dayananda Dissanayake*, p. 177.
31. A. Jeyaratnam Wilson, *The Gaullist System in Sri Lanka*, London, The Macmillan Press Ltd., 1980, p. 55.
32. *Silva vs Bandaranayake* (1997) 1 SLR, p. 92.
33. K.M. de Silva, 'Electoral Systems: The Sri Lankan Case' in Devendra Raj Panday and Anand Aditya (eds), *Democracy and Empowerment in South Asia*, Kathmandu, Nepal South Asia Centre, 1995, p. 94.
34. A.J. Wilson, *The Gaullist System*, p. 18.
35. (1992) 2 SLR 1.
36. Ibid., p. 12.
37. Ibid., p. 64.
38. (1989) 1 SLR 240, p. 247.
39. K.M. de Silva, 'Electoral Systems: The Sri Lankan Case', p. 90.
40. Ibid., p. 92.
41. Ibid., p. 93.
42. *Parliamentary Series*, No. 14, 1978, p. 143.
43. K.M. de Silva, 'Electoral Systems: The Sri Lankan Case', p. 93.
44. For instance see the discussion of this point in Sundari de Alwis, P. Saravanamuttu and Rohan Edrisinha, 'The Electoral Process in Sri Lanka Recent Developments', in Devendra Raj Panday, Anand Aditya and Dev Raj Dahal (eds), *Comparative Electoral Processes in South Asia*, Nepal South Asia Centre (NESAC), July 1999, p. 107.

45. (1987) 2 SLR 312 at p. 323.
46. (1999) 1 SLR 157 at p. 181.
47. Ibid., pp. 165–66.
48. Ibid., p. 171.
49. Planning Secretariat, papers by visiting Economists, Colombo, 1957, p. 107.
50. K.M. de Silva, 'Decentralization: The Sri Lankan Case', in Devendra Raj Panday and Anand Aditya (eds), *Democracy and...*, p. 118.
51. G.R. Tressie Leitan, *Political Integration through Decentralisation and Devolution of Power: The Sri Lankan Experience*, Colombo, 1990, pp. 26–27.
52. Ibid.
53. Ibid., p. 29.
54. Ibid.
55. Ibid., p. 24.
56. Cooray, *Constitutional and Administrative* op. cit., p. 306.
57. (1999) 1 SLR at p. 170.
58. See Kishali Pinto-Jayawardena, 'The Egodawela Judgement: A Judicial Response to Executive Indifference', *Moot Point*, Vol. 5, Colombo, Center for Policy Alternatives, 2001, p. 3.
59. R.K. Chandananda de Silva, *Comparative Electoral Systems in South Asia*, Monograph No. 5, Sri Lanka, Colombo, International Centre for Ethnic Studies, 1997, p. 29.
60. Report of the Commissioner of Elections on the Ninth Parliamentary General Election of Sri Lanka held on 15.02.1989, *Sessional Paper No. 1*, 1993, pp. 118–19.
61. Frederica Jansz, 'His Head on a Platter', *The Sunday Leader*, 24 September 2000, p. 9.
62. Ibid.
63. Kishali Pinto-Jayawardena, 'Returning to Some Electoral Sanity' (an instalment of the author's regular weekly column, 'Focus on Rights'), *The Sunday Times*, 21 October 2001, p. 10.
64. Kishali Pinto-Jayawardena, 'Extent and Limitations of the 17th Amendment' (an instalment of the author's regular weekly column, 'Focus on Rights'), *The Sunday Times*, 28 October 2001.
65. C.A. Writ Application No. 1396/2003.
66. SC Application No. 271/2003.

Part IV

GROUP DISCRIMINATION AT
ELECTIONS

12

BANGLADESH

Sohela Nazneen

Introduction

Formal democratic institutions[1] in Bangladesh do not legally exclude minorities (that is, religious and ethnic) from participating in the electoral process. However, the high incidence of minority voter intimidation and post-election violence against minority groups as well as boycotting of elections by the Hill people in Chittagong Hill Tracts (CHT) in 2001, raise questions about the quality[2] of democracy in Bangladesh. The minority groups (especially the religious and ethnic minorities living in the plains) have been marginalised from participating in mainstream politics as a result of the hegemonic state building process based on the Bengali–Muslim identity, 'criminalisation'[3] of politics and the lack of effective organisation of these minority groups. The minority communities assert that the state generally overlooks discriminatory practices, both violent (that is, prevention from voting) and non-violent (that is, non-registration of voters) because their (particularly the Hindus') right to exercise their citizenship (that is, vote or participate in decision-making) is questioned by the majority because of the Hindu groups' alleged 'links' with India which undermine the sovereignty of Bangladesh.[4]

They also argue that the fear of losing territorial control is used to justify the electoral malpractices against the Hill people in the CHT.

The objective of this chapter is to study group discrimination with particular reference to religious minorities in the parliamentary elections of 2001 in Bangladesh. The experience of the Hill people is not extensively discussed in this chapter because of the lack of secondary data and scarcity of time for collecting adequate information from primary sources.

The chapter will focus on pre-election malpractices as well as election day and post-election violence. Pre-election malpractices against minorities have been identified as voter intimidation (using physical threat, threat of destruction of property, extortion, looting, threat of rape and the actual carrying out of such threats) and non-registration. Use of violence to prevent minority voters from voting, and discrimination by election officials are malpractices which occur on election day. Post-election violence occurs in the form of looting, destruction of property, assault and rape, and these incidents are closely linked to pre-election voter intimidation. The position of minorities in Bangladesh and the attitude and reaction of government and civil society towards minority issues have implications for minority participation in the electoral process.

While exploring the experience of religious minorities at elections, it is important to note that the experience of women belonging to minority groups would differ from that of the men belonging to these communities and women belonging to majority groups. Women's participation in the electoral process and their experience of violence would be affected by norms involving community honour and shame.

This chapter focuses on selected case study sites on which pre- and post-election information is available and has five sections. The first section briefly describes the methods used for collecting data. An overview of the minority position within the state of Bangladesh is presented in the second section. The third section details the types of non-violent discriminatory as well as violent discriminatory practices related to elections against minority groups and tries to identify patterns and trends. The fourth section identifies the various immediate and underlying causes behind group discrimination and how these are linked to state building policies and the changes that took place in Bangladeshi politics (that is, the re-emergence of sectarian politics and criminalisation). Identification of the immediate causes is useful for understanding the ways in which informal discriminatory practices take place. Analysis of structural causes helps in exploring the links between electoral politics and other socio-economic factors. The fifth section focuses on the responses of both the minority groups themselves and those of the state and political elite. Analysis of these issues identifies the obstacles that need to be overcome for formulating strategies for advocacy and prevention of violation of rights.

I

Research Methods

The chapter uses data collected from secondary sources and key informant interviews. Four electoral constituencies: Gouranadi and Agoiljhara Upzillas in Barisal-1, Lalmohan Upzilla in Bhola-1, Keshabpur Upzilla in Jessore-6 and Chandina Upzilla in Comilla-6, where a large number of pre- and post-election malpractices took place and data is available from fact-finding reports prepared by several human rights organisations, were selected as case study areas. The quantitative data on malpractices was collected from news scan of five newspapers (*The Daily Star, Prothom Alo, Bhorer Kagoj, Sangbad, Jugantor*) from July 2001 to November 2001. The newspapers were selected keeping in mind the political leanings of the dailies. Moreover, fact-finding reports and election-monitoring reports prepared by several non-partisan human rights and legal aid organisations such as Ain O Shalish Kendra *(ASK)*, Bangladesh Mohila Parishad *(BMP)*, *Brotee*, Fair Election Monitoring Association (FEMA) and Coordinating Council for Human Rights in Bangladesh (CCHRB) were collected in order to gather information on pre- and post-election violence. These reports focused on collecting data on the types, extent and nature of violence experienced by the minority communities and their perceptions about the causes that led to such high levels of violence at the case study sites. Furthermore, reports on minority violence in elections of 1991 and 1996 were collected for supplementary evidence. Key informants such as members of the NGO fact-finding teams, journalists and selected researchers and academics who work on minority issues were interviewed in order to cross check the findings in these reports and gain insights.

II

An Overview of the State of Minorities in Bangladesh

Compared to other states in South Asia, Bangladesh has projected itself as having greater uniformity of culture and religion. Bangladesh is ethnically almost homogenous as 98 per cent of the population is Bengali. The ethnic minorities compose 1.13 per cent of the population (1.2 million). The Bengalis are predominantly Muslim while the largest religious minority group, the Hindus, is approximately 10.3 per cent of the population. The Constitution guarantees equal citizenship and non-discrimination for all citizens (Articles 27 and 28). However, in various other Articles of the Constitution the state identifies itself with the dominant Bengali community. The Bengali language and culture are emphasised in the Constitution because the national ethos is based on the Bengali nationalist movement.[5] This state-building process has created a gulf between the majority (Bengali Muslims) and the minority communities. In fact, it is the debate over state-building stressing Bengali identity that gave rise to the *Jumma* nationalist movement in CHT. State management of resources based on hegemonic ideas has also marginalised the minorities.[6] The non-recognition of communal landholding and nationalisation of forests have adversely affected the Hill people and other minorities in the plains. Moreover, settlement policies followed in CHT have economically marginalised the Hill people.[7]

The citizenship rights of religious minorities[8] were not undermined after Bangladesh became independent because they were Bengalis, and secularism was identified as one of the pillars of the state by the Constitution.[9] However, the rights of religious minorities have undergone structural changes as a result of constitutional amendments and legislative changes[10] and emergence of sectarian politics. The Constitution established Islam as one of the pillars of the state building process (Eighth Amendment).[11] The minority communities feel that this has significantly undermined all religious and ethnic identities except the Muslim identity.[12] The enactment of *Vested Property Act (VPA)[13]* in 1974 has made the Hindus secondary citizens because it has been exploited by local influentials (in most cases local level politicians) to grab property and has resulted in mass out-migration of Hindus.[14] The collective memory of communalism (pre- and post-partition) coupled with rise of sectarian politics in South Asia contribute significantly to the perception that Hindus do not truly belong to Bangladesh.[15]

It is also believed that the increase in migration of workers, especially unskilled workers, to Middle Eastern countries who return home with notions about 'true Islamic culture' and the role Middle Eastern donors play in deciding Bangladesh's policy towards Islam have indirectly contributed to the current politics based on religious identity.[16] Furthermore, the majoritarian (single representative 'first-past-the-post') system makes it difficult for effective political representation within the political system.[17] It has also been argued that after the success of the anti-autocracy movement in 1990, the state/political and civil society actors have only focused on ensuring continuation of free elections whereas issues related to inclusion (vital for minority participation) were not given serious attention by the state and political elite.[18]

III

An Overview of the Findings on Electoral Malpractices Experienced by the Minority Community in the Pre- and Post-Election Period

After the parliamentary elections of 2001, the various national and international election observation missions[19] asserted that in 96 to 98 per cent of the polling centres observed by their monitors, the minority voters were able to cast their ballots without any obstruction or harassment by officials or political violence. In fact, analysis of data by polling centre presented in these reports show that in several of the constituencies some of the data regarding false votes, violence and so on, is missing, and that observers had indicated harassment of minority voters in certain centres. The low incidence of discrimination experienced by minority communities and an overall peaceful election day cannot be interpreted as an indication that minority communities had not been discriminated against in the parliamentary elections of 2001.

The electoral process covers the three-month-long pre-election phase followed by the post-election period.[20] News scan analysis and fact finding reports of the various human rights organisations show that the pre- and post-election periods have been traumatic for the religious and ethnic minority communities in some electoral constituencies where they were systematically targeted and victimised. It is interesting to note that pre-election malpractices (voter intimidation, assault, looting, and so on) and post-election violence against the minority community have been limited to pockets mainly in the south and south-west of Bangladesh (Barisal and Khulna division), the most violent being Barisal, Bhola and Bagerhat districts. News scan analysis also shows that from mid-August the news about minority voter intimidation and violence against minority communities was filtering through. In the second half of September the number of such incidents had dramatically increased. The caretaker government tried to reassure the minority voters by issuing a statement that warned the 'criminals'.[21] Pre-election malpractice against minority groups, mainly the Hindus, was supposedly limited to voter intimidation, whereas allegations about non-registration were made to journalists and long-term election monitors in Sherpur, Manikganj (Debalaya) and Barisal. The ethnic minority community, the Santals, also made the same complaints in Dinajpur and Rajshahi areas where their numbers are quite high.[22]

Analysis of incidents of voter intimidation shows that the aggressors used threat of physical assault, rape, destruction of property, looting and extortion to intimidate voters. Interestingly, the areas where post-election violence was high had also reported the highest number of pre-election incidents of voter intimidation. News scan shows that there were about 164 reports of violence and threat against minority communities and that physical assault and threat of assault ranked the highest (see Table 12.1). About 110 people had been injured in these assaults.

Election day was comparatively violence free, although in some centres in certain constituencies (Barisal-1 and 5, Bhola-1, Barguna) minority voters were harassed by officials and were prevented from voting.[23] Election observers, however, claimed that these centres were aberrations given that the minorities were able to exercise their voting right freely in most of the polling centres in these constituencies. What the election observers' reports and the other data sources do not highlight is that the minority community in villages situated at a distance from the polling centres had in fact opted out of casting their ballots due to threats of post-election reprisals. For example, the ASK fact-finding team reported that in Annadaprashad and

Fatemabad villages in Lalmohan Upzilla, Bhola, many had not cast their vote.[24] The CCHRB team in one of the villages in Chandina reported that about 200 Hindu voters claimed that they had not voted.[25] However, an analysis of the percentage of votes cast vis-à-vis the total population of several constituencies where the Hindus constitute a significant number revealed that 66 per cent of the Hindu voters had cast their votes.[26] But this analysis does not include Bhola and Barisal where pre- and post-election violence were the highest.

The post-election phase had been the most violent in the history of Bangladeshi elections. The high incidence of pre-election violence, both against minority groups and in general, was perhaps an indication that the post-election phase would be bloody as well. News scan analysis shows that the incidence of violence against minorities, especially Hindus, rose dramatically in the span of four weeks in October and that 17 Hindus were murdered, a total of 701 were injured, and 64 women were raped.[27] The victims stated that the perpetrators were between the ages of 15 and 35 and had claimed that they were supporters of the Bangladesh Nationalist Party (BNP). Another interesting fact was that the attacks on Hindu villages in Bhola and Barisal took place on the same night although these villages were at a considerable distance from each other. The fact-finding teams sent by BMP and ASK to Bhola (Annadaprashad and Fatemabad villages) reported that the perpetrators had assembled beforehand at Betuar Khal and Lord Hardinge Bazar to prepare for the attacks. These facts perhaps indicate that the attacks were 'organised' and that they were probably committed with the blessings of local influentials.

Table 12.1

Violence against Hindus and Ethnic Minorities in Pre-/Post-election Phase

Time Period	Attack	Threat	Physical Assault	Loot	Destruction of Property	Extortion	Bomb	Other	Total
15/09–30/09	21	52	24	11	19	11	4	22	164
1/10–15/10	38	42	41	37	54	21	3	10	246
16/10–30/10	32	16	29	39	57	15	2	13	203
Total	91	110	94	87	130	47	9	45	613
Adivasi	3	9	1	0	1	0	0	1	–

Source: ASK, 2001b.

News scan also reveals that incidents of looting, extortion and destruction of property belonging to minorities were highest (54 incidents of arson, 34 of looting, 38 assaults) in the immediate aftermath of the elections in October. Furthermore, about 611 Hindu households were attacked in the first two weeks and then the numbers declined in the last two weeks of October. There were also sporadic reports of looting of property belonging to ethnic minorities (see Table 12.2). The number of attacks on property perhaps indicates that these attacks were linked to materialistic aspirations.

Attacks on temples and destruction of deities increased in the last two weeks of October. This rise in attacks on temples may be due to the fact that the Durga Puja had taken place recently and that in the last two weeks of October communal sentiments had taken hold in selecting targets (see Table 12.2). Given the fact that many of the temples are rich, the attackers may have also had an economic incentive to loot these temples.

Table 12.2
Incidence of Looting and Destruction of Property Belonging to Hindus

Day	Households	Shops/Businesses	Temples/ Deity	Other
15/09–30/09	61	25	5	180
01/10–15/10	611	91	28	15
16/10–30/10	291	32	42	1
TOTAL	963	148	70	196

Source: ASK, 2001b.

Electoral Malpractice against Minority Women

News scan analysis shows that in September and October 64 Hindu women were raped and another 64 sexually harassed, and that most of these incidents took place in the aftermath of the elections. Fact-finding reports prepared by NGOs and civil society organisations reveal that incidents of rape in certain villages would be higher than those revealed in the news scan. For example, in Annadaprashad and Fatemabad villages it was alleged that between 50 to 60 women were raped.[28] Violence against women was highest in Bhola, Barisal and Patuakhali districts. The fact-finding teams sent by BMP found that threat of rape and sexual harassment of women were effective weapons for intimidating minority voters to deter them from voting.[29] In Bhola and Barisal many families who could afford to do so had sent the women away to their natal families in the pre-election period fearing post-election reprisals.[30] In fact, out-migration of women from rural areas where Hindus constitute a significant number was found to be a good indicator of the level of pre-/post-election violence against Hindus in these areas. Moreover, most women who had stayed behind in these areas did not cast their votes for fear of violence,[31] and those who did were harassed at various polling centres.[32]

During the post-election reprisals the perpetrators specifically targeted women. Members of fact finding teams sent to Bhola and Barisal were told that the perpetrators called the women by name and demanded that they come out of their hiding places.[33] Some women fell into the hands of the aggressors when they had come out to save their men from severe beatings.[34]

IV

Causes for Discrimination against Minorities in Elections

Many hypotheses were put forward by the media and analysts to explain the high incidence of pre- and post-election malpractice experienced by the religious minority communities, particularly the Hindus, in 2001. These can be generally placed under three categories: (a) since religious minority communities are identified as Awami League (AL) vote banks, the BNP cadres tried to intimidate them during the pre-election period; (b) certain 'opportunist elements' took advantage of the vulnerable position of the religious minorities and engaged in violent activities during the post-election phase; and (c) post-election violence against minorities is a result of communal tendencies in Bangladeshi society. Analysis of the data collected from the case study sites and long-term election monitoring reports reveal that each of these hypotheses has some truth in it although none fully explains the overall situation. It should be noted that clashes between the two parties and the level of violence has been high in other constituencies as well. For example, although minorities have been victimised in constituencies such as Feni 2 and 3, the general opinion was that AL supporters were harassed and that the minority identity did not act as a contributing factor to their experience of pre- and post-election harassment.[35] This indicates that there are other structural reasons behind minority exclusion in the case study areas.

In order to unravel the experience of minority discrimination in the elections of 2001, the findings and trends identified by analysing the case study areas are divided into two categories. The section which follows discusses the immediate issues related to the electoral process such as security arrangements, voting patterns and the various dimensions of local politics that had contributed to discrimination against minorities. The subsequent section explores the structural issues such as criminalisation of politics and kinship-based political structure and how these are linked to electoral malpractice against minorities.

Immediate Causes

The popular perception that the Hindus are a vote bank for the AL does contribute to the discrimination they face in the electoral process.[36] In the case study areas, minority opinion and election monitors' observations confirm the view that during the pre- and post-election period, minorities were *specifically* targeted by BNP activists in a political vendetta mainly because of their association with the AL.[37] No extensive study has been conducted to find out whether the perception is accurate. However, given that historically the AL is identified as secular,[38] Ziaur Rahman's role in bringing Islam into politics and the BNP's alliance with Jamaat-i-Islam in the parliamentary elections of 2001,[39] the decision of Hindus and other religious minorities to vote for the AL seems rational.[40] Although identification as a vote bank by itself does not mean that a group would face discrimination. Factors such as close competition between the two dominant parties as well as the presence of a significant number of Hindu voters may lead to the targeting and victimisation of minorities because the election results can be altered if a significant number of minority voters can be prevented from casting their votes. In fact, one election observer stated that voter intimidation and post-election violence would take place in areas where the chances of winning for each party is close and the minority community constitutes above 10 per cent of the total votes.[41] The findings from the selected case study areas support this observation.

The significant finding that emerged from the case study areas (where pre- and post-election violence was high) is that in all of these areas the Hindus constituted about 15 to 40 per cent of the total voting population and the villages that were attacked were Hindu villages. In three of the four constituencies that were chosen, for which statistics are available, the demographic composition of Hindu voters is as follows: 37 per cent in Bhola-1, 42 per cent in Barisal-1 and 20 per cent in Keshabpur. In all of these areas the competition between the main parties was close. In 1991 and 1996, the AL had won in Bhola, Barisal, Keshabpur (Jessore-6) and Chandina Upzilla (Comilla-6).

Fact-finding teams reported that in previous elections the Hindu voters in these areas had traditionally voted for the AL. This perhaps indicates why in the pre-election phase of 2001, the Hindus were threatened against casting their votes and incidents of pre-election violence were also high. These factors also indicate that the perpetrators perhaps assumed that if the minorities were not allowed to vote, the result would be different in 2001. In fact, the fact-finding teams reported that the victims had alleged that the attackers had identified themselves with the BNP or were known to be members of BNP.[42] They also found that in some of the villages in these areas (for example, Bhola and Chandina) none of the minority community members had cast their ballot for fear of post-election reprisals. This is likely to have had an effect on the outcome of the elections in an area where competition is very tight. In fact, in 2001 the BNP did win the elections in Bhola, Barisal and Chandina.[43] This line of argument seems to hold true for other ethnic minorities as well because in Dinajpur, where the presence of the Santal (the second largest ethnic minority community in Bangladesh) was significant (one-fourth of total voters), news reports were filed detailing complaints about intimidation by AL cadres. It was assumed that AL candidates would lose the votes of this minority group since they had their own independent candidates fielded on these seats (Dinajpur-6 and Dinajpur-2).

It is important to note that the presence of a significant number of religious minority voters in a constituency alone would not mean that pre-election malpractices and post-election violence against them would automatically take place. An analysis of 12 constituencies where minority voters constitute a significant percentage reveal that in seven[44] constituencies the number of incidents of violence against minorities in the pre- and post-election phase was very low.[45] However, five out of these seven constituencies were either in traditionally AL-dominated areas (for example, Gopalganj, the birth district of Sheikh Mujibur Rahman, the founder leader of AL in its current form) or AL top leader Sheikh Hasina ran in these seats

(Narail). It may be argued that the absence of competition and the fact that AL offered protection to minorities explain why violence against a community identified as an AL vote bank would be low.[46]

Local level political dynamics also emerged as an important factor that had contributed to pre- and post-election violence against minorities in Bhola and Barisal. The nature of politics in Bhola and Barisal is generally described as '*char dokhol er* politics' (meaning extremely violent and bloody politics). In both areas, there were allegations that the incumbent AL MPs had turned a blind eye to widespread oppression of BNP workers and extortion of money from and violence against local people by some AL party leaders and workers.[47] The BNP leaders and workers including BNP *mastans* (political thugs) were forced to leave the area unless they joined the AL or were compelled to remain inactive. Furthermore, the elected AL MPs had given more importance to the new political recruits who had dubious backgrounds which distanced these MPs from the committed older rank of workers. The caretaker government, when it took over power, arrested those who had been involved in violent activities in these areas, especially *mastans* belonging to the AL. This created an insecure situation for the identified AL supporters including minorities and the general public. As one voter stated, 'the local leader had done a lot of development work, but he failed to curb violence and as a result we have reasons to feel insecure'.[48] A long-term monitoring report states that during the pre-election period (September) 94 incidents of violence and 68 incidents of looting had taken place in Barisal.[49]

The general perception in the case study areas was that the presence of the army reassured voters about security arrangements and in some areas where minority voters were harassed the army was able to intervene successfully. However, this was not the case in all minority areas. Fact-finding teams reported that the Hindus living in remote areas in Bhola had decided not to vote despite the presence of the army because they felt that the army would not be there to protect them in the post-election period. The CCHRB observer in Barisal reported that although security forces reached the troubled areas promptly their numbers were not adequate to tackle the situation.[50] Furthermore, the minority voters pointed out that the majority of the security forces were stationed at or were placed close to the polling centres which enabled 'miscreants' to prevent voters who lived in remote areas from coming to the polling centres. In the post-election phase in Bhola, the attacks took place on 2 October

2001 and the victims pointed out that most of the security forces were guarding the ballot boxes and were not available to prevent the attacks.[51]

Yet another factor that may have contributed to the high level of electoral discrimination and post-election violence is the unpreparedness of the local administration in tackling the situation. This may have been partly due to the fact that inclusion of minority voters or discrimination against minorities was not included as indicators in identifying vulnerable polling centres. Though the caretaker government had anticipated high levels of violence in several constituencies, systemic attacks on minorities in certain constituencies were not anticipated. The vulnerable centres were selected on the basis of: (a) level of electoral competition; (b) criminal record; and (c) whether that area had a record of election violence. The EC had identified 77 constituencies as highly vulnerable to violence, 170 as violence-prone constituencies and 53 as risk-free constituencies. In fact, 50 out of 79 centres in Barisal-1 had been marked as vulnerable because of the high level of violence in 1996.[52] However, neither the election monitors nor the EC thought that violence against minorities in the pre- and post-election periods would be a significant issue in 2001.[53]

Underlying/Structural Causes

At a very general level, one of the reasons behind the systematic targeting of religious minorities in the case study areas may be the rise of sectarian politics at the local and national levels after the Babri Masjid riots in India and Bangladesh in 1992.[54] Both in Bhola and Barisal, pro-Islamic, anti-Hindu and anti-India rhetoric had been used. Some election monitors pointed out that sectarian politics had particularly taken root in Bhola where the riots had been quite severe in 1992. Other areas where sectarian politics is present are areas where ethnic minority populations and other non-Hindu religious minorities live in significant numbers. For example, in Rangunia, Chittagong-7, where Hindus, Buddhists and ethnic minorities constitute a significant number of the voters, one candidate openly stated that if the minority voters were unable to cast their ballots he would win the election.[55] Although this is an extreme example, the equating of the unworthiness of an opponent with a religious identity other than Muslim had, in fact, triggered anti-minority feelings. The use of sectarian rhetoric is also evident in the election campaign at the national level in 1996 and 2001. Both the AL and BNP expressed their commitment to not enact any laws or adopt any policy that contradicted the Quran and Sunnah.[56]

Pre-election malpractices and post-election violence also need to be studied in the context of the materialistic aspirations of local influentials and political cadres. News scan analysis reveals that incidents of extortion and looting of Hindu property increased over time, particularly in the immediate aftermath of the elections (see Table 12.2). The fact-finding reports on the case study areas stated that Hindu houses were stripped of all their possessions, both valuable and non-valuable, which perhaps indicates a desire to inflict as much damage as possible on the victims.[57] The victims also pointed out that in the pre-election phase political cadres had taken away their cattle, poultry and fish, and also demanded large sums of money. Minorities in the case study area perceived land grabbing to be a prime motive behind the attacks. Many Hindu families were internally displaced by these attacks. At least 5,000 Hindus took shelter in Ramshil and Gopalganj and some families left for India.[58]

It is not that the houses of Muslim AL supporters were not attacked during the post-election phase, but that the Muslim supporters of the AL were not targeted and attacked as a group as the Hindus were in these areas.[59]

Fact-finding reports prepared by ASK, CCHRB and BMP reveal that the victims and their Muslim neighbours expressed two reasons behind the widespread destruction of Hindu property. First, the 'local good-for-nothings had claimed they belonged to BNP'[60] and taken advantage of the vulnerable position of the Hindu community in the post-election phase as they had no 'protectors or patrons' and 'reaped as much benefit as possible'.[61] Second, the underlying motivation behind these attacks was to grab Hindu land, create insecurity and initiate mass out-migration. Analysis of the nature of these incidents indicates that both these explanations are plausible and linked to the kinship-based patron–client power structure of Bangladeshi politics.

The existence of VPA of 1974 for 27 years had led to the systematic encroachment of Hindu and minority property by local influentials, irrespective of which political party they belong to,[62] and mass out-migration from all districts of Bangladesh. Local groups have a vested interest in communalising politics since land is a scarce commodity in Bangladesh.[63]

Fact-finding teams found that some of the well-off Hindu households were left untouched by the attackers.[64] Deeper investigation revealed that either these households had ties with local BNP influentials or were able to buy protection. However, buying protection was not an option that was open to the majority of the poor Hindu households. Moreover, traditionally the elite of the Hindu community who offered protection to poor Hindu households either belonged to the AL (for example, in Gouranadi) or had connections with local/senior AL leaders (in Chandina). These vertical ties were of no use when the attacks came from people claiming to be opposition political cadres. Historically Bangladeshi Hindus have not had vertical ties with the BNP. In areas where poor Muslims came under attack they were mostly protected by local leaders as a result of kinship-based ties.[65] However, this option based on kinship is not open to the Hindus which left them vulnerable to attacks from local opportunists, political thugs and influentials. This is not to say that Hindus had not sought help from local leaders or supporters of BNP. Reports from case study areas show that in some areas (particularly Bhola) neighbours who were supporters or activists of BNP, sheltered the Hindus although they were unable to save them from attacks. In many cases their own houses were set on fire and looted.[66] In Bhola, a local BNP worker reported that he had taken the matter up to senior party leaders and was told that 'you do not truly belong to [the] BNP, because real BNP workers would never give shelter to Hindus'.[67]

Criminalisation of politics[68] and the centralised party structure paralleled with a geographic concentration of power in the capital had contributed to the escalation of post-election violence.[69] The impact of geographical concentration of power was evident in the post-election scenario in Bhola and Barisal where there was no scope for both parties to control the situation because the losing candidates were not available to assess the situation, rein in the political cadres, and prevent violence.[70] Experts speculate that the investment made by each candidate for nomination and election[71] compels the elected MPs to leave their constituencies in search of privilege and positions and much of the political control/local administration over constituencies is left to the local henchmen. Since election victory is seen as a means of distributing the 'spoils of electoral combat', the elected candidates turn a blind eye to the extortion and looting that takes place in their localities. In fact, fact-finding teams alleged that in some case study areas high ranking local party cadres had divided the looted goods among themselves.[72]

V

Response

State and Political Response

The absence of effective response from the state and political parties regarding the violence perpetrated on religious and ethnic minorities in the pre- and post-election periods indicates the marginalisation of these groups in electoral politics. Both the major political parties and the left and right wing parties had stated in their election manifestos that they would uphold the rights of minority communities and the principles of non-discrimination stated in the Constitution.[73] This promise had been made by the AL and the BNP since 1991. However, most senior political officials had not publicly made any statements regarding ensuring the political rights of religious and ethnic minorities when news about discrimination against minorities was being published by the media. The AL leaders in Barisal-1 and Bagerhat-2 had complained to the newspapers about intimidation of minority voters. In some cases, the local BNP leaders had denied any involvement with minority voter intimidation. The AL had sent a delegation to the EC in order to prevent pre-election malpractices against minorities. However, the delegation was sent just four days before the elections and did not consist of high-ranking AL members.[74]

This indifferent political response can be termed as short-sighted and as an evasion of responsibility to the voter. Human rights activists point out that a responsible reaction would have been for the ruling party to rein in their cadres and reach out to the losing party so that both sides could have worked to maintain peace, law and order.[75]

Instead, top AL leaders were busy rejecting the poll results and accusing the caretaker government of being biased. Only after civil society organisations and the international media drew its attention to minority repression did the AL begin to issue statements against it.[76] Although the attacks on Gournadi and Agoiljhara Upzilla had taken place on 2 October 2001, none of the top AL leaders had gone to these areas till 20 October 2001. In fact, some analysts had interpreted the AL complaints as opportunistic because they had tried to present the repression of minorities within the broader context of repression against AL workers, in order to contest the legitimacy of 2001 elections.[77]

Initially the BNP Government had overlooked post-election violence against minorities and made no attempt to contain the disaster.
The Minister of Home Affairs, after a much publicised visit to
Ramshil and Gopalganj, where the minorities from Barisal had taken
refuge, claimed that the stories were exaggerated, concocted and a
conspiracy against the BNP,[78] which was also the position taken by
several ministers. The Minister of Finance, at a meeting in Delhi,
alleged that the attacks were 'contrived by [the] AL against [the]
BNP'.[79] In the case study areas local BNP leaders also toed the party
line by stating that some 'isolated events' had taken place and the
attacks were planned by the AL to 'blacken the image of BNP'.[80]
However, the government was spurred into action and promised
protection for *puja mandaps* (area where *puja* is performed) and temples
when the *puja udjapon* committee (committee for celebrating the
puja) announced that they would hold *ghot pujas* (ritual performed
during *puja* where household idols are worshipped),[81] but this promise was not effective in several areas (see Table 12.2).

Only after much publicising of the issue in the media and pressure
from donors and civil society organisations did the government
decide to form a four-member enquiry committee. This was a closed
committee consisting of government secretaries and no deadline was
set for submission of their report.[82]

These are probably indicators of the government's desire to side-
line the issue. A member of the Hindu–Buddha–Christian Oikya
Parishad (HBCOP) clearly explained the reasons behind the apathy
of both political parties: 'Why should AL or BNP care? If we stay
[the] AL is happy because they get votes and if we leave they get the
land. [The] BNP does not care, because if we leave they get the land
and [the] AL loses votes'.[83]

Local Administration

Fact-finding reports and news reports point to the apathy of the local
administration in the face of post-election violence against minorities. Under orders from the caretaker government, the local government had tried to reassure the minority voter in the pre-election
period. In Bhola, the district commissioner and additional district
commissioner had held meetings in several areas with minority
voters. However, the voters did not feel very secure with their
assurances.[84] In the post-election period the apathy shown by both
of the major parties, especially statements made by BNP leaders

suggesting that minority repression was a conspiracy by the AL, had a negative impact on the local administration.[85] The fact-finding teams found that the local administration was unwilling to draw attention to minority repression in their areas because they feared that it would invoke the 'displeasure' of the ruling party (see next section for the explanation offered by local administration on minority repression and their action regarding this). In addition, the involvement of locally powerful persons deterred any police action. The victims in the case study areas alleged that without the involvement of local influentials, the perpetrators could not have acted with such impunity.[86] One of the victims in Chandina stated, 'if the big leaders are not behind these acts then how can the perpetrators go on terrorising us?[87] Very few arrests were made in the selected case study areas. In some areas, Bhola for example, police failed to file specific charge sheets.[88]

Local administration had also been ineffective in providing relief to the victims in the form of food, clothes, medicine and medical treatment.[89] The BMP team found that none of the rape victims in Bhola had received any medical treatment.[90] The local health personnel refused to administer medical treatment because rape cases would have to be filed and the police refused to file rape cases. However, the police was compelled to register the case of a seven-year-old who was raped and required immediate medical attention.[91] In many instances the local administration denied any incidents of post-election violence against minorities. In one instance, when asked why Hindus had left their villages, a local administrator replied 'Only those who are criminals ran away'.[92] In another instance the officer-in-charge (OIC) tried to undermine the seriousness of the situation by stating that there were a few violent incidents and those were due to personal reasons or previous disputes.[93] In areas where local administrators had admitted to post-election violence, they had tried to explain the ineffectiveness of the administration by claiming surprise and unpreparedness.[94] This claim is perhaps highly debatable given the level of pre-election violence and voter intimidation in these areas.

Civil Society

Civil society organisations, especially human rights organisations and the print media at the local and national levels played a proactive role in drawing attention to post-election violence, collecting evidence and providing relief to the victims. The civil society organisations that solely represented minority interests had tried to draw attention to the repression against minorities in the pre-election phase at the local level. The premier organisation of religious minorities, HBCOP, had met with the caretaker government in September to express its concern. However, its efforts failed to garner a strong response from the government and particularly the political parties which may have been because this organisation is perceived as 'an insignificant *lejur* (appendage) of [the] AL'.[95] Immediately after elections, HBCOP called a press conference to highlight the plight of minority voters. However, their efforts did not gain momentum until other civil society organisations began to focus on this issue.

Through collection and publication of evidence from the field, press conferences and their proactive role in the media, civil society organisations forced the government out of inertia. ASK had filed a writ petition at the High Court based on which a show cause notice was served to the government and the inspector general (IG) of police, asking the government to explain why it had failed to provide security to minority citizens. The government is yet to present an enquiry report.[96] Fact-finding teams also reported that their presence in the affected areas had made the local administration conscious of bad publicity and this helped in the collection of evidence, and in some instances the filing of cases (the BMP has filed two cases and is fighting them in court). They also found that in some areas local civil society groups had campaigned for communal harmony and had managed to ensure peace during the pre- and post-election periods. In Bhola, for instance, the lawyers association had campaigned in selected areas where, as a result, communal harmony has been maintained.[97] These developments indicate perhaps the starting points for ensuring minority right to participation.

However, civil society in Bangladesh is mostly partisan.[98] Polarisation of civil society organisations into two political camps has weakened their initiative on the issue of inclusion of minorities.[99] Moreover, the government took a defensive stance against the pressure created by civil society organisations partly because of the presence of some organisations that were marked as appendages of the AL.[100] The government also tried to harass some workers of these particular organisations[101] by stating that they were involved in the conspiracy hatched by the AL to undermine the BNP. In fact, certain reports of these organisations on post-election violence sensationalised the issue by presenting minority repression as part of a conspiracy against the AL. All these undermined the effort by the civil society to raise public outcry against electoral violence.

It should be noted that these efforts by civil society organisations drew the attention of the intellectuals and the academia to the type of democracy prevalent in Bangladesh and the issue of minority voice and their inclusion in the political process. Having separate electorates for religious and ethnic minorities was suggested in order to ensure their participation in policy-making. This has been vehemently criticised by the HBCOP and academics. Many pointed out that this was against the provisions made in the Bangladesh Constitution and that it would further instigate communal feelings as it had during the Pakistan period.[102] Proportionate nomination by political parties and representation of religious minorities in the Parliament was favourably received. Whether this is politically feasible and whether the parties would reach a consensus on this remains highly debatable.

Conclusion

The extent of violence and brute force experienced by minority communities, especially the Hindus, during 2001 elections in certain areas of Bangladesh, was very intense. An analysis of causes shows that pre- and post-election malpractice experienced by the minorities was due to the culmination of various factors such as the rise of sectarian politics, marginalisation of minority issues in political and social life, indifference shown by local administration and political leaders, and criminalisation of politics. These certainly point to the fact that the issue of group discrimination in elections in Bangladesh is enmeshed in a complex web of issues related to power relations and the nature of 'democratic' politics.[103] It also points to the fact that while Bangladesh may have functioning democratic institutions, questions can be raised about the quality of democracy in Bangladesh.

Furthermore, the attempts made by the AL to 'capitalise' on minority repression to gain political mileage and the BNP's attempt to sweep the issue under the carpet have further marginalised the position of minorities as the issue of inclusion would now be identified as a partisan (AL) issue and undermine efforts to restore minority confidence in democracy. Although the efforts made by local and national civil society groups indicate that steps can be taken to curb violence and provide crucial support to minority groups, identification of strategies and institutional measures for ensuring minority participation have yet to be placed on the agenda for building a democratic polity.

The impact of pre- and post-election malpractice, especially violence, has implications for minority participation in the future. Many Hindus in the case study areas have already asked to be written off the voter list[104] and want the government to 'abolish' the minorities' right to vote and participate in the electoral process. For Bangladesh to become a flourishing plural democracy, measures need to be taken to punish the perpetrators and develop practices that encourage inclusion.

Notes

1. Institutions are defined here as a set of arrangements for organising political competition, legitimising rulers and implementing rules. R. Luckham, A.M. Goetz and M. Kaldor, 'Democratic, Institutions and Transition in the Context of Inequality, Poverty and Conflict,' IDS Discussion Paper No. 104.
2. Quality refers to creating mechanisms for inclusion that would help to create a stable, legitimate and effective government. This means that the powerful groups cannot use power to subvert, co-opt or corrupt the process of democracy.
3. Basically refers to the use of thugs and muscle power and black money. Connection to marginalisation of minority community will be discussed in a later section (interview with Prof. M. Guhathakurta, Dept. of International Relations, University of Dhaka, 23 Feburary 2002).
4. A. Chowdhury 'State and the Minority: The Case of Hindus in Bangladesh', in C. Abrar (ed.), *On the Margin: Refugees, Migrants, Minorities*, Dhaka, Refugee and Migratory Movements Research Unit (RMMRU), 2000.
5. A. Mohsin, 'Rights of Ethnic Minorities', *Human Rights in Bangladesh 2002*, Dhaka, ASK, 2001.
6. A. Mohsin, *The Politics of Nationalism: The Case of CHT, Bangladesh*, Dhaka, UPL, 1997.
7. Ibid.
8. The poor members belonging to any religious minority community had less access to the state and their exercise of citizenship was limited. However, this was the same for a poor person belonging to the dominant community.
9. There is debate on whether inclusion of secularism as one of the state principles in the Constitution had any effective impact on the society or political culture since the ideals of secularism were not reflected in the educational curricula or any other matters (interview with A. Khanam, general secretary, Bangladesh Mohila Parishad, 28 May 2002).
10. S. Moral, 'Rights of Religions Minorities.

11. The Eighth Amendment was challenged by women's groups at the High Court in 1988. The matter still remains *subcommittees judice*.

12. S. Nazneen, 'Bangladesh Rastre Santal Shomprodai: Prantikaroner Shikar?' *Somaj Nirikhkhon* No. 74, November 1999; MLAA, 'Collective Rights of Ethnic Minorities: A Report Prepared for Sasawaka Project' (Unpublished), New Town, Madaripur, 1996.

13. VPA, 1974 was repealed by AL in 2001.

14. A. Barakat and Shafique uz Zaman, 'Forced Migration of Hindu Minority: Human Deprivation due to Vested Property Act,' in C. Abrar (ed.), *On the Margin: Refugees, Migrants, Minorities*, Dhaka RMMRU, 2000. A. Barakat et al., estimate that about 164 million acres were affected by VPA over the years and more than 40 per cent of total Hindu households were affected. The study also found out that in 92 per cent of the cases the beneficiaries of VPA were the local members or chairpersons of the union parishads. In about 45 per cent of the cases the beneficiaries belonged to a party with religious sentiments.

15. See A. Chowdhury 'State and the Minority...' for the Hindu community's perception on citizenship.

16. Guhathakurta interview, and Khanam interview.

17. H. Hossain, 'Violence Against Minorities in Bangladesh: An Analysis', *Combating Communalism (Draft)*, 2001; J. Achariya, 'Nirapattahin Shonkhyalaghu', *Saptahik 2000, Weekly Magazine*, 19 October 2001. The percentage of minority representation in the Parliament in 1991 was 3.63 per cent (12 seats); in 1996 it was 4.24 per cent (14 seats) and in 2001 it was 1.25 per cent (4 seats).

18. It is interesting to note that in the 2001 parliamentary election and various other local level elections, women have been successfully integrated in the political process (related to participation and voting) because of the proactive effort of the election commission, local administration, NGOs and women's rights group. In the parliamentary elections of 2001, women have voted for the first time in many years in 12 constituencies (see Guhathakurta interview).

19. Reports of 14 monitoring organisations funded by the Asia Foundation (that is, Brotee, FEMA, BNPS, Democracy Watch, MMS, Odhikar, Banchte Shekha, etc.) and observation report submitted by the European Union and UNDP.

20. This was very succinctly put by a local election observer: 'Ensuring "shanti" on election day is only part of it. If voter intimidation takes place beforehand and if voters are afraid of reprisals, do you think election will be free and fair? But very few observers and monitors will think about this' (CCHRB, *The CCHRB Election Observation Report: The Eighth Parliamentary Election 2001*, Dhaka, SEHD, 2002).

21. *The Daily Star*, 17 September 2001.

22. *Prothom Alo*, 19 September 2001.

23. Brotee, 'Eighth Parliamentary Election 2001: Election Monitoring   Report' (Draft), Dhaka, Brotee, 2001.

24. M. Guhathakurta, 'A Report from Bhola', Dhaka, 11 February 2002, ASK.

25. Q.A. Tahmina, 'Dhormiyo Shonkhyaloghu-r Opor Hamla: Otironjon na Nishthur Sattya?' *Dainik Ekota*, 5 November 2001.

26. A. Nazrul, 'Minority Voting Issues: When Shamsur Rahman Protests', *The Daily Star*, 9 October 2001.
27. The news scan does not reveal the true extent of rape. The numbers would be higher but many incidents were not reported to the media. The fact-finding teams, especially teams sent by Bangladesh Mohila Parishad to Bhola and news reports on Barisal found that in several villages, all women (more than 50/60 in each village), regardless of age, have been raped. (M. Banu, 'Sarejomine Bholar Protibendon', *Mohila Samachar, Bangladesh Mohila Parishad Bulletin*, October–December 2001; Sammilito Samajik Andolon, Nirjatoner Dolil–2001: Nirbachon Purba and Nirbachan Uttar Shanghkyaloghu Nipiron, Dhaka, 2002).
28. The medical team of BMP found evidence of physical injury that suggests rape had taken place. They also found other corroborating evidence that indicates that the incidents narrated by the women were true. (that is, marks on their bodies where leeches had attached themselves, where the women had taken refuge in the water).
29. M. Banu, 'Sarejomine Bholar....'.
30. Guhathakurta interview, interview with S. Moral, Human Rights activist, CCHRB, 19, April 2002; Sammilito Samajik Andolon.
31. Fear of violence had also deterred women in other constituencies that did not have a significant number of Hindu voters (for example, Feni). An overall 73 per cent of the female voters had cast their ballots in 2001 parliamentary elections, which is a significant number.
32. Brotee, 'Eighth Parliamentary Elections...'.
33. See M. Guhathakurta, 'A Report from Bhola'.
34. Ibid.
35. *The CCHRB Election Observation Report.*
36. Amnesty International, *Bangladesh: Attacks on Members of Hindu Minority*, December 2001.
37. Q.A. Tahmina, 'Sarjomion Protibedon: Barisal', *Dainik Ekota*, 12 November 2001; M. Guhathakurata, 'Assault on Minorities in Bangladesh. An Analysis', *www. dristipath.org*, 2002; 'The CCHRB...' Election Observation Report.
38. There is very little ideological difference between AL and BNP. AL has also used Islam to garner votes. (This will be discussed later.)
39. Alliance building emerged as a crucial factor for securing election victory ever since AL benefited from a tacit alliance with Jammat in the parliamentary election of 1996.
40. Generally the majority interprets this Pro-AL stance of the Hindu community as the result of AL's pro-India policy.
41. Interview with P. Gain, Human Rights Activist, CCHRB, 21 April 2002.
42. ASK, *Draft Report on Violence against Minorities in September and October in Bangladesh*, Dhaka, 2001; Q.A. Tahmina, 'Sarjomion Protibedon...'; M. Guhathakurta, 'A Report from Bhola'.
43. The difference in Keshabpur between candidates is very slim though AL won. In Barisal the difference between AL and BNP is around 14,000 (quite slim considering the total votes). In Bhola the difference seems to be large, about 40,000.

44. These are 3 seats in Gopalganj; 2 in Narail.
45. A. Nazrul, 'Minority Voting Issues'.
46. A recent report identified 134 constituencies where the minority community has 'swing vote', analysed the voting patterns in elections and claimed that party affiliation of the candidates have become less important and that identity of the candidate has become the determining factor in who wins in these constituencies (*Prothom Alo*, 26 January 2004). Arefin also provides statistics which reveal that in 2001, the four party alliance (BNP and others) have won 90 seats out of the 134 constituencies which is more than thrice the number they had won in 1996. (However, the news report did not state how the researcher had identified these 134 constituencies as where the minority has swing vote, hence the author is unable to comment further on these findings.)
47. *The CCHRB ... Report*, B.A. Nabil, 'Shatti Ashone Lorai: Barisal and Patuakhali', *Saptahik 2000*, 14 October 2001.
48. *The CCHRB ... Report*, p. 86.
49. *The CCHRB ... Report*.
50. Ibid.
51. M. Guhathakurta, 'A Report from Bhola'.
52. *The CCHRB ... Report*.
53. Debates took place over whether to include the question on 'whether minorities had voted freely' in the election observation forms prepared for the election monitors. The number of dissenters among election monitoring organisations was significant (interview with P. Gain, 21 April 2002).
54. M. Guhathakurta, 'A Report from Bhola'.
55. *Prothom Alo*, 25 September 2001.
56. J. Achariya and M. Adnan, 'Eto Mukh Noi Jeno', *Saptahik 2000*, 14 September 2001.
57. H. Hossain, 'Violence against Minorities...'.
58. *Prothom Alo*; M. Guhathakurta, 'A Report from Bhola'.
59. Q.A. Tahmina, 'Dhormiyo ... Hamla'.
60. Q.A. Tahmina, 'Sarjomion Protibedon...'.
61. Ibid.
62. A. Barakat et al., 'Forced Migration of Hindu Minority...'.
63. M. Guhathakurta, 'A Report from Bhola'.
64. Interview with Q.A. Tahmina, associate professor, Dept. of Journalism, University of Dhaka, 21 April 2002.
65. Ibid.
66. M. Guhathakurta 'A Report from Bhola'; *The CCHRB ... Report*.
67. M. Guhathakurta, 'A Report from Bhola'.
68. In Bhola 20 political cadres were arrested based on complaints, but released by the police. In interviews conducted by *Saptahik 2000*, the cadres stated that all types of arms, including the latest models were brought in for the election. (B.A. Nabil, 'Shatti Ashone ...'). Of the 2 lakh licensed arms only 6,000 were surrendered at various police stations before the election (*Prothom Alo*, 26 September 2001).
69. H. Hossain, 'Violence against Minorities...'.

70. Ibid.
71. Investment for nomination may cost a prospective candidate between 10 lakh to 50 lakh taka (see *Saptahik*, *2000*, 7 September 2001).
72. Guhathakurta interview.
73. J. Achariya and M. Adnan, 'Eto Mukh ...'.
74. *Prothom Alo*, 26 September 2001.
75. Whether the party leaders would have been able to control the violence and looting is debatable. Recent political events show that criminalisation of politics and lack of internal democracy within the parties has led to a situation where the *mastans* are able to restrict actions against them taken by the top party officials.
76. H. Hossain, 'Violence against Minorities ...'.
77. Ibid.
78. Ibid.
79. ASK, *Draft Report* ....
80. Q.A. Tahmina, 'Dhormiyo ... Hamla,' M. Guhathakurta, 'A Report from Bhola'.
81. Instead of making deities of Durga and her children, only a *ghot* (pot) would be used to symbolise the deities.
82. H. Hossain, 'Violence against Minorities...'.
83. J. Achariya, 'Nirapattahin ...'.
84. *Prothom Alo*, 1 October 2002.
85. H. Hossain, 'Violence against Minorities ...'.
86. Q.A. Tahmina, 'Sarjomion Protibedon ...'; ASK, *Draft Report*....
87. Q.A. Tahmina, 'Sarjomion Protibedon...'.
88. M. Guhathakurta, 'A Report from Bhola'.
89. Ibid., Q.A. Tahmina, 'Dhormiyo, ... Hamla'; 'Sarjomion Protibedon...'.
90. M. Banu, 'Sarejomine ... Protibendon'.
91. Ibid.
92. Q.A. Tahmina, 'Sarjomion Protibedon...'.
93. Ibid.
94. M. Guhathakurta, 'A Report from Bhola'.
95. Quoted by a member of the organisation in J. Achariya, 'Nirapattahin ...'.
96. H. Hossain, 'Violence against Minorities ...'.
97. M. Guhathakurta interview.
98. M. Hassan, 'Supply of and Demand for Second Generation Reform: The Case of Bangladesh', PhD thesis, Institute of Commonwealth Studies, University of London, 2001; K. Stiles, 'International Support for NGOs in Bangladesh: Some Unintended Consequences', *World Development*, Vol. 30, No. 5, 2002.
99. Khanam interview.
100. Ibid.
101. Government arrested a worker of Proshika (a large development NGO), carrying reports prepared by NGOs on minority repression. He was later released. The most publicised case is the one of Shahriar Kabir, who was arrested after he came back from West Bengal where he showed the videos he had made on minority repression. The government has filed a case against him. Kabir had actively campaigned for AL during election.

102. J. Achariya, 'Nirapattahin ...'.
103. M. Guhathakurta 'A Report from Bhola'.
104. *The CCHRB ... Report*.

13

INDIA

Amit Prakash

Electoral processes have taken various forms the world over but in a representative democracy its fundamental role remains that of ensuring free and equal exercise of political rights by all citizens. The issue which arises therefore is the extent to which citizens have equal access to an equal role in the political system.

Representative democracy is not the only mechanism through which interests of the citizens are aggregated. Social aggregation of interest is expressed in the political system via the formal institutions of representative democracy—the elections. However, social groups are an equally important mechanism through which the interests of the citizens are aggregated and articulated. The interface between the political and social systems contains many contradictions which often sharpen to such an extent that the inequality of the social system starts to reflect in the formally equal political system. This expression of social inequality in the political system may take many forms: from formal institutionalisation of political inequality on the lines of social groups to informal inequality of the political process. Whatever form such a process may take, it constitutes discrimination against some section of the citizenry.

This chapter aspires to examine the issue in the context of India and analyse the operation of discrimination in elections at the formal–constitutional level as well as at the level of the actual political process.

I

In a plural society like India, there are multiple and overlapping group identities around numerous premises such as caste, religion, community, ethnic identity, tribe, language, gender and so on. Such plurality offers a rich field for political mobilisation along and across any number of these socio-political fault lines. Political mobilisation based on any one or more of these premises has an inherent tendency of engendering a politics of discrimination. Various groups mobilised into political identities[1] on any such group premise compete with other similarly mobilised groups for the same political and electoral space. Consequently, in the case of a competing political claim, the politics of electoral space leads to the domination of the larger (usually, but not necessarily, numerically larger) socio-political identity. The smaller/weaker socio-political identity is unable to find adequate political and electoral space and the net result is electoral and political discrimination against the marginalised social groups/ political identities. In this political process, some degree of discrimination against a certain social group is institutionalised into formal legal structures. More often than not, such discrimination is targeted at minorities and the marginalised sections of the society.

In India the historically disadvantaged and marginalised social communities and minorities are the Scheduled Castes (SCs), Scheduled Tribes (STs) and Women. They also include ethnic and religious-based identities such as Muslims, the Dravidian identity in south India, Sikhs and so on.

As far as ethnic and religious-based identities in India vis-à-vis the electoral system are concerned, the absence of positive discrimination for these identities was a conscious choice made by the representatives of these communities in the Constituent Assembly (CA). While historically these social groups enjoyed special provisions under the British rule, they voluntarily relinquished their claim to positive discrimination during the process of the framing of the Constitution owing to the perceived need to stress a common citizenship. However, this does not imply that these communities have equal access to the electoral system. These social groups have no legal or formal impediment to the enjoyment of equal political rights and any discrimination that might exist against them is not directly attributable to any actual desire by the state to reduce or eliminate the election of citizens who happen to belong to a minority. The problem is rather a manifestation of a structural difficulty or flaw in many political systems, including majoritarian democracies; owing to their smaller numbers and territorial dispersion, minorities are systematically outvoted in terms of their participation and representation in public life. This constitutes an impediment to their enjoyment of individual political rights and, hence, discrimination in the political process. Here, it must also be noted that the institutional structures as well as the political process operate within a set of discursive structures, which encourage or hinder the operation of discrimination.

The SCs and STs, however, have been beneficiaries of constitutionally mandated positive discrimination. It is widely agreed that positive discrimination in the Indian context has led to a wave of democratisation. For instance, the growing assertiveness of hitherto marginalised sections of the society (especially in the north Indian states) is testimony to the fact that such positive discrimination has been of immense value in fostering democratisation of the polity. This has not only challenged old structures of domination which had discriminated against the marginalised sections for centuries, but has also set in motion a pattern of socio-economic and political empowerment which is irreversible and will significantly alter the popular political discourse, the political idiom and the patterns of discrimination.

However, there are significant problems with the way in which such positive discrimination has been implemented. There is a valid criticism that such positive discrimination in favour of the marginalised population has, over the past half century, led to serious discrimination against the majority and non-marginalised sections of the population. Positive discrimination for women has also been hanging fire for more than a decade.

Section II will examine the process of the framing of the Constitution of India in order to underline the broad contours of the discussion on equality of political rights and discrimination in the post-colonial discourse in India. Section III will delineate the emergent constitutional provisions embodying the central principles of this discourse. Section IV will analyse the support base of various political formations during the 1990s in terms of the social categories to examine if discriminatory practices have been operating in the political process. Section V will examine the infirmities of the institutional structure of political equality leading to discriminatory practices of the non-conventional kind. Some conclusions will be offered in Section VI.

II

Framework of Equality and Discrimination: Concerns in the Constituent Assembly

The Constitution of India lays down the parameters within which the electoral system of the country must operate and also provides the institutional structures for the same. The laws enacted by the Parliament attempt to further the constitutional design and implement the spirit of the provisions of the Constitution in all fields of public life, the electoral system included. Thus, while the details of the electoral system are provided by the various parliamentary enactments (such as the *Representation of the People Act, 1951*), these enactments are designed to provide an enabling framework for enforcing the constitutional provisions. The constitutional provisions lay down the basic framework of the electoral system (see Section III) but the provisions that deal with group discrimination (or, more accurately, the portions which outlaw such discrimination on any ground) during the electoral process in particular and the political process in general is not directly a part of the electoral scheme laid out in the Constitution. These provisions flow from the constitutional provisions and framework dealing with Citizenship, Fundamental Rights, Administration of Scheduled Areas and the Directive Principles of State Policy. Hence, in order to isolate the constitutional framework vis-à-vis group discrimination in India, attention must be paid to Parts II, III and XVI of the Constitution of India (see Section III).

Further, in order to understand the structures which buttress the constitutional provisions, it is crucial to analyse the ideational framework in which these provisions were framed. Hence, adequate attention needs to be focused on the CA debates. These debates provide an insight into the reasons why a certain framework was preferred in place of other possible options and also provide background to the content of the Constitution.

The CA and the political leaders who formed the CA were acutely conscious of the central role that such rights would play in the future political and administrative set-up of the country. Consequently, the Experts Committee appointed by the Indian National Congress (INC) to recommend and prepare materials for the CA decided in its meeting on 20–22 July 1946 that in consonance with the Cabinet Mission Plan, the first session of the CA should appoint an Advisory Committee on Fundamental Rights, Minorities, and Tribal and Excluded Areas to recommend to the CA the scheme of fundamental rights which must form an integral part of the future administrative and constitutional arrangements for India. This centrality of fundamental rights was seen as important to guarantee full and equal political rights to all citizens of India, including minorities.

The Experts Committee of the INC also recommended that immediately after the appointment of the Committee on Fundamental Rights, a Resolution regarding Aims and Objects must be adopted by the CA in order to clearly lay down the goals towards which the Constitution being framed must aspire. In pursuance of this recommendation, an 'Objectives Resolution' was moved in the CA by Jawaharlal Nehru on 13 December 1946 which proclaimed that the Constitution to be framed would be such,

> Wherein shall be guaranteed and secured to all the people of India justice, social, economic and political; equality of status, of opportunity, and before the law...
> [and]
> ... adequate safeguards shall be provided for minorities, backward and tribal areas, and depressed and other backward classes...[2]

Stressing the importance of the Objectives Resolution, Nehru had observed that while this resolution does not seek to circumscribe the freedom of the CA to frame and adopt a Constitution as it thought fit, it 'lays down only certain fundamentals which ... no group or party and hardly any individual in India can dispute'.[3]

The inextricable link between the Indian polity and full and equal rights to the minorities, at least at the institutional and legal level, was thus firmly established in the very first act of the CA. The mindfulness of the CA towards the minorities was also stressed by Dr S. Radhakrishnan, who while commending the Objectives Resolution to the CA, stressed that the CA will endeavour to 'abolish every vestige of despotism ... bring about real satisfaction of the fundamental needs of the common man of this country, irrespective of race, religion or community....'[4]

The foundations of a fundamental feature of the Indian Constitution—that of full and equal political rights to all sections of the society—was thus laid in very steady ground indeed. The following discussion analyses the main contours of the CA debates with respect to those sections in the Indian Constitution that buttress this idea of political equality.

Single and Equal Citizenship

The provisions concerning citizenship were incorporated into the Draft Constitution which was presented before the CA for detailed consideration.[5] While moving the Draft Constitution, B.R. Ambedkar stressed that unlike the US, where a dual citizenship obtains (federal and state), in the proposed Indian Constitution, 'there is only one citizenship for the whole of India ... every citizen of India has the same rights of citizenship, no matter in what State he resides'.[6] The stress on ruling out any discrimination in the rights of citizenship and rejection of more than one citizenship is quite clear. Throughout a protracted debate on this issue before the provisions were finalised, there was hardly any doubt that all citizens of India were to be treated equally. The debate centred on various definitions to exclude persons of alien origin from Indian citizenship and defining parameters for the same. In other words, the CA was convinced that there must only be one citizenship of India wherein all citizens of India would have equal rights.[7]

Universal Adult Suffrage

Once the question of single and equal citizenship was settled and agreed upon by the CA, the next relevant question was that of equal political rights to all citizens. While there was substantial opinion in the CA on the desirability of universal adult suffrage, there was no unanimity on this issue.[8]

Article 67(6) of the Draft Constitution prepared by the Drafting Committee had proposed that

> The election to the House of the People shall be on the basis of adult suffrage; that is to say, every citizen who is not less than

twenty-one years of age and is not otherwise disqualified ... on the ground of non-residence, unsoundness of mind, crime or corrupt or illegal practice shall be entitled to be registered as a voter at such elections.[9]

When this Article was discussed in the CA on 3 and 4 January 1949,[10] though a number of Amendments were moved, none of them questioned the desirability of the provision for universal adult franchise. However, when Article 149(2)[11] of the Draft Constitution, dealing with similar provisions for the states' legislative assemblies was taken up for discussion, K.T. Shah proposed an Amendment that sought to add a new clause which, amongst other things, provided that no person shall be entitled to be a candidate or offer himself for election to either House of a state legislature

> ... who is unable to read or write or speak the principal language spoken in the State for a seat in whose legislature he offers himself for election, or after a period of ten years from the date of coming into operation of this constitution, is unable to read or write or speak the National Language of India, shall be entitled to be a candidate for or offer himself to be elected to a seat in the State Legislature....[12]

This Amendment tried to institute a qualification of literacy and lingual proficiency for the exercise of the citizen's right to be elected to the state legislatures. Given the rich diversity of languages, culture and educational levels in the country, such a provision might have discriminated against certain groups, particularly the historically disadvantaged ones. However, this amendment was rejected by the CA and the exercise of their political rights by the citizens was to be subject to the tests of Indian citizenship, soundness of mind and of not being a criminal or corrupt person. Thus, the CA continued the pattern of not prescribing any qualification that might have discriminated against any set of persons on any socio-economic, cultural or ascriptive premise.

Thus, great care was taken by the CA to ensure that there is no institutional, legal or formal disability for any section of the population as far as the exercise of their political rights as citizens was concerned. No discrimination was allowed on any ground and universal adult suffrage became the framework for the operation of the electoral process.

Minorities, SCs and STs:
Joint Electorates and Positive Discrimination

The CA was also acutely aware of two other factors which had the possibility of playing havoc with the non-discriminatory scheme of political rights that was envisaged by its members. The first was the issue of separate electorates for religious minorities and the second was the issue of equal participation in the electoral process by the historically disadvantaged sections of the population, namely, the SCs and the STs. Since discriminatory electoral practices usually affect these very sections of the population, the CA felt that some enabling provisions were required. The rationale for such provisions was that in a political system wherein all individuals have equal political and civic rights, majoritarian impulses can lead to the denial of rights to minorities and the disadvantaged sections of the society, which would undermine the very scheme of equal and fair representation to all sections of the population.

Therefore, in order to arrive at a well-considered decision vis-à-vis the question of a separate electorate for the various religious minorities and other minority rights, a Subcommittee on Minorities was appointed by the Advisory Committee on Fundamental Rights, Minorities and Tribal and Excluded Areas on 27 February 1947 and its membership represented all minority interests. The Subcommittee discussed a wide variety of issues concerning the minorities such as the removal of all disabilities which might hinder their participation in public life (especially in the case of SCs and STs) and at the same time stressed the need for preserving the cultural and educational rights of all minorities, especially the religious minorities. The issues of relevance to this discussion were those of political safeguards for the minorities: separate/joint electorates and reservation of seats for minorities in the Parliament and state legislatures. As may be expected, a wide variety of opinions were articulated on these issues and there was no unanimity in the Subcommittee and many decisions were arrived at by voting. Vallabhbhai Patel, in his covering letter forwarding the report to the CA, noted that:

> ... from the very nature of things, it was difficult to expect complete unanimity on all points ... however, [it may be noted] that our recommendations, where they were not unanimous, were taken by very large majorities composed substantially of members belonging to minority communities themselves.[13]

On the question of separate/joint electorates, the subcommittee

> ... by an overwhelming majority ... came to the conclusion that the system of separate electorates must be abolished in the new Constitution. In our judgement, this system has in the past sharpened communal differences to a dangerous extent and has proved one of the main stumbling blocks to the development of a healthy national life....
>
> ... we recommend accordingly that all elections to Central and Provincial Legislatures should be held on the basis of joint electorates. In order that minorities may not feel apprehensive about the effects of a system to unrestricted joint electorates on the quantum of their representation in the Legislature, we recommend as a general rule that seats for different recognised minorities shall be reserved in the various legislatures on the basis of their population. This reservation should initially be for a period of 10 years, the position to be reconsidered at the end of that period. We recommend also that members of a minority community who have reserved seats shall have a right to contest unreserved seats as well. As a matter of general principle, we are opposed to weightage for any minority community.[14]

Thus, the Subcommittee on Minorities favoured reservation of seats for the minorities but did not find it desirable to recommend separate electorates for the various minority communities. Besides, any kind of proportional representation for the minorities was also ruled out by the Subcommittee on Minorities.

Accordingly, the provisions recommended by the subcommittee for inclusion in the Constitution were:

Electorates: All elections to the Central and Provincial Legislatures will be held on the basis of joint electorate:

Provided that as a general rule, there shall be reservation of seats for the minorities shown in the schedule in the various legislatures on the basis of their population:

Provided further that such representation shall be for 10 years, the position to be reconsidered at the end of the period.[15]

The Report of the Subcommittee on Minorities was considered in the Advisory Committee on Fundamental Rights, Minorities and Tribal and Excluded Areas on 28–31 July 1947. While most of the recommendations of the Subcommittee on Minorities were endorsed by the advisory committee, a separate subcommittee was appointed to report on the case of Indian Christians and Anglo-Indian population in the country. The reports of these subcommittees were incorporated into the Draft Constitution prepared by the constitutional advisor. However, in every meeting of the Advisory Committee, some of the issues with regard to political safeguards for the minorities were raised by various members, especially on the issues of separate electorates and that of reservations.

In the meeting of the Advisory Committee on 30 December 1948, some suggestions of a fundamental nature were made. Some members had given notice of resolutions seeking to do away with reservations for all minorities. Despite a decision of the CA that there must be reservation of seats in the Union and state legislatures for Muslims, SCs, STs, Indian Christians, Sikhs and so on, in view of the vastly changed situation after Partition, it was decided that the report of the Advisory Committee of 1947, on the basis of which provision had been made for reservation for the minorities, was no longer valid.

Consequently, the Advisory Committee reconvened on 11 May 1949 where the resolution for the abolition of reservation for all minorities other than SCs found wholehearted support from an overwhelming majority of the members of the Advisory Committee.[16] It was recognised, however, that the peculiar position of the SCs would make it necessary to give them reservations for a period of 10 years. Besides, the Advisory Committee further decided that the reservation of seats made by the North East Frontier (Assam) Tribal and Excluded Areas Subcommittee and the Excluded and Partially Excluded Areas (other than Assam) Subcommittee[17] would stand.

This 'finalised' report was moved in the CA on 25 May 1949 by Vallabhbhai Patel, where he observed there had been

> ... a considerable change in the attitude of the minorities themselves.[18] [Members from the minority communities themselves] ... moved a motion for dropping of the clause on reservation of seats in legislature on population basis. When this proposal was moved, Mr Muniswamy Pillai, who was representing the Scheduled Castes, moved an amendment to the effect that provision for reservation, so far as the Scheduled Castes are concerned, may be continued for a period of ten years. The general opinion in the

Advisory Committee was, which was almost unanimous, that this reservation so far as the Scheduled Castes are concerned, should be continued for that period and Mr Muniswamy Pillai's amendment was accepted.... The Committee considering the whole situation came to the conclusion that the time has come when the vast majority of the minority communities have themselves realised after great reflection the evil effects in the past of such reservation on the minorities themselves, and the reservations should be dropped.[19]

In the charged debate in the CA on this issue lasting for two days, some amendments were moved to recommend both separate electorates as well as reservation of seats for the minorities. However, the majority of the CA members felt that since the minorities had themselves proposed abolition of these measures, it was a welcome step towards a secular India. Clearly, the concern about centrifugal tendencies emerging from such special political rights being granted to minorities had a role to play in the matter.

The net result of all the above processes concerning political safeguards for minorities was that the Constitution did not envisage any kind or degree of discrimination against any of the minorities. Thus, while no special political rights were envisaged for the religious minorities, the provisions on fundamental rights sought to protect and safeguard all the cultural and social rights of all minorities.

Scheduled Castes and Tribes

As far as the question of the STs was concerned (along with the case of SCs discussed above), the CA took an entirely different view. The case of SCs and STs were treated as different from all other questions before the CA. While there seems to have been hardly any disagreement on the question of special political rights for the SCs in view of their peculiar historical trajectories, the issues related to the STs and administration of excluded areas were examined by two subcommittees.[20] These subcommittees recommended various safeguards, which were incorporated into the constitutional scheme of administration. Of the many safeguards recommended for the STs, only one is of relevance to the present discussion—reservation of seats for the STs in accordance with their population.

The Assam Subcommittee proposed that the excluded and partially excluded areas, which were not represented or only partially represented in the legislatures, must be given full representation on the basis of a joint electorate, universal adult franchise and reservation of seats in accordance with their population. The 'Other than Assam Subcommittee', on the other hand, recommended direct universal franchise with reservation of seats and strongly opposed nomination or indirect election.[21]

This became the ground for one significant digression from the framework of equal political rights: that of additional political rights and safeguards for SCs and STs.[22] There seems to have been near unanimity in the Advisory Committee and the CA that these two communities, on account of historical injustices suffered and/or having been excluded from normal administration under the British rule, were entitled to additional political rights in order to secure adequate representation of their interests in the legislatures. This strand of the framework of the CA debates cannot be construed to act as a discriminating factor against the wider communities concerned. However, the way in which this provision has been operationalised may act as a source of discrimination against non-SC/non-ST communities. This discussion shall be taken up in a subsequent section.

The Drafting Committee included suitable provisions to incorporate the recommendations of these two subcommittees. While discussing the relevant sections of the Draft Constitution (Articles 292 and 293), there seemed to have been no disagreement in the CA as far as the electoral provisions for the STs were concerned.

Thus, the overall framework which emerged from the process of Constitution-making over the period of functioning of the CA and its Advisory Committees was that of conscious removal of all possible disabilities which might hinder or retard the exercise of full political rights by any member of any minority community. Universal adult franchise and joint electorates were repeatedly emphasised by various bodies concerned with the framing of the Constitution. These two concepts emerged as the bulwark of the democratic set-up of India.

The framework of equal citizenship and political rights for all individuals, irrespective of community, sex or creed was tempered by cultural and educational rights for the minorities. This ensured that while political equality was emphasised, such equality would not translate into majority-led homogenisation of the polity.

III

Constitutional Framework: Equal Electoral Rights and Positive Discrimination

The framework of equality and positive discrimination that emerged from the CA has been embodied in the Constitution, adopted on 26 November 1949 and brought into force from 26 January 1950, as amended from time to time. The constitutional provisions along with the framework of the CA debates lay down the parameters for the operation of the electoral process in India. Hence, before discussing the operational dynamics of the framework of non-discrimination and equality of political rights enunciated by the CA, it is imperative to briefly enumerate the constitutional provisions that emerged from the labours of the CA and provide the overall institutional–legal framework for the electoral process in India.

The constitutional emphasis on the requirement for removal of all disability in the exercise of full political rights by all citizens of India starts from the Preamble to the Constitution, which proclaims that:

We, the People of India, having solemnly resolved ... *to secure to all its citizens*:
Justice, social, economic and political;
Liberty of thought, expression, belief, faith and worship;
Equality of status and of opportunity;
and to promote among them all ... (emphasis added).[23]

The discursive emphasis of the National Movement on the removal of the 'Rule of Difference'[24] thus finds a clear expression right at the beginning of the Constitution.

While the Preamble clearly lays down the ideological apparatus of the Constitution and in that sense has significant importance in the operation of the constitutional process, the actual provisions of the Constitution are of more crucial importance. As was pointed out in the preceding pages, the framework of discrimination (or the lack thereof) starts from the provisions of citizenship in Article 5, which provides that:

At the commencement of this Constitution every person who has his domicile in the territory of India and

(a) who was born in the territory of India; or
(b) either of whose parents was born in the territory of India; or
(c) who has been ordinarily resident in the territory of India for not less than five years preceding such commencement, shall be a citizen of India.[25]

Thus, the emphasis on single and uniform citizenship noticed in the CA debates was embodied in this Article of the Constitution. Care was also taken that the large number of persons who migrated from the territories of present-day Pakistan and Bangladesh or elsewhere, or those who acquired Indian citizenship by virtue of naturalisation, did not suffer any disability in citizenship.[26]
While the creation of a single citizenship for all citizens of India, was an important part of the creation of a non-discriminatory framework for the electoral process, the latter was buttressed by the provisions on fundamental rights contained in Part III of the Constitution. While the Constitution envisages eight fundamental rights[27] available to all citizens of India,[28] this discussion will confine itself to those relevant to the electoral process.
The provisions of Part III, amongst others, provide that:

The State shall not deny to any person equality before the law or the equal protection of the laws within the territory of India.
… Prohibition of discrimination on grounds of religion, race, caste, sex or place of birth.
(1) The State shall not discriminate against any citizen on grounds only of religion, race, caste, sex, place of birth or any of them.
(2) No citizen shall, on grounds only of religion, race, caste, sex, place of birth or any of them, be subject to any disability, liability, restriction or condition….[29]

While ensuring that there must be no institutionalised discrimination in the exercise of the rights of all citizens of India, the CA was alive to the fact that merely outlawing all discrimination will not have the desired effect of achieving equal political rights for all sections of the population, especially in the case of marginalised and disadvantaged groups such as the SCs, STs, women and other backward sections of the population. Consequently, there was almost a consensus in the CA and its Subcommittees that special enabling provisions were required as far as the full exercise of their political rights by these sections of the provisions were concerned. Hence, the

Constitution lays down that while all citizens of India shall have
equal rights,

> Nothing ... shall prevent the State from making any special pro-
> visions for women....
> Nothing ... shall prevent the State from making any special pro-
> vision for the advancement of any socially and educationally
> backward classes of citizens or for the Scheduled Castes and the
> Scheduled Tribes.[30]

In order to enforce these rights, the Constitution provides that all
citizens of India will have:

> (1) The right to move the Supreme Court by appropriate proceed-
> ings for the enforcement of the rights conferred by this Part is
> guaranteed.
> (2) The Supreme Court shall have power to issue directions or
> orders or writs, including writs in the nature of *habeas corpus,*
> *mandamus,* prohibition, *quo warranto* and *certiorari,* whichever
> may be appropriate, for the enforcement of any of the rights
> conferred by this Part.

The above-discussed constitutional provisions on citizenship and
fundamental rights provide the background framework for the operation of an electoral framework of non-discrimination. Moreover,
these provisions notwithstanding, the Constitution also clearly provides for such a framework for the electoral process by laying down
universal adult franchise, single electoral rolls and the absence of
discrimination on any ground therein:

> No person to be ineligible for inclusion in, or to claim to be
> included in a special, electoral roll on grounds of religion, race,
> caste or sex. There shall be one general electoral roll for every
> territorial constituency for election to either House of Parliament
> or to the House or either House of the Legislature of a State and
> no person shall be ineligible for inclusion in any such roll or claim
> to be included in any special electoral roll for any such constitu-
> ency on grounds only of religion, race, caste, sex or any of them.
> The elections to the House of the People and to the Legislative
> Assembly of every State shall be on the basis of adult suffrage;
> that is to say, every person who is a citizen of India and who is
> not less than eighteen years of age on such date as may be fixed

in that behalf by or under any law made by the appropriate legislature and is not otherwise disqualified under this constitution or any law made by the appropriate Legislature on the ground of non-residence, unsoundness of mind, crime or corrupt or illegal practice, shall be entitled to be registered as a voter at any such election.[31]

Thus, the Constitution does not allow for the operation of any discrimination on any ground, as far as the electoral system is concerned. However, as has been noted above, the CA was alive to the fact that there may be a requirement for special provision for certain disadvantaged and marginalised sections of the population. Consequently, special provisions were laid down for ensuring and enabling full and equal participation of the SCs and STs in the electoral process of the country. These provisions were clearly seen as a temporary measure by the CA and are, therefore, not a part of the main provisions on elections but are contained separately in Part XVI of the Constitution. This part provides for various affirmative action policies for the backward and marginalised sections of the population. The portions of this part that are relevant to the elections are as follows:

Seats shall be reserved in the House of the People for
(a) the Scheduled Castes;
(b) the Scheduled Tribes except the Scheduled Tribes in the autonomous districts of Assam; and
(c) the Scheduled Tribes in the autonomous districts of Assam. The number of seats reserved in any State or Union territory for the Scheduled Castes or the Scheduled Tribes ... shall bear, as nearly as may be, the same proportion to the total number of seats allotted to that State or Union territory in the House of the People as the population of the Scheduled Castes in the State or Union territory or of the Scheduled Tribes in the State or Union territory or part of the State or Union territory, as the case may be, in respect of which seats are so reserved, bears to the total population of the State or Union territory.[32]

Besides, keeping in view the special historical circumstances and the numerical strength of the Anglo-Indian community in the country, a special provision has been made for them: '... the President may, if he is of opinion that the Anglo-Indian community is not adequately represented in the House of the People, nominate not more than two members of that community to the House of the People'.[33]

Here, it must be noted that while the CA had recommended that the reservation of seats in the legislative assemblies must cease after 10 years of the operation of the Constitution, the peculiar political economy of reservation and elections which emerged has ensured that the system was extended for another 10 years every time the expiry date approached. The result has been that, as it stands now, the reservations must cease to operate in the year 2010.

This fact itself testifies to some extent of the importance that the SCs and STs have in the Indian electoral system; it is very difficult to argue that electoral discrimination operates in India, at least as far as the two most significant minorities—the SCs and STs, are concerned.

Overall, there seems to be little scope for any institutionalised discrimination against any societal group in the country. The Constitution and, thereby, all enactments of the Parliament, have been geared towards ensuring that (*a*) all the individual citizens enjoy full and equal political rights, which they must be able to exercise without let or hindrance and (*b*) the historically disadvantaged communities must have larger than average electoral space to exercise their political rights through the mechanism of seats reserved specially for them.

IV

The Political Process and Discrimination

In India, over the past decade or so, political mobilisation has increased substantially. While on the one hand, there has been a Right-wing mobilisation on the premise of Hindutva, which seeks special group rights for the historically advanced social groups, there has also been a concomitant mobilisation by the historically disadvantaged groups, as can be seen in the recent electoral history of almost all states in India, especially Uttar Pradesh, Rajasthan, Madhya Pradesh and Bihar. These mobilisations have been aided by the constitutional provisions of reservations but have not been limited to these seats alone.

The cumulative effect of such mobilisation has largely been an increasing level of participation of the disadvantaged sections of the society, ensuring that their political and electoral role is magnified manifold, sometimes far beyond the proportion of their numbers in the population. Thus, there is hardly any ground for deducing that any kind of discriminatory framework operates vis-à-vis such societal groups. However, the case of religious minorities is quite different. This section will analyse the role of the votes of these marginalised and disadvantaged groups in the electoral process at the national level.

An analysis of the available data for the national elections 1996, 1998, 1999 and 2004 (Figures 13.1–13.25)[34] does not support a hypothesis that any particular group, except religious minorities, is unable to find sufficient electoral space in the political system and therefore, is discriminated against. In fact, as will be discussed below, most societal groups not only have adequate space in the electoral system but often the marginalised and backward sections of the population are the most crucial support base of the dominant political parties. Considering the large role played by these groups in the electoral chances of the dominant parties, it is difficult to see how a politics of discrimination can operate in the political system. The only exception seems to be the Muslims and Christians in a Bharatiya Janata Party (BJP+)-led political process. This complex process will be elucidated later in this section.

Here it must be pointed out that direct data on the presence or absence of discrimination has not been collected and collated. In fact, while the study of electoral support for various dominant political parties amongst the various social groups has been a subject of study for a long time, empirical data in support of such formulations has been thin. Election Commission (EC) data does not give us much insight into these factors and other studies which may give us some data on these areas are too micro-oriented to be of much use in any generalisation. National Election Studies (NES) conducted by the Centre for the Study of Developing Societies (CSDS), New Delhi are the only source for such data. Hence, the chapter depends heavily on the published data (for the 2004 elections, largely unpublished data)[35] of the CSDS election studies for empirical data.[36] While this data provides a fairly convincing picture of the support base of the various political parties, the logic of discrimination can only tangentially be deduced from this data. The following sections will therefore examine the support base of the various dominant political parties and draw up a picture of the degree of significance of the weaker and marginalised social groups in the electoral success of these political parties.

Gender

Gender discrimination is perhaps the most widespread kind of discrimination not only in India and South Asia, but the world at large. Absence of such discrimination is important for the overall health of the electoral system and also reflects the general state of women's development in the country—a factor which has important connotations for the developmental profile of the country concerned. The lack of discrimination on this count is attested to by the fact that voting rights for women was extended in the UK only in 1928. As far as gender discrimination in the Indian electoral scenario is concerned, there is no formal disability on any adult citizen, man or woman, from fully participating in the elections—as voters as well as candidates. However, the operational electoral reality is not as evenly balanced. As Figure 13.1 demonstrates, since the third general election in 1962,[37] there has been about a 10 per cent difference between the voting pattern of male and female voters. Simultaneously, this difference has been narrowing with every election. While the gap between participation of male and female voters was 16.68 per cent in the 1957 elections, the same declined to about 11 per cent for the 1967 and 1971 elections.

During the 1977, 1980 and 1984 elections, this gap hovered around the 10 per cent mark before declining to 8.81 per cent in the 1989 elections. Since the 1989 elections, the difference between the male voting percentage and the female voting percentage has stayed between 8 and 11 per cent, with the narrowest gap in the election of 2004 when the gap had declined to only 7.29 per cent. Thus, it may be concluded that the participation of women in the elections is on a rising curve.

As far as the participation of women in the electoral process as candidates is concerned, the picture is quite a mixed one. Table 13.1 delineates the number of women candidates in the elections since the 1990s in the 543 Lok Sabha constituencies. While the number of women contesting in these elections has fluctuated between 284 and 599 over the five elections held since the 1990s, the number of women elected has stayed almost constant at about 40–50. The main inference which may be drawn from this pattern is that while there is no formal impediment on women contesting elections, their chances of winning the election has not increased substantially over the past decade or so. Thus, while there may be no discrimination against women as far as the right to vote and contest elections is

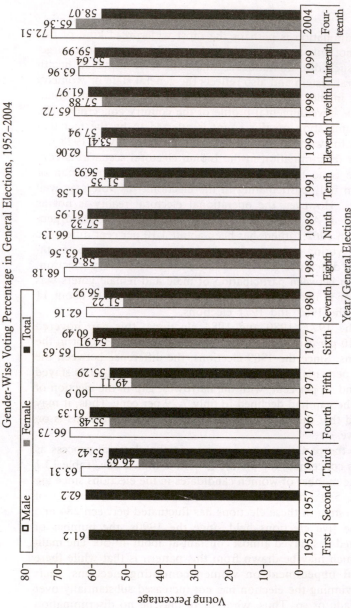

Figure 13.1

Gender-Wise Voting Percentage in General Elections, 1952–2004

Source: Data collated and published by the Election Commission of India on its website http://www.eci.gov.in/; *Statistical Report on General Elections, 1999 to the Thirteenth Lok Sabha*, Volume I (National and State Abstracts & Detailed Results), New Delhi, Election Commission of India, 2000; and *Statistical Report on General Elections, 2004 to the Fourteenth Lok Sabha*, Volume I (National and State Abstracts & Detailed Results), New Delhi, Election Commission of India, n.d.

Notes: The figures in each bar chart may not add up to 100. The difference being taken up by the percentage of votes cast for all the parties.

Table 13.1
Women Candidates in Elections, 1991–2004

	Number of Women Candidates	Number of Women Elected	Percentage of Women Candidates Elected
1991	314	43	13.69
1996	599	40	6.68
1998	274	43	15.69
1999	284	49	17.25
2004	355	45	12.68

Source: Various reports of the Election Commission of India and its website at
http://www.eci.gov.in/

concerned, the system does not seem to be ready for electing a
substantial number of women to political office. This is also attested
by the fact that the present proposal to reserve seats for women in
the legislatures does not have wide support across the political spectrum.

Figure 13.2
Support for Main Political Parties in 1996 Elections According to Gender

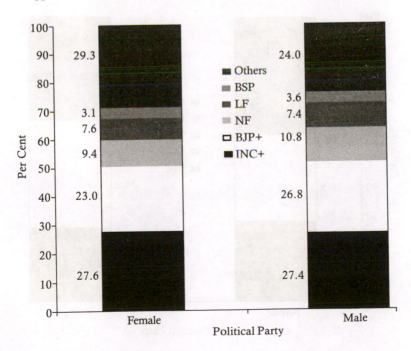

Apart from this direct data on the performance of women in the elections, other data available on the support base of the various political parties is also instructive. Figure 13.2 depicts the voting behaviour of the electorate according to gender. The support base of the Indian National Congress (INC+) in the 1996 elections was equally balanced as far as gender was concerned.

Approximately, 27 per cent of the men as well as women exercised their franchise in favour of the INC+. However, by the 1998 elections, the picture was changing when 28 per cent of the female voters chose to vote for the INC but the support amongst male voters declined by almost 1 per cent (Figure 13.3). On the other hand, the support for the BJP and its allies (even though the composition of allies changed between these two elections) saw a rather steep rise in their vote share amongst the men as well as the women. While 23 per cent of the women voted for the BJP+ in 1996, by the 1998 elections 29.5 per cent of them were exercising their franchise in favour of the BJP+. Similarly, the support of the male electorate for

Figure 13.3

Support for Main Political Parties in 1998 Elections According to Gender

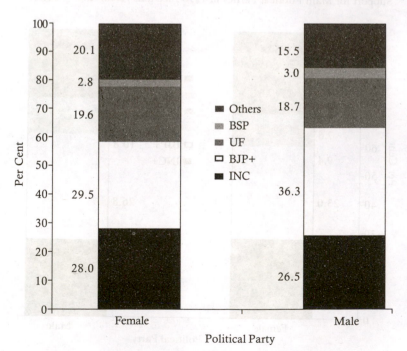

the BJP+ rose steeply from 26.8 per cent in 1996 to 36.3 per cent in 1998.

Further, electoral support for the coalition of parties that formed the National Front (NF) in 1996 and the United Front (UF) in 1998 elections also increased rather steeply. While the NF had secured 9.4 per cent of the female votes in 1996, by 1998, 19.6 per cent of the women were voting for the UF. Similarly, 10.8 per cent of the male voters had supported the NF in 1996 but by 1998 Left Front (LF) secured 18.7 per cent of the male votes.

What is significant in this pattern of support for the various political parties is the fact that the dependence of all the three dominant political formations on the support of women voters increased during the 1990s. All the three political formations saw a larger proportion of female votes being cast for them. In such a scenario of increased electoral dependence on the women voters, it

Figure 13.4
Support for Main Political Parties in 1999 Elections According to Gender

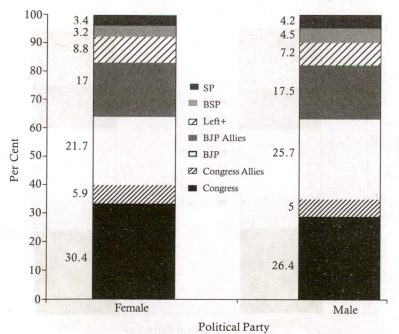

Note: The figures in each bar chart may not add up to 100, the difference being taken up by the percentage of votes cast for all other parties.

is unlikely that any political formation would be inclined or be able to discriminate against women in the electoral system.

Turning to the 1999 general elections (Figure 13.4), the proportion of female voters that opted for INC and its allies[38] crossed 36 per cent while that of male voters approached 31 per cent. This pattern of larger support amongst the female voters was repeated for the BJP and its allies as well. Together, BJP and its allies secured support of more than 37 per cent of the female voters while 43.2 per cent of the male voters supported the BJP and its allies. Similarly, the Left parties found greater support from the female voters (8.8 per cent) than male voters (7.2 per cent). This trend of a larger dependence on female voters amongst all political parties/formations did not continue across other political parties such as the SP and the BSP in the 1999 elections, nor did it extend to the 2004 elections (Figures 13.4 and 13.5).

Figure 13.5

Support for Main Political Parties in 2004 Elections According to Gender

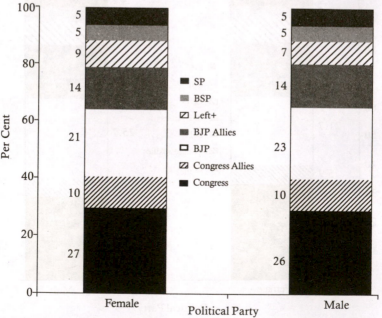

Note: The figures in each bar chart may not add up to 100, the difference being taken up by the percentage of votes cast for all other parties.

The pattern of significant dependence of all parties on female voters continued in the 2004 elections although the pattern of a larger proportion of support for all the major political formations coming from female voters did not continue (Figure 13.5). In the 2004 elections, INC and its allies secured the support of 37 per cent of the female voters compared with the support of 36 per cent of the male voters—a larger support for the INC+ across both categories of voters compared with the 1999 elections. BJP and its allies secured the support of 35 per cent female and 33 per cent male voters—a downswing from its performance since the 1999 elections across both categories. However, this downturn in the support for BJP+ was lower amongst the female voters than male voters. The Left parties continued to find greater support amongst the female voters (9 per cent) than male voters (7 per cent) while the Bahujan Samaj Party (BSP) and the Samajwadi Party (SP) found equal support amongst both male and female voters.

The overall pattern in the elections analysed above—the changes in support of the female voters—appears to be a lynchpin in the 'winability' of a particular political alliance or formation. Thus, the question of discrimination against female voters in the political process seems to be at best marginal.

Educational Levels of Voters

While the educational level of a citizen is not a ground on which discrimination can operate in the Indian electoral system, it is often argued that the illiterate voters, not being aware of their rights, may be discriminated against by the political system. However, the available data clearly argues against any such formulation.

Figures 13.6–13.9 represent the level of electoral support for the various political parties according to the educational level of the voters. The largest support for the INC+ was amongst the illiterate and poorly educated voters. While 28.6 per cent of the illiterate voters and 28.4 per cent of the voters educated up to the middle school supported the INC+, the largest support for the BJP came from voters with higher education. Voters who have attended college with or without degree qualifications predominantly voted for the BJP in the 1996 elections (Figure 13.6). While 31.3 per cent of the voters who had attended college without acquiring a degree voted for the BJP, 36.7 per cent of the voters with degree qualifications supported it.

Figure 13.6
Support for Main Political Parties in 1996 Elections
According to Educational Level

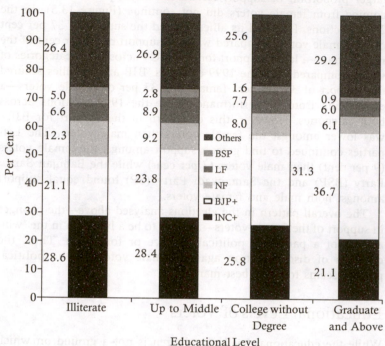

The pattern of the BJP's support base lying largely with the educated electorate was reinforced by the 1998 election when 34.3 per cent of the voters educated up to middle school voted for the BJP while 36.5 per cent of the voters who have attended college without degrees voted for the party. The voters possessing degree qualifications who voted for the BJP amounted to 42.5 per cent of the voters in this category (Figure 13.7).

Besides, any possible discrimination against the illiterate voters by one of the dominant political formations, the BJP+, was not likely in the scenario of the 1998 election, wherein there was a swell in support for the BJP amongst the illiterate voters as well. While 21.1 per cent of the illiterate voters voted for the BJP in 1996, in the 1998 elections, 28.9 per cent of the illiterate voters supported the party.

The third dominant political formation, the LF/NF were also not in a position to ignore the illiterate and poorly educated voters.

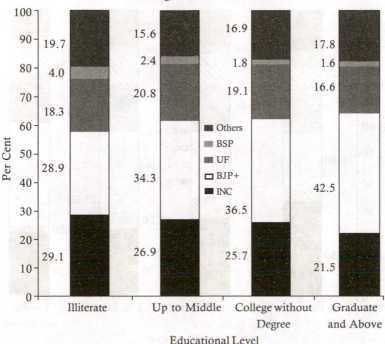

Figure 13.7
Support for Main Political Parties in 1998 Elections
According to Educational Level

While in 1996, 12.3 per cent of the illiterate and 9.2 per cent of those with middle school education supported the NF, the same figures for electoral support for the UF in the 1998 elections were 18.3 per cent and 20.8 per cent.

Similar patterns were repeated for the 1999 and 2004 elections as well (Figure 13.8 and Figure 13.9). INC and its allies secured the support of 38.5 per cent of the illiterate voters and 34.5 per cent of those voters who were educated up to primary school in the 1999 elections. The BJP and its allies on the other hand secured the support of 53.2 per cent of the voters with college education and above while 45.1 per cent of the voters with educational qualifications up to the matric level supported the BJP and its allies. On the other hand, 29.7 per cent of those with education up to matric supported the INC and its allies. As far as support for the BJP and its allies amongst the illiterate and poorly educated voters is

Figure 13.8
Support for Main Political Parties in 1999 Elections
According to Educational Level

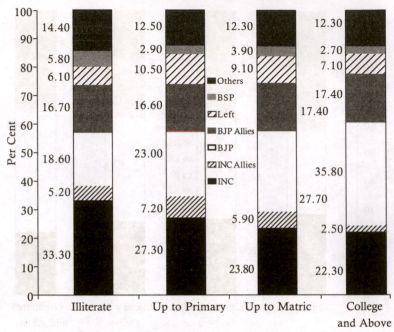

Educational Level

concerned, 35.3 per cent of illiterate and 39.6 per cent of those educated up to the primary level supported the BJP and its allies. Thus, while the BJP found larger support amongst the educated voters, substantial support also existed for it amongst the illiterate and poorly educated voters.

Interestingly, support for the Left parties was largest amongst those voters who were educated up to the primary (10.5 per cent) and matric level (9.1 per cent) but perhaps a little counter-intuitively, support for these parties amongst illiterate and well-educated voters was smaller. On the other hand, as may be expected, the BSP had its largest following amongst the illiterate voters with 5.8 per cent of such voters supporting the party.

Similarly, in the 2004 elections, INC and its allies found the support of 39.7 per cent of illiterate voters and 42.9 per cent of those educated up to the primary level. On the other hand, like the earlier elections, the better educated voters continued to extend large support to the BJP and its allies with 46.7 per cent of the voters with college education or above supporting the BJP and its allies. Repeating trends noted earlier, the BJP and its allies found support of a smaller but substantial 34.3 per cent of the illiterate and 35.6 per cent of those educated up to the primary level in the 2004 elections.

The largest degree of support for the smaller parties on the national electoral scene such as BSP and SP was found amongst the illiterate voters with 7.8 per cent and 6.5 per cent respectively supporting these two parties. The patterns of those voters who were educated up to primary or matric levels offering the largest degree of support to the Left parties continued in the 2004 elections as well (Figure 13.9).

Thus, electoral support of the illiterate and poorly educated voters was significant for all the dominant political formations in these

Figure 13.9
Support for Main Political Parties in 2004 Elections
According to Educational Level

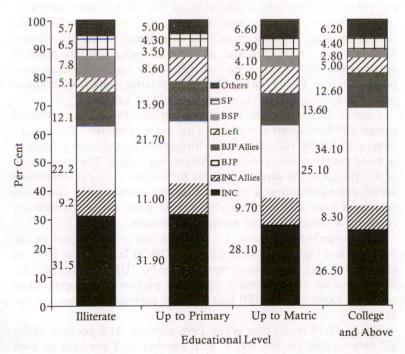

two elections. The fact that such illiterate and poorly educated voters supported both the major political parties/formations in such substantial numbers precludes any possibility of systemic discrimination against them in the political process.

Scheduled Castes, Scheduled Tribes and Other Backward Castes[39]

It may not be an exaggeration to state that perhaps caste is the most important category wherein electoral discrimination may operate. This social category is not only rooted in the historical dynamics of Indian public life but has also been the bedrock of all kinds of social discrimination. Owing to the inherently exploitative and inegalitarian nature of the caste hierarchy, this social category is perhaps most amenable to discriminatory practices in the electoral realm as well.

Although caste-based political mobilisation has been a part of Indian political reality since at least independence,[40] it has acquired a greater salience during recent decades. Indian electoral system and the polity have provided a special space for the backward castes by the mechanism of reserved seats since the first general elections, but it is in the past 10 years or so that caste-based politically-relevant identities have crystallised and are now claiming separate political space rather than being a part of the larger national mainstream political parties. Hence, an analysis of the relative support for political parties according to the caste categories is of salience.

Figures 13.10–13.13 represent the support for various political parties and formations according to the caste categories. The pattern of support for the various political formations across caste categories is more complex than gender or educational levels. The main point of divergence in the support patterns for various political formations across caste categories is the fact that the various caste categories exercise a more differentiated choice with some castes traditionally choosing a certain kind of political formation.

As is depicted in Figures 13.10–13.13, the main support of the SCs, STs and Other Backward Castes[41] (OBCs) lay with the INC, its allies and the set of parties comprising the NF/UF. Interestingly, the NF/UF parties also secured a significant portion of the upper caste votes. As expected, the BSP had its main support base amongst the SCs.

Figure 13.10 shows that in the 1996 election, 31.6 per cent of the SC voters opted for the INC+ with another 14.4 per cent of such

Figure 13.10
Support for Main Political Parties in 1996 Elections According to Caste

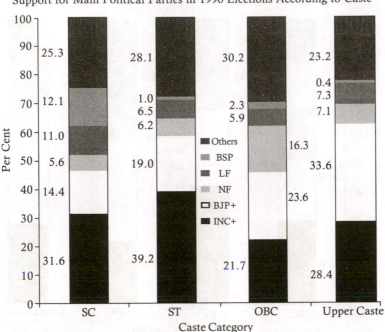

voters opting for the BJP+. Thus, 46 per cent of the SC voters had opted for the first two dominant political formations. This figure becomes even larger if the support for NF and LF (5.6 per cent and 11 per cent, respectively) amongst the SC voters is accounted for.

The fact that such a large proportion of SC voters had extended electoral support for these parties reflects conscious voting by these voters in favour of these parties—a situation which does not reflect discrimination against this electoral section. Besides, with the SC voters exercising their franchise in favour of these parties in such large numbers, the resultant electoral dependence of these parties on SC voters would strengthen the hands of SC voters in securing greater political and electoral space for themselves.

In the 1998 elections (Figure 13.11), the same pattern continued with INC being the choice of 29.6 per cent of the SC voters while BJP was voted by 20.9 per cent. Cumulatively, more than half of the SC voters supported these two political formations, while UF was supported by more than a fifth of the SC voters. Again, the voting

Figure 13.11

Support for Main Political Parties in 1998 Elections According to Caste

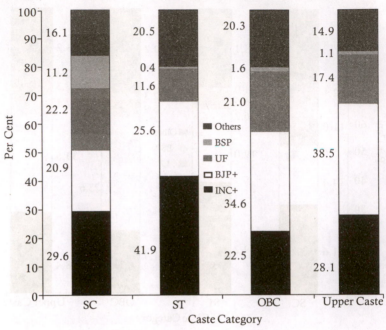

Caste Category

pattern reflects a conscious participation and choice on the part of the SC voters.

The dependence which emerges for any political formation when such large scale support is offered to it by any one social category was further strengthened in the 1999 elections wherein the INC+ was the preferred choice of 29.6 per cent of the SC voters. However, the support amongst the SCs for the BJP and its allies more than doubled with 42.2 per cent of the SC voters exercising their franchise in favour of this particular political formation. While there were a host of reasons for this splendid increase in the support for BJP+ amongst the SC voters (such as the electoral benefits reaped by the BJP from the regional support bases of many of the allies), it does not detract from the fact that the political space available to SCs in the national election was increasing over the 1990s. In such a scenario, concern about electoral discrimination against the SCs in the national elections seems to be unfounded.[42]

In the 2004 elections,[42] the pattern of support for the major political formation amongst the SC voters did not show any drastic change. The INC and its allies secured the support of 29 per cent of the Dalit (SC) voters, while BJP and its allies were supported by 23 per cent of the voters from this social category. BSP was supported by 29 per cent of the Dalit voters. Thus, the major political formation found the support of more than three-fourths of all Dalit/SC voters in the 2004 elections, buttressing the formulation that any political process that finds such large degree of support amongst any social group cannot afford to ignore or discriminate against that social group.

Turning attention to the STs, the pattern of support for the dominant political parties amongst the SCs is more or less repeated amongst the STs. In the 1996 elections (Figure 13.10), 39.2 per cent of the ST voters extended their support to the INC+ while 19 per cent of them voted for the BJP+. Thus, about 60 per cent of the ST electorate extended their support to the two dominant political formations in the 1996 elections. In the 1998 elections (Figure 13.11), the support for these two political formations amongst the ST voters increased, as was the case with the SC voters. The INC+ was voted by 41.9 per cent of the ST voters while 25.6 per cent of the ST voters supported the BJP+. Thus, in the 1998 elections, more than two-thirds of the ST voters supported the two dominant political formations, a pattern which further strengthened in the 1999 elections (Figure 13.12).

In the 1999 elections, a small but significant proportion of the ST voters shifted their support from the INC+ to BJP+. The INC+ found support of 36.8 per cent of the voters in the 1999 elections while the proportion of ST voters which voted for the BJP+ increased to 40 per cent. Turning to the 2004 election (Figure 13.13), the support of Adivasi/ST voters shifted back to INC and its allies, who were supported by 43 per cent of the Adivasi electorate. BJP and its allies were supported by 33 per cent of the Adivasi/ST voters.

The total support of ST voters to these two dominant political formations stayed stable at a little over two-thirds of the ST electorate all through the 1990s and the first general elections of the new millennium. As has been indicated earlier in the case of the SC voters, such large and active support of the ST/Adivasi electorate for the dominant political formation is bound to increase the dependence of these political parties/formations on ST votes leading to a better and more important political space for these marginalised groups in the electoral politics of the day. The political process born out of these patterns is unlikely to lead to a politics of discrimination against these social groups.

Figure 13.12
Support for Main Political Parties in 1999 Elections According to Caste

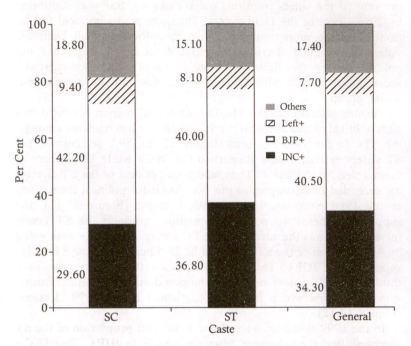

Another important link which completes the picture in the above discussed political process is that of the support of OBCs and the upper castes for the dominant political formations. Unfortunately, differentiated data for these two categories is unavailable for the 1999 elections but the data for 1996, 1998 and 2004 elections (Figures 13.10, 13.11 and 13.13) is instructive as far as the patterns of dominance and discrimination against certain social groups is concerned.

In the 1996 elections, about 45 per cent of the OBC voters supported the INC+ and the BJP+ (these two political formations individually found support from 21.7 and 23.6 per cent of the OBC voters, respectively). Significantly, 16.3 per cent of such voters supported the NF and 5.9 per cent supported the LF. Thus, while a sizeable proportion of the OBC voters supported the two dominant political formations, not an insignificant proportion of them also supported the political formations representing the 'third alternative'.

Figure 13.13

Support for Main Political Parties in 2004 Elections According to Caste

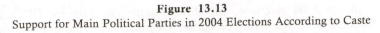

■ SP   ■ BSP   ☒ Left+   ■ BJP Allies □ BJP   ☒ INC Allies   ■ INC

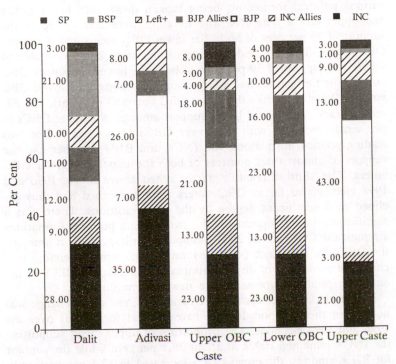

Notes: The figures in each bar chart may not add up to 100, the difference being taken up by the percentage of votes cast for all other parties.

In the 1998 elections, the proportion of OBC voters which supported the two dominant political formations added up to about 57 per cent (INC+: 22.5 per cent, BJP+: 34.6 per cent), while the support for the 'third alternative' remained stable at about 21 per cent. This is a pattern which clearly differentiates OBC voters from the SC and ST voters, indicating that the OBC voters did not feel that they would be able to get adequate political space in the dominant political formations and hence, strengthened the 'third alternative'. Keeping in mind the coalitional politics of the country over the 1990s, the OBCs, despite not being a part of the dominant political formations, were in a position to exercise sufficient autonomy and carve out an adequate political space in the political system.

In the 2004 elections, the differentiation of data for OBCs is different from the data for earlier elections with the support for various political formations being broken down into lower OBCs and upper OBCs. The INC and its allies were able to secure the support of 36 per cent of both, the lower OBC voters and the upper OBC voters. The BJP and its allies on the other hand were able to secure the support of 39 per cent of both the lower and upper OBC voters. The Left parties had a larger support amongst the lower OBC voters (10 per cent) than the upper OBC voters (4 per cent). The SP, on the other hand, had a larger support amongst the upper OBCs (8 per cent) compared with the lower OBCs (4 per cent). The two leading political formations, the INC+ and BJP+ together had the support of almost three-quarters of both the upper and lower OBC voters. The 'third alternative' factor noted above in the 1996 and 1998 elections as far as OBC voters were concerned had thus declined to a significant degree by the 2004 elections. There was a significantly larger support for the two leading political formations amongst the OBCs in the 2004 election. Such large support amongst the OBCs for the major political formulations would therefore preclude the possibility of any discrimination against the OBCs in the emerging political process of the new millennium.

As far as the upper castes were concerned, not much change was noticed in their support for the two political formations over the 1996 and 1998 elections. The proportion of upper castes supporting the INC+ remained stable at about 28.1 per cent while the support for BJP+ amongst the upper castes increased to 38.5 per cent, indicating a greater polarisation of the upper caste votes for the BJP+. The 2004 elections continued this pattern of support amongst upper caste voters with INC and its allies being voted by a slightly lower 24 per cent of the voters while the support for the BJP and its allies was polarised ever further with the support (56 per cent) of such voters. However, keeping in mind the much smaller numerical strength of the upper castes, such polarisation is not of as much consequence as the shifting of the support base amongst the other caste categories.

The patterns of support amongst the upper castes also buttresses the argument of the dependence of the dominant political formations on the support of other castes. The support for both the dominant political formations amongst the upper caste voters has been more or less static in the two elections for which differentiated data is available. This indicates that for victory in the elections, both these political formations must mobilise the SC, ST and OBC votes in their favour. This adds to the pattern of dependence which augurs well for the ability of these caste categories to carve out political and electoral space for themselves and effectively oppose any discrimination that might be present in the political process. Further, the voting patterns along caste categories have also strengthened plurality in the political process. This allows the smaller and marginalised social categories to find a voice and representation in the political process, besides strengthening democracy. Hence, the operation of the political process does not support a hypothesis of any substantial degree of discrimination against the marginalised and backward caste categories.

Religion

In the half century of post-colonial political history of India, not to mention the pre-partition political dynamics of the subcontinent, religion has played an important role in crystallisation and mobilisation of political identities. In light of this, it is crucial to focus attention on the support for the various political parties according to the religious affiliation of the voters in order to analyse if it forms the ground for political discrimination. Figures 13.14–13.17 represent the pattern of support for the main political parties according to religion, which is complex as well as far more polarised compared to any other social category. Besides, in light of the socio-political history of India over the past decade, this category is, perhaps, also the most significant.

Two patterns hold true in the data available for the 1996 and 1998 elections: first, the support for the BJP+ has substantially increased amongst the Hindus and Sikhs. Second, all other religious categories continued to extend large-scale support to the INC+. The implications of this pattern are of serious consequence to the political process in India but, first, a brief survey must be made of the pattern of support for the various political formations across the religious categories. Here it must also be noted that the data available for the 1999 and 2004 elections does not lend themselves to a comparative analysis with the data for the 1996 and 1998 elections. While the data sets for the first two elections are differentiated by major religions only, the same data sets, responding to the criticisms of clubbing certain social categories into contested religious categories, present a far more disaggregated data set. In view of this, the analysis of religion as a factor of discrimination will be broken down into

Figure 13.14
Support for Main Political Parties in 1996 Elections According to Religion

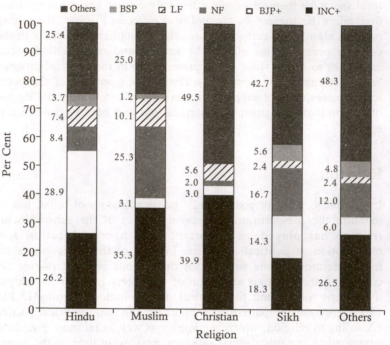

two threads so as to remain true to the available data sets: 1996 and
1998 elections; and 1999 and 2004 elections.

In the 1996 elections (Figure 13.14), 26.2 per cent of the Hindu
voters supported the INC+, which declined marginally to 25.6 per
cent in the 1998 elections. Despite this small decline in the support
for the INC+ amongst the Hindu voters, there was a substantial
increase in the proportion of Hindu voters which supported the
BJP+, from 28.9 per cent in 1996 to 37.4 per cent in 1998. This
increase in the support for the BJP+ indicates a rising polarisation
in the political process on religious lines, a formulation supported
by the fact that apart from the two largest political formations, the
smaller political formations were all but squeezed out of electoral
existence as far as support from the Hindu votes were concerned.

This pattern of extreme electoral polarisation can be noticed in
the Muslim votes as well. In the 1996 elections, 35.4 per cent of
Muslim voters supported the INC+ whereas only 3.1 per cent of

Figure 13.15

Support for Main Political Parties in 1998 Elections According to Religion

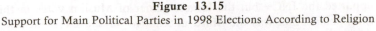

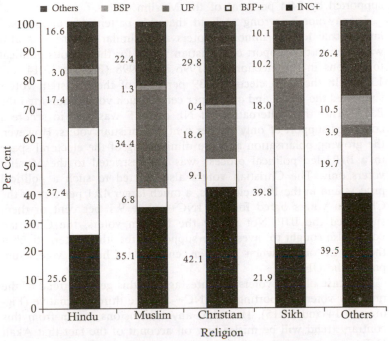

them opted for BJP+. While this voting pattern can well be explained by the character and nature of BJP's mobilisation strategies premised on Hindutva, this kind of voting pattern does leave out substantial electoral space that is not available to Muslim voters. Conceptually, such extreme polarisation would indicate a declining plurality in the political process and, hence, the possibility of some discrimination against the Muslims. However, this discrimination was tempered by one factor: the 'third alternative'. This 'third alternative' representing electoral space not occupied by either the INC+ or the BJP+, and constituted largely by the NF and the LF, found electoral support of 25.3 per cent and 10.1 per cent of the Muslim voters, respectively.

In the 1998 elections, these patterns of electoral polarisation further sharpened, a larger support of 6.8 per cent of the Muslim voters for the BJP+ notwithstanding. In the 1998 elections (Figure 13.15), a larger proportion of the Muslim voters (35.1 per cent) supported the INC+ but the largest gainer of Muslim votes in this rising polarisation was the 'third alternative' of the UF, which was supported by 34.4 per cent of the Muslim voters.

It may not be wrong to hold that this pattern of support was largely true for the minority voters as a similar pattern was also witnessed in the support of Christian voters for the various political formations in the elections of 1996 and 1998 (Figures 13.14 and 13.15). In the 1996 elections, 39 per cent of the Christian voters supported the INC+ and only 3 per cent of such voters supported the BJP+. The 'third alternative' of NF and LF was able to secure a combined support of only 7.6 per cent of Christian voters. However, the growing polarisation and the diminishing of the electoral space in a BJP+-led political process was not restricted to the Muslim voters only. The Christian voters also reacted to such a political process and in the 1998 elections, a much larger 42.1 per cent of the Christian voters opted for the INC+ while 9.1 per cent of them supported the BJP. Not unlike the Muslim voters, the Christian voters also sought to invest their support in the 'third alternative' of the NF, LF or UF when 18.6 per cent of the Christian voters supported the UF.

The case of Sikh voters militates against this general trend of the minority voters supporting the INC+ and the third alternative (Figures 13.14 and 13.15). However, any conclusions drawn from this contrary trend will be misleading on account of the fact that Akali Dal was a part of the alliance led by the BJP.

Moving on to the 1999 and 2004 elections, as has been noted earlier, the data set available does not facilitate a comparison of the support base of various political formations as far as the Hindu voters are concerned. The data set available has disaggregated the data for Hindu voters by various social subgroups with caste as the main criterion. Since caste-wise support for various political parties has already been analysed, it is of little value in reanalysing the same within the rubric of religion.

However, the data sets for 1999 and 2004 can be gainfully employed to analyse the changes in support for various political formations amongst the Muslim, Christian and Sikh voters. As far as Muslim voters were concerned, there was a further polarisation of their support in favour of the INC and its allies with 54.9 per cent of Muslim voters supporting the INC+. There was also a rise in the proportion of Muslim voters supporting the BJP and its allies at 14.7 per cent. The possible 'third alternative' that was visible in the data sets for 1998 was squeezed out of the political system with only the

Figure 13.16

Support for Main Political Parties in 1999 Elections According to Religion

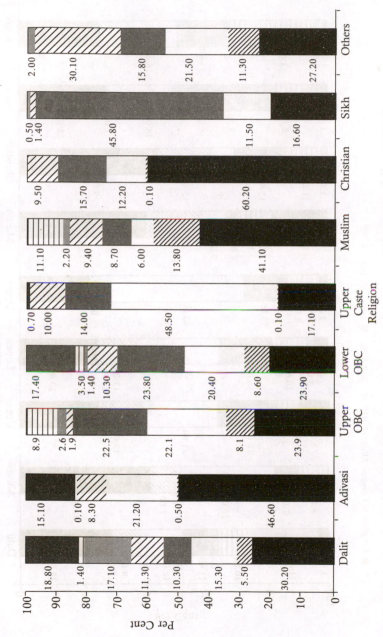

Notes: The figures in each bar chart may not add up to 100, the difference being taken up by the percentage of votes cast for all other parties.

Figure 13.17

Support for Main Political Parties in 2004 Elections According to Religion

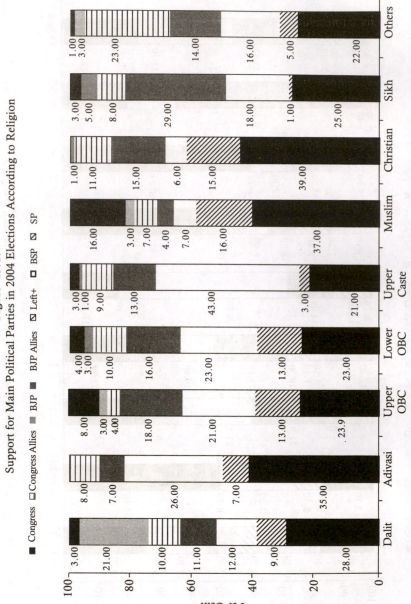

Notes: The figures in each bar chart may not add up to 100, the difference being taken up by the percentage of votes cast for all other parties.

Left parties polling 9.4 per cent of the Muslim votes in the 1999 elections.

There was no substantial change in the voting patterns of Muslim voters in the 2004 elections. The support for INC and its allies amongst Muslim voters continued at 53 per cent while that for BJP and its allies also stayed at about 13 per cent. The alternatives to these two political formations remained peripheral as far as the Muslim voters were concerned. A small decline can be noted as far as Muslim support for Left parties is concerned (Figure 13.17).

As far as Sikh voters in the 1999 elections were concerned, the support for the INC and its allies declined to 16.6 per cent while 57.3 per cent of the Sikh voters supported the BJP and its allies. Similarly, in the 2004 elections, INC and its allies doubled its support by securing support of 26 per cent of Sikh voters. The BJP and its allies on the other hand saw a decline in their support amongst Sikhs and secured support of only 47 per cent of the Sikh electorate.

The proposition that much of the Sikh votes that are cast for BJP+ is a spiral effect of the votes cast for the BJP's ally, the Shiromani Akali Dal, is proved by the data for 1999 and 2004 elections. A vast proportion of Sikh support for the BJP+ is due to the support for its allies (Figures 13.16 and 13.17).

Similarly, a vast proportion of Christians supported the INC and its allies. In the 1999 elections, 60.3 per cent of the Christians supported the INC and its allies while the 2004 elections, the same proportion had declined to 54 per cent. The support for BJP and its allies amongst Christian voters in the 1999 election was at 27.9 per cent, which declined to 21 per cent in the 2004 elections. Thus, the decline in the support for INC+ amongst the Christian voters was not a gain for the BJP+ but for other smaller parties (Figures 13.16 and 13.17).

Overall, there was a high degree of polarisation of electoral support amongst the voters from various social categories on the lines of religion. With the low degree of support for the BJP+ amongst Muslims across all elections, there is a possibility of some degree of discrimination against them by the political process. While BJP+ as an electoral alternative to the INC+ seems to be more or less closed to Muslim voters, the decline in the support for the possible 'third alternative' (some of which was rooted in the decline in the electoral and political presence of the parties themselves), indicates the emergence of a rather polarised political process. This polarisation undermines the possible plurality of political choice and thereby restricts options for the Muslim electorate in particular and the voters of religious minority groups in general.

Locality: Urban Versus Rural Support Base

Moving on to the distribution of support for various political parties across the urban and rural areas of India (Figures 13.18–13.21), once again the INC and its allies seem to have strengthened their support base in both urban and rural areas of the country between 1996 and 2004. Interestingly, against conventional understanding of the INC having a larger following amongst the rural voters, the urban voters were the ones who have shown a continuously increasing preference for the INC. Rural voters on the other had opted for other parties, particularly the BJP+ (something which continued until 1999 but declined in 2004) and the UF in 1998, before marginally increasing their support for the INC in 1999.

Figure 13.18

Support for Main Political Parties in 1996 Elections According to Locality

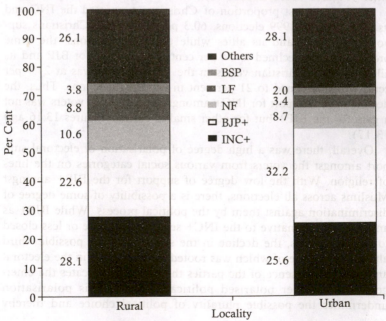

Figure 13.19
Support for Main Political Parties in 1998 Elections According to Locality

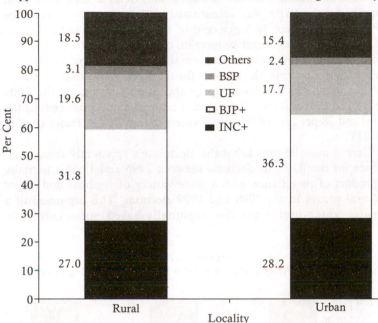

While in 1996, 28.1 per cent of the rural voters had voted for the INC+, the same declined to 27 per cent in 1998 but increased substantially to 34.30 per cent in 1999 elections and to 37 per cent in 2004. On the other hand, 25.6 per cent of the urban voters had opted for the INC+ in 1996 but by 1998 elections, 28.2 per cent of these voters preferred to vote for the INC+ while by 1999 elections, 30.8 per cent of the urban voters were voting for the party. In the 2004 elections, 38 per cent of the urban voters supported the INC+.

The support base of the BJP and its allies on the other hand, shows a continuous upward trend until the 1999 (Figures 13.18–13.21) and a pattern of some decline in 2004. Not only did the support for the BJP and its allies grow both in urban and rural areas of the country, the rate of growth of this support far surpasses that of any other party. In 1996, 22.6 per cent of the rural voters opted for the BJP+ while a much higher 32.2 per cent of the urban voters supported the party. In 1998, the same figures had grown to 31.8 per cent and 36.3 per cent, respectively. This reflects a faster growth in the support for the BJP+ in the rural areas, in addition to its traditional support amongst the middle class urban voters. This trend of increasing rural support for the BJP+ was accentuated in the voting patterns of the 1999 election where 39.5 per cent of the rural voters opted for the BJP+ while an even larger proportion of urban voters (43.7 per cent) along with 45.9 per cent of semi-rural voters voted for the BJP+.[43] In the 2004 elections, the support for the BJP and its allies declined substantially, which showed up in the overall results of the 2004 polls. The BJP and its allies found the support of 27 per cent of the rural and 38 per cent of the urban voters in the 2004 elections (Figure 13.21).

Here it must be noted that the electorate's apparently rising preference for the BJP+ in elections between 1996 and 1999 is partially a product of its alliance with a wide variety of regional and socio-cultural parties in the 1998 and 1999 elections. This argument of a greater voter preference for regionally-based socio-culturally

Figure 13.20
Support for Main Political Parties in 1999 Elections According to Locality

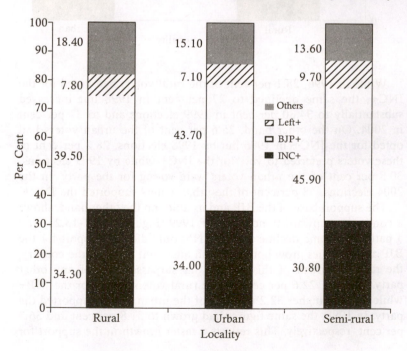

located parties with mobilisation base in a distinct economic group-
ing in the society is bolstered by the rest of the data in Figures 13.19
and 13.20. The other Figures also underline this formulation.

The political parties and groups that formed the NF in 1996 and
the UF in 1998 were largely such socio-cultural parties with a regional base, representing the interests of a certain economic section
of the society. As is represented in Figures 13.18 and 13.19, the
electoral preference for the NF/UF rose appreciably between the
1996 and 1998 elections. In the urban areas, 8.7 per cent of the
voters preferred the NF in 1996, which rose to 17.7 per cent in 1998.
However, in view of the fact that the parties and political groups,
which comprised the NF/UF, were representative of rural economic
and socio-cultural interests, it is not surprising that the level of
support for these parties in rural areas saw a larger growth. While
10.6 per cent of the rural electorate voted for the NF in 1996, in

Figure 13.21

Support for Main Political Parties in 2004 Elections According to Locality

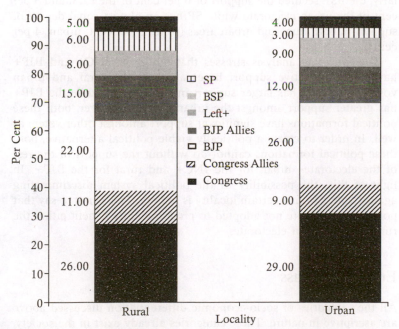

Notes: The figures in each bar chart may not add up to 100, the difference being
taken up by the percentage of votes cast for all other parties.

1998 elections the NF saw support of 19.6 per cent of the rural electorate.

Similarly, despite the various components of the NF/UF representing the rural socio-economic interests, the BSP as the party representing particular social and economic interests of the most backward voters continued to find increasing support amongst the rural as well as the urban voters. In the 1996 elections, 3.8 per cent of the rural and 2 per cent of the urban voters extended their support to the BSP while in 1998, 3.1 per cent of the rural and 2.4 per cent of the urban voters opted for the BSP.

In the 1999 elections, Left parties found support of 9.3 per cent of the rural voters (compared with only 2.3 per cent of the urban voters). The SP was able to secure only marginal support amongst the rural voters with merely 4.8 per cent of the votes (only 1.7 per cent in urban areas).

In comparison to this in the 2004 elections, the Left parties secured the support of only 8 per cent of the rural voters but found a much larger support amongst the urban voters at 9 per cent. Similarly, the BSP secured the support of 6 per cent of the rural and 3 per cent of the urban electorate while SP has an almost equal degree of support in both rural and urban areas (rural, 5 per cent; urban, 4 per cent).

The foregoing analysis stresses that while the INC+ and BJP+ have their respective support bases amongst the rural and urban voters, the INC+ has larger support in rural voters while the BJP+ has greater support amongst the urban voters. However, both these political formations have significant support amongst other voters as well. In order to create a politically viable political alternative, both these political formations cannot do without the support of the rest of the electorate—urban for the INC+ and rural for the BJP+. In light of this, the possibility of the political system discriminating against voters from a certain locality is remote. This is not to say that policy measures are not adopted to predominantly benefit either the rural or the urban electorate.

Economic Class

All the categories of socio-economic differentiation discussed above are ascriptive in nature. These categories already exist in the society, which the political processes and actors often use as premises to aggregate political interests and mobilise political support. One

Figure 13.22
Support for Main Political Parties in 1996 Elections
According to Economic Class

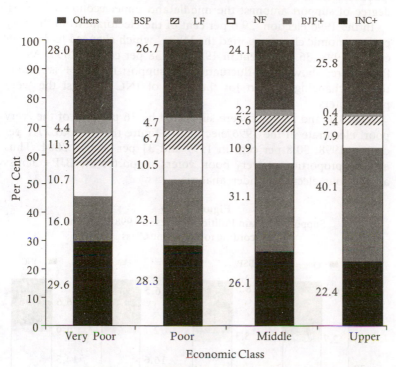

category that is of an entirely different nature is that of economic class and any analysis that seeks to delineate and analyse the possibility of discrimination in the political process cannot ignore the pattern of political support for various political formations across economic class. The data sets of electoral support for the different political parties across economic class amongst the electorate has been tabulated in Figures 13.22–13.25.

Figures 13.22–13.25 show that the support base for the INC was rather evenly distributed across all economic classes in all the four elections under analysis. There are some variations in the support offered by the various classes to the INC+ over the four elections under analysis but the support for INC remains constant between 20 to 30 per cent across all economic classes. However, the support for INC's allies does not follow the same pattern, neither is a similar pattern repeated for any other political party/formation. Besides, INC+ had the largest degree of support from the 'very poor' and 'poor' economic classes. On the other hand, the BJP+ shows a rising degree of support amongst the middle and upper economic classes.

In the 1996 election, 29.6 per cent of the electorate from the very poor economic class supported the INC+, which changed to 27.3 per cent in 1998, 36.8 per cent in 1999 and 38 per cent in 2004. As the four figures show, these fluctuations in support for INC+ is a function of changing support for the allies of INC amongst the 'very poor' voters.

The BJP and its allies were supported by 16 per cent of the 'very poor' electorate in the 1996 election—a figure that rose to 27.1 per cent in 1998, 30.8 per cent in 1999 and 31 per cent in 2004. Thus a rising proportion of 'very poor' voters supported the BJP+ across all the four elections under analysis.

Figure 13.23
Support for Main Political Parties in 1998 Elections
According to Economic Class

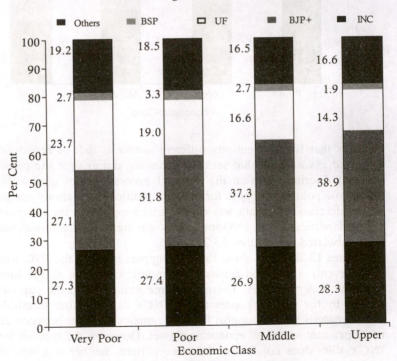

The LF was supported by 10.7 per cent of the 'very poor' voters in the 1996 elections while the Left parties were supported by 11.3 per cent of the 'very poor' voters in this election. The degree of support amongst the 'very poor' voters for these 'third alternative' parties increased in the 1998 elections to 23.7 per cent for UF and 2.7 per cent for BSP. However, unlike other categories discussed earlier, the degree of support for non-INC, non-BJP political formation amongst the 'very poor' voters increased over the 1999 and 2004 elections. In the 1999 elections, the 11.2 per cent of the 'very poor' voters supported the Left parties, while 6.2 per cent and 3.1 per cent supported the BSP and SP, respectively. In the 2004 elections as well, 9 per cent of the 'very poor' voters supported the

Figure 13.24

Support for Main Political Parties in 1999 Elections
According to Economic Class

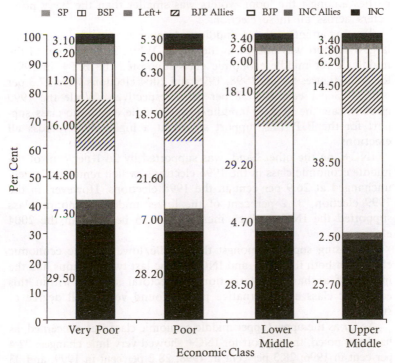

Notes: The figures in each bar chart may not add up to 100, the difference being taken up by the percentage of votes cast for all other parties.

Left parties, 8 per cent supported the BSP and 5 per cent chose the SP.

Clearly, the issue of a 'third alternative' may be peripheral for the other categories analysed earlier but the 'very poor' voters were keen to keep their electoral choices alive in terms of possible alternatives for the dominant political formations.

As far as the 'poor' economic class was concerned, the largest support was once again offered to INC+. In the 1996 election, 28.3 per cent of the 'poor' electorate supported the INC+, which declined to 27.4 per cent in 1998 before climbing to 35.2 per cent in 1999 and 38 per cent in 2004. This rise in the support for the INC and its allies amongst the 'poor' voters was largely a function of the rising electoral support for its allies.

The BJP+, on the other hand, was supported by 23.1 per cent of the 'poor' voters in 1996; 31.8 per cent in 1998; 40.1 per cent in 1999; and, 36 per cent in 2004. The degree of support for alternative parties amongst the 'poor' voters was smaller than the 'very poor' voters across all these elections.

Turning attention to the middle and upper economic classes,[44] the largest support was offered to the BJP+. While 31.1 per cent of the middle/lower middle economic class supported the BJP+ in 1996, the same figures for the 1998, 1999 and 2004 elections were 37.3 per cent, 47.3 per cent and 38 per cent, respectively. While the 1999 election saw the peak of middle/lower middle economic class support for the BJP, this support stayed at a higher level across all elections.

INC+, on the other hand, was supported by 26.1 per cent of the middle economic class in the 1996 elections, which remained largely unchanged at 26.9 per cent in the 1998 elections. However, in the 1999 election, 33.2 per cent of the lower middle economic class supported the INC+, which increased to 36 per cent in the 2004 election.

The rising support amongst the middle/lower middle economic classes for both the BJP+ and INC+ in the last two elections had the impact of a sharper polarisation of electoral support within this economic class and alternative parties found very small degree of support.

As far as the upper/upper middle economic class was concerned, as has been noted, the support for INC+ showed very little changes: 22.4 per cent in 1996; 28.3 per cent in 1998; 28.2 per cent in 1999; and 33 per cent in 2004 elections. On the other hand, the support for BJP+ in the upper/upper middle economic class increased substantially.

Figure 13.25
Support for Main Political Parties in 2004 Elections
According to Economic Class

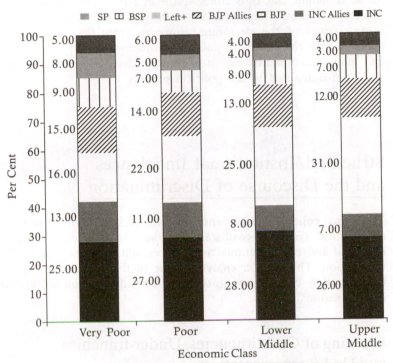

Notes: The figures in each bar chart may not add up to 100, the difference being taken up by the percentage of votes cast for all other parties.

While 40.1 per cent of the upper/upper middle economic class supported the BJP+ in the 1996 election, in the 1998 election the support of the same class declined to 38.9 per cent before rising to 53 per cent in 1999 and then declining again to 43 per cent in 2004. These fluctuations in the support amongst the upper/upper middle economic class for the BJP+ notwithstanding, the degree of support for the BJP+ in this economic class is without question. The inevitable impact of this pattern has also been the increasing marginalisation of alternative political formations in the electoral support of the upper/upper middle economic classes.

The foregoing analysis underlines that all political formations depend heavily across all economic classes for their electoral support.

In such a scenario, it is unlikely that discriminatory political processes can operate. However, there is also a pattern of increasing
political polarisation across all economic classes in which the choices
for all economic classes is either INC+ or BJP+. Such polarisation
reflects declining choices and can have the possibility of marginalising
some sections of the electorate. However, given the large dependence of both the dominant political formations on the 'very poor'
and 'poor' economic classes, it is unlikely that the economic class
will be marginalised in the political process.

V

Structural/Institutional Imbalances
and the Discourse of Discrimination

The formal political equality and the stress on non-discrimination in
the political system notwithstanding, there have emerged certain
structural and/or institutional imbalances that may amount to discrimination. This section analyses some of these issues and questions, which cannot be ignored in any discussion of group
discrimination in India.

Freezing of Constituencies, Under-franchise
and Under-representation

The Constitution provides for each state of the Union to be allotted
seats in the Lok Sabha on the basis of population in such a way that
the ratio between the seats and population shall be the same in all the
states and that the ratio will be the same throughout the state. Further,
the Constitution provides for the delimitation of constituencies in this
manner after every census. However, the 42nd Amendment in 1976
had frozen the delimitation exercise constitutionally mandated after
every census until the 'relevant figures for the first census taken after
the year 2000 have been published....'[45] Thus, in effect, the constituencies for the election of the representatives of the citizens for the Lok
Sabha and the state legislative assemblies were frozen in the shape that
they had acquired after delimitation after the 1971 Census. This has
serious implication for the conceptual premises of the electoral

system and the operation of the conceptual paradigm of equal political rights for all citizens.

The provisions of Articles 326 and 327 (and parliamentary laws framed under it to govern the process of delimitation of constituencies) attempt to put in place an essential requirement of democratic theory and practice: the value of the vote of every citizen must be the same, as far as practicable. The effects of the freezing of constituencies have been that this very principle has been grossly violated.

As the figures in Table 13.2 demonstrate, the delimitation of constituencies as per the figures of the 1971 Census had led to each seat representing 0.593 million voters, a figure that had more than doubled to 1.237 million voters per seat by the 2004 elections. This malady introduced in the electoral system in 1976 has constantly and consistently undermined the value of each vote since the 1977 elections. Further, it has also undermined a central tenet of democratic theory: namely adequate representation. Each member has been representing an exponentially growing number of constituents, which means the degree of representativeness of the electoral system has been undermined.

Table 13.2
Declining Value of Votes in Elections, 1977–2004

	1977	1980	1984	1989	1994	1996	1998	1999	2004
Electors[*]	321.2	356.2	400.1	498.9	511.5	592.6	605.9	619.6	671.49
Average per Seat[*]	0.593	0.673	0.738	0.943	0.953	1.091	1.116	1.141	1.237

Source: Various Reports of the Election Commission and its Website at http://www.eci.gov.in/
Note: [*]In million.

To address some of these issues, the exercise of fresh delimitation of electoral constituencies is underway under the provisions of the *Constitution (84th Amendment) Act, 2001*; *Constitution (87th Amendment) Act, 2003*; the *Delimitation Act, 2002 (Act 33 of 2002)*; and the *Delimitation (Amendment) Act, 2003 (Act 3 of 2004)*. The Delimitation Commission appointed under the provisions of the *Delimitation Act of 2002* has already published the draft of the delimitation.

However, there are certain fundamental issues with the delimitation exercise currently under way. First, the delimitation exercise would keep the number of seats assigned to each state at the same level as the earlier delimitation carried out on the basis of the 1971

Census. This will create an imbalance in the representativeness of each constituency across the various states of India. The argument being put forth is that if such a freeze is not implemented, it will amount to a disincentive to the states which have had a more successful population control policy. While the party–political nature of this proposal is clear, the government seems to be arguing that the representation in Lok Sabha has a link to the choice of family size amongst voters!

Second, delimitation is being carried out on the basis of 1991 Census when the results of the 2001 Census are available and the next census is scheduled in barely four years in 2011. There has been a substantial growth in the population of India since the 1991 Census besides fundamental changes in the distribution of the population across the country.

Third, perhaps most importantly, the next delimitation will not be undertaken until 2026. This will compound an already bad situation as far as representativeness of constituencies is concerned. Thus, delimitation is frozen for at least another 36 years (1991 to 2026). The ostensible justification for this freeze is that by that date the population growth would have stabilised and, hence, an optimum size of Lok Sabha may be created at that date! Clearly, the requirements of democratic theory and procedural democracy are being subjected to the diktat of developmental goals, which may not at all be achieved.

Besides, these national averages mask the extreme case of very large constituencies, some of whom have been tabulated in Table 13.3. The largest constituency is that of outer Delhi in the national capital which has an electorate of 2.82 million—more than two and a half times of the national average, as was the case of Thane constituency in Maharashtra with 2.771 million electors. Amongst the 9 most imbalanced constituencies in the country tabulated in Table 13.3, almost all of them have an electorate of more than the national average. This also implies that owing to the natural growth pattern of the population, there would be constituencies with an electorate being far lower than the national average. Thus, the cardinal rule of equality of the value of all votes is violated. In other words, there is under-representation in the constituencies with larger electorates constituting discrimination against the voters in these constituencies, while unduly privileging constituencies with a smaller electorate.

Clearly, discrimination is evident in this new kind of gerrymandering being used in India for the past three decades and promises to continue for at least another three decades.

Table 13.3
Select Constituencies with Largest Disparities

Constituency	Electorate Size (in million)
Outer Delhi, Delhi	2.820
Thane, Maharashtra	2.771
Mumbai North, Maharashtra	2.222
East Delhi, Delhi	2.220
Madras South, Tamil Nadu	2.074
Secundrabad, Andhra Pradesh	1.769
Siddipet, Andhra Pradesh	1.621
Dum Dum, West Bengal	1.597
Mayiladuthurai	1.030

Source: *The Boundaries of Indian Democracy: Delimitation of Constituencies and Related Issues*, New Delhi, Centre for Policy Research, 2002.

Constituencies Reserved for SCs/STs and Reverse Discrimination

This source of discrimination flows from the first but promises to acquire a serious character. One effect of the freeze in the delimitation of constituencies has been that the seats which had once been designated as reserved for the SCs/STs have continued to be so for the past three decades. The original idea was that with a new delimitation every 10 years, these seats would be rotated in accordance with the patterns in the growth of population. However, with the freeze in delimitation, all the reserved constituencies were also frozen in time, irrespective of the changing character of the population in the constituency. The net result has been that in all the reserved constituencies, there has been no representation for the non-scheduled population for the past three decades. This is certainly a violation of the fundamental and political rights of non-scheduled citizens residing in the reserved constituencies, irrespective of the social group to which they belong. The reverse discrimination has been the result whereby, unimaginative and mechanical implementation of the letter of the Constitution vis-à-vis positive discrimination for the SC/ST population has led to an under-franchise for the non-SC/ST population.

An aligned issue is that of the continued reservation for the SCs/STs. As is evident in the discussion of the CA debates above, the reservation of seats for the SCs and STs was clearly a temporary measure for assisting these historically disadvantaged communities.

However, owing to the close contest for election between various political formations, the SCs and STs have become an important support base for all the political parties. Consequently, a politics of reservation has emerged by virtue of which the reservation of seats for SCs and STs has been extended whenever it comes up for re-examination.

While the greater participation of the SCs/STs may have partially been the original reason behind providing for reservation for these social communities, this option was perhaps a devise to opt for the politically most convenient tool for positive discrimination. With this policy operating for a substantial number of years, there has emerged a 'politics of backwardness' whose net result has been that even simple and more elegant options such as that of multi-member constituencies (as was the case until the 1962 elections) are not considered in the political discourse of the country.

VI

Conclusions: Broad Patterns in the Political Process and Discrimination

The dependence of the political formations on the large supports extended to them by the various marginalised social groups largely ensures that they may not be discriminated against. The logic for this formulation is that a political formation is a part of the political process for the purpose of being elected to office. Discrimination against one particular group by a political formation is likely in two scenarios: (*a*) it is of electoral advantage to discriminate against such a group; and (*b*) there is a strong *a priori* ideological apparatus which encourages such discrimination.

Taking the second reason first, while it is likely that some political formations, especially like the BJP, may have a strong ideological reason to discriminate against some social group such as the religious minorities, SCs or the OBCs, the constitutional framework of universal adult franchise does not allow such a course of action. Any attempt to discriminate on ideological grounds will patently be *ultra vires* of the Constitution and would fall within the realm of illegality and malpractices. It is unlikely that any party in a keenly contested electoral space will run the risk of any large-scale discrimination against any social group and in the process be disqualified from holding office. The case of religious minorities is more complex and will be taken up presently.

The first scenario of discrimination against any particular group, while continuing to fall within the realm of illegality and malpractices, being capable of delivering electoral advantage, might be sufficient to tempt the political formations to adopt such a course of action, whatever the costs to be paid if found guilty. However, the data discussed above may not bear out such a formulation. The large amount of active electoral support for the two largest political formations across all the social categories, except religious minorities, in more than one election in a keenly contested electoral space cannot be interpreted to be operating under covert discrimination. The electoral arithmetic does not offer much scope for any such large scale discrimination.

Thus, the constitutional framework combined with a contested and increasingly democratised political space does not leave much scope for large-scale discrimination against any social group, except the case of religious minorities in a BJP+-led political process.

Religious Minorities and Discrimination

As has been discussed earlier, the case of religious minorities is one of acutely polarised electoral space wherein not much room for manoeuvre is left for the voters of the minority communities. While discrimination by any political party on grounds of religion will again be *ultra vires* of the Constitution, this is a peculiar case wherein the political formation concerned does not actively discriminate against any particular social group. Instead, it constructs a public discourse in which the social groups concerned (religious minorities) would themselves find it difficult to support the party concerned. This difficulty on the part of the social groups is expressed in the data sets discussed above wherein the religious minorities support the INC+ or the 'third alternative'. In a polity led by the BJP+, if any particular social group finds it difficult to vote for this particular political formation on account of the latter's public discourse, there is clearly a prima facie case of operation of discrimination against the former.

In this analysis, while the BJP+ may stand accused of discrimination, since no such policy may be actively enforced, little legal action is possible against this political formation. However, such discrimination does not become systemic on account of the presence of electoral and political space for a third alternative and the coalition politics within which such a process has been operating. While the third alternative political formations offer an alternative electoral space for the representation of these discriminated social groups without making them over-dependent on only the INC+, they may also play a substantial role in legislative bodies and policy-making. This is so by virtue of the coalitional political process of the past decade which has thrown up these patterns.

Further, the apparent discrimination by BJP is also tempered by the rising plurality in Indian politics across multiple levels (national, regional, subregional and so on). In fact, the large and rising support for the BJP+ can also be attributed in substantially large measure to the coalitional politics characterised by the rising importance of regional parties (who often play a role disproportionate to their size or electoral support). While the support of these regional parties may give the BJP+ its electoral support base, it is the presence of these regional parties which ensures that discrimination against any one social group does not become state policy. These regional parties, with support base in a particular geographic region or social group, are perhaps the most fundamental reality of Indian political process which will ensure that discrimination against any one social group will never be institutionalised since these smaller parties fracture any discursive structure which might be emerging in the BJP to justify discrimination against any social group. The regional parties with their support bases premised on these socio-cultural and economic cleavages in the society represent these cleavages in the society. As long as these cleavages are represented in the political process,[46] plural politics in India has a bright future, polarisation of electoral space in religious lines in past few years notwithstanding.

As far as the issues of structural and institutional imbalances creeping into the political process over the past three decades are concerned, it has the potential to spiral into more serious crisis of representation. However, the political process (and thereby the institutional–legal process) seems to have no interest in resolving these issues. A fundamental delimitation every decade is likely to upset the political configurations of all political formations. While of some of the issues raised in Section V are likely to be addressed by the ongoing delimitation exercise (for instance, the imbalances between representativeness of the various constituencies within a state), the rest of the issues will only see collective inertia for the next three decades.

Notes

1. None of the above social groups are per se political identities. Each of these terms is a descriptive term to refer to the relevant individual. However, any of these terms has the potential to become a politically relevant identity. For instance, the term woman may be used to distinguish between genders and remain a descriptive term. However, during the last few decades it has also acquired a certain degree of political currency and has emerged as a politically relevant identity. Similarly, the term Hindu pertains to the relevant individuals belonging to a religious group in the society. However, the mobilisation of a large number of persons on the grounds of Hindutva in the recent years by the Bharatiya Janata Party in India has led to its emergence as a politically significant identity.

2. *Resolution regarding Aims and Objects* moved in the Constituent Assembly on 13 December 1946 by Jawaharlal Nehru and adopted unanimously after eight days of debate on 20 January 1947; *Constituent Assembly Debates*, Vol. I, 9 December 1946–23 December 1946, New Delhi, Lok Sabha Secretariat, 1950 (Third Reprint 1999), p. 59.

3. Speech by Jawaharlal Nehru while moving the *Resolution regarding Aims and Objects* in the Constituent Assembly on 13 December 1946; *Constituent Assembly Debates*, ibid., p. 62.

4. Speech by S. Radhakrishnan on 20 January 1947 commending the Objectives Resolution to the CA; *Constituent Assembly Debates*, Vol. II, 20 January 1947–25 January 1947, ibid., p. 270.

5. There were a number of avenues through which various ideas entered the Constitution. One important avenue was the debates in the CA. The resolutions adopted were treated as decisions of the CA by the Drafting Committee and incorporated into the Draft. Besides, a more substantial influence was exercised by the various committees and subcommittees-committees appointed to examine particular issues such as the Advisory Committee on Fundamental Rights, Minorities and Tribal and Excluded Areas and its subcommittees-committees on minorities, excluded areas in Assam and the rest of India, Union Powers Committee, Provincial Constitution Committee, etc. The reports of these committees were either discussed in the CA or their recommendations were incorporated in the Draft Constitution and presented for the consideration of the CA. The Draft Constitution thus drafted by Constitutional Advisor B.N. Rau and presented to the Drafting Committee on 27 October 1947 was perhaps the first coherent formulation about many of the issues we are concerned with. Thereon, this Draft Constitution formed the basic document and working paper for the Drafting Committee. The Drafting Committee, in turn, examined the Constitutional Adviser's draft in the light of the various materials—notes, memoranda, reports, etc.—placed before it and a revised Draft Constitution was communicated to the President of the CA on 21 February 1948 and moved in the CA on 4 November 1948 by Dr B.R. Ambedkar, the chairman of the Drafting Committee, for clause by clause consideration and adoption, with amendments, if any.

6. Speech by Dr B.R. Ambedkar while moving the Draft Constitution in the CA on 4 November 1948, *Constituent Assembly Debates*, Vol. VII, 4 November 1948–8 January 1949, p. 34.

7. Constituent Assembly Debates of 10–12 August 1949, *Constituent Assembly Debates*, Vol. IX, 30 July 1949–18 September 1949, pp. 313–430.

8. The significance of the near-unanimity in the CA on the issue of universal suffrage lies in the fact that universal male suffrage was granted in the UK in 1918 while universal female suffrage was granted only in 1928. Similarly, not all women had a right to vote in the US until 1920. However, universal women suffrage was granted in New Zealand as early as 1893.

9. Article 67(6) of the Draft Constitution prepared by the Drafting Committee, reproduced in B. Shiva Rao, *The Framing of India s Constitution: Select Documents*, Vol. III, New Delhi, IIPA, 1967, p. 540.

10. Constituent Assembly Debates of 3–4 January 1949, *Constituent Assembly Debates*, Vol. VII, 4 November 1948–8 January 1949, pp. 1195–265.

11. Article 149(2) of the Draft Constitution prepared by the Drafting Committee, reproduced in Rao, *The Framing of India s Constitution...*, Vol. III, p. 571.

12. Amendment No. 2247 moved by K.T. Shah on 6 January 1949, *Constituent Assembly Debates*, Vol. VII, 4 November 1948–8 January 1949, p. 1319.

13. Letter dated 8 August 1947 from Vallabhbhai Patel to the President, Constituent Assembly of India, forwarding the report on minority rights, reproduced in B. Shiva Rao, *The Framing of India s Constitution: Select Documents*, Vol. II, New Delhi, IIPA, 1967, pp. 411–18.

14. Ibid., para 3.

15. Appendix to ibid.

16. The Sikhs had already indicated their willingness to forego their claim to reservation of seats in East Punjab if Sikh SCs (such as Mazhabis, Kabirpanthis, Ramdasias, Baurias, Sikligars, etc.) and Hindu SCs are lumped together and seats reserved for them on the strength of their population, *Minutes of the Meeting of the Sikh Members of the East Punjab Legislative Assembly and of the Constituent Assembly*, 10 May 1949, reproduced in Rao, *The Framing of India s Constitution...*, Vol. IV, pp. 598–99.

17. *Report of the Advisory Committee on Minorities*, 11 May 1949, *Constituent Assembly Debates*, Vol. VIII, 16 May 1949–16 June 1949, pp. 310–12.

18. Since 27 August 1947 when the first report of the minorities subcommittees-committee was moved in the CA.

19. Constituent Assembly Debates of 25–26 May 1949, *Constituent Assembly Debates*, Vol. VIII, 16 May 1949–16 June 1949, pp. 1195–269–355.

20. Subcommittee on Excluded and the Partially Excluded Areas (other than Assam), and the Subcommittee on North-east Frontier (Assam) Tribal and Excluded Areas examined the issues related to the administration of excluded and partially excluded areas but the Subcommittee on Minorities reported in the question of political rights for the SCs, STs and minorities.

21. Reports of the Subcommittee on Excluded and the Partially Excluded Areas (other than Assam), and the Subcommittee on North-East Frontier (Assam) Tribal and Excluded Areas, Constituent Assembly Debates 4 November 1948, *Constituent Assembly Debates*, Vol. VII, 4 November, 1948–8 January 1949, pp. 101–201.

22. And the provision for nomination of two representatives of the Anglo-Indian community to the Lok Sabha, if the president thinks that they are not properly represented in the House (Article 331 of Constitution of India).

23. Preamble to the *Constitution of India*, New Delhi, Ministry of Law and Justice, 1991 (as on 1 September 1991).

24. The 'rule of difference' dwelt on the superiority of the European race and their cultural practices over the Indian population and their practices. Examples of this include barring of all Indians from certain areas of Indian cities and the outcry from the European population living in India over the Ilbert Bill whereby an Indian judge could try European offenders.

25. Constitution of India, Article 5.

26. In order to ensure that the naturalised citizens of India and those who migrated from the erstwhile Pakistan (today's Pakistan and Bangladesh) did not suffer any disability in the exercise of their political rights, Articles 6–11 of the Constitution provide that:

Notwithstanding anything in Article 5, a person who has migrated to the territory of India from the territory now included in Pakistan [including what was then East Pakistan] shall be deemed to be a citizen of India at the commencement of this Constitution if:

(a) he or either of his parents or any of his grandparents was born in India...

(b) (i) in the case where such person has so migrated before the nineteenth day of July 1948, he has been ordinarily resident in the territory of India since the date of his migration, or

(ii) in the case where such person has so migrated on or after the nineteenth day of July 1948, he has been registered as a citizen of India by an officer appointed in that behalf by the Government of the Dominion of India on an application made by him therefore to such officer before the commencement of this Constitution in the form and manner prescribed by that Government:

Provided that nothing in this article shall apply to a person who, after having so migrated to the territory now included in Pakistan, has returned to the territory of India under a permit for resettlement or permanent return issued by or under the authority of any law and every such person shall for the purposes of clause (b) of Article 6 be deemed to have migrated to the territory of India after the nineteenth day of July 1948.

Notwithstanding anything in Article 5, any person who or either of whose parents or any of whose grandparents was born in India as defined in the Government of India Act, 1935 (as originally enacted), and who is ordinarily residing in any country outside India as so defined shall be deemed to be a citizen of India if he has been registered as a citizen of India by the diplomatic or consular representative of India in the country where he is for the time being residing on an application made by him therefore to such diplomatic or consular representative, whether before or after the commencement of this Constitution, in the form and manner prescribed by the Government of the Dominion of India or the Government of India.

27. Including the Right to Property, which was abridged by the 7th and 42nd Amendments and the Right to Education, included by the Constitution (93rd Amendment) Bill 2002.
28. Including Right Against Exploitation (Articles 23 and 24), Right to Freedom of Religion (Articles 25–28), and, Cultural and Educational Rights (Articles 29 and 30). All of these are particularly relevant to the minorities and the marginalised populations. However, for the present discussion on the electoral processes, the ones relevant are the Right to Equality, Right to Freedom and Right to Constitutional Remedies.
29. Ibid., Articles 14 and 15.
30. Ibid., clauses 3 and 4 of Article 15.
31. Ibid., Articles 325 and 326.
32. Ibid., Article 330. Similar provisions have also been made for the state legislative assemblies under Article 332.
33. Ibid., Article 332. Similar provisions have also been made for the state legislative assemblies under Article 333.
34. In the data discussed in this chapter, the components of the political formations are as follows:

1996 elections:

INC+ = INC + AIADMK
BJP+ = BJP + Samata Party + Shiv Sena + Haryana Vikas Party
NF   = JD + Samajwadi Party
LF   = CPM + CPI + RSP + FBL

1998 elections:

BJP+ = BJP + Samata Party + Shiv Sena + Haryana Vikas Party + AIADMK + Akali Dal + Trinamool Congress + Lok Shakti + Biju Janata Dal + TDP(NTR)
UF   = Janata Dal + SP (Mulayam) + TDP(NTR) + AGP + TMC + DMK + MGP +CPI + CPI(M) +RSP + FBL

1999 elections:

INC+ = INC + RJD + AIADMK + Muslim League + Rashtriya Lok Dal + Kerala Congress (Mani)
BJP += BJP + JD(U)+ Trinamool Congress + TDP + BJD + Loktantrik Congress + Shiv Sena + Jantantrik Congress + DMK + PMK + MDMK + Rashtriya Lok Dal + Himachal Vikas Congress + Shiromani Akali Dal + Sikkim Democratic Front + Tamizhaga Rajiv Congress + Democratic Bahujan Samaj Morcha + MGR-ADMK + MGR-Kazhagam + Arunachal Congress + Manipur State Congress Party + Independent (Maneka Gandhi)

2004 elections:

INC+ = New allies of the Congress in 2004 were NCP, TRS, DMK, MDMK, PMK, LJNP, PDP and JMM. Old allies no longer allies in 2004 elections were RLD and AIADMK.
BJP+ = New allies of BJP were AIADMK, SDF, MNF, IFDP and NPF. Old NDA allies who were no longer allies were DMK, MDMK, PMK, INLD and LJNP.

Some minor errors that have crept into this data cannot be eliminated since detailed break-up is unavailable.

35. Comparable published data for the 2004 elections is rather thin. Therefore, recourse was made to the unpublished data generated by the NES at CSDS. Yogendra Yadav and Sanjay Kumar at the CSDS, Delhi have very graciously made this data available for this chapter, for which the author is grateful.

36. Most data about the support for political parties amongst the various social groups has been taken from Subrata K. Mitra and V.B. Singh, *Democracy and Social Change in India: A Cross-Sectional Analysis of the National Electorate*, New Delhi, Sage, 1999, pp. 134–35 and Yogendra Yadav and Sanjay Kumar, 'Interpreting the Mandate', *Frontline*, Vol. 16, No. 22, 23 October–5 November 1999, pp. 120–25.

37. Gender-wise distribution of voting pattern is not available for the first two general elections held in 1950–52 and 1957.

38. The data set available for the 1999 and 2004 elections delineate INC, BJP and their allies separately, which has been reflected in the figures. However, to arrive at a comparison with earlier years, the support for INC and its allies have been added for these two general elections.

39. In this analysis, ST has been listed as a caste category. While such a comparison is useful for the study of political dynamics, there is no effort to represent the STs as a caste of the Hindu fold. The author is conscious of the fact that there are significant differences in the political mobilisations based on caste lines and those on the basis of a shared tribal cultural heritage.

40. Quite a large amount of literature examines the caste–political mobilisation interlinkages. For instance, see Francine R. Frankel and M.S.A. Rao (eds), *Dominance and State Power in Modern India*, 2 Vols, New Delhi, Oxford University Press, 1989/1990 and Zoya Hasan, *Dominance and Mobilisation: Rural Politics in Western Uttar Pradesh 1930–1980*, New Delhi, Sage, 1989.

41. The category of 'Other Backward Castes' has a long history in India and many of these castes have traditionally played a significant political role. However, these castes acquired a great deal of political (and socio-economic) importance in the aftermath of the implementation the Mandal Commission Report in 1990. The provisions of this report provided for reservation of a certain proportion of government jobs for the designated OBCs, which sparked off widespread and, occasionally, violent protests. Owing to the vast amount of resources controlled by the government in India (including employment opportunities), reservation of jobs for the OBCs has inevitably had significant influence on the political process in India, especially in the northern states.

42. In the 2004 elections, the available data is disaggregated differently than those for earlier elections. Instead of SCs, STs, OBCs, and upper castes (or general in some of the data for other elections), the data for 2004 presents Dalits, Adivasis, upper OBCs, lower OBCs and upper castes. However, the category of Dalits can be taken to correspond to SCs for the purpose of this analysis, the Adivasis are STs while the two categories of OBCs can be clubbed together to offer a comparison with the category of OBCs in the data for earlier elections.

43. The available data for 1999 has an additional category of 'semi-rural voters,' which is not available for the 1996 and 1998 elections.
44. The data sets for the four elections are not strictly comparable across economic class. While the 1996 and 1998 data set uses categories of middle and upper economic classes, the data set for 1999 and 2004 elections uses the categories of lower middle and upper middle economic classes. For the purpose of this analysis, the middle economic class used in the 1996 and 1998 elections has been taken to correspond to the lower middle economic class of 1999 and 2004 elections. Similarly, the upper economic class has been taken to correspond to the upper middle economic class.
45. Article 81, as amended by the *Forty-second Amendment Act, 1976*. Similar provisions for the state legislative assemblies are provided in Article 170 and were similarly amended by the same amendment.
46. The vote share of the regional political parties has been rising over past three elections at the cost of monolithic national parties. See Amit Prakash, 'Social, Cultural and Economic Dimensions of the Party System', in Ajay Mehra, D.D. Khanna and Gert W. Kueck (eds), *Political Parties and the Party System: The Indian Experience*, New Delhi, Sage, 2002, pp. 129–61.

14

NEPAL

Hari Prasad Bhattarai

Introduction

Nepal's electorate is predominantly rural, multi-ethnic, multi-cultural and of unequal economic status, and therefore provides a fertile ground for political parties to exploit the grievances and aspirations of racial, ethnic, caste, class, tribal, religious, linguistic, regional and gender groups for political expediency. The discrimination against such groups could be overt or covert, legal or illegal.

According to a global report on voter turnout in 2002 by the International Institute for Democracy and Electoral Assistance (IDEA), Nepal ranks 110th (at 61.25 per cent) among the 169 countries with a relatively good voter turnout. However, this figure does not take into account the prevailing social biases against the political participation of socially deprived groups. Furthermore, when poverty and social injustice are rampant, a majority of the electorate do not consider elections as an act of political empowerment but rather as an opportunity to trade votes for material gain. This kind of discrimination is one where even those included can be deprived of the actual participation and decision-making process[1].

This chapter reviews the existing electoral laws and regulations of the electoral process to identify discriminatory provisions and is based primarily on secondary data as available. The analysis has been enriched through interviews with a number of election experts, officials and political leaders in the country. Discussions were also held with voters in selected election constituencies to gain in-depth insight about the problem under investigation.

Definition of the Concepts

The concept 'group' has been defined as a number of people regarded as forming a unit or a whole on the grounds of some mutual or common relation or purpose, or classed together because of a degree of similarity.[2] However, the term can be broadly used to describe a category of people that behaves cohesively or is perceived to behave cohesively as a distinct entity in the political realm.

The word 'discrimination' is often used to mean illegal discriminatory acts. The concept of discrimination, thus, connotes the unfavourable or unfair treatment of a person or class of persons on the grounds of race, colour, religion, sex, social status, age, or handicap. For the present purpose, the term discrimination is used to describe any departure from legally established practice or norms, or a deviation from what is generally accepted as democratic norms in the treatment of a particular category of people with regard to the conduct of all aspects of elections. This type of discrimination thus includes denying a particular group the right to exercise what it is entitled to under the law as well as making legal or administrative or forceful impositions on a group of people.

There is also the issue of 'automatic discrimination' due to poverty and illiteracy. The Constitution of 1990 guarantees the right to vote for all citizens over the age of 18 years irrespective of any distinction of property, class, caste or religion. However, the fact that more than 50 per cent of the electorate is illiterate, while 60 per cent lives below the poverty line cannot be overlooked. Under these conditions it is doubtful whether a significant portion of the population exercises the right of franchise in any meaningful sense.

Electorate of Nepal: An Overview

Nepal is characterised by a mosaic of religions, languages, castes, ethnic groups and indigenous peoples. Presently 101 ethnic and caste groups and subgroups and 93 living languages have been documented in Nepal.[3] These groups are further divided into eight major religions, that is, Hinduism, Buddhism, Islam, Kirat, Jainism, Sikhism, Christianity and the Baha'i faith. Table 14.1 represents the population composition[4] of the diverse groups of the country.

Table 14.1
Percentage Distribution of Nepalese Population by
Social Category/Group, 2001

Groups	Description of Groups	Percentage
Parbatiyas	Groups considered as Hindu castes (twice-born, ascetic castes as well as the 'untouchables') speaking Nepali as their mother tongue	38.9
Janajatis	Hill and Mountain ethnic groups of Tibeto-Burman speakers	21.88
Newars	Various Hindu and Buddhist castes	5.48
Madhises	People of the plains: 18.27% caste Hindus; 9.55% plain ethnic group; 4.3% Muslims (approximate figures)	32.11
Others	Marwaris, Bengalis, Sikhs, Christians and unidentified caste and ethnic groups	2.02

Source: Based on CBS, 2002.

The complex diversity of the electorate has serious implications for the just and equal political participation of all the citizens. In any pluralistic society, the challenge of designing and implementing an electoral system transcends the functional requirement of merely electing a government or its assemblies. The system has to guarantee the participation of the entire electorate and everyone should have equal access to the electoral process without discrimination.

Past Elections

Since the restoration of democracy in 1990, Nepalese citizens have participated in three national elections in 1991, 1994 and 1999 and two local elections in 1993 and 1997.

The number of voters has increased significantly from 11.1 million in 1991 to 12.1 million in 1994 and 13.5 million in 1999. The electoral turnout was highest (65.8 per cent) in 1999. However, the only data available are on voter registration and valid votes cast during the elections, whereas there is no classified data on voter participation according to gender, caste, ethnicity, residence, or other social and political groupings. Statistics relating to total number of votes and voter turnout at elections from 1959–99 are set out in Table 14.2.

Table 14.2
Voter Turnout Rates of Past General Elections

Year of Elections	Total Voter Age	Total Registered Voters	Total Votes Cast	Percentage of Total Votes Cast	Percentage of Valid Votes	Percentage of Invalid Votes
1959	4,341,120	4,246,468	1,791,381	42.20	–	–
1981	–	7,192,451	4,813,486	66.92	92.27	7.72
1991	9,567,476	11,191,777	7,291,084	65.15	95.58	4.42
1994	–	12,327,329	7,626,348	61.86	96.84	3.16
1999	–	13,518,839	8,894,566	65.79	97.25	2.79

Source: Elections Commission, 1991, 1994 and 1999, and CBS, 1991.

Following International IDEA report, reported registration rate as well as the voting age population, which includes all citizens above the legal voting age, have been used to calculate voter turnout percentages. The use of Voting Age Population (VAP) figures provides a clearer picture of participation because they can indicate any problems with the voter registration system. However, it is important to note that registration figures are updated more often than population figures. Interestingly, the national voter registration rate for the 1991 elections exceeded the VAP of the 1991 Census. A possible explanation for this anomaly could be the political pressure to register underage and non-eligible voters. Moreover, multiple registration, deaths or movement of people from one district to another have not been taken into consideration.[5]

However, there are many districts and villages where the opposite has been reported. The register has under-represented the true size of the eligible voter pool, omitting names of illiterate persons, women, new voters who have come of age and certain other sections of society.[6] Although such discrimination may occur at any point in the electoral process, preparation of the electoral roll deserves special attention.

Group Discrimination

Very few empirical studies have been conducted on electoral discrimination in Nepal. Some relevant empirical data from a study[7] conducted by Development Associates for Regional and Rural Development (DEVA) in May 2000 has been utilised in this chapter. Although the study was mainly concerned with the voter registration process, some inferences can be drawn to understand the nature and extent of group discrimination in the electoral process.

In order to ascertain the ethnic/caste patterns of voting behaviour, respondents were asked if they voted in any of the past elections. Table 14.3 shows the responses.

Table 14.3

Voting in Past Elections by Caste/Ethnic Categories (N = 433)

Responses	Brahmin/ Chhetri = 152 (%)	Ethnic Group = 137 (%)	Dalit = 79 (%)	Others = 65 (%)
Yes	97.4	94.9	91.1	87.7
No	2.6	5.1	8.9	12.3
Total	100.0	100.0	100.0	100.0

Source: DEVA, 2000.
Note: N = Total no. of respondents.

On analysing the responses, it is possible to conclude that although the variation in voter participation may not be statistically significant, the pattern followed a descending order in terms of Brahmin/Chhetri/ethnic groups/Dalit/others. This seems to validate the commonly held belief that the Brahmin/Chhetri category is politically more conscious than the remaining categories and that the ethnic group category is more politically active than the Dalit and 'others' categories.

The respondents were also asked if they had encountered any problems in casting their vote in the last elections despite having their names in the voters' list. Table 14.4 lists the responses across the caste/ethnic categories.

Table 14.4 shows that the 'others' category reported the highest proportion of voters who encountered such problems. This was due to the fluid identity situation as well as the marginal position of the Tarai population in politics. The ethnic and Dalit categories were the next group who had problems in this respect. Being the most

Table 14.4

Presence/Absence of Problems in Casting Votes in the Last
Election by Caste/Ethnic Categories (N = 433)

Responses	Brahmin/ Chhetri = 152 (%)	Ethnic Group = 137 (%)	Dalit = 79 (%)	Others = 65 (%)	Total %
Affirmative	4.1	9.0	9.3	13.3	7.9
Negative	95.9	91.0	90.7	86.7	92.1
Total	100.0	100.0	100.0	100.0	100.0

Source: DEVA, 2000.
Note: N = Total no. of respondents.

politically conscious category, the Brahmin/Chhetri group had the lowest proportion of voters who encountered problems whilst casting their votes in the last elections.

Table 14.5 lists responses as to whether respondents' names were excluded from the voters' list during voter registration.

Table 14.5 illustrates that overall, around 12 per cent of the respondents found that their names were excluded from the voters' list. Significantly, there is no noticeable difference between the Brahmin/Chhetri, ethnic and Dalit categories. However, the 'others' category reported the highest proportion (28 per cent) of such exclusions. The probable reasons for this could be the yet unsettled issues of birth and citizenship registration in the Tarai as well as migration and political issues.

The study also shows that overall 6.8 per cent of the respondents (N = 427) believed that women did not have equal access to register as voters. Although the difference in opinion was not significant, a greater percentage of the Brahmin/Chhetri and ethnic categories

Table 14.5

Magnitude of Exclusion from and Inclusion in Voters'
List by Caste/Ethnic Categories (N = 433)

Responses	Brahmin/ Chhetri = 152 (%)	Ethnic Group = 137 (%)	Dalit = 79 (%)	Others = 65 (%)	Total %
Yes (Inclusion)	90.8	91.2	90.9	72.3	88.1
No (Exclusion)	9.2	8.8	9.1	27.7	11.9
Total	100.0	100.0	100.0	100.0	100.0

Source: DEVA, 2000.
Note: N = Total no. of respondents.

believed that women had less access to registration than the Dalit and 'others' categories. We may infer from this that the most often excluded or non-included categories in elections are peasants, ethnic minorities, *Madhise* (original inhabitants of Tarai plains), women, the illiterate, the poor and people belonging to the low castes.

Due to the lack of reliable data it is not possible to present the exact magnitude of discrimination. Nevertheless, based on the above information and discussions with election experts, officials, political leaders and voters in selected election constituencies, the following groups can be identified as the most discriminated against in the electoral process in Nepal.

Marginalised Castes and Ethnic Groups

Several linguistic groups, ethnic minorities and indigenous peoples, Dalits or low caste people, and people of Tarai origin such as the *Chepang, Satars, Dhimals, Rajbanshis, Kusundas, Rautes, Doms, Musahar* and *Chamars* belong to this category of people who do not receive equal access to the electoral process.

Table 14.6 shows that the number of candidates in the three parliamentary elections since the restoration of parliamentary democracy has considerably increased. However, the corresponding share of the marginalised castes and ethnic groups in the list of candidates has remained insignificant.

Table 14.6

Castes/Ethnic Composition of Candidates in General
Elections, 1991 to 1999

Category	1991		1994		1999	
	No.	(%)	No.	(%)	No.	(%)
1. Caste Group	879	65.3	950	65.9	1,466	65.5
Hill	615	45.7	692	48.0	1,003	44.9
Tarai	264	19.6	258	17.9	463	20.6
2. Ethnic Group	422	31.3	459	31.6	689	30.8
Hill	339	25.2	358	24.8	555	24.8
Tarai+Inner Tarai	83	6.1	101	7.0	134	6.0
3. Muslim	41	3.0	82	2.1	65	2.9
4. Unclassified	3	0.2	3	0.2	18	0.8
Total	1,345	100.0	1,442	100.0	2,238	100.0

Source: Gurung, 1998 and Election Commission, 1999.

The 1994 elections had candidates from 42 caste/ethnic groups and in 1999 the number increased to 52. However, indigenous population groups such as the *Chepang, Kumal, Kumar, Majhi* and *Rajbanshi* were not in the list of candidates even though these groups were represented in the 1994 elections. A total of 81 Dalit candidates contested the 1999 elections but none of them were elected.[8] Only 10 ethnic groups and a lesser number of caste groups were elected.

Out of a total of 205 Members of Parliament (MPs) in the 1999 House of Representatives (HOR), 56 or 27.31 per cent belonged to ethnic groups (Annexure-2). There were 62 (30.2 per cent) and 51 (24.8 per cent) ethnic community MPs in 1991 and 1994, respectively. However, the Mountain/Hill caste group, including Brahmin and Chhetri, which constituted only 31.6 per cent of the total population, dominated the HOR with 59 per cent of elected members in 1999, 61.5 per cent in 1994 and 57.1 per cent in 1991 (Annexure-2). The proportion of Mountain/Hill ethnic group representation in the HOR declined from 22 per cent in 1991 to 18.5 per cent in 1994 and went up to 22 per cent in 1999. However, the two major Hill ethnic groups, the *Magar* and the *Tamang*, which constituted 7.2 per cent and 5.5 per cent of the total population of the country, respectively, have a low representation in the HOR compared to their population share (Annexure-2).

The people of Mountain/Hill origin, who comprise approximately two-thirds of the population of the country (Annexure-1) had more than 80 per cent representation in the HOR in 1999, while the people of Tarai origin, with nearly a third of the population, had just 19.5 per cent representation. The proportion was more or less the same in the 1991 and 1994 elections. The Dalits who constitute more than 15 per cent of the total population (including Dalits of Tarai origin) did not have representation in the HOR in 1994 and 1999 and only one MP from a Hill Dalit group was elected in 1991 (Annexures 1 and 2).

A similar trend is apparent in the caste/ethnic representation in both Houses of Parliament. Out of a total of 265 members of both Houses of Parliament in 1999, ethnic groups constituted only 27.55 per cent (Annexure-3) while the Hill Brahmins dominated the Parliament with 39.6 per cent (Annexure-3) of elected members. The representation of hill Brahmins is three times more than their population share of 12.9 per cent (Annexure-1). Similarly, the representation of Hill Dalits such as *Kami and Damai* is just 1.5 per cent (Annexure-3) while their population share is 8.7 per cent (Annexure-1). On the other hand, the

Newars have a better participation with 8.3 per cent (Annexure-3), whereas their population share is only 5.6 per cent (Annexure-1).

Although the Tarai caste representation increased from 25 members in the 1991 Parliament[9] to 31 in 1999 (Annexure-3), representation from the Tarai ethnic group decreased from 20 in 1991[10] to 12 in 1999 (Annexure-3).

The above discussion should provide an adequate empirical base to argue that some ethnic groups are to some extent excluded and therefore discriminated against in electoral politics.

Language, illiteracy, poverty and backwardness are some of the reasons for the exclusion of these sections of society in electoral politics and governance. It has been reported that on many occasions the notices issued by the Election Commission (EC) with regard to voter registration and taking of photographs for voter identity (ID) cards are not communicated properly to these people and even if they do get registered and have their ID cards prepared, they still have difficulty in understanding the concept of general elections or the value of their vote. Therefore, they often succumb to the lure of money, coercion and other instruments of power used against their interests. For this reason, the role of civic education for the illiterate, minorities, ethnic groups, bonded labourers and lower caste people can be critical.

Women

Women account for almost 50 per cent of the total electorate. However, there were only 143 (6.39 per cent) female candidates out of a total of 2,238 in the general elections of 1999. Likewise, 80 (5.95 per cent) and 86 (5.96 per cent) out of 1,345 and 1,442 candidates were women in the general elections of 1991 and 1994, respectively. Although the total number of candidates has increased by 66 per cent since the parliamentary elections in 1994, the proportion of women candidates in relation to men has remained almost the same. Table 14.7 sets out statistics relating to caste/ethnic representations in the House of Representatives from 1991–99.

Table 14.8 illustrates female representation by major parties in the HOR during the general elections of 1991, 1994 and 1999.

Only seven women were elected in the 1991 and 1994 general elections, comprising 3.4 per cent of the members of the HOR. In 1999, 12 out of a total of 143 female candidates who contested the

Table 14.7

Female Candidates of Major Parties in General Elections, 1991 to 1999

Political Parties	1991		1994		1999	
	No.	(%)	No.	(%)	No.	(%)
Nepali Congress (NC)	11	5.39	11	5.37	14	6.83
Rastriya Prajatantra Party (RPP)	17	5.39	13	6.44	14	7.18
Communist Party of Nepal Unified Marxist-Leninist CPN(UML)	9	5.08	11	5.61	12	6.15
Nepal Sadbhawana Party (NSP)	5	5.59	9	10.47	5	7.35
Others	38	6.64	42	5.58	98	6.22
Total	80	5.95	86	5.96	143	6.39

Source: IIDS, 2001.

Note: Column percentages are taken from the total candidates of each party in each general election and the last row percentages are taken from the total candidates of each general elections.

elections were elected, which is the largest representation by women in the parliamentary history of Nepal. Although the increase in the number of women MPs is a positive sign, the ratio in terms of their total population is not satisfactory.

In the 1999 elections, out of a total of 13.5 million registered voters, 6.6 and 6.8 million were women and men, respectively. Although women comprise 49 per cent of the total vote base, they do not vote with the same frequency as men. Whilst the gap between male and female registration has decreased, significant gender imbalances still exist, particularly in those regions with a large Muslim population and in those with high illiteracy rates.

Table 14.8

Female Representation in House of Representatives by Major Parties, 1991 to 1999

Political Parties	1991		1994		1999	
	No.	(%)	No.	(%)	No.	(%)
Nepali Congress (NC)	5	4.5	4	4.8	5	4.5
Rastriya Prajatantra Party (RPP)	–	–	–	–	1	9.1
Communist Party of Nepal Unified Marxist-Leninist CPN(UML)	2	3.0	3	3.4	6	8.5
Total	7	3.4	7	3.4	12	5.9

Source: IIDS, 2000.

Note: Percentages are taken from the total elected MPs of each party in each general elections.

A newly married woman is also more likely to be deprived of her right to vote because very often she is unable to produce the necessary documentation (that is, marriage certificate) in order to register herself in the constituency she resides in after marriage, unless her family members help her achieve her civic rights.

Various factors such as traditions or customs which propagate the idea that political activities are unfeminine or inappropriate for women and that women should be confined only to the domestic sphere of social life are responsible for the low turnout of women during elections. The patriarchal system in Nepal has also contributed towards the discrimination of females. Rural women, in particular, face numerous impediments such as lack of political consciousness, socially enforced dependency on males, illiteracy, suppression, and poverty, which prevent them from participating in elections on an equal footing with their male counterparts. These factors affect the exposure of women to the media, political information, partisan identities, image of party/candidates, civic attitudes, and participation in various activities. For instance, women are not allowed to cast their votes in some villages of the Tarai. In the Mahottary district, women's votes are cast by their relatives.[11] This indicates that women in rural Nepal are unaware of their voting rights and allow the abuse of these rights because of the influence of *thulabad* (local influential persons), their relatives or male members of the family.

The high turnout of women voters does not therefore imply the socio-economic and political empowerment of Nepalese women. Their empowerment is part of the wider issue of women's rights which has to be resolved as part of the larger struggle against the oppressive role of state and society against women.

Socially and Physically Underprivileged Groups

There is a severe lack of information about the electoral participation of the physically and socially underprivileged groups in Nepal. This category includes the disabled, the aged, and the poor, as well as the inhabitants of remote areas. It is estimated that about 4.5 per cent of the total population of Nepal is disabled. With an average family size of 6.6 persons, nearly 30 per cent of the people are directly affected themselves or through a family member. However, the   electoral rights of this section of society have so far received little attention.

A significant number of voters in Nepal, especially in the hill and mountain regions, reside in remote areas and have to walk for five or even eight hours and sometimes through forests and formidable terrain in order to reach the polling stations. Under these circumstances, a large number of dwellers in remote areas, the aged and the disabled, in particular, can be deprived of their right of franchise.

According to the census figures of 1991 and 2001, the share of aged people (between 60 to 74 years) in the total population increased from 4.7 per cent to 5.19 per cent, respectively. The number of people above 75 years was 184,000 in 1991 and 295,000 in 2001.[12] Since there is no provision for the special needs of aged voters during elections, they are very likely to lose their right to vote.

Instead of developing suitable mechanisms for bringing the physically and socially underprivileged into the electoral process, the number of polling booths was reduced from 7,412 in 1994 to 6,821 in 1999 with an allocation of one polling station for every 3,000 voters, which increases the average distance between households and polling centres. This is too rigid a formula for the remote districts, considering their geophysical condition and sparse population.

Electoral Fraud

Electoral fraud deprives a great number of people from participating in the elections. Most often the victims of electoral fraud are the illiterate, the poor, the Dalits, and the indigenous peoples. Although these people participate in the electoral process, their votes are directly or indirectly routed in favour of a particular party or candidate through fraudulent means. Amartya Sen terms this type of discrimination as 'unfair inclusion' rather than an outright exclusion in the electoral process.[13]

Buying votes, threatening, obstructing, harassing and otherwise intimidating are some of the prevailing malpractices. There are also charges of distributing ballot papers before the election day, distributing ballot papers without the signature of the election commission officer (ECO), vote casting by polling officers/police and volunteers on behalf of the voters and exerting pressure on the ECO to conduct a re-election without a valid reason.[14] Allegations regarding distribution of clothes and money by certain candidates belonging to major parties have also been received. For example, it was alleged that the Nepali Congress and the Rastriya Prajatantra Party (RPP) candidates distributed up to Rs 1,000 for a vote in the Sindhupalchok district.[15]

The major political parties, whether they are in government or in the opposition, have failed to bring any positive change to the economic status of the poor. Little attempt has been made to educate the poor and the illiterate in order that they may understand the importance of the electoral process for better governance. Instead, most politicians exploit the poverty of the people for political gain. Acute poverty, unemployment, illiteracy and backwardness compel the masses to sell their rights in exchange for handouts. Adhikari[16] describes the emerging election pattern of Nepal 'as a time of buying and selling of mandate'. Until and unless this condition improves, free and fair elections in Nepal will continue to be only a distant possibility.

Nepali Citizens of Foreign Residence

A large number of professional and skilled workers from Nepal seek overseas employment due to the lack of lucrative employment opportunities locally. The major world regions where Nepalese citizens currently live and work are Northern Europe and North America, South-East Asia and the Far East, the Arabian Gulf and India. Apart from migrant workers, students, diplomats, administrative staff in foreign missions, and their families also reside abroad.

The official number of Nepalese living and working abroad in 1991 was about 660,000, which is about 3.5 per cent of the total population.[17] However, independent researchers claim that more than one million Nepalese work in India alone as agri-labourers, service workers, police and military personnel, porters, and gatemen.[18] However, there is a lack of reliable information on the exact number of Nepalese migrant workers due to the open Nepal–India border.

All these non-resident Nepalese citizens are discriminated against because they have been denied franchise under the prevailing electoral laws and practices.

Internal Temporary Migrants

The current legal provision for preparing electoral rolls entails residential requirements for voter registration. This poses a serious problem for the large number of rural migrants working on temporary jobs in urban areas. They cannot go back to their villages to vote. However, they are not allowed to register their names in their place of temporary residence/work. This group also includes a large number of students who temporarily reside in cities where they are pursuing higher education.

The introduction of ID cards in some constituencies has further complicated this issue since the residency requirement for ID cards is a problem for the homeless, temporary migrants and students. For example, only 312,348 voters out of an estimated 468,000 eligible voters in the Kathmandu district were issued voter ID cards. Nearly 18,000 voters in the Kathmandu district could not participate in the general elections of 1999 because they were denied voter ID cards due to this rigid residency criterion.[19]

Earlier, there was a provision for 'temporary voters' but it was done away with after the enactment of the *Act Relating to Electoral Rolls, 1996*. This has posed problems for those who do not have a permanent residence; for instance, most of the Satar of Jhapa district are homeless and frequently migrate from one location to another in search of a livelihood. Consequently, many of them are deprived of registration in any location and are automatically prevented from voting.[20] However, those voters who have houses in two or three constituencies can theoretically vote in all of those constituencies.

Civil Servants, Security Personnel and Others

For the same reason, civil servants, public officials and certain other job-holders are also deprived of their voting rights. Thousands of citizens belonging to this group cannot vote since they do not live and work in areas of their permanent residence. There are 105,000 civil servants, an equal number of private and public sector employees, NGO and International Non-Governmental Organisation (INGO) workers, and their family members of 18 years of age and above who cannot fulfil the residency requirement for voting. Similarly, about 50,000 army personnel, 50,000 civil police personnel and 9,000 armed police personnel who work in areas other than their place of permanent residence are not allowed to cast their votes. Even an election official who has duties in a constituency other than his own is not permitted to cast his vote. The 59,516 civil and 75,000 security personnel involved in conducting and providing security for the 1999 elections were all prevented from exercising their democratic rights.

The 'others' category, which includes prisoners, urban house-renters, inmates of rehabilitation centres (for example, AIDS patients, drug addicts, orphans, the aged), industrial workers, school teachers, patients, and medical staff belonging to hospitals, clinics and nursing homes, are also disfranchised if their permanent residence is in a different location from where they reside/work. Although there are no accurate figures for the number of people who fall into this category, this group of people certainly face discrimination in the electoral process.

Maoist Insurgency and its Impact on Elections

The Maoist insurgency in Nepal is both the cause for and effect of group discrimination in all democratic processes including elections. The caste system has a social hierarchy which restricts claims to social opportunities by those who are considered low caste, impure and 'untouchable'. Traditionally, the country has been ruled by the dominant hill Hindu groups following the Hindu ethical code. The ethnic groups along with the *Madhise* and the Dalits have been largely marginalised and excluded from overall development processes in Nepal. Even after the establishment of the democratic regime in 1990, the state has continued to reinforce the existing social structure.

Despite the reformatory measures undertaken by the government in the socio-economic and political spheres, there appears to be a lack of commitment to change the existing system.[21] Instead, corruption and incompetence have marred the political system. Thus, the inability to effect structural reform through the parliamentary system and the continued deterioration of the economic well being of the majority of the people provided the impetus for the Maoist movement which has major agendas with regard to nationalism and public welfare; the Maoists have obtained a high degree of support and many recruits from the socially and economically marginalised sections of society.

The eight-year-old Maoist insurgency has prevented a large

number of people from participating in the electoral process. Despite the imposition of national emergency and mobilisation of counter-insurgency armed forces, the government has failed to contain Maoist violence. During the 1999 elections, although the EC declared some districts affected by Maoist insurgency as 'very sensitive' and sought to provide special protection for these areas, the government was unable to provide sufficient security for the candidates or voters. For example, only 43.98 per cent of 100,970 voters in Rukum, 31.81 per cent of 124,662 voters in Rolpa and 47.58 per cent of 118,012 voters in Salyan districts were able to cast their votes in the 1999 parliamentary elections.[22] The low voter turnout was due to the boycott of elections by Maoists since 1994 and the insurgency in these districts. The caretaker government of 2002 could not hold national elections for the HOR, as stipulated in the Constitution of 1990, due to Maoist violence.

People abstained from elections fearing the Maoists. Some candidates were kidnapped and others intimidated into withdrawing their nominations and 13 people were killed. Nomination papers could not be filed in 81 village development committees (VDCs) of 17 districts in the western and far-western regions during the local elections of 1997 due to Maoist threats. In the local elections, the Maoists mostly targeted Nepali Congress (NC) candidates. Subsequently, candidates and party workers belonging to other parties including the Communist Party of Nepal (Unified Marxist-Leninist) CPN(UML) also came under attack. Overall, local elections for 2.04 per cent of the seats could not be held due to Maoists' violence.[23]

Conclusion

Nepal has seen little change in its socio-political make-up since 1990. The political parties are still dominated by those elite sections of society which have ruled the country for centuries, and even though they may articulate values of equality and progress, the hierarchical values and traditions which are deeply rooted in these elitist groups are an impediment to the development of a fully-fledged democratic system.

Krämer[24] has rightly asserted that democracy, above all, means participation and equality of all sections of society. A precondition for building an inclusive democracy is to ensure the right to elect people's representatives and the development of a legal framework that protects the right to participation and freedom of expression and association of all people. This requires a more enlightened sharing of economic and political resources than is possible in the simple majoritarian democracy that Nepal follows today.

Policy Recommendations

- The current electoral laws need to be revamped and reformed because they do not accommodate all social groups and potential voters.
- Proper registration of electors is a critical precondition for free and fair elections. The current registration system needs to be expanded and improved to give women and the indigenous and rural population access to their right to franchise. Widespread illiteracy and inadequate information about the importance of, and methods and duties with regard to registration and voting should not be a barrier to participation in elections and the development of true citizenship.
- A long-term awareness campaign is necessary to educate the people about the importance of the electoral process. The message needs to be communicated in multiple languages in order to be meaningful for the diverse electorate in the country.
- The problem of illiteracy should be addressed.
- Polling stations should be made more accessible to the rural population because inaccessibility prevents a large section of the populace from voting (especially the elderly, the sick, or single parents who cannot leave their children at home).
- Facilitating absentee voting with the use of postal voting and also the new system of internet voting for foreign residents and disabled persons could also increase the level of direct participation in elections.
- Customs and traditions which are the major obstacles to women's participation in public and civic affairs should be modified. Long-term awareness campaigns led by civil society and the full commitment of the major political parties in this regard are necessary in order to make an effective impact on the people, particularly in rural areas.
- Since polling booths are usually located in schools, offices, or even outdoors, they most often do not cater to voters with special needs, for example, physically handicapped people. Ramps at stairs, increased space around the polling stands and

low voting tables will enable voters in wheelchairs or those with other disabilities to cast their vote with ease. All possible measures, such as having large symbols on ballot papers for those with bad eyesight or low literacy levels, should be taken to enable disabled voters to mark their ballot papers without assistance, thereby ensuring the secrecy of their vote.

Notes

1. Amartya Sen, 'Exclusion and Inclusion', a Paper presented at the Conference on 'Including the Excluded', South Asians for Human Rights, New Delhi, 11–12 November 2001.
2. Oxford Talking Dictionary, 1998.
3. Central Bureau of Statistics (CBS), *Population Census of Nepal 2001: National Report*, Kathmandu, HMQ/CBS in collaboration with UNFPA Nepal, 2002.
4. 2001, Census Data (Population Census 2001: National Report, Central Bureau of Statistics and UNFPA 2002, Table 16 of form 1).
5. DEVA, *Action Research on the Development and Establishment of a Revised Voters Registration Scheme for the Election Commission of Nepal*, A Final Report Submitted to DANIDA/HUGOU, Kathmandu, 2000.
6. Elections Commission, *General Election in Nepal 1991*, Kathmandu; DEVA, *Action Research....*
7. The study was based on a household survey of 466 persons of different caste, ethnic, educational, economic, marital and gender background in five districts, namely Morang, Makawanpur, Kaski, Banke and Kailali. The male/female representation of the survey was 53 and 47 per cent, respectively. Approximately 92 per cent were married. Of the sample, 64 per cent were literate and 36 per cent illiterate. Brahmin/Chhetri (35.1 per cent), ethnic group (31.6 per cent), Dalit (18.3 per cent) and 'others' (15.0 per cent) were the major caste/ethnic composition of the respondents. The 'others' category mainly consisted of *madhise* people of Tarai, that is, Yadav, Koiri, Gupta, Mahato, Kurmi, etc.
8. H. Gurung, *Nepal: Social Demography and Expression*, Kathmandu, New Era, 1998.
9. IIDS, *Fourth Parliamentary Election: A study of the Evolving Democratic Process in Nepal*, Kathmandu, Institute for Integrated Development Studies (IIDS), 2000.
10. Ibid.
11. Shanta Thapaliya, in a discussion at the Seminar on Comparative Electoral Processes in South Asia, 1999.
12. CBS, 1991 and 2002.
13. Amartya Sen, 'Exclusion and Inclusion', a Paper Presented at the Conference on 'Including the Excluded', South Asians for Human Rights New Delhi, 11–12 November 2001.

14. P.N. Maharjan, 'Local Election in Nepal, 1997, CNAS Professional Paper, Kathmandu, Center for Nepal and Asian Studies, 1998.
15. B.P. Adhikari, 'Evolution of Election Code of Conduct and its Violation in the General Election—1999', *Nepali Journal of Contemporary Studies*, Kathmandu, Nepal Center for Contemporary Studies, 2001.
16. Ibid.
17. David Seddon, Ganesh Gurung and Jagannath Adhikari, 'Foreign Labor Migration and the Remittance Economy of Nepal', *Himalayan Research Bulletin, XVIII (2)*, 1998, pp. 1–10; H. Gurung, *Nepal: Social Demography*.
18. K.M. Dixit et al., 'Lowly Labor in the Lowlands', *Himal South Asian*, 10(1), 1997.
19. IIDS, *Fourth Parliamentary Election*: A Study of the Evolving Democratic Process in Nepal, Kathmandu, Institute for Integrated Development Studies (IIDS), 2001.
20. H.P. Bhattarai, 'Identities in the Making: Cultural Pluralism and Politics of Imagined Communities in the Lowlands of Nepal', Unpublished M. Phil Dissertation, Dept. of Social Anthropology, University of Bergen, Norway, 2000.
21. D. Kumar, 'Consequences of the Militarized Conflict and the Cost of Violence in Nepal', *Contribution to Nepalese Studies*, 30(2), 2003, pp. 167–216.
22. Election Commission, *Election Result of House of Representative Election 1999*, Kathmandu, Election Commission, 1999.
23. P.N. Maharjan 'Local Election...'
24. Karl-Heinz Krämer, 'Elections in Nepal: 1999 and Before', Informal Sector Service Center (ed.), *Human Rights Yearbook 2000*, Kathmandu, INSEC, 2000, pp. 29–47.

Annexure–1

Table 14.A1
Percentage Distribution of Castes and Ethnicity
in the Population of Nepal

(1) Parbatiyas		(38.9%)
Twice-born:	Brahman	12.74%
	Chhetri (formerly Khas)	15.8%
	Thakuri	1.47%
Renouncers:	Dashnami Sanyasi and Kanphata Yogi	0.88%
*Untouchables**	Kami (iron-workers)	3.94%
	Damai (tailors)	1.720%
	Sarki (cobblers)	1.40%
	Gaine (singers)	0.03%
	Badi (dancers and drum makers)	0.02%
(2) Newars**		(5.48%)
Entitled to full		
Initiation:	Brahman	0.1%
	Bajracharya/Shakya	0.5%
	Shrestha	1.2%
	Uray	0.3%
Other Pure Castes:	Maharjan (Jyapu)	2.4%
	'Ekthariya' etc.	0.7%
Untouchable Castes:	Khadgi (Kasai), Dyahla (Pore) etc.	0.3%
(3) The Hill/Mountain ethnic groups or Janajati		(21.88%)
	Magar	7.14%
	Tamang	5.64%
	Rai	2.79%
	Gurung	2.39%
	Limbu	1.58%
	Sherpa	0.68%
	Sunuwar	0.42%
	Chepang (Praja)	0.23%
	Loda	0.11%
	Thami	0.10%
	Bhote	0.08%
	Nurang	0.08%
	Yakkha	0.07%
	Thakali	0.06%
	Pahari	0.05%
	Chhantel	0.04%
	Brahmu/Baramu	0.03%
	Jirel	0.02%
	Dura	0.02%
	Lepcha	0.02%
	Byangsi	0.01%
	Hayu	0.01%

	Walung	0.01%
	Raute	0.001%
	Yehlmo	0.001%
	Kusunda	0.0001%
	Adhibasi/Janajati	0.02%
(4) Madheshis		(32.11%)
(a) Castes Hindus		(18.27%)
Twice-born:	Brahman	0.59%
	Baniya (Vaishya)	0.56%
	Rajput (Kshatriya)	0.21%
	Kayastha (Kshatriya)	0.20%
	Rajbhat[§] (Kshatriya)	0.11%
Other Pure Castes:	Yadav/Ahir (herdsmen)	3.94%
	Khushawaha[§§] (vegetable-growers)	1.11%
	Kurmi (cultivators)	0.94%
	Kewat (fishermen)	0.60%
	Mallah (fishermen)	0.51%
	Lohar (iron workers)	0.36%
	Nunia	0.29%
	Kumhar/Kamhar (potters)	0.28%
	Halwai (confectioners)	0.22%
	Badhae	0.20%
	Mali	0.05%
Impure, but	Teli (oil pressers)	1.34%
Touchable:	Kalawar (brewers/merchants)	0.51%
	Hajam/Thakur	0.44%
	Kanu (oil pressers)	0.42%
	Sudhi	0.40%
	Barae	0.16%
	Bhediyar/Gaderi	0.08%
	Bing/Binda	0.08%
	Chidimar	0.05%
	Kusbadiya	0.001%
Untouchable:	Chamar (leather workers)	1.19%
	Musahar (basket weaver)	0.76%
	Dushadh/Paswan/Pasi	0.70%
	Tamta	0.34%
	Khatawe (labourers)	0.33%
	Dhobi (washermen)	0.32%
	Kahar	0.15%
	Dom	0.04%
	Halkhor	0.02%
(b) Madheshi ethnic or Janajati groups		(9.55%)
Inner Tarai:	Kumal	0.44%
	Majhi	0.32%
	Danuwar	0.23%
	Darai	0.07%
	Bote	0.04%

Tarai Proper:	Tharu	6.75%
	Dhanuk	0.83%
	Rajbanshi	0.42%
	Satar/Santhal	0.19%
	Dhangar/Jhangar	0.16%
	Gangai	0.14%
	Dhimal	0.09%
	Tajpuriya	0.06%
	Meche	0.02%
	Kisan	0.01%
	Raji	0.01%
	Koche	0.01%
	Munda	0.001%
(c) Muslims/Churaute/Dhunia		(4.3%)
(d) Marwaris/Jain¶		(0.2%)
(e) Panjabi/Sikhs		(0.01%)
(f) Bangali		(0.04%)
(g) Unidentified caste/ethnic groups		(1.78%)

Source: 2001, Census data (Population Census 2001: National Report, Central Bureau of Statistics and UNFPA 2002, Table 16 of Form 1).

Notes: * They are commonly known as Dalits. There are significant numbers of untouchables among the Newars and the Tarai Hindu communities of Nepal, which together account for approximately 15 per cent of the total population of the country.

** The census treats the Newars as a single group. Figures for the main subdivisions are calculated from the estimates of the relative size of the different subdivisions in J. Whelpton, 'Political Identity in Nepal: State, Nation and Community', in David N. Gellner, J. Pfaff-Czarnecka and J. Whelpton (eds), *Nationalism and Ethnicity in a Hindu Kingdom: The Politics of Culture in Contemporary Nepal,* London, Harwood Academic Publishers, 1997.

§ They are also known as Rajbhar or Bhat. Though classified as a Tarai group in the census, they are also found in the hills. Both in the Tarai and western hills, they still function as genealogists and matchmakers for the other twice-born castes, though Bhat elsewhere in the hills are more usually the offspring of irregular unions between Brahmans and Sanyasis (Gaborieau, 1978: 180 and 217–18, cited in Whelpton, 'Political Identity in Nepal...').

§§ Formerly known as Koiris, their new name indicates a connection to Lord Ram's second son, Kusha, and thus a claim to being Kshatriyas, but this has not yet been accepted by other groups.

¶ Harka Gurung (*Nepal: Social Demography and Expression,* Kathmandu, New Era, 1998) has treated the Marwaris as a category outside the Tarai caste hierarchy because many are Jains and also because they are generally seen as outsiders by the Tarai population. Many do, however, claim to be Hindus.

Annexure–2

Table 14.A2

Caste/Ethnic Representation in the House of Representatives, 1991 to 1999

Caste/Ethnicity	1991 No.	1991 %	Change 1991–94	1994 No.	1994 %	Change 1994–99	1999 No.	1999 %	% of the Total Population*
Mountain/Hill	162	79.0	+2	164	80	+1	166	80.9	67.9
A. Caste Group	117	57.1	+9	126	61.5	−5	121	59.0	40.3
Brahmin	77	37.6	+9	86	42.0	−9	77	37.6	12.9
Chhetri	28	13.7	+1	29	14.1	0	29	14.2	16.1
Thakuri	11	5.4	0	11	5.4	+2	13	6.3	1.6
Sanyasi	–	–	–	–	–	+2	2	1.0	1.0
Damai	1	0.5	−1	–	–	–	–	–	2.0
B. Ethnic Group	45	22.0	−7	38	18.5	+6	45	21.5	27.5
Gurung	7	3.4	−2	5	2.4	+1	6	2.9	2.4
Magar	3	1.5	+2	5	2.4	+1	6	2.9	7.2
Rai	5	2.4	0	5	2.4	0	5	2.4	2.8
Limbu	7	3.4	−3	4	2.0	+3	7	3.4	1.6
Tamang	5	2.4	−1	4	2.0	0	4	2.0	5.5
Newar	14	6.8	−1	13	6.3	+1	14	6.8	5.6
Sherpa	–	–	+1	1	0.5	−1	–	–	0.6
Thakali	3	1.5	−2	1	0.5	0	1	0.5	0.1
Bhote	1	0.5	−1	–	–	–	–	–	0.1
Sunuwar	–	–	–	–	–	+1	1	0.5	0.2

(Table 14.A2 Contd.)

(Table 14.A2 Contd.)

Caste/Ethnicity	1991		1994		Change 1991–94	1999		Change 1994–99	% of the Total Population*
	No.	%	No.	%		No.	%		
Tarai/Inner Tarai	43	21.0	41	20.0	–2	39	19.02	–2	32.0
A. Caste Group	21	10.2	24	11.7	+3	25	12.1	+1	16.1
Brahmin	5	2.4	6	2.9	+1	3	1.5	–3	0.9
Bhumihar	1	0.5	1	0.5	0	2	1.0	+1	NA
Rajput	5	2.4	3	1.5	–2	–	–	–	0.4
Kayastha	4	2.0	5	2.4	+1	–	–	–	0.3
Yadav	5	2.4	8	3.9	+3	12	5.9	+4	4.1
Halwai	–	–	–	–	–	3	1.5	+3	0.2
Teli	–	–	–	–	–	2	1.0	+2	1.4
Others	1	0.5	1	0.5	0	4	2.0	+3	NA
B. Ethnic Group	17	8.3	13	6.3	–4	11	5.4	–2	9.0
Dhanuwar	1	0.5	–	–	–1	–	–	–	0.3
Rajbanshi	1	0.5	–	–	–1	–	–	–	0.4
Tharu	15	7.3	13	6.3	–2	10	4.9	–3	6.5
Dhanuk	–	–	–	–	–	1	0.5	–1	0.7
C. Others	5	2.4	4	2.0	–1	3	1.5	–1	7.0
Muslims	5	2.4	4	2.0	–1	2	1.0	–2	3.5
Marwari	–	–	–	–	–	1	0.5	+1	0.2
Total	205	100.0	205	100.0		205	100.0		100.0

Source: Gurung 1998 for 1991 and 1994, and IIDS 2000 for 1999 figures.
Notes: *1991 Census data, Central Bureau of Statistics 1993, Vol. 2, Part VII, Table 25.

Annexure–3

Table 14.A3
Caste/Ethnic Composition of Parliament 1999

Caste/Ethnicity	Number	Percentage of the Total	Percentage of the Total Population (as of 1991)
Mountain/Hill	219	82.6	67.9
A. Caste Group	158	59.6	40.3
Brahmin	105	39.6	12.9
Chhetri	30	11.3	16.1
Thakuri	16	6.0	1.6
Sanyasi	3	1.1	1.0
Damai	1	0.4	2.0
Kami	3	1.1	5.2
B. Ethnic Group	61	23.0	27.5
Gurung	7	2.6	2.4
Magar	9	3.4	7.2
Rai	6	2.3	2.8
Limbu	9	3.4	1.6
Tamang	4	1.5	5.5
Newar	22	8.3	5.6
Thakali	2	0.8	0.1
Sunuwar	1	0.4	0.2
Muslim (Hill Origin)	1	0.4	NA
Tarai/Inner Tarai	46	17.4	32.0
A. Caste Group	31	11.7	16.1
Brahmin	5	1.9	0.9
Bhumihar	2	0.8	NA
Rajput	1	0.4	0.4
Yadav	14	5.3	4.1
Halwai	3	1.1	0.2
Teli	2	0.8	1.4
Others	4	1.5	NA
B. Ethnic Group	12	4.5	9.0
Tharu	11	4.2	6.5
Dhanuk	1	0.4	0.7
C. Others	3	1.1	7.0
Muslims	2	0.8	3.5
Marwari	1	0.4	0.2
Total	265	100.0	100

Source: IIDS, 2000.

15

PAKISTAN

Rasul Bakhsh Rais

Introduction

Building democracy in any country, including Pakistan, is not only about holding elections—which in this case were few in number and mostly controversial—but about laying the true foundation of democratic polity and society. For any student of democratic thought, fundamental to such an enterprise would be institutions and systems, citizenship, equality, inalienable fundamental rights and empowerment of all individuals without any discrimination. In most postcolonial states, ethnic, linguistic and religious minorities have found themselves at the receiving end of political discrimination. Some saw their decline from a privileged to a marginalised group, while others found themselves reduced in number or as a new minority after the redrawing of boundaries. The examples of Muslims in India, and Hindus and Sikhs in Pakistan fit this description.

This chapter discusses how the minorities, women and lower castes have been discriminated against, the discriminatory legal regimes, and how informal social structures, values and culture have sustained these discriminatory regimes. An indication of the relating numerical strength of the different religious groups in Pakistan is set out in Table 15.1.

Table 15.1
Number of Minorities

Religion/Community	No.	Percentage
Muslims	127,433,409	96.28
Christians	2,002,902	(1.58)
Hindus	2,111,271	(1.60)
Ahmadis	289,212	(0.22)
Scheduled Castes	332,343	(0.25)
Others	96,142	(0.07)
Total Population	132,352,279	(100)

Source: Government of Pakistan, Statistics Division, No. SD. PER.E (53)/99-449, Islamabad, 16 July 2001.

Religious Minorities and Separate Electorates

Central to the question of the political status of the minorities in Pakistan is the contested issue of the country's identity as an Islamic state or a secular state. It is pertinent to commence our study of discrimination against minorities in Pakistan with the famous and oft-quoted statement of the founder of Pakistan before the Constituent Assembly:

> You may belong to any religion or caste or creed—that has nothing to do with the business of the state.... We are starting in the days when there is no discrimination between one caste or creed and another. We are starting with this fundamental principle that we are all citizens and equal citizens of one state ... you will find that in the course of time Hindus would cease to be Hindus and Muslims would cease to be Muslims, not in the religious sense because that is the personal faith of each individual but in the political sense as citizens of the state.[1]

There cannot be a more lucid and forceful expression of the founder of Pakistan's political ideology than this address to the Constituent Assembly. The liberal sections of society and minorities in Pakistan have taken this statement as the fundamental principle of the country's political structure. All those who believe in liberal, secular and democratic values cite this historic address to support their vision of Pakistan.

However, in the formative phase of the country some members of Jinnah's own party began to present a distorted, non-liberal and retrogressive political map for the country.

Until the changes in the election laws brought about by the military regime of Pervez Musharraf in 2002, Pakistan had mainly employed a system of separate electorates. The political roots of separate electorates go back to pre-partition Muslim politics in the subcontinent and also to early debates after the creation of the country about how best to protect minority rights. One of the most important planks of Muslim politics under British rule was to ensure that the Muslims scattered around the length and width of India were represented in the elected councils in proportion to their numbers. The Muslims were a substantial minority, comprising about 25 per cent of the population of undivided India. They demanded a system of separate electorates, meaning that Muslims would be allocated seats in the local, provincial, and central legislative bodies according to their percentage in the population, and that only Muslims would vote for Muslim candidates. The British finally accepted this demand in the Minto–Marley Reforms of 1909 for India, though the Indian National Congress vehemently opposed it.[2] After the introduction of these reforms, all elections were held according to this system. Some historians have rightly argued that the establishment of the separate electorates system further strengthened the Muslim separatism that led to the creation of Pakistan.[3]

The question of separate electorates was one of the focal points of debate and controversy in the Constituent Assembly of Pakistan when the first post-Independence Constitution was under discussion and lines were drawn between liberal politicians and regional parties on one side and religious parties on the other. The *Jamat-i-Islami* (Islamic party) and its founder and prominent leader Maulana Abul Aala Maudoodi were at the forefront of opposition to the joint electorates. Some other religious political parties and some sections of the Muslim League also supported separate electorates. Most of them thought that separate electorates would be consistent with the two-nation ideology of Pakistan,[4] which had been at the heart of the political struggle for the creation of Pakistan. Some of them even questioned the loyalty of the Hindu minority to Pakistan and openly expressed their distrust of them. Many of them hid their ideological bias by pleading that under a system of joint electorates the minorities might not get adequate representation in the national Parliament and provincial assemblies.

The views of the leaders of East Pakistan, where there was a sizeable Hindu minority, differed on the issue of separate electorates from those of the leaders of West Pakistan. While the West Pakistanis stressed the need for separate electorates, the East Pakistanis insisted on joint electorates.[5] The members of the Constituent Assembly from East Pakistan rightly argued that separate electorates would leave the minorities in both the wings of the country disenfranchised, and that the system would work against national integration and inclusive politics. Those opposing the views of the East Pakistani members argued that some pro-India parties and groups would capture power with the support of the Hindu minority in a system of single member electoral constituencies in East Pakistan. In their judgement, more Hindus would get elected to the Provincial Assembly in East Pakistan and to the National Assembly under the joint electorates than their number would justify. They also argued that with the influence of Hindu lawmakers and their prominence in the political arena, Bengali nationalism would gain strength, undermine Pakistan's position on Kashmir and gradually erode the country's ideological foundations.[6]

The members of minority communities believed that separate electorates would cast them off from mainstream national politics. They demanded equal political, civic and legal rights that could only be guaranteed under the joint electorates system.

In a very contentious atmosphere, the Constituent Assembly failed to reach any agreement on whether to have separate or joint electorates when framing the 1956 Constitution. The assembly left the matter for the future Parliament to settle after ascertaining the views of the Provincial Assemblies. When the issue was referred to the East and West Provincial Assemblies, they passed different resolutions: East Pakistan for joint and West Pakistan for separate electorates. The National Assembly, feeling the political pulse and opposition from the East Pakistani parties, decided to approve two different methods, joint electorates for East Pakistan and separate electorates for West Pakistan.

When elections were about to be held under the 1956 Constitution the military imposed its first episode of martial law in the country, abrogated the Constitution and set about implementing a new one that would be 'appropriate to the genius' of the people of Pakistan. The issue of separate or joint electorates lingered on in political debates. The commission that was set up to frame the 1962 Constitution recommended separate electorates for the minorities. The military ruler General Mohammad Ayub Khan did not accept the recommendation and decided to opt for joint electorates. Pakistan held all subsequent elections under the system of joint electorates. Formal marginalisation of minorities in elections was ended. After the break-up of Pakistan in 1971, Parliament framed a new Constitution more or less on the same lines as the 1956 Constitution, putting an end to the presidential system that Ayub Khan had introduced. Pakistan went back to a parliamentary system, but this time around, even in the face of opposition from the religious parties, procedures for joint electorates were adopted. After the separation of East Pakistan, the population of religious minorities shrank to nearly 5 per cent of the population. The new government of Zulfikar Ali Bhutto introduced additional safeguards into the 1973 Constitution to ensure representation of the minorities in the national and provincial assemblies. Six seats were reserved for the religious minorities in the national assembly. They were also given representation in the provincial assemblies: five seats in the Punjab, two in Sindh and one each in Baluchistan and the North-west Frontier Province. However, the minority legislators were not elected directly, but by the electoral college of their provincial assemblies. To provide further evidence to the international community that minorities were well-represented in the power structure of Pakistan, the Bhutto Government, and almost all subsequent governments, have appointed at least one federal minister from the minority communities to some unimportant ministry. The minorities had greater participation within this system, but it was far from being equal in the real sense as discrimination against them continued in many other forms.

The Bhutto Government created many controversies, but one of the most crippling was the move to declare the Ahmadi sect, which had been known as Muslim since it was founded in 19th century in India, as non-Muslim. This was done through a constitutional amendment.[7] Subsequent to the national Parliament determining the religiosity of the community, religious parties and groups organised pogroms against known Ahmadi families and prominent figures, and burnt their houses and businesses. Thousands of Ahmadis—who had a following of millions and well-funded and well-organised religious and social networks—lost their lives and Pakistan created yet another marginalised community. Their mosques were closed down and they were debarred from congregational prayers or showing any sign of being a Muslim in their places of worship. They were added to the list of other minorities, which included Buddhists, Hindus and Sikhs, and required by law to declare in all official documentation that they were Ahmadis. The anti-Ahmadi movement was an old one in the country, and had led to civil disturbance in the city of Lahore in 1951, but this was quelled by the intervention of the military. The real persecution of this community started with their declaration as non-Muslims. Officially, the leadership of the Ahmadi community refused to participate in any elections in protest, but those who hid their religious affiliation for fear of persecution cast their votes by forging identity.

Under the joint electorate system of the 1973 Constitution, members of minority communities could vote as any other citizen. Therefore, the system did not affect the Ahmadis as far as the casting of votes was concerned; they could vote for any candidate. But with the imposition of third martial law in the country in July 1977, the government of General Zia-ul-Haq—which had cultivated the religious constituency for political support against the mainstream political parties—decided to enforce separate electorates in the country through an ordinance in 1979. His vision of Pakistan was not very different from that of most of the religious political parties. Since he had plans to stay in power longer than he had promised the nation, he believed that, besides the military, the religious groups could provide the main base of his support. He had the personal image of a pious, God-fearing, patriotic Pakistani. His Islamisation agenda for the Pakistani state would have little credibility without acceding to the long-standing demands of the religious right for making provisions for a separate system of elections for the minorities. As an unchallenged military ruler, General Zia-ul-Haq began to give an altogether different orientation to Pakistan's political system, which was selectively Islamic in the most conservative tradition. His ordinances, laws, and acts of omission and commission were passed through the 8th Amendment into the Constitution when the national assembly convened after the 1985 non-party elections. In this way, separate electorates became part of the 1973 Constitution.

The Zia regime increased the number of seats for the minorities in the national assembly from five to 10, but maintained the same numbers in the provincial assemblies. There was also a change in how the seats in the legislatures were to be filled. The entire country was divided into 10 constituencies for the minorities, which made it utterly impossible for candidates to effectively contest or voters to cast their votes because of the long distances and fragmented concentration of the minorities in different parts of the country. Since the religious minorities were dispersed throughout the length of the country, drawing up large territorial constituencies reduced the exercise of separate electorates to a mockery. Only a few influential, wealthy and well-connected minority figures could win in such a rough and unlevelled electoral field.

Following the restoration of democracy in the country after the death of General Zia-ul-Haq and fresh elections in 1988, the political leaders from the mainstream political parties did not bother to address the issue of the marginalisation of minorities in electoral politics. Even with the removal of some parts of the 8th Amendment unanimously through the 13th Amendment in 1997, the issue of separate electorates was not touched.

In the bouts of political struggle for power, even liberal politicians remained silent on the issue of separate electorates. Most of the political parties decided not to push the issue fearing that a reversal of separate electorates would anger the religious political parties and create a backlash. Their vision of democracy was confined to getting to the assemblies, obtaining ministerial positions and making fortunes at the expense of laying the foundations for true democracy or addressing the issue of the rights of minorities.

Formal and informal discrimination against the minorities went hand in hand; the former encouraged and deepened the latter. Separate electorates were more than separate electoral constituencies for the religious minorities. In practical terms they amounted to their disenfranchisement, furthering their marginalisation and deepening a sense among them of being second-class Pakistanis. The mainstream political parties had no interest in courting the minorities and ensuring that they gained prominent leadership positions, as the latter could not vote for them. They were left to form their own parties if they wished to, and it was only the Christians who set up some loosely organised parties. Other minorities had notable figures but no political organisations.

In traditional Islamic societies such as Pakistan, non-Muslims do not enjoy equality of social or religious status. Pakistan's minorities have never supported separate electorates, and have, for decades, struggled with whatever meagre political capital they have had to attempt to get joint electorates restored. In a large number of urban constituencies where the mainstream political parties have traditionally close contests, the balance held by the minorities would make a major difference under a system of joint electorates. Compared to the noisy religious parties, minority groups had neither adequate forums nor organisations to get back into mainstream national politics. The minorities kept the issue of separate electorates in the public sphere through regular press coverage, seminars and publications, yet their struggle met with no success. Pakistan has received a lot of foreign attention during the past few years, and this has focused particularly on the issues of the status of women and the plight of minorities. Foreign media, human rights organisations, and civil society organisations in Pakistan have kept consistent pressure on the government for a change in the electorates system.

The military government of Pervez Musharraf, under a programme of political restructuring that has included many controversial changes, finally reversed the practice of separate electorates and held elections in October 2002 on the basis of joint electorates. Seats have also been reserved for the minorities in Parliament, as they were in the original 1973 Constitution. Thus the first and most important step toward empowering the minorities and bringing them back into mainstream national politics has been taken.

There is also an informal, social aspect to discrimination against minorities, which is subtler than the formal, legal process of restricting their access to the political arena. Unfortunately, Pakistan has a long way to go before minorities are integrated into electoral politics. Although Muslims and non-Muslims voted in joint electorates in October 2002, not a single member from the minority communities won any seat. This continued the pattern that began with the 1970 and 1977 elections, which were also held on the basis of joint electorates. The political parties avoided the risk of fielding candidates from minority groups out of a concern for winning seats. Given the social climate of the country, it is hard to believe that the political parties will grant members of minority communities tickets to contest elections on open seats even in the future. The policy of reserving seats for minority members in the provincial and national Assemblies partly addresses the problem of their representation in the legislature. However, minority members who are selected generally belong to the elite category and move in elite networks rather than build grassroots support among their communities.

Women and Discrimination

No other issue is so contentious and well-debated in the politics of contemporary societies as the question of sex and politics. Female activists all over the world are questioning political inequality among the sexes. They have raised fundamental questions about the legitimacy of male-dominated democratic systems in which women find themselves formally or informally excluded from political power. In

recent decades, they have focused on the vital issues of empowerment, rights, social and political equality, and an end to discrimination in all its forms. Even in male-dominated, socially conservative
societies like Pakistan, the feminist movement has brought into
sharp focus more or less the same issues relating to the social status
and inadequate representation of women in politics.

Women in Pakistan are more disadvantaged than women in modern
western democratic societies, mainly due to the social and cultural
conditions in which they live. The values, social structures and
cultural orientations of the Pakistani population point to women as
the most oppressed social and political group in Pakistan. Their
general status is characterised by dependence, passivity, low self-
esteem and even denial of some of the basic rights. The political
culture of traditionally male-dominated Pakistan has meant that
very little has been done to empower women. Exclusion from, and
low voluntary participation of women in the political process are
culturally and socially determined traits of the society. Women are
constrained by the socially and culturally determined self-image of
the role of the woman lying within the boundaries of the house: to
serve a husband, raise children and stay at home as the honour of the
family. The biggest barrier to women's involvement in public affairs
in general and in electoral politics in particular is posed by the low
social status of women in the society, mainly because of the customs
of a largely feudal and tribal culture. *Report of the Pakistan Women s
Rights Committee*, published in 1996 by the Government of Pakistan,
lamented the fact that Muslim women who had participated in the
independence movement of the country seemed to have since retired
from direct involvement in public affairs.[8] Among other factors,
such as military rule and absence of democratic politics in the country, the report cited 'deep rooted usages and customs, which are
without religious or ethical sanctions' as preventing women from
exercising constitutional rights.[9]

Yet there are also variations in the status and roles of women
depending on their social circumstances. Studies on political participation have repeatedly confirmed a positive link between social status
and participation in electoral politics.[10] Educated and professional
women in urban areas and from upper classes enjoy much better status
and rights than illiterate women in rural areas. Women in the tribal
areas of Baluchistan, North-west Frontier Province and remote areas
of southern Punjab and interior Sindh live in more adverse social
conditions than women in other parts of the country. In these areas,
honour killings, domestic violence and discrimination by male

members of the families are common, and such acts are not confined to these areas alone. Many educated Pakistani women have shunned the role traditionally assigned to them, yet they are an exception.[11] Even women with better levels of education and from the upper classes of the society have found the system closed to them. However, female activists in Pakistan are highly educated, skilled and articulate. Their groups have clearer visions, more convincing agendas and more forward-looking politics than the men in Pakistan do. Yet they have a long distance to travel before they will be able to achieve equal rights, fair participation in different professions and their share of political power.

Constitutionally and legally, women can contest elections in any open seat at any level and vote for candidates of their own choice in any elections. There is no legal discrimination against them. However, in practice, fewer women than men have been registered as voters, smaller numbers have come to polling booths on election days and the number of women who have contested elections against men is minute. A very tiny number have been elected, owing more to the social status and standing of their families or its political legacy than purely individual attributes and capabilities.

All women's groups throughout the history of Pakistan have time and again suggested that the state must take the lead in increasing women's participation in politics through reserving seats for them in the elected assemblies. Another area flagged by women's groups relates to the removal or amendment of discriminatory laws against them, particularly the *Hudood* laws.[12] The National Commission on the Status of Women has also recommended the repealing of these laws.[13] All women's rights activists consider the state as the primary agent of bringing about change in their social and political status, as the slow evolution from within society takes much longer. This has been quite a consistent theme in the feminist movement, although with the recent expansion of civil society networks women have found a larger number of independent forums in which to articulate their demands and seek and expand participation in the informal sectors of political power.

All Pakistani constitutions have had a provision reserving seats for women in the legislatures. In the post-Independence Constitutional Assembly, there were only two seats reserved for women. The 1956 Constitution reserved 10 seats for women in the national assembly of Pakistan, five each to be elected from West Pakistan and East Pakistan, respectively. However, the Constitution was abrogated in October 1958 before any elections could be held.[14] At that time, there were the two provinces of East and West Pakistan. The four provinces of today's Pakistan were then merged together into West Pakistan. Similarly, in each provincial assembly, 10 women legislators were to be elected. This arrangement was to continue for only 10 years in the hope that the country would not need affirmative action. The 1962 Constitution reduced the number of seats reserved for women in the national and provincial assemblies to three from each province in the national assembly, and five in the provincial assemblies. It also changed the mode of their elections from direct to indirect. The provincial assemblies acted as their electoral colleges.

Women had nominal representation in the local governments that Ayub Khan introduced under the 1962 Constitution. The councillors who elected the president and members of the provincial and national legislatures—40,000 from each province—were predominantly men. But Ayub Khan's period was very distinctive in terms of codifying family laws that gave substantial rights to women that were previously not recognised or protected by the state. His was a progressive era for women's rights.[15] State actions increased awareness among women's groups and strengthened their movement. Many religious groups including the *Jamat-i-Islami* were very critical of the general for introducing family laws and family-planning programmes which they thought were un-Islamic.

The progressive involvement further increased with the political campaign of Zulfikar Ali Bhutto and the 1970 elections. However, none of the political parties in West Pakistan granted a ticket to any female candidate to contest in the provincial or national elections in 1970. Bhutto promised to grant more rights to the oppressed sections of the society, including women. Under the 1973 Constitution women were allocated 5 per cent of the seats in Parliament, which amounted to 10 seats in the national assembly for the next 10 years. It was only in the 1977 elections that a woman was granted a ticket to contest. But the lady was the wife of the sitting prime minister of the country.[16] The entire electoral exercise became controversial and resulted in political chaos and finally the imposition of martial law.

Women's groups in Pakistan contend that their movement and rights suffered with the Islamisation programme of General Zia. They have argued that their status suffered and their vulnerability to injustice increased because the Islamisation process strengthened the attitudes and values that hindered their progress.[17] Ironically, it was under his rule that new women's organisations were launched and women became more active in the political sphere, perhaps fearing that what they had gained could be taken back. In response, some religious scholars who were allotted prime-time slots on national television attacked the notion of women's freedoms, and their social and political rights. This fuelled more fire in the women's movement.

During much of the decade of democracy when elected governments were in power, the question of women's participation remained unsettled, particularly the amendment of the Constitution to extend the initial period of 10 years and the mode of elections. The government of General Pervez Musharraf has taken some radical measures to increase women's participation. Under the new arrangements, women have been allocated 30 per cent of the seats in the national and provincial assemblies. Around 73 female members have been elected to the national assembly, the federal legislature, by the electoral college of the provincial assembly members according to the principle of proportional representation based on lists of candidates provided by each party to the Election Commission. Through reserving seats or affirmative action, women now have a substantial presence in the assemblies. Likewise, in the local government elections held in 2001, women were allocated 30 per cent of seats in the local councils. These were formal affirmative actions that the women's movement in Pakistan had demanded for a long time. Will their status, role and participation in elections increase? Will discrimination against them come to an end?

Answers to these questions must focus on social structures, the rural agrarian environment and the feudal and tribal characteristics of the society. In the local elections, there were hardly any contests among female candidates, most of them being elected unopposed because of pre-election bargaining among the local groups. In certain areas in Baluchistan and the North-west Frontier Province, the local populations decided not to nominate any female candidates.[18] Large proportions of women voted according to the preferences of the men in their families. They were not exposed to political debates and the question of political choice was left to the male members of the families. Thus, formal measures taken by the military government to end discrimination against women are important but the real change will come when the social barriers gradually come down.[19] Women's equality as candidates and voters continue to suffer not because of state policy, but primarily due to tradition, social structures, lower levels of education, and a male-dominated society.

The Lower Castes

The social background of individuals and groups generally determines their political inclination and capacities to utilise opportunities to participate in any political action.

In feudal agrarian political cultures, groups of different social status develop and fail to develop the necessary skills to articulate interest in, and seek access to power. Are the lower castes in Pakistan well-equipped to participate in the political process? Have they been sensitised or granted enough opportunities? Most people of lower castes seldom exercise independent judgement on whom to vote for. Their individual and family choices in this respect are made in line with the political preferences of locally influential persons. The democratic principles of free will and self-determination are idealistic propositions in the traditionally caste- and class-based society of Pakistan. Caste differentiation, though not the same as in India, remains a strong social marker.

Lower-caste members have traditionally adopted menial professions such as shoemaking, carpentry, hairdressing, weaving, and cleaning the streets and toilets in public buildings and private homes. The other category of lower-caste families consists of those who work on agricultural farms and in the households of major landowners. They are not wage earners, but get some grain and meagre amounts of cash for clothing and other necessities at the end of each crop. Known as *kammis* (domestic, agricultural workers), they survive mainly as semi-slave dependants of the feudal lords or even work in the households of families with medium-sized agricultural farms. There is also the pervasive phenomenon of bonded-labour in the agriculture sector with entire families working to pay back loans they have taken either to feed themselves or for social or other reasons.

Household servants in both urban and rural areas of Pakistan are a much under-observed and neglected group in research terms. The question of the political rights of these castes and social groups is very important. Their dependent economic and social status make them a political appendage of the lords they serve. They are restricted from making political opinions or exercising choices different from those of the lord. It was only during the populist era of Zulfikar Ali Bhutto, though himself a feudal lord, and his populist politics that the lower classes had their first awakening. They defied their lords for the first time in the 1970 elections to vote for the candidates of Bhutto's parties against the wishes of their masters. That spirit and sense of freedom among the lower castes and classes did not last very long after the elimination of the founder of the people's struggle in Pakistani politics.

Discrimination against lower castes is deeply rooted in the society and takes place at an informal level. The masters and lords use economic bondage along with fear of the state agencies such as the police to keep the lower castes they preside over in servitude. Even a slight sign of rebellion is suppressed with the most severe punishment, which may take many forms, such as theft of animals; registration of false cases with the police; harassment by the lord's goon squads; and in more severe cases, abduction of women. Illegal confinement and even jailing of lower castes in the private jails that still exist in the interior of Sindh and Baluchistan is not uncommon. Their unconditional social and political obedience is a prerequisite for their social and economic survival where the state laws and institutions are too weak to protect them.

Political liberty and the exercise of free will in elections, let alone contesting them, would be an unrealistic expectation for the lower castes in the feudal agrarian conditions of Pakistan. Even with the harsh and oppressive environment within which the lower castes survive, they are not trusted. To make sure they vote, they are hauled to the polling stations early in the morning.[20] They remain under close vigil by the workers of the lords until they have cast their votes and are taken back to their villages. Personal observation and many reports suggest that most of them vote due to fear and intimidation. Elections put the lower castes in real dilemmas where they are caught between many rival local influentials. They essentially have to make a choice between a more harmful and less harmful party and tend to be forced to vote for the one who might have a greater capacity to do evil to them in the case of their disobedience. They do not have the effective legal remedies or local institutions to protect them, or the independent economic means to move away to better places. However, physical movement and relocation is a part of economic and social mobility. There is a growing trend among lower castes of moving to major towns and industrial cities for better economic opportunities. Many families that have done so have shown others the way. However, a real transformation is yet to take place, and will depend on how Pakistan's economy performs in the coming years. Such a transformation will be the only way to end discrimination in the rural setting of the village. It is the feudal political culture that has sustained group discrimination against the lower castes. But once democracy becomes a consistent functional political pattern, it will help to create a new political culture of equal rights and provide a political space and institutional remedies for various groups to act against discrimination.

Recommendations

- Pakistan needs to invest more in social sector development so that disadvantaged groups like minorities, women and lower castes achieve social and economic mobility, which is a prerequisite for ending all forms of discrimination against them.
- The question of social structures, values and customs is troublesome. It is the responsibility of the government to create better legal regimes and effective institutions to negate the adverse effects of tradition on social relations.
- Periodic elections on the basis of adult franchise and democracy are the best tools for the empowerment of different groups in the society. Pakistan's democratic experience has been disjointed, controversial and interrupted by the military's intervention. The strengthening of democracy in the country would gradually empower women and marginalised groups.
- Ending separate electorates is a welcome step for the minorities. But in order to ensure that they have some representation in the elected assemblies, some seats must be reserved for them in the provincial and national assemblies.
- Minorities, particularly Christians, have demanded repeal of the Blasphemy Law, which they believe has been an instrument of social and legal victimisation of their community. It is suggested that either the law be repealed or amended to make it difficult for anyone to register cases of blasphemy.
- Political parties must be required by law to allocate a portion of their party tickets to minority and female candidates. These should be in addition to the reserved seats.
- To improve the conditions of lower castes and marginalised groups, Pakistan needs to strengthen its governmental institutions, increase the efficiency of the police and invest more in education and rights-awareness campaigns.

Notes

1. Government of Pakistan, *Constituent Assembly Debates Constituted under Punjab Act 11 of 1954 to Enquire into the Punjab Disturbances of 1953*, Vol. 1, No. 2, Lahore, Government of Pakistan, p. 255.

2. H.V. Hodson, *The Great Divide: Britain–India–Pakistan*, Karachi, Oxford University Press, 1985, pp. 12–17.

3. It seems that without separate electorates, the Muslims' political identity would not have taken the shape that it did in undivided British India. It was a factor that contributed to their struggle for political representation and, later, in the demand for the creation of Pakistan as an independent homeland.

4. On the early debates on these issues, see Khalid Bin Sayeed, *Pakistan: The Formative Phase*, Karachi, Oxford University Press, 1978.

5. G.W. Choudhury, *Constitutional Development in Pakistan*, Vancouver, University of British Columbia Publication Centre, 1969.

6. For details see, M. Rafique Afzal, *Political Parties in Pakistan, 1947–58*, Vol. 1, Islamabad, National Institute of Historical and Cultural Research, 1986, pp. 185–89.

7. Second Amendment of 1974, Section 3, which read: 'A person who does not believe in the absolute and unqualified finality of the Prophethood of Muhammad (Peace be upon him) of the Prophets or claims to be a Prophet in any sense of the word or of any description whatsoever after Muhammad (Peace be upon him), or recognises such a claimant as a Prophet or a religious reformer, is not a Muslim for the purposes of the Constitution or law'. See Asif Saeed Khan Khosa, *The Constitution of Pakistan, 1973 (With all Amendments up to 1990)*, Lahore, Kausar Brothers, 1990, p. 142.

8. Government of Pakistan, Ministry of Law and Parliamentary Affairs (Law Division), *Report of the Pakistan Women s Rights Committee*, Islamabad, 1976, pp. 95–96.

9. Ibid., p. I.

10. Lester Milbrath, *Political Participation*, Chicago, Rand MacNally, 1965.

11. Khawar Mumtaz and Farida Shaheed, *Women of Pakistan: Two Steps Forward, One Step Back?*, Lahore, Vanguard Books, 1987, p. 7.

12. These laws relate to Islamic punishment for moral crimes, like adultery. 'Sherry for Repeal of Hudood Laws', *Dawn*, 30 March 2004.

13. Adil Zareef, 'Why Inaction on Women's Issues', *Dawn*, 8 April 2004.

14. 'History of Women's Reserved Seats in Leglislatures of Pakistan,' *Legislative Watch*, Lahore, Aurat Publication and Information Service Foundation, (November–December 2001).

15. On this period, see for instance, Lawrence Ziring, *Pakistan: The Enigma of Political Development*, Boulder, CO, Westview Press, 1980.

16. Begum Nusrat Bhutto was given a ticket.

17. Asma Jahangir, Hina Jilani and Shahla Zia, *Muslims Family Laws and their Implementation in Pakistan*, Islamabad, Ministry of Women Development, Government of Pakistan, 1988, p. 11.

18. See for instance the news item 'Jirga (local assembly of elders) Bars Women from Voting', *Dawn*, 28 March 2004.
19. See some damning comments by Ardeshir Cowasjee, 'Suffering On, and On', *Dawn* 28 March 2004.
20. Authors' observation in southern Punjab districts, Rajanpur and Dera Ghazi Khan.

SELECT BIBLIOGRAPHY

I

Court Judgements, India

S.S. Dhanoa vs *Union of India*, S.C. 1745, *All India Reporter*, 1991.
Dasappa vs *Election Commission*, Kant 230, *All India Reporter*, 1992.
Narayan vs *Purushottam*, UJSC 297, *All India Reporter*, 1992.
Nawab vs *Viswanath*, All 109, *All India Reporter*, 1993.
Union of India vs *Association for Democratic Reforms and Anr.*, S.C. 249, 2002.
Peoples Union for Civil Liberties (PUCL) & Another vs *Union of India and Another*, *Judgements Today*, Vol. 2, No. 10, 20 March 2003.

Reports, India

Report of the Committee on Electoral Reforms, Ministry of Law and Justice, Government of India, May, 1990.
One Hundred and Seventieth Report on Reform of the Electoral Laws, Law Commission of India, May, 1999.
Report of Citizens for Democracy (Tarkunde Committee Report), 1975.

Reports, Nepal

The Constitution of the Kingdom of Nepal 2047 (1990).
Member of the House of Representatives Election Act, 2047 (MHRE Act).

Member of the National Assembly Election Act, 2048.
Local Bodies (Election process) Act, 2048.
Election Constituency Delimitation Act, 2047 (ECD Act).
Election Commission Act, 2047 (EC Act).
Election Offences and Punishment Act, 2047 (EOP Act).
Voters List Act, 2052.
Rules on Voters List, 2052.
Directives on Election of Member of the House of Representatives, 2055.
Directives on Election of Member of the National Assembly, 2055.
Code of Conduct, 2053.
Rules on Voters Identity Card, 2053.
Local Bodies Election Directives, 2049.
Election Commission s Instruction to Chief Officer for Voters Name Registration, 2057.
Bill on Political Parties.

II

Acharya, Nilamber, 'Prospects of the Constitution Reforms' in Bhimsen Thapa (ed.), *Prospects of the Constitution Reforms*, Kathmandu, 1996.

——, *Consolidation of Democracy and Electoral Process*, NESAC Paper, Kathmandu, 1996.

Achariya, J., 'Nirapattahin Shonkhyalaghu', *Sapthahik 2000: Weekly Magazine*, 19 October 2001.

Achariya, J. and M. Adnan, 'Eto Mukh Noi Jeno', *Sapthahik 2000*, 14 September 2001.

Adhikari, Bishnu P., 'Evolution of Election Code of Conduct and its Violation in the General Elections—1999', *Nepali Journal of Contemporary Studies*, Vol. 1, No. 1, March 2001, pp. 29–56.

Aditya, Anand, 'Restructuring Elections in Nepal: A Case of the Misrepresented Mandate' in Devendra Raj Panday and Anand Aditya (eds), *Democracy and Empowerment in South Asia*, Kathmandu, NESAC, 1995.

Ahmed, Nizam, U., 'Party Politics in Bangladesh's Local Government: 1994 City Corporation Elections', *Asian Survey*, 1995.

Ahmed, N., G. Mortaza and A. Kibria, 'Haoae Urche Ekhon Nirbachoni Hazar Koti Taka', *Sapthahik 2000*, 7 September 2001.

Akhter, Yahya, *Electoral Corruption in Bangladesh*, London, Ashgate, 2000.

Amnesty International, *Bangladesh: Attacks on Members of Hindu Minority*, December 2001.

ASK, *Draft Report on Violence Against Minorities in September and October in Bangladesh*, Dhaka, ASK, 2001a.

ASK, *ASK Bulletin*, December 2001b.

Austin, Granville, 'The Expected and the Unintended in Working a Democratic Constitution' in Zoya Hasan, E. Sridharan and R. Sudarshan (eds), *India s Living Constitution: Ideas, Practices, Controversies*, New Delhi, Permanent Black, 2002.

Banu, M., 'Sarejomine Bholar Protibendon', *Mohila Samachar, Bangladesh Mohila Parishad Bulletin*, October–December 2001.

Barakat, A. and Shafique uz-Zaman., 'Forced Migration of Hindu Minority: Human Deprivation due to Vested Property Act', in C. Abrar (ed.), *On the Margin: Refugees, Migrants, Minorities*, Dhaka, RMMRU, 2000.

Basu, D.D., *Shorter Constitution of India*, New Delhi, Prentice Hall of India, 1996.

Baxi, P.M., *The Constitution of India*, Delhi, Universal Law Publishing Company, 2001.

Baxter, Craig, 'Bangladesh in 1991. A Parliamentary System', *Asian Survey*, 1992.

Baxter, Craig and S. Rahman, 'Bangladesh Votes—1991, Building Democratic Institutions', *Asian Survey*, 1991.

Bertocci, Peter J., 'Bangladesh in the Early 1980s: Pratorian Politics in an Intermediate Regime', *Asian Survey*, 1982.

———, 'Bangladesh in 1985: Resolute Against the Storms', *Asian Survey*, 1986.

Bhattarai, H.P., *Identities in the Making: Cultural Pluralism and Politics of Imagined Communities in the Lowlands of Nepal*, Unpublished M.Phil. Dissertation, Department of Social Anthropology, University of Bergen, Norway, 2000.

Bista, D.B., 'The Process of Nepalisation', in S. Iijima (ed.), *Anthropological and Linguistic Studies of the Gandaki Area in Nepal*, Tokyo, Institute for the Study of Languages and Cultures of Asia and Africa, 1982.

Borre, Ole, Sushil R. Pandey and Chitra K. Tiwari, *Nepalese Political Behaviour*, New Delhi, Sterling, 1994.

Brotee, 'Eighth Parliamentary Elections, 2001: Election Monitoring Report', (*Draft*) Dhaka, Brotee, 2001.

CCHRB, *The CCHRB Election Observation Report: The Eighth Parliamentary Elections 2001*, Dhaka, SEHD, 2002.

Central Bureau of Statistics (CBS), *Population Monograph*, Vol. 2, Part VII, Table 25, Kathmandu, HMG, National Planning Commission Secretariat, 1993.

———, *Population Census of Nepal 2001: National Report*, Kathmandu, HMG/CBS in collaboration with UNFPA Nepal, 2002.

Chaube, S.K., *Constituent Assembly of India: Springboard of a Revolution*, New Delhi, People's Publishing House, 1973.

Choudhury, Dilara, 'Evaluation of Bangladesh Parliamentary Election Monitoring, 2001', Paper Presented at International Conference on Electoral Processes and Governance in South Asia, Colombo, 2002.

Chowdhury, A., 'State and the Minority: The Case of Hindus in Bangladesh' in C. Abrar (ed.), *On the Margin: Refugees, Migrants, Minorities*, Dhaka, RMMRU 2000.

Coomaraswamy, Radhika, *Sri Lanka: The Crisis of the Anglo-American Constitutional Traditions in a Developing Society*, Delhi, Vikas, 1984.

———, 'The Constitution and Constitutional Reform', *Sri Lanka: The Problems of Governance*, Kandy, ICES, 1993, pp. 127–47.

Cooray, Joseph A.L., *Constitutional and Administrative Law of Sri Lanka*, Colombo, Sumathi Publishers, 1995, p. 116.

Cooray, L.J.M., *Constitutional Government in Sri Lanka*, Colombo, Lake House, 1984.

Dahal, D.R., 'Ethnic Cauldron, Demography and Minority Politics: The Case of Nepal', in D. Kumar (ed.), *State Leadership and Politics in Nepal*, Kathmandu, Centre for Nepal and Asian Studies (CNAS), Tribhuvan University, 1995.

————, 'Reforms in the Electoral Process of Nepal', in Devendra Raj Panday, Anand Aditya and Dev Raj Dahal (eds), *Comparative Electoral Processes in South Asia*, Kathmandu, Nepal South Asia Center (NESAC), 1999, pp. 55–76,.

Dahal, R.K., 'Candidate Selection in the 1999 Parliamentary Elections in Nepal', *NCCS Occasional Papers 1*, Kathmandu, Nepal Center for Contemporary Studies, 2000.

De Alwis, Sundari (ed.), *The Right to Vote and the Law Relating to Election Petitions*, Colombo, Centre for Policy Alternatives, 2000.

de Silva, K.M. (ed.), *Sri Lanka: A Survey*, London, C. Hurst, 1977.

————, *Sri Lanka: The Problems of Governance*, Kandy, International Centre for Ethnic Studies (ICES), 1993.

De Souza, Peter Ronald, 'The Election Commission and Electoral Reforms in India' in D.D. Khanna et al. (eds), *Democracy, Diversity and Stability in India*, New Delhi, Macmillan,1998.

————, 'Elections, Parties and Democracy in India', in Peter Ronald de Souza (ed.), *Contemporary India: Transitions*, New Delhi, Sage, 2000.

DEVA, *Action Research on the Development and Establishment of a Revised Voters Registration Scheme for the Election Commission of Nepal*, Final Report Submitted to DANIDA/HUGOU, Kathmandu, 2000.

Devendra Raj Panday and Anand Aditya (eds), *Democracy and Empowerment in South Asia*, Kathmandu, Nepal South Asia Centre, 1995.

Devendra Raj Panday and Dev Raj Dahal (eds), *Comparative Electoral Processes in South Asia*, Nepal South Asia Centre (NESAC), July 1999.

Dixit, K.M. et al., 'Lowly Labor in the Lowlands', *Himal South Asia*, 10(1), 1997.

DREFDEN, *Report on the Study and Research on the Local Elections in Nepal, 1992*, Kathmandu, Development Research for a Democratic Nepal, 1992.

Election Cell, 'Sthaniya Nikaya Nirbachan 2054 ko Ghatna Sambandhi Bibaran', (*Details Relating to the Local Elections 1997 Events*), Ministry of Home Affairs, HMG/Nepal.

Elections Commission, *General Election in Nepal 1991*, Kathmandu, Election Commission, 1991.

————, *Pratinidhi Sabha Sadasya Nirbachan—2051 Parinam Bibarana* (*Election Result of House of Representative Election 1994*), Kathmandu, Elections Commission, 1994.

————, *Nirbachan Sambandhi Sudharharu* (Reforms Related to Election), (Kathmandu, 1997).

————, *Electoral Process in Nepal*, Kathmandu, Election Commission, 1998.

————, Kathmandu Declaration on Free and Fair Election adopted by the first meeting of the Chief Election Commissioners of SAARC Countries, February 1999.

Election Commission, *The Election Code of Conduct, 1996*, Kathmandu, 1999.

————, *Pratinidhi Sabha Sadasya Nirbachan—2056 Parinam Bibarana (Election Result of House of Representative Election 1999)*, Kathmandu, Election Commission, 1999.

Election Commission, (1999), *http://www.cybermatha.net/ec.*

Enskat, Mike, Subrata K. Mitra and Vijay Bahadur Singh, 'India', in Dieter Nohlen, Florian Grotz and Christof Hartmann (eds), *Elections in Asia and the Pacific*, Oxford, Oxford University Press, 2001.

Gadkari, S.S., *Electoral Reforms in India*, New Delhi, Wheeler Publishing, 1996.

Gain, P., Human Rights Activist, CCHRB, Interview, 21 April 2002.

Guha, Ramchandra, 'The Biggest Gamble in History', *The Hindu Magazine*, 27 January 2002.

Guhathakurta, M. 'Assault on Minorities in Bangladesh: An Analysis', www.dristipath.org, 2002a.

———, 'A Report from Bhola', 11 February 2002, Dhaka, ASK, 2002b.

———, M. Professor, Department of International Relations, University of Dhaka, Interview, 23 February 2002.

Gurung, H., *Nepal: Social Demography and Expression*, Kathmandu, New Era, 1998.

Gurung, H. and Jan Salter, *Faces of Nepal*, Kathmandu, Himal Associates, 1996.

Hassan, M., 'Supply of and Demand for Second Generation Reform: The Case of Bangladesh', Ph.D. Thesis, Institute of Commonwealth Studies, University of London, 2001.

Hasan, Mirza M., 'Electoral Malpractices in Bangladesh: An Empirical Assessment of the 8th Parliamentary Elections', Paper Presented at International Conference on Electoral Processes and Governance in South Asia, Colombo, 2002.

High Level Committee Headed by the Prime Minister 2002 (2058 BS), *Report on Suggestion on Electoral Reform*, Kathmandu (in Nepali).

Himal, 16–31 Chaitra, 2058 BS (March 2002) (in Nepali).

His Majesty's Government (HMG) of Nepal, *The Act Relating to Electoral Rolls*, Kathmandu, HMG, Ministry of Law and Justice, Law Books Management Board, 1996.

Hossain, Golam, 'Bangladesh in 1994, Democracy at Risk', *Asian Survey*, 1995.

Hossain, H., 'Violence Against Minorities in Bangladesh: An Analysis' in *Combating Communalism (Draft)*, 2001.

Hoque, Azizul, 'Bangladesh 1979: Cry for a Sovereign Parliament', *Asian Survey*, 1980.

Huntington, S., *The Third Wave: Democratisation in the Late Twentieth Century*, Norman, University of Oklahoma Press, 1991.

IIDS, *Fourth Parliamentary Election: A Study of the Evolving Democratic Process in Nepal*, Kathmandu, Institute for Integrated Development Studies (IIDS), 2000.

International IDEA, *Voter Turnout since 1945: A Global Report*, Halmstad, International Institute for Democracy and Electoral Assistance (International IDEA), 2002.

IPU, Universal Declaration on Democracy, Cairo, 16 September 1997.

Islam, Syed S., 'The State in Bangladesh under Zia, (1975–81)', *Asian Survey*, 1982.

———, 'Bangladesh in 1986: Entering a New Phase', *Asian Survey*, 1987.

———, 'Bangladesh in 1987. A Spectrum of Uncertainties', *Asian Survey*, 1988.

Jacob, Lucy M., *Sri Lanka, From Dominion to Republic*, Delhi, 1973.

Jahan, Rounaq, *Politics in Bangladesh*, Dhaka, University Press Limited, 1980.

Jennings, W.I., *The Constitution of Ceylon*, Bombay, 1949.

Jennings, W.I., and H.W. Tambiah, *The Dominion of Ceylon: The Development of its Laws and Constitution*, London, 1952.

Jupp, J., 'Constitutional Developments in Ceylon since Independence', *Pacific Affairs*, Vol. XLI, No. 2, 1968, pp. 169–83.

Kanesalingam, V., *A Hundred Years of Local Government in Ceylon 1865–1965*, Colombo, 1971, p. 8.

Khan, Zillur R., 'Bangladesh in 1981: Change, Stability, and Leadership', *Asian Survey*, 1982.

———, 'Bangladesh's Experiments with Parliamentary Democracy', *Asian Survey*, 1997.

Khanal, Krishna P., '*Nirbachan Sudhar tatha Suddhikaranka kehi Pakshyaharu*', Paper Presented at a Seminar Organised by NCCS on Kartik 26, 2053, 10 November 1996.

Khanam, A., General Secretary, Bangladesh Mohila Parishad, Interview, 28 May 2002.

Kochanek, S.A., 'Bangladesh in 1996: The 25th Year of Independence', *Asian Survey*, 1997.

———, *Business and Politics in Bangladesh*, Dhaka, University Press Limited, 1997.

———, 'Bangladesh in 1997: The Honeymoon is Over', *Asian Survey*, 1998.

Krämer, Karl-Heinz, 'Elections in Nepal: 1999 and Before', Informal Sector Service Center (ed.), *Human Rights Yearbook 2000*, Kathmandu, INSEC, 2000, pp. 29–47.

Kumar, Dhruba, 'What Ails Democracy in Nepal?', in Dhruba Kumar (ed.), *Domestic Conflict and Governability in Nepal*, Kathmandu, Centre for Nepal and Asian Studies, 2000.

———, 'Consequences of the Militarized Conflict and the Cost of Violence in Nepal', *Contribution to Nepalese Studies*, 30(2), 2003, pp. 167–216.

Leitan, G.R. Tressie, *Local Government and Decentralized Administration in Sri Lanka*, Colombo, Lake House Investments Ltd., 1979, p. 49.

Luckham, R., A.M. Goetz and M. Kaldor, 'Democratic Institutions and Transition in the Context of Inequality, Poverty and Conflict', IDS Discussion Paper 104, Brighton, IDS, 2000.

Maharjan, Pancha Narayan, *Local Elections in Nepal, 1997*, Kathmandu, Centre for Nepal and Asian Studies, 1998.

Mehta, Pratap Bhanu, *The Burden of Democracy*, New Delhi, Penguin, 2003.

Ministry of Law, Justice and Parliamentary Affairs, *The Constitution of the Kingdom of Nepal 2047 (1990)*, Kathmandu, Law Books Management Board, HMG/Nepal, 1992.

Mishra, Birendra Prasad, '*Nirbachan Sudhar Kehi Sujhav*', Paper Presented at a Seminar Organised by NCCS on Kartik 26, 2053 (10 November 1996).

Mishra, Birendra Prasad, 2058 BS, 'A Suggestion on the Electoral System', *Kantipur* daily of 23 10 2058 BS, Kathmandu (in Nepali) 5 February 2002.

———, *Sudridh/Sashakta Nirbachan Aayog ki Sarbadaliya Chunabi Sarkar?*, (Consolidated/Empowered Election Commission or All-Party Election Government?), *Kantipur*, 20 March 2002.

MLAA, 'Collective Rights of Ethnic Minorities: A Report Prepared for Sasawaka Project', New Town, Madaripur (unpublished report), 1996.

Mohsin, A., *The Politics of Nationalism: The Case of CHT, Bangladesh*, Dhaka, UPL, 1997.

———, 'Rights of Ethnic Minorities', *Human Rights in Bangladesh 2000*, Dhaka, ASK, 2001.

Moral, S., 'Rights of Religious Minorities', *Human Rights in Bangladesh 2000*, Dhaka, ASK, 2001.

———, Human Rights Activist, CCHRB, Interview, 19 April 2002.

Mozaffar, Shaheen and Andreas Schedler, 'The Comparative Study of Electoral Governance: Introduction', *International Political Science Review*, Vol. 23, No. 1, 2002, pp. 5–27.

Nabil, B.A., 'Shatti Ashone Lorai: Barisal and Patuakhali', *Saptahik 2000*, 14 October 2001.

Nair, Jeevan and U.C. Jain, *Electoral System in India*, Jaipur, Pointer Publications, 2000.

Nazneen, S., 'Bangladesh Rastre Santal Shomprodai: Prantikaroner Shikar?', *Somaj Nirikhkhon*, No. 74, November 1999.

Nazrul, A., 'Minority Voting Issues: When Shamsur Rahman Protests', *The Daily Star*, 9 October 2001.

Communist Party of Nepal (CPN-UML), 'Description of Irregularities and Events of Local Election 1997', Kathmandu, November 1997.

Nepali Congress, *Report on Riggings of the Local Elections 1997*, Kathmandu, August 1997.

Neupane, *Nepalko Jatiya Prashna: Samajik Banot ra Sajedariko Sambhawana* (*Question of Caste/Ethnicity in Nepal: Social Structure and Possibility of Collaboration*), Kathmandu, Center for Development Studies, 2000.

Panday, Devendra Raj and Anand Aditya (eds), *Democracy and Empowerment in South Asia*, Kathmandu, Nepal South Asia Centre, 1995.

Panday, Devendra Raj, et al., *Comparative Electoral Processes in South Asia*, Kathmandu, Nepal South Asia Centre, 1999.

Partho, S., 'Bangladesh at the Crossroads: Religion and Politics', Asian Survey, 1993.

Pokharel, Iswor, *Nirbachan Byabasthanka Bibidh Pakshya, Tyasaka Samasya ra Sudhar*, NCCS Occasional Paper, No. 3, Kathmandu, 2001.

POLSAN, *Political Parties and the Parliamentary Process in Nepal*, Kathmandu, Political Science Association of Nepal, 1992.

Poudel, Jagannath, *Samyukta Samiti ra Nispakshya Nirbachan ko Sandarbha*, Paper Presented at a Seminar Organised by National Democratic Institute in Kathmandu on Mangsir 15–16, 2053, (30 November 1996).

Powell, Bingham G., *Elections as Instruments of Democracy*, New Haven, Yale University Press, 2000.

Rahman, Md. Ataur, 'Bangladesh in 1983: A Turning Point for the Military', *Asian Survey*, 1982.

Rao, B. Shiva, *The Framing of India s Constitution: Select Documents*, Vol. IV, New Delhi, Indian Institute of Public Administration, 1968.

Rashiduzzaman, M., 'Political Unrest and Democracy in Bangladesh', *Asian Survey*, 1997.

Reilly, B., *Democracy in Divided Societies: Electoral Engineering for Conflict Management*, Cambridge, Cambridge University Press, 2001.

Report of Commissioner of Elections on the Ninth Parliamentary General Election of Sri Lanka held on 15 February 1989, *Sessional Paper No. 1*, 1993, pp. 118–19.

Report of High-Level Committee formed under the Chairmanship of the Prime Minister, 2001.

Report of Joint Parliamentary Committee, 1998, Sangsad Bhavan, Singhdurbar.

Rudolph L.I. and S.H. Rudolph, 'Redoing the Constitutional Design: From an Interventionist to a Regulatory State', in Atul Kohli (ed.), *The Success of India s Democracy*, Cambridge, Cambridge University Press, 2001.

Sammilito Samajik Andolon, Nirjatoner Dolil—2001: Nirbachon Purba and Nirbachon Uttar Shanghkyaloghu Nipiron, Dhaka, 2002.

Seddon, David, Ganesh Gurung and Jagannath Adhikari, 'Foreign Labor Migration and the Remittance Economy of Nepal', *Himalayan Research Bulletin*, XVIII(2): 1998, pp. 1–10.

Sen, Amartya, 'Exclusion and Inclusion', Paper Presented at the Conference on 'Including the Excluded', South Asians for Human Rights, New Delhi, 11–12 November 2001.

Sezhiyan, Era, 'Appointment of Election Commissioners', *The Hindu*, 21 May 2001, p. 11.

Shah, B.P., 'Inaugural Address: Study and Training/Workshop on Electoral System and Research Methodology', *Nepali Journal of Contemporary Studies*, Kathmandu, Nepal Center for Contemporary Studies, 2001.

Shah, Bishnu P., *Nirbachan Pranali ra Loktantrako Sudridhikaran*, Paper Presented at a Seminar Organized by NCCS on Kartik 26, 2053 (10 November 1996).

Sharma, S. and P. Sen, *Politics, Political Party and Politician in the Eyes of Electors: An Opinion Poll Survey of 1999 General Election*, Kathmandu, Himal Associates, 1999.

Sharma, Thakur P., '*Pratinidhi Sabhama Sadasya Nirbachanko Kanuni ebam Byabaharik Pakshya*' NCCS Occasional Paper, No. 3, Kathmandu, 2001.

Shrestha, K., 'Minority Politics in Nepal: A Human Right Perspective', in D. Kumar (ed.), *Domestic Conflict and Crisis of Governability in Nepal*, Kathmandu, CNAS, Tribhuvan University, 2000.

Stiles, K., 'International Support for NGOs in Bangladesh: Some Unintended Consequences', *World Development*, Vol. 30, No. 5, 2002.

Sunny, K.C., 'Election Laws' in S.K. Verma and Kusum (eds), *Fifty Years of the Supreme Court in India*, New Delhi, Oxford University Press, 2000.

Tahmina, Q.A., 'Dhormiyo Shonkhyaloghu-r Opor Hamla: Otironjon na Nisthur Sattya?', *Dainik Ekota*, 5 November 2001.

Tahmina, Q.A., 'Sarjomion Protibedon: Barisal', *Dainik Ekota*, 12 November 2001.

———, Associate Professor, Department of Journalism, University of Dhaka, Interview, 21 April 2002.

Thiagarajah, J. (ed.), *Governance and Electoral Process in Pakistan*, Colombo, International Centre for Ethnic Studies, 1998.

Whelpton, J., 'Political Identity in Nepal: State, Nation, and Community', in David N. Gellner, Joanna Pfaff-Czarnecka and John Whelpton (eds), *Nationalism and Ethnicity in a Hindu Kingdom: The Politics of Culture in Contemporary Nepal*, London, Harwood Academic Publishers, 1997.

Wilson, A. Jeyaratnam, *Politics in Sri Lanka, 1947–1979*, London, Macmillan, 1974.

———, *The Gaullist System in Sri Lanka*, London, The Macmillan Press Ltd., 1980.

Yadav, Yogendra, 'India's Electoral Democracy, 1952–2000', Paper Presented at International Symposium on 'Global Dimensions of Electoral Democracy', Election Commission of India, Golden Jubilee Celebrations, 18 January 2001, New Delhi.

Yamanaka, Keiko, 'Nepalese Labour Migration to Japan: From Global Warriors to Global Worker', *Ethnic and Racial Studies*, 23(1): 2000, pp. 62–93.

ABOUT THE EDITOR AND CONTRIBUTORS

EDITOR

Dushyantha Mendis is Director, International Centre for Ethnic Studies (ICES). He has degrees in Economics and Law and is a Sri Lankan Attorney-at-Law. He has held senior management positions in Sri Lanka's private sector and also briefly practiced Law prior to joining the ICES in 2002. His research interests lie in economic history, governance issues and ethnic conflict. He has presented several papers on these topics at many international conferences. He is editor of *Ethnic Studies Report, XX*, (Nos 1 & 2), 2002—Special Issue on 'Electoral Processes in South Asia: Statutory Framework and Institutional Arrangements'. He is a contributor to and editor of *Christians and Spices: The Portuguese in Sri Lanka and Goa* (forthcoming) and is also currently engaged in researching and writing a work on the economic history of Sri Lanka.

CONTRIBUTORS

Nilamber Acharya is a constitutional expert and political thinker. He was Minister for Law, Justice and Parliamentary Affairs; Labour and Social Welfare in the Interim Government after the restoration of democracy in Nepal 1990. He has also served as the Royal Nepalese Ambassador in Sri Lanka from 1996 to 2000.

Muzaffer Ahmad is currently Chairman of Transparency International Bangladesh (TIB), Bangladesh Environment Movement (BAPA), and Citizens for Fair Election (Sujon). He was president of Bangladesh Economic Association. Formerly a professor of Economics at Dhaka University, he has contributed articles to various national and international journals, as well as books edited on special topics in various countries. He has researched in different areas of Economics and Management, Political Economy and issues related to Human Rights and Freedom and International relations, etc., over the last 40 years. He has attended many International conferences and delivered conference and/or invited papers. His current Interest of Research relates to Poverty, Education, Health, Social Security, Governance and Dynamics of Development.

Hari Prasad Bhattarai is Lecturer in Social Anthropology at the Department of Sociology/Anthropology, Patan Multiple Campus, Tribhuvan University, Kathmandu, Nepal. He received his MA (1994) from Tribhuvan University and his M.Phil (2000) from University of Bergen, Norway. His main research has been with Tarai communities, with whom he has carried out fieldwork for his degrees. Since then he has carried out fieldwork with the community at regular intervals. He has published several papers on various issues (changing survival strategies, politics of identity, poverty, citizenship, national integration, cultural diversity and pluralism, cultural injustice and unfair inclusion) of the Tarai communities.

K.M. de Silva is Professor Emeritus, Department of History, University of Peradeniya, and Chairman, ICES, and has been the Executive Director of the International Centre for Ethnic Studies, Kandy/Colombo since its establishment in 1982 until 2006. He was Foundation Professor of Sri Lankan History at the University of Peradeniya (1969–95) and is a historian, political analyst, and a specialist in ethnic studies and conflict resolution. His publications include: *A History of Sri Lanka* (Penguin, India, 2005); *Regional Powers and Small State Security: India and Sri Lanka, 1977–1990* (Johns Hopkins University Press, Washington DC, 1995); and *Reaping the Whirlwind: Ethnic Politics, Ethnic Conflict in Sri Lanka* (Penguin, India, 1998). He has held several distinguished fellowships in British and US universities, and was a Fellow of the Woodrow Wilson Center, Washington, DC. He was selected as the Academic Prize Laureate (2002) of the 13th Fukuoka Asian Culture Prize.

Partha S. Ghosh is Professor of South Asian Studies at the School of International Studies, Jawaharlal Nehru University, New Delhi. His areas of interest are South Asian politics, ethnicity, and foreign policy. Ghosh was earlier a Visiting Professor at the OKD Institute of Social Change and Development, Guwahati, a Humboldt Fellow at the Heidelberg University, a Ford Visiting Scholar at the University of Illinois, Urbana-Champaign, and a Visiting Fellow at the Centre for Policy Research, New Delhi. He served as the Research Director at the Indian Council of Social Science Research, New Delhi for several years.

His books include *Unwanted and Uprooted: A Political Study of Refugees, Migrants, Stateless and Displaced in South Asia* [2004], *Ethnicity versus Nationalism: The Devolution Discourse in Sri Lanka* [2003], *BJP and the Evolution of Hindu Nationalism* [1999, 2000], *Pluralism and Equality: Values in Indian Society and Politics* [2000, co-edited], *Rivalry and Revolution in South and East Asia* [1997, edited], *Cooperation and Conflict in South Asia* [1989, 1995] and *Sino-Soviet Relations: US Perceptions and Policy Responses* (1849–1959) [1981]. Besides, he has written many research articles for eminent journals. Ghosh is currently finalizing a book tentatively titled as *Politics of Law in South Asia* to be published by Routledge of the Taylor and Francis Group of London.

Krishna P. Khanal is Professor of Political Science at Tribhuvan University, Kathmandu. He has been engaged in teaching and research for more than two decades. He has written extensively on issues related to Nepal's democracy and contributed papers at various seminars. His latest publications include *Nepal s Discourse on Constituent Assembly (2005), Future of Democracy in Nepal (2005)*. Professor Khanal has been active in the advocacy of democracy and human rights in Nepal.

Zulfikar Khalid Maluka is practising lawyer at the Supreme Court of Pakistan and is a member of the Supreme Court Bar Association. He has a strong academic background in International Law and Politics with a Masters Degree in 'Futuristics' from The American University in London (UK) and another Master's Degree from the Quaid-e-Azam University, Islamabad. His foreign academic pursuits include courses at The Australian National University, The Institute of International Studies, the Geneva University, and the Asian Institute of Technology, Bangkok.

He has also worked as a research fellow with various Academic institutions of international repute like the Islamabad-based Institute of Regional Studies and the National Institute of Historical and Cultural Research, Islamabad. Most recently, he has served as a Legal and Constitutional Consultant with the National Reconstruction Bureau (Government of Pakistan) 2000–2001.

As a writer he has authored over 40 international publications on international and regional politics as well as three books, the most recent one being the *Myth of Constitutionalism in Pakistan* (Oxford University Press, 1995). His earlier academic endeavours include his two books, *Pakistan in the Pamir Knot: Geo Strategic Imperatives* (Vanguard Books) and *Pakistan-China Security Relations* (Progressive Publishers), published in the early 1980s.

Recently he contributed a paper titled 'Restructuring the Constitution for a COAS President: Pakistan 1999–2002' for a book *Pakistan on the Brink: Politics, Economics and Society* (Oxford University Press, 2004), edited by Craig Baxter.

Birendra Prasad Mishra is Coordinator, Peace Monitoring Committee. Prior to this, he was the Coordinator for National Peace Monitoring Committee for Ceasefire Code of Conduct which functioned until the Maoists and the Prime Minister signed the Comprehensive Peace Accord in November 2006. A retired Professor of Philosophy, Mishra was also the Election Commissioner from 1994 to 2000 and has served as an international observer at parliamentary elections in India, Pakistan and the UK. He has authored four books, the most recent one being *Rebuilding Nepal* (July 2007).

Sohela Nazneen is Assistant Professor at the Department of International Relations, University of Dhaka. She has academic and policy-based research experience on gender and minority rights, mostly with Bangladeshi and international development organisations and think tanks such as CARE, ICES, Bangladesh Legal Aid Services Trust (BLAST), Ain O. Salish Kendra (ASK). She has a Ph.D. from the Institute of Development Studies (IDS), Sussex. Her Ph.D. research focused on accountability relations, mainly incentives and mechanisms that influence NGO frontline workers to promote gender equity during service delivery in Bangladesh.

Amit Prakash is Associate Professor, Centre for the Study of Law and Governance, Jawaharlal Nehru University, New Delhi, He has published widely in the areas of politics of development; dynamics of socio-political and ethnic identity mobilisation and its inter-linkages with the processes of public policy; Indian politics; governance and development; and global governance. Dr Prakash is the author of *Jharkhand: Politics of Development of Identity* (New Delhi: Orient Longman, 2001) and *Politics and International Security* (Mumbai: Popular, 2004) and co-editor (along .with Niraja Gopal Jayal and Pradeep K. Sharma) of *Local Governance in India: Decentralisation and Beyond* (OUP, New Delhi, 2006).

Rasul Bakhsh Rais is Professor of Political Science at Lahore University of Management Sciences (LUMS). He has held fellowships at Wake Forest University, Harvard University and University of California, Berkeley, and was Professor of Pakistan Studies at Columbia University, New York, during 1991–94. Dr Rais is author of *War Without Winners: Afghanistans Uncertain Transition after the Cold War* (OUP, 1996), *Indian Ocean and the Superpowers: Economic, Political and Strategic Perspectives* (Croom Helm, 1986), and editor of *State, Society and Democratic Change in Pakistan* (OUP 1997). He has published widely in professional journals on political and security issues pertaining to South Asia, Indian Ocean and Afghanistan.

Ujjwal Kumar Singh is presently a Reader in the Department of Political Science, University of Delhi, New Delhi. Prior to that, he was a Fellow at the Centre for Contemporary Studies, Nehru Memorial Museum and Library, Teen Murti Bhavan, New Delhi. He has authored the book *Political Prisoners in India,* which was published by the Oxford University Press in 1998. His writings have appeared in *Economic and Political Weekly*, *Diogenes, Scienza & Politica, Ethnic Studies Report, Contemporary India* and *Indian Journal of Human Rights*. His forthcoming book titled *The State, Democracy and Anti-Terror Laws in India* is being published by Sage Publications.

INDEX